Volumes previously published by the University of California Press, Berkeley, Los Angeles, London, for the Center for Chinese Studies of The University of Michigan:

MICHIGAN STUDIES ON CHINA

Communications and National Integration in Communist China, by Alan P. L. Liu

Mao's Revolution and the Chinese Political Culture, by Richard Solomon

Capital Formation in Mainland China, 1952–1965, by Kang Chao

Small Groups and Political Rituals in China, by Martin King Whyte

Backward Toward Revolution: The Chinese Revolutionary Party, by Edward Friedman

Peking Politics, 1918–1923: Factionalism and the Failure of Constitutionalism, by Andrew Nathan

THE PRESIDENCY OF YUAN SHIH-K'AI

Michigan Studies on China
Published for the Center for Chinese Studies
of The University of Michigan

MICHIGAN STUDIES ON CHINA

The research on which these books are based was supported by the Center for Chinese Studies of The University of Michigan.

The Presidency of
Yuan Shih-k'ai

*Liberalism and Dictatorship in
Early Republican China*

ERNEST P. YOUNG

Ann Arbor   The University of Michigan Press

Grateful acknowledgment is made to the following publisher for permission to reprint copyrighted material:

The Bobbs-Merrill Company, Inc., for material from *China Revolutionized* by John Stuart Thomson, Copyright, 1913, R. 1940 by John Stuart Thomson. Reprinted by permission of the publisher.

For my beloved parents
Evelyn Orne Young
Lorin Bradford Young

Acknowledgments

My interest in the period of China's 1911 Revolution began in seminars at Harvard University. It led to work on the late Ch'ing revolutionary movement and to a dissertation on Liang Ch'i-ch'ao, the writer and politician, during the 1911 Revolution and the immediately following years. Liang's essays and letters provided a convenient point of entry into the politics of the period. But a wider view was necessary, it seemed to me, if one were to interpret adequately the various political forces and their interaction during the early years of the Chinese republic. After publishing some of this earlier work in articles, I turned to the task of researching a fuller range of political movement when Yuan Shih-k'ai was Chinese president. This book is the result.

I have gained inestimably from the careful reading and perspicacious criticisms of the manuscript by Joe Esherick, Stephen MacKinnon, Donald Sutton, and Marilyn Blatt Young. Ch'i Hsi-sheng, John Fairbank, Albert Feuerwerker, Andrew Nathan, and Keith Schoppa also read the manuscript in whole or in part, and I am grateful for their comments and suggestions. Chang Hao and George Sun-Chain Lin provided extraordinary linguistic assistance at different stages of my research, although neither they nor any of the readers are responsible for errors of fact, interpretation, or translation.

While pursuing this project, I was courteously served by the staffs of these libraries and archives: Asia Library, University of Michigan; East Asiatic Library, University of California at Berkeley; Eisenhower Library, Johns Hopkins University; Gaikō Shiryōkan, Ministry of Foreign Affairs, Tokyo; Harvard-Yenching Library, Harvard University; Hoover Library, Stanford; Houghton Library, Harvard University; Institute of Modern History, Academia Sinica, Taipei; Kensei Shiryōshitsu, Diet Library, Tokyo; Kuomintang Archives, Taiwan; Mitchell Library, Sydney; National Archives, Washington, D. C.; Library of Congress, Washington, D. C.; Public Record Office, London; and Tōyō Bunko, Tokyo. For guiding me to libraries and archives in their countries and for their generous hospitality, I wish to thank Professors Banno Masataka, Chang P'eng-yuan, Ichiko Chūzō, Ikei Masaru, Katō Yūzō, and Nakamura Tadashi.

The extensive traveling and the research leaves, without which this study could not have been completed, were sustained by grants from the Center for Chinese Studies at the University of Michigan, the East Asian Research Center at Harvard University, the U. S. Office of Education, and the Social Science Research Council.

I am grateful to Penny Greene and Eva Chan for their patience and perseverance in typing the manuscript. The work of Elnor Parker and her staff at the University of Michigan Press has been careful and creative, as they have wrestled with the special problems of scholarly publishing on China.

To Chang Ch'un-shu, friend and colleague, I owe a special debt for his calligraphic contribution to the design of the book jacket.

Finally, I should note that I follow the customary adaptations of the Wade-Giles system of transliterating Chinese. I am perhaps more sparing than most with the umlaut, which I reserve for circumstances where it is phonemically necessary. Hence, Li Lieh-chün, but Yuan Shih-k'ai.

Contents

Tables

Maps

Introduction

China's last dynasty, the Ch'ing, showed signs of a declining vigor as early as the end of the eighteenth century. For the next one hundred ten years, the court and its political system were subjected to a qualitatively unprecedented combination of internal and external assaults. In the face of rebellion and encroachment by Western imperialism, the dynasty's capacity to survive was remarkable. One price was major concessions to the desires of Western nations during the latter half of the nineteenth century. Another price was conceding greater scope to the local power of the social elite outside the government. Meanwhile, a variety of efforts were made to reverse the unfavorable trend, notably during the 1860s and the first decade of the twentieth century. But apparent achievement bred further difficulties. The Ch'ing dynasty, the result of a seventeenth-century conquest by Manchus, who nonetheless had ruled in established Chinese patterns and with Chinese assistance, was overthrown by a republican revolution that broke out in 1911. A newly formulated nationalism was a conspicuous ingredient in the agitation surrounding the revolution.

This book is about Chinese politics in the aftermath of the 1911 Revolution. In particular, it concerns the problems prominent in the period defined by the presidency of Yuan Shih-k'ai, which emerged in the wake of the revolution and lasted four and one-half years. It describes and evaluates the strategies devised by political leaders to deal with these problems, with special attention to the policies of Yuan Shih-k'ai and their fate.

By the early twentieth century, the overriding issue in Chinese politics was how to stop and turn back foreign encroachments on China's political and economic autonomy. The issue was not new but had been developing since the Opium War (1839–42). The changing strategy of China's leadership can be analyzed in terms of both its external and internal aspect. That

is, there was the question of what policy to adopt toward foreign states and their impingement on China, and there was the question of how to organize forces within China in support of the policy.

By the time of the 1911 Revolution, the government had already undertaken a variety of external policies: war (five times between 1839 and 1900), footdragging and evasion, accommodation, and militant resistance short of war. In brief, it had tried just about everything. But the results seemed not to vary with the policy. Deterioration remained almost constant, with some marginal improvement after 1901. Indeed, between 1839 and 1949, only the first decade of the twentieth century and the 1920s registered any appreciable recovery of sovereignty, and that quite partial. (The wartime termination of Anglo-American extraterritoriality in 1943 was accompanied by so much American intervention in Chinese affairs that it signified no overall advance.) Yuan's presidency employed virtually the whole stock of external strategies but that of war. It was marked by the same failure in resisting foreign pressure that characterized most other years.

The internal aspect of China's strategy is usually discussed in terms of the pace of the adoption of Western technology and institutions, that is, reform or modernization. The pace was slow and jerky, but the trend was growth in the size of this "reformed" sector from the 1860s onward. The correspondence between the advance of Western-style reforms and the recovery of rights was reasonably high in the first decade of the twentieth century, but reform of this sort turned out, by itself, not to hold the key to sovereignty. The Western powers and Japan were, after all, "reforming" at a much faster rate. Competition in this category was, to say the least, unequal.

China's strategy toward foreign encroachment had another internal aspect that changed over time. That was the portion of the society asked or allowed to participate. The people at the top would presumably have preferred to continue to handle the question by themselves. But this luxury was denied them, as the pressure of imperialism increased. What began in the first half of the nineteenth century as a matter for court politics soon became a subject of general concern in the bureaucracy.[1] Regional officials took the initiative and in an extreme case operated independently of the court in foreign relations. A crucial further breakthrough occurred in the 1890s when elite members of the society outside the bureaucracy began to advocate and organize around questions of high policy in foreign affairs.

After 1900, the government cautiously invited this sort of participation in a variety of ways. The modest achievements in the recovery of rights between the Boxer affair and the 1911 Revolution owed as much to the energy thereby elicited as they did to the adoption of Western technology or institutions. A significant increase in the portion of the society mobilized behind the government's foreign policy had occurred.

Despite this increase in energy, the imperialist position was too strong to be seriously shaken. Perhaps in an earlier decade, when the Western presence was smaller and more tentative, a movement to recover rights that was based in the social elite might have succeeded, in the manner of Meiji Japan. By the early twentieth century, it was insufficient. Political leaders among the extrabureaucratic elite blamed the government (and this contributed largely to the overthrow of Ch'ing power in 1911 and 1912). Many bureaucrats, including some who survived the 1911 Revolution in power, blamed the uncontrolled and undisciplined political activity of the social elite. Once again, there was the smell of failure in the air.

For those grappling with the continuing issue of foreign imperialism in China, there were two options remaining. One, favored by certain intellectuals and officials, was to recover authority from the nonbureaucratic elite and centralize power in the national government. The other was to consolidate, and perhaps even broaden further, the social base of organized political movement.

In the period with which this book is concerned, between the 1911 Revolution and the onset of warlordism, the prominent political events were marked by the conflict between two tendencies: the continuing demand for political participation and power by the social elite (with a decentralizing effect on the national political structure), and the efforts by some, especially Yuan Shih-k'ai, to recentralize. The leading advocates of both positions were nationalist and defended their strategies as the best means of attaining sufficient Chinese power to turn back foreign encroachments.

The comparative advantages of centralized or decentralized authority (*chün-hsien* versus *feng-chien*) have enjoyed centuries of debate among China's political thinkers.[2] The main theme of this book is how the problems China faced in the early twentieth century became enmeshed in this old tension in the Chinese polity. Advocates of administrative centralization gained confidence and a sense of urgency from the demands of nationalism. It seemed self-evident to some that political power had to be concentrated in order to stave off foreign encroachment. It was not enough merely to regain those levels of centralization that had characterized the Ch'ing and earlier dynasties. The new character of the external challenge required unprecedented degrees of centralization. On the other hand, the heightened desire among the elite outside the government for participation in politics—a desire traceable in part to nationalist concerns and abetted by reforms stimulated by nationalism—invigorated institutions and movements that seemingly reduced the center's power. Nationalism, the liberal call for participation in government, the appeal to the efficiency of concentrated autocratic power—these issues entered into the old debate about degrees of centralization. The debate was not closed in Yuan Shih-k'ai's time, nor is it yet.

In this sense, then, the period is a further chapter in an ancient question about China's polity. But the new circumstances in which the question was restated mark off the contemporary answers as conspicuously twentieth century. The towering presence of Western and Japanese imperialism means that, as we look back, Yuan's presidency also partakes of patterns that refer not so much to a Chinese past as to a Third World future. Its problems and its policies often evoke the experience of other Asian countries and some African ones as they have struggled in recent decades for national autonomy. My understanding of Yuan's presidency comes from looking at China's experience in the aftermath of the 1911 Revolution in both a Chinese and a global context.

Chapter 1

China in the Early Twentieth Century

After the 1911 Revolution, the republican president Yuan Shih-k'ai established a bureau for the compilation of an official history of the Ch'ing dynasty. As he did so, he praised the Ch'ing for having "abolished its old
ways and reformed itself, effecting a revival in its declining years."[1] This
evaluation, rare among Chinese, was common before the revolution among
foreign observers, who were partly admiring, partly fearful. For foreigners,
that China had finally undertaken the voluntary adoption of Western institutions confirmed feelings of cultural superiority. After decades of resistance or paltry modifications, it seemed that China was, in the first years
of the twentieth century, seriously altering her institutions along Western
lines. On the other hand, with the flattery of imitation went demands for
equality and redress of grievances and, more disturbing, the beginnings of
means to exact attention for her demands.

Impressive as the reforms of the late Ch'ing may have been compared
with past efforts, they were not for all Chinese. At the elite level, the effects of the reforms were apparent. New political relationships (notably
through representative institutions of government) were being established.
New methods of administering the law (a new court system) with new laws
(modifications in old codes) were spreading from the top down, with a
great distance to go to reach many ordinary people. New security agencies
(a modernized army and police system) were in partial operation by the
end of the dynasty, protecting the elite from its foreign and domestic challengers. New schools with new curricula, new professions, new ideas, new
styles of life were emerging. The urban environment was acquiring a new
face. A foreigner with long experience in China commented on Peking's
aspect on the eve of the revolution: ". . . I find that the city is being transformed. Macadamised roads are being made everywhere; every important

5

house is lit with electricity; there is an excellent telephone system; there is a postal service with delivery eight times a day. The police force cannot be too highly praised—a well-paid, well-equipped, well-disciplined body of men." The water supply was good, some Chinese were taking to buying English bedsteads, rickshaws were now rubber tired, and there were a few motor cars.[2] For those participating in these changes, both monumental and trivial, the feeling of movement, of expectancy, of potential achievement was quickening.

At the same time there was a stifling sameness for the majority, for whom political relationships, the law, security, schooling, and style of life had barely been touched. An official British medical report on China in 1911 noted an improvement in draining and cleaning the streets in Peking, but also a terrible toll from disease: "The number of infant deaths is so great that it is beyond individual burial, and the small bodies are simply wrapped in matting and placed in carts which go through each district collecting bundles, which are afterwards thrown *en masse* into a hole outside the city gates."[3] The gap between an elite conscious of moving into a new age and a mass left even further behind by changes toward which it contributes its labor and taxes but from which it gains nothing—this gap, which characterizes many countries drawn into Western ways without changes in social structure, also characterized China in 1911.

Chinese society on the eve of the revolution contained several divergent tendencies, as well as significant continuities. As background to an investigation of politics in the early republic, we need to identify the main features of the period and their relationships one to another. The discussion in this chapter concerns aspects of Chinese society in the early twentieth century that set the terms and boundaries of politics.

The Social Elite

In contemplating the changes sweeping China from the end of the nineteenth century, we must not lose sight of the endurance of a particular species of social and economic elite, the Chinese gentry. This historical class had persisted for centuries through different circumstances.[4] Under the special requirements of a China besieged by the industrial nations, it was forced to adapt to a new set of demands. But it was not forced to step down with the demise of the empire. On the contrary, it adapted most adroitly to the changing circumstances of the period surrounding the 1911 Revolution. To understand the politics of the first years of the republic, two characteristics of the gentry must be marked: their continuing social predominance and their considerable cohesion despite a growing diversity of interests and activity.

The question of what constituted the elite in the late empire (Ming and Ch'ing) and how it maintained its status has been controversial. The controversy extends to nomenclature. Deviations from the unsatisfactory but well-established term "gentry" (in Chinese, commonly *shen-shih*), although handy as variants, either remove the particularity inherent in the gentry's cultural distinctiveness (for example, "local elite") or emphasize too much only one feature, albeit an important one, to be generally useful (for instance, "landlord class"). The gentry in each successive period was not quite what it had been in the previous one. An argument could be made for changing the name for the twentieth century. But for the first two decades, at least, the importance of the continuities warrants retention of the traditional term. This issue here is, of course, the degree of the continuity of this dominant social class, not the terminology.

A member of the Chinese gentry was distinguishable from someone lower down the social scale by a combination of education, a cultured manner that was concretely expressed in cultural talents acquired by years of classical studies, and abstention from physical labor and petty commerce. The majority of gentry sustained this special style of life by securing annually a disproportionate per capita share of the output of agriculture—and agriculture was and continued to be the overwhelmingly dominant economic activity. Most gentry, then, were landlords, moneylenders, or managers of enterprises (often related to charity or to clan) that directly tied in with the peasant economy. This dependence on access to the returns from peasant farming and the social control to ensure access characterized them as a class, even though individuals with the proper educational and cultural attainments might prosper as gentry by other means. Although commerce was frowned upon and most traders were far from gentry levels of prestige and power, gentry did participate as investors in commercial enterprises, and wealthy merchants strived for and often attained gentry social characteristics. The exact point of division blurred, especially in the early twentieth century. In the larger cities gentry and prosperous merchants joined together in an amalgamated community leadership or in friendly alliance. In the country as a whole, however, the gentry retained its numerical and social dominance over potentially competing social elites.

Before 1905 the central government, with its regional branches, both reinforced and regulated the gentry through a system of examinations and degrees. By certifying their educational attainments (and making these attainments more valuable), the government enhanced the gentry's legitimacy in the society (and its own legitimacy with the gentry). It also provided satisfaction for the wealthy by selling the less valuable degrees. Meanwhile, for a small number who successfully scaled the higher reaches of the examination ladder, it offered government jobs and enormous economic rewards. The achievement of these few reflected glory on those of similar cultural attainment who stayed at home.

Since the degrees granted through the examination system and by purchase clearly separated the possessors from those without, and since they are readily counted, they were a major yardstick for determining gentry status and have been an important quantitative tool in Chinese social history before 1905. By this measure, gentry and their families numbered over seven million, or about 2 percent of the population in the late nineteenth century.[5] But the degrees were one aspect of the gentry, not the entire content of their social and economic role. Indeed, the social functions and characteristics that have been ascribed to the gentry were in the nineteenth century by no means confined to degree holders.[6] Hence, if we look at this culturally distinctive elite from the vantage point of their relationship to the larger society rather than of their formal links to the government, the gentry class extends beyond the degree holders even before 1905. As landowners of education and cultural talents, roughly the same group remained the dominant social element on the local scene after the examinations were no more. They remained the people with whom governmental authority, whether extending out of Peking or from some closer source, had to make its peace or perish. They remained those in most direct competition with the peasant for the agricultural product and who had the most personally at stake in containing "disruptive elements" in the countryside.

Things could not be quite the same after the ancient manner of awarding the old degrees was terminated in 1905. But neither could a profound change occur in the social structure without either social revolution or a change in the economic structure through rapid development. A country-wide revolution in the social structure came only after 1949, and rapid economic development still later. The gentry had recovered smartly from the Taiping Rebellion of the 1850s and 1860s and in the first two decades of the twentieth century enjoyed a notable flowering of activity and influence.

The continuing dominance of the gentry well into the twentieth century despite storms of rebellion, reform, and revolution underlines the peculiarity of change in modern China when measured against familiar Western models. (Whether these models accurately state the realities of change in the West is a separate question.) We find radically new ideas penetrating the literate population without a substantial rising "middle class" to advocate them. We find a new range of prestigious occupations—military officer, newspaperman, politican, engineer, scientist, even lawyer—but recruited largely from the same class which had in the past aspired chiefly to roles in education and the government bureaucracy. We find strong movements for reform and revolution without any profound change in the structure of the early twentieth-century economy. Foreign trade and the few new industries in the treaty ports had made little penetrating impact, quantitatively, on the agrarian economy and its traditional commercial adjuncts, where the center of economic gravity remained.[7] The political changes sweeping China did not arise from some new economic system, from altered relations in the factors of production, or from a new layer in the social system. Such as there was that was new in these respects played its role in advancing change, but its limited strength could not account for the turmoil that was occurring even before the May Fourth Movement. (The meagerness of structural change in society and the economy also helps explain gentry success in maintaining ultimate control over political movement until after World War I.) The main stimulus to change came in these years not from structural alterations already accomplished within the society but from imperialism. More accurately, the demand for change stemmed from Chinese perceptions of imperialist threats and of the remedies required.

The demand for change did not leave the gentry elite untouched. The old cultural qualifications for membership in the gentry seemed unsuitable for leadership in a world of competing nations—a world where, it was finally admitted, China was far behind in the competition. "Western learning," science, industrial entrepreneurship, modern military expertise, the talents of a publicist—these challenged a classical education as the skills useful for social advancement. As more gentry (or their sons) acquired the new skills, the content of the elite culture was modified.

One might conceive of this process as the end of the gentry, or at least its division into a modernizing, essentially nongentry offshoot, an intelligentsia without class character, and a traditional, generally reactionary gentry branch. The degree to which one stresses the separation and autonomy of the Westernized intelligentsia (including students in Western-style schools) depends on the point one wishes to make. Certainly attending school in Japan and writing stirring editorials in urban newspapers, for example, were new styles of life for sons of gentry, and fathered new attitudes. In the absence of any new, broad, economically based class, one is tempted to attribute political change to the activities of this small intellectual stratum. There is a partial truth in the attribution, and as individuals they are interesting, identifiable, accessible spokesmen for some of the currents of the larger society.

But there are problems with isolating and elevating the social and political roles of this group. To do so exaggerates on both sides the gap between the gentry left at home and the son pursuing his quest for "Western learning." While the son was imbibing nationalism in Tokyo, the father was often learning its meaning back in Hunan, Kwangtung, Shantung, Szechwan, or wherever, as a variety of gentry and merchant-based political movements swept the provinces, especially after 1904. The gentry and their merchant allies were classes in motion, historical products but not mired in the past. On the other hand, in the years surrounding the 1911 Revolution, the intellectual generally remained bound to gentry social attitudes. He often scurried home when trouble threatened and helped maintain order in time-honored gentry style.

Take, for example, the case of Ting Wen-chiang (1887—1936). Born of Kiangsu gentry parents, Ting excelled in the intensive classical training proper to his station, until in 1902 at age fifteen he joined the swelling stream of youth seeking Western knowledge in Japan. Two years later he went to Britain, and eventually acquired degrees in both geology and biology at Glasgow. In the 1920s, he became China's leading exponent of the scientific outlook. Hu Shih described him as "the most Westernized Chinese" and "most under the influence of science." Fu Ssu-nien considered him "truly the best and most useful representative of China in the new age. He is the purest product of the Europeanization of China." His return from his foreign education occurred in 1911, before the revolution, when he published, at age twenty-five, an early version of the scientifically based view of life for which he was later famous.[8] Here, surely, was a young product of the new spirit who was as well advanced along the road of Westernization and as distant from "the old gentry" as any person of privilege in China at the end of the Ch'ing.

But in that same year, when the revolution erupted, Ting returned to his native town, T'ai-hsing, just north of the Yangtze River between Shanghai and Nanking. In his own words, written six months after the event:

> On arriving home I found that the people were also in a great panic, for the town had declared for the Revolutionaries after the fall of Soochow, and the disorderly element began to take full advantage of the change. The gentry asked me to organize a local guard, thinking that since I had been abroad I was capable of doing anything and everything in the world. This I did with the help of my trusted servant, an ex-sergeant in Chao Er Fong's army. I was greatly astonished at the easiness with which order could be kept, for though the crops were especially bad last year and there were many unemployed people about town, we kept perfect order for more than a month with nothing better than rusty old swords.[9]

A British academic degree had supplemented, in the local conceptions of prestige and authority, the exalted *chü-jen* and *chin-shih* degrees of the Chinese imperial system. The gentry had not closed their minds to the changes in the air. And the role in his home community of the gentry lad who had made good in the new style was still molded by old patterns of expected behavior. Insofar as he conformed to these expectations, his ties to a gentry outlook were by no means severed. The Westernized intellectual stratum was not independent of its social origins.

Nor could the Westernized intelligentsia effect its programs without eliciting support from the rest of society, or some major section of it. Not unexpectedly, its primary relationship was with the gentry. Leaders of the new political movements of the early twentieth century only spottily advocated programs benefiting peasants and petty traders and readily abandoned them. Programs fortifying gentry interests found numerous and determined advocates. Merchant interests were remembered but secondary. Despite the bitter struggles among groups within the Westernized fold (notably between associates of Liang Ch'i-ch'ao and those of Sun Yat-sen), they agreed on much, and both could find allies in the reforming (and therefore partly Westernized) segments of the bureaucracy. After all, each of these groups recruited much of its membership from the gentry and was therefore naturally close to gentry concerns. Although the first thoughts of a political leader were not to serve the selfish interests of any particular group, pressures in that direction were formidable. To be effective without challenging the social order, he had to adjust to a social structure in which gentry still carried the greatest weight. Even Sun Yat-sen, not himself of gentry origin, accommodated. The intelligentsia was impelled from behind even as it led.

The persistence of the gentry should not be taken to mean an undifferentiated class without internal divisions or differences. Although relatively few gentry actually inhabited villages, there was quite a range of urban environments in China. The administrative importance of the town in which a gentry family lived probably corresponded roughly to a hierarchy among gentry.[10] A number of attributes may have been apportioned unequally along this hierarchy: wealth, level of academic degrees, exposure to new ideas and Western-style learning, influence with the bureaucracy. His position on this scale and his place of residence would determine whether a particular gentry acted as a member of the local, provincial or national elite. His role might substantially influence his views about the apportionment of formal power among local, provincial, and national political units.

Those from the narrow upper reaches of the gentry could hope for national or provincial power and might be cushioned from local social struggles by commercial and rent-collecting agencies. The large number of lesser gentry looked first to local politics for reinforcement and, because of their proximity to the front lines of the gentry-peasant class struggle, might appear to the top political elite excessively acquisitive and therefore socially disruptive. Substantial tensions might develop between these two groups. We shall observe Yuan Shih-k'ai as president acting, in his view of it, to restrain the local gentry exploiter.

From 1895 onward, as political activism increased among the gentry, different political tendencies flourished at all levels of the gentry hierarchy. Although sharing both nationalism and a gentry social base, the reformer and the revolutionary might end up in deadly competition. Further, determined gentry conservatives were still important in some provinces after the Boxer affair, even if their political power slipped remarkably by the eve of the revolution. There were many lines along which the gentry could be divided.[11]

These divisions within the gentry were counterbalanced by circumstances encouraging class cohesion. Gentry solidarity in face of challenges from below remained firm. (This was to change in later decades, when elements of the elite youth defected to the social revolution.) Even as politics and occupations were diversifying, interaction within the social elite was increasing. The telegraph permitted national debates on immediate issues. Communication nets spread more widely through newspapers and magazines, reaching well beyond the provincial capitals and major cities into small towns.[12] The reform programs brought the gentry into province-wide activities more frequently and intensively than in the past. Elections, and the preparation for them, induced efforts to strengthen linkages among gentry from the local through the provincial and even national levels.[13] Politicization of the social elite led to divergent and competing political programs but at the same time probably increased the degree of active coordination up and down the gentry hierarchy.[14] Despite differing strategies, the sense of common engagement in great causes and in defense of class interests may have been intensified.

Local and provincial politics were subject to struggles for power reflecting social differences within the gentry. But in a national perspective, these differences were overshadowed by achievement of what appears to have been substantial consensus regarding the major issues: during the first decade of the century, agreement on the desirability of institutional reforms; in 1911, agreement on the dispensibility of the Ch'ing; and in 1916, agreement on the rejection of Yuan Shih-k'ai's rule. During 1912 and 1913, the upper gentry seemed on the whole inclined to support Yuan Shih-k'ai more than his enemies. But it was hardly the case that the lesser gentry in broad sections of the country rallied to the opposition when the first test came. The political divisions marking the Second Revolution of 1913 do not seem to have been determined by social cleavages in the gentry that cut across provincial boundaries. In other words, the political consequences of social differentiation among the gentry were to a great extent contained until after Yuan's demise, when the reformist élan of the late Ch'ing and early republic had subsided.

We should not project the social effect of a commercial or industrial revolution onto the changes occurring in China before World War I. The fact that the broad outlines of the economic and social structures had not changed had political meaning. The gentry continued through its education and its lien on the agricultural product to be in the best position to exploit the new opportunities that change was bringing. Moreover, it had not lost its historical self-image as the natural font of leadership. Wealthy city-based merchants had good opportunities to participate in the new movements, but their numbers and prestige in most parts of the country were insufficient to compete with the social force of the gentry.[15] Outside the handful of large commercial centers, where participation was shared with the commercial class, most leadership as well as support for the variety of political movements in the late Ch'ing and early republic was imbedded in or was recently connected with the gentry class. There were some important exceptions, which will be noted, but in general this shared characteristic cut across the diversity of politics.

Political Movement in the Late Ch'ing

Although the dominance of an agriculturally based, urban-dwelling, classically educated gentry persisted into the twentieth century, some of its roles and attitudes, and those of merchants in a few large urban centers, were startlingly new. What was radical and confined to a few in the abortive 1898 reform movement became ordinary and widespread. Reform, resistance to foreign incursions, national sovereignty, self-government—these slogans became so common that within a few years of the turn of the century they were looked on by some intellectuals as platitudes.

The striking features of the new atmosphere were the spread of political activity and its nationalistic tenor. Gentry, by virtue of their local leadership, had always had what might be described as a political role in matters affecting the area circumscribed by the extent of their personal social power. They were not only extralegal adjudicators of local disputes and intermediaries between community and government. They also managed or collaborated with officialdom in managing a variety of local good works, such as orphanages, bridge building, schools, and dikes. In the nineteenth century, they became supervisors of local military units. Merchants, particularly in the eighteenth and nineteenth centuries, had organized themselves in protective associations, not only on their home ground, but in guilds or Landsmannschaften (*hui-kuan*) in cities far from their place of origin. But these characteristic activities of the late empire, both gentry and merchant, were limited to a very narrow conception of the proper sphere of concern. Politics broadly conceived was not precisely a government monopoly, but the arena in which those outside the bureaucracy were allowed to exercise leadership was small. Handling large issues, which affected a province, region, or whole class, was, before the 1890s, exclusively the prerogative of the emperor and his servitors. Even within the bureaucracy, the channels of communication on a particular subject might be closed.[16]

Philip Kuhn has shown how gentry were entrusted with local administrative powers in the mid-nineteenth century in certain regions. What began as a military response to the Taiping Rebellion become extended to tax collecting and police authority. Kuhn suggests that this enhancement of the local power of the social elite was the practical basis for the institution of local self-government in the early twentieth century, which legitimized what had been customary functions for many years.[17] The mid-nineteenth-century growth of local unofficial powers, particularly if they can be shown to have persisted to the end of the century, helps explain the energy and confidence with which the gentry took matters into their own hands later on. But, until their powers were enlarged to allow for political organization beyond the locality, throughout their social class, and for breaking down the political insulation of the county or region, the gentry as a class were still at a disadvantage before central government power.

With the crisis of confidence induced by the defeat by Japan in 1895 and the subsequent Western scramble for concessions, large-scale political movement outside the government (short of rebellion) became noticeable for the first time since the end of the Ming dynasty. In Hunan, there were gentry-led reform societies. In Peking in 1898, K'ang Yu-wei organized an extragovernmental association addressing itself to the largest issues besetting the country. Dormant during two years of reaction, the seeds planted by the 1898 reform movement grew astonishingly after the Boxer Rebellion. Associations to defend the nation, to create a modern school system, to build railways, to develop organs of self-government, to put pressure on foreign governments through boycotts—a whole panoply of movements, broadly based in the gentry and merchant elite, flourished with government toleration. Indeed, in many cases, the governmental posture was rather that of stimulation and cooperation. Needless to say, this greatly advanced the enthusiasm and degree of gentry and merchant participation. But political motion was not easily controlled. Before the end of the decade, it was frequently turned against the government, especially the central organs in Peking.

Politics on the march was, of course, not a new phenomenon in Chinese history, although the society's nonbureaucratic elite had not been so assertive since the founding of the Ch'ing two and one-half centuries earlier. It bears analogy with the last decades of the Ming, when scholars out of office banded together to influence the policy of the central government. There is something here symptomatic of an expiring dynasty: when the gentry are out of control, the mandate to rule is slipping.

Seen as a whole, however, the early twentieth-century politicization of the nonbureaucratic elite, especially the gentry, was an unprecedented event. It contained a new element—a large quotient of nationalism.

Chinese were responding to the incursions of Western power along their ocean and land frontiers well before they were recognizably nationalist in their outlook. They responded with warfare, with old techniques of manipulation (the Western barbarians, though unfathomable, were also simple people, easy to fool, readily placated with concessions of unimportant land and lucre), with bloody antiforeign riots. But what we recognize as the mainstream of twentieth-century nationalism did not emerge coherently until about the time of the Sino-Japanese War (1894–95).

John Schrecker has persuasively argued that the key concept heralding the birth of Chinese nationalism was the claim to sovereignty, that is, the declaration of the aspiration to exclusive jurisdiction over all affairs (no matter how trivial) conducted within the country's borders and the sacred nature of the territory (no matter how barren or remote) so governed. To acquire the power necessary to fulfill this aspiration, reform in domestic affairs was necessary, reform which would release the people's energies and weld them into a unified force.[18] Militant antiforeignism and the advocacy of reform along Western lines, which had developed independently in the decades before the Sino-Japanese War, were wedded at that time, notably in the writings of K'ang Yu-wei. Then, the catastrophe of the Boxer Rebellion sounded the deathknell for antiforeignism without reform. The union of the two was henceforth indissoluble in all major political movements. A nationalism, insisting on the recovery of sovereign rights (most of which, when lost, had not been considered in such terms) and on the creation of instrumentalities to that end through reform, was the main ideological content of the politicization of gentry and merchant after 1900.

The late Ch'ing expressions of the nationalist movement in the area of sovereign rights were drives to recover old railway and mining concessions and to prevent new ones, militant defense of frontiers, and campaigns in response to particular incidents of foreign insult. In the effort to recover concessions, the populace was at first following government initiative and later compelling government action, or some mixture of the two.

In the area of domestic institutional and social reform, the chief efforts were in the creation of new schools to dispense Western learning, the building of a modern army, the establishment of a separate judiciary with new law codes to go with it, the institution of partially elected representative bodies to embody new concepts of self-government, a campaign to reduce and within a few years abolish the habit of opium smoking, the formation of a modern police force, and the extensive reorganization of the administrative organs of government, both in Peking and in the provinces. Some of these activities, especially the last, were programs where initiation and execution were almost entirely governmental. But in most of them, participation by the unofficial elite of the society, often in highly organized forms, played a large part. There was a great deal to be excited about, then, if you were a leader in or out of government in the last ten years of the Ch'ing.

The programs of anti-imperialism and institutional reform, which in the late Ch'ing were the leading political concerns of those working within the system, had social meanings. As might be expected, the social implications were less explicitly acknowledged by those benefiting than by those disadvantaged or left behind. The new school system was advanced as (among other things) a step toward universal education. In practice, it fell far short of the goal and to a great extent served to retread the old elites, equipping them or their children to preserve their elite status in times of change.[19] The New Army (the Western-style divisions and brigades of the late Ch'ing) was dedicated, in theory, to national defense. It no doubt had some value as a deterrent to thoughts of invasion. But before the revolution it actually fired its weapons only in the suppression of unrest among the rural and urban poor. The organs of representative government were established on the theory that participation would mobilize the people behind the government and produce greater unity in the country. Or, especially among those outside the government, it was held that self-government could do better for national strength what the centralized bureaucracy did poorly. The first Chinese self-government organ in Shanghai was founded, according to its chroniclers, because of "apprehension at the

growth of foreign power and the loss of sovereignty."[20] In practice, however, organs of self-government were also instruments for confirming or augmenting gentry power at the expense of both the central government and the peasantry.

These points are, of course, only of very general application.[21] But an incident in rural Honan about a year before the revolution illustrates a widespread pattern. Owing to a lack of funding for the reform programs of Yeh county, the self-governing body undertook to raise money from the villages. The gentry went forth to persuade the people of the justice of this course and to give speeches on the benefits of self-government. The common people at one rural gathering were unpersuaded. Their spokesman was quoted as saying: "Before, when you weren't managing these new policies, the people remained undisturbed. Now, the management of self-government, the police, the schools—all seek their support from the backs of the people." Certain taxes had risen two and one-half times as a consequence, he said, and the officials and gentry were now conspiring together to extort further funds from the people. The considerable crowd which had assembled for the lecture by the reforming gentry, it was reported, expressed agreement with their spokesman. But another tax was imposed anyway. The villages became immensely agitated and approached a state of insurrection. Within a day, it was said, some ten to twenty thousand had gathered and planned to march on the county capital. Meanwhile, the gentry had taken to their heels and petitioned the county magistrate for help, who felt it was too big for him and appealed to the provincial governor. A brigade of the New Army (pride of reformers, weapon of national defense) was sent to suppress the peasant demonstrators. We are spared the details of precisely how that was done.[22]

The reform programs, including self-government offices, became special objects of popular hostility in the waning years of the Ch'ing. In its second year of existence, the Shanghai self-governing board, a gentry-run affair, complained: "For some peculiar reason we are feared by the common people and cannot win their trust."[23] In Szechwan, the first attack on reform policies occurred in 1904, with the destruction of a Western-style school. As attacks on reformist institutions increased, those on missionaries and Chinese Catholics declined.[24] In 59 recorded cases of rural uprisings between 1908 and 1911 in Kiangsu and Chekiang, the main issues were the census investigation, which provided the excuse for a tax collected exclusively by the gentry; new taxes for schools, the police, and self-government offices; the rising price of rice; and the prohibition of poppy cultivation. In one disturbance in March, 1911, not far from Shanghai, occasioned by a self-government bureau taking over a temple, twelve self-government offices and twenty-nine schools were destroyed.[25] Almost every section of the country experienced numerous cases of violent peasant hostility to the reform projects, their gentry beneficiaries, and the resulting tax burdens.

One need not stress corruption on the part of self-governing institutions (almost everywhere gentry dominated), though it was frequently charged and undoubtedly occurred. More fundamental was the fact that the reforms served not only nationalist aspirations, but also particular social groups, notably the gentry. A powerful conjunction of idealism and material interest occurred. National salvation (*chiu-kuo*) and nation building (*chien-kuo*) became bywords. And the social benefits of programs launched in their name were distributed in a manner skewed in favor of the old elites. This conjunction served to lift the gentry out of their local preoccupations, to mobilize them into a more self-conscious class, and to propel them into a frantic period of assertive political leadership.

Provincialism

The degree to which many gentry and merchants were imbued with nationalist spirit has been masked by the phenomenon of provincialism. Almost instinctively assuming that devotion to province and dedication to nation must be mutually exclusive, contrary attitudes, students of the early twentieth century have generally measured the progress of a man or movement out of traditionalism into modernism at least in part by his repudiation of provincial interests in favor of national ones.

This view, when applied to the actual politics of the early twentieth century. immediately faces a contradiction. Admittedly, provincialism had links with the past and there were retrograde varieties. (The disparaging meanings in English specifying narrow attitudes and lack of refinement are, of course, not contained in my use of the word.) But many ardent nationalists were, in theory or practice or both, enthusiastic provincialists. Some leading revolutionaries behaved at times in a provincial mode. Provincialism was strong among many of the most active and articulate bearers of the new thought and the new politics of the time. Indeed, there was not a major political movement that escaped being marked by provincialism. A politically oriented provincialism—or the disposition to pursue one's political goals through the provincial unit—was much more than an inheritance from the past. Rather, in the early twentieth century, it reached unprecedented heights of importance. It is more properly considered a largely new or remade phenomenon.

This new version of provincialism emerged as dissatisfaction with the Peking government's failure to stem foreign encroachment spread. Seeking an arena for responding effectively to foreign encroachment, portions of the literate population began to focus attention on the province. The provincialism that resulted was a devotion to one's province as a vehicle for reform and for protection against foreign power. It was the infusion of what we would call nationalist goals into a provincial framework. Its conception of China's political organization was implicitly federalistic.

This politically oriented provincialism with its nationalist programs bore a relation to older localism similar to nationalism's relation to Sino-centric culturalism (that is, the view that "the significant unit was really the whole civilization rather than the narrower political unit of a nation within a larger cultural whole).[26] Localism, or particularistic attachment to one's native area, was a diffuse sentiment, strongest with respect to the village or town of one's family seat and progressively weaker as applied to larger units. It was still perceptible at the provincial and even supraprovincial level. Officials like Tseng Kuo-fan and Li Hung-chang used it in building their bureaucratic power, just as Chinese cultural loyalties lent cohesion to the empire. By contrast, provincialism and nationalism grew out of the new politicization of unofficial elites (gentry and merchant), which required a new definition of instrumentalities.

At one level, the province (*sheng*) became the most frequently chosen instrument of the new movements of the early twentieth century—not the county or department (*hsien* or *chou*), not the prefecture or circuit (*fu* or *tao*), and not the supraprovincial combinations of Ch'ing viceregal administration. At another level, the nation (*kuo-chia*)—more difficult to define territorially—became a focus for the new, more broadly based politics. (At yet another level, the whole Asian or East Asian area was seen as a potential base for an alliance against Western imperialism. This pan-Asian conception deserves treatment, but remained a relatively minor theme at this time.) Although in the sphere of practical policy provincialism and nationalism often conflicted (as did nationalism and pan-Asianism), they were similar products of the same circumstances and had similar goals. They frequently coexisted in the mind of one person or the program of one party and were easily reconciled through federalist structures.

The provincialism that flourished around the time of the 1911 Revolution must be distinguished from notions of regionalism that have been applied to bureaucratic politics in the last decades of the nineteenth century or to the warlord period that was to come. Whatever the extent of accumulations of personal power by high regional officials in the late Ch'ing—and its importance has been hotly disputed—the phenomenon bears little resemblance to the extrabureaucratic and highly ideological movement of provincialism of the early twentieth century.[27] Although traces of provincialism were ingredients in the sort of regionalism Diana Lary describes as underlying warlord strength in the 1920s and 1930s, the main features of the two tendencies were starkly different. Among the contrasts were provincialism's function as a response to imperialism, its ideological assertiveness (with its share of intellectual advocates), and its elite social base.[28]

Provincialism naturally incorporated particularistic interests and cultural inheritances. The great rights-recovery and railway-building movements of the provincial gentry and merchants in the first decade of the twentieth century were devoted to regaining concessions granted to foreigners by the central government. But ideas of modernization and patriotism were accompanied in these movements by much profit taking and power seeking. Provincialism, like regionalism, also fed on historical differences of language and customs. It has been usual to dwell on such apparently corrupting and "antimodern" features of provincialism when discussing its political manifestations in the early part of the century.[29] But these features in no way distinguish provincialism from nationalism. The quest for privilege and the exploitation of cultural differences (real or manufactured) are, if not the essence of nationalism, at least among its common attributes.[30]

Concrete expressions of politically oriented provincialism began appearing in the late nineteenth century as a response to the interrelated desires for internal reform and external defense. In the Hunan reform effort of the 1890s—the first reform movement with important popular as well as official backing—the proposition was advanced that the local Hunanese gentry were more qualified to rule than were officials imported from elsewhere, as the regulations of the dynasty demanded.[31] One could trace the suggestion to much earlier rounds in the debate on degrees of administrative centralization, but this time it merged with certain selected Western notions about self-government. Liang Ch'i-ch'ao, a leading popularizer of Western thought, endorsed provincial autonomy in late 1897 and 1898. Despairing at the court's inability to institute reforms and cope with foreign aggression, he was ready to consider the need for Hunan to secede from the empire, carry out reform, and become a base area for China's ultimate liberation. In 1901 he gave theoretical underpinnings to the idea of provincial autonomy by applying Rousseau's advocacy of small states in federal relationships to the Chinese situation.[32] The commonest justification was not the nurture of democracy and individual freedom, but rather the release of people's energies on behalf of reforms leading to social and military strength. Some political writers, such as K'ang Yu-wei and Liang Ch'i-ch'ao himself, soon rejected the emerging enthusiasm for provincial autonomy. Despite objections, the idea of self-government became closely, though by no means exclusively, linked to the provincial unit.

In the decade before the 1911 Revolution, provincialism commonly served explicitly nationwide objectives but with means sought within the province. As a provincial journal noted in 1903: "The spirit of self-government lies in taking the nation's affairs as the purposes of the locality's existence and in using the strength of the locality to effect [these purposes]."[33] In addition to provincially focused journals, often published by Chinese students in Tokyo (and not solely devoted to provincialism), works with provocative titles like *New Kwangtung* and *New Hunan* were circulated. As in the case of Liang Ch'i-ch'ao's toying in late 1897 with the notion of Hunan's independence, extreme proposals were aired: for example, in the wake of the Boxer affair, that Kwangtung should secede from China to prevent Peking contracting a French takeover; or in 1909, that the Yunnanese should sever relations with the central government and proceed to liberate Vietnam, Burma, and India from Western rule, in order to prevent the otherwise inevitable submission of Yunnan.[34] The underlying assumptions were that the Ch'ing government in Peking had failed, that there was in fact no nation in being, only a dynastic empire, and that through self-rule and local initiative one's own province could begin to rectify the situation. Through federalist conceptions, provincialism generally stayed within the framework of a larger Chinese nationalism. But it was an immensely powerful force in its own right.

As political movements spread in the first decade of the new century, aspects of the imperial reform program abetted the growth and organization of provincial sentiment. Elective provincial assemblies became centers for the articulation of provincial interests immediately upon their establishment in 1909. The New Army, whose purpose was ostensibly national defense, had provincial adjuncts. In addition to the central divisions raised and financed by Peking, each province was instructed to develop local military formations on the same model. Though centrally inspired, they acquired strong provincial identification (and also, of course, some local uses, as in the suppression of a peasant demonstration described earlier).[35] The same can be said of parts of the new school system. These reforms became vehicles for provincial sentiment to different degrees in different provinces, but in general there was this side to them.

Apparent success in various provincial endeavors created a favorable atmosphere for forging more links at that level. Foreign mining concessions were revoked in part through agitation by provincial organizations. Railway building rights were similarly retrieved. Provincial companies for various purposes were formed. Provincial assemblies played politically prominent roles. Only time would reveal that, without drastic changes in social policies, the province, like the central government, was unable satisfactorily to achieve goals of reform and defense.

In the formal revolutionary organizations of the time, provincialism was resisted by some but continued as a powerful influence. The founding of the interprovincial T'ung-meng hui under Sun Yat-sen's leadership in 1905 represented a victory over provincial divisions among revolutionaries. Sun's main argument in persuading the important Hunanese contingent to join with him was the need for unity among the provinces to prevent foreign meddling during the revolution.[36] In the first issue of the party organ, a call was issued for a truce in what was seen as growing provincial exclusiveness.[37] A small group of supraprovincial leaders cleaved to the aim of a centralized republican order, overriding provincial privilege. But in practice the T'ung-meng hui membership divided into autonomous provincial branches.[38] The linkage of local self-government with provincial autonomy persisted among many young radicals. It was this provincialist undertone to the T'ung-meng hui, perhaps, which in October, 1911, induced Liang Ch'i-ch'ao, by then a confirmed centralizer, to dismiss the revolutionaries as "regionalists," incapable of unifying the country.[39]

If obvious nationalists, such as revolutionary students in Japan, could be at the same time provincialists, then it is not inconceivable that obvious provincialists could also be nationalists. The provincial movements of gentry and merchants in the last decade of the Ch'ing shared the mixture of nationalism and provincialism that I have characterized and need not be considered less progressive or less patriotic because of it. In Szechwan, for example, the vigorous opposition to the nationalization of provincial railway projects in the summer of 1911 arose from nationalist protest against the foreign financing that Peking proposed and from provincialist resentment at central interference in local affairs (including local profits). Szechwan by herself, it was asserted, could better protect national honor. Hence, Peking's nationalization of the Szechwan trunk line project in May, 1911, was not only interference in local privilege, from a Szechwanese point of view; it was also unpatriotic.

As the confrontation in Szechwan illustrated, the spread of provincialist sentiment was accompanied by a determination in the court to centralize wherever possible. From Peking's viewpoint, the reforms of the previous ten years had been intended to increase the power of the central state, not to dissipate it. Plans to further the authority and penetration of the center were in preparation on the eve of revolution, especially in the sensitive area of taxation. Even as theories justifying provincial initiative and autonomy were flourishing, contrary proposals were emerging. K'ang Yu-wei, in exile from 1898 until the 1911 Revolution but reaching a Chinese audience, learned to distinguish self-government at a local level, which he vigorously espoused, from provincial autonomy, which he quickly came to abhor. Governors-general in the provinces already had too much power, he argued, and even greater provincial independence would aggravate national weakness, abet civil war, and induce foreign intervention. He struggled against ideas of provincial separatism when they appeared within his own circle in the first years of the century. By 1908 K'ang was advocating the displacement of provinces by smaller units to heighten the government's authority in the country.[40] The proposal to abolish the provincial unit was not adopted by the court before its collapse, but the centralizing principle informing it was shared.

Provincialist and centralizer pursued in opposite directions their search for structural remedies to China's weakness. Their angry recoil from each other widened the political gap between them and hastened the ultimate confrontations. The 1911 Revolution was, among other things, the climax of the first round of conflict over this issue. Other rounds soon followed during Yuan Shih-k'ai's presidency.

This discussion of China on the eve of the 1911 Revolution has been necessarily selective. The purpose has been to emphasize a few features of the scene that are key to what immediately follows. Peasants, for example, who became in later decades central actors in China's unfolding revolutionary drama, remained in only subsidiary political roles in the years with which we are concerned. Like the petty traders and rural unemployed or the small numbers of industrial workers, they were not entirely passive and enter the story at certain junctures. But their collective power was unformed and they did not yet decide the direction of the main events. And it would be another work altogether to attempt a summary of all the intellectual currents and political movements preceding the revolution. What I consider the most important features of the late Ch'ing—most important for what was to come under the presidency of Yuan Shih-k'ai—are now apparent: the continuing social dominance of the gentry class, even as it modified somewhat its shape and cultural content; the politicization of the unofficial elites of the gentry and wealthy merchants; and the spread of nationalism combined with a new, political provincialism as the content of political concern.

Related to the last two, and never to be forgotten, is the continuing pressure of Western and Japanese power on Chinese society and sovereignty. We shall have several occasions to return to the subject of the specific role of foreign imperialism in the events of the early republic. Its relationship with Chinese politics had become so intricate by this period that it is often difficult to isolate the effect of its influence. The foreign presence, in other words, was so entrenched that it had become almost domestic to China. This is not to say that the presence was accepted. The one main motivating force in Chinese politics which cut across all political complexions was the desire to remove that presence, or at least subordinate it to Chinese power and dignity. No one at this time had discovered how to do this; the problem was rather staving off further losses of sovereignty. This immense fact cast a pall over all political efforts and constantly undermined the legitimacy of any leadership.

Westerners or Japanese, however, were not in control. They aspired to be, in one way or another, but China was too large, too complex, with too much social momentum, for simple manipulation from outside. Chinese politics remained largely in Chinese hands, even as foreigners looked for opportunities to tip the scales in their own favor.

Chapter 2

The Birth of the Republic

The founding of the republic, most educated Chinese have felt, represented progress. Although some updated, constitutional versions of monarchy were quite respectable in the world of 1911, republican institutions and the ideas attached to them were considered the vanguard of political development. Once a serious revolt broke out against the Ch'ing dynasty in October, 1911, the judgment that Manchu rule was an anathema and an anachronism spread rapidly and widely among the social elite of the country. Almost as many readily accepted a republic as the proper alternative. With only a decade of widespread discussion of the possibility, China rushed headlong into republicanism.

But for whom was the republic? The republic was progress, but from what vantage point in the society was progress to be defined? One might hope that it was progress for everyone—for the nation, in fact, where new energies would be released and universally beneficial achievements recorded. This is what the leaders of the revolution, and those who joined in as it succeeded, spoke of. In contemplating the revolution and its aftermath, it is worth exploring the conditions and expectations, perhaps the special pleading, which underlay this optimism. Who participated and why? And who survived in power to consolidate? There is no single set of answers for all parts of China, but these are questions underlying the following brief review of the revolution and of some of the main themes that emerged during it.

The Ch'ing imperial government proved in the end to be an easy mark for the revolutionary movement because it had failed to satisfy the ever-growing demand for redressing the imbalance of power with the West. The measure of failure lay both in foreign relations and in the domestic reforms which might promise future success in foreign relations. The question,

"How can China acquire the wealth and power to save herself?" eventually raised the question, "Is the Ch'ing government a contributor or an impediment to national salvation?" As the government raced to meet the rising expectations of performance (an aspect of the spread of nationalism), it precipitated new conflicts within the society, which disposed Chinese to doubt further the virtue of the existing order. Spectacular successes in foreign relations or domestic remodeling might have contained the conflicts. But by 1911 expectations were such that the modest successes of the previous decade, though surpassing anything since the Opium War, were insufficient to stem disaffection. Domestic conflict, therefore, occupied center stage.

Like the reforms of the late Ch'ing, the 1911 Revolution was an affair ultimately dominated by the elite social strata. In most places (I shall note some important exceptions) revolution was achieved not by mass force but by coup d'etat, not by a great social turmoil where the conflict of class interests produces a reordering of privilege, but by the rapid defection of most leading social elements, with social conflict contained. Agitated for the most part by China's political failure rather than social injustice, the formal revolutionary leadership worked to dampen down any evidences that the social order was combustible. Where alliances had been struck during the revolution with lower class groups (secret societies, bandits), concerted efforts were made almost everywhere after the revolution to sever the alliance and reimpose their subordination. Within five months the efforts had succeeded.

Aside from small numbers at the very peak of the Ch'ing political system and apart from the casualties of the revolutionary violence, most life patterns were not profoundly altered by the experience of 1911. The villages were particularly untouched, though there might have been a great deal of gentry uneasiness about them during the uncertainty of the revolution. Commerce was only briefly interrupted and recovery was rapid. Those who were pursuing new educational or professional careers, if they had been diverted by the revolution, seemed generally to have returned shortly to their prerevolutionary pattern once the settlement came. In contrast to the May Fourth Movement, which was a turning point in the lives of many in the elite, the 1911 Revolution was for most only an incident, an interruption. This would not have been obvious during the excitement that accompanied the revolution. Enthusiasm was great among those involved, from the turbulence in Szechwan in the summer of 1911, to the

RUSSIA

MANCHURIA

HEILUNGCHIANG

KIRIN

Vladivostok

OUTER MONGOLIA

INNER MONGOLIA

CHIHLI

Peking

Mukden

FENGTIEN

KOREA (J.)

Tientsin

Talien (J.)

SHANSI

Taiyuan

Tsinan

TSINGHAI

KANSU

SHENSI

Yellow River

SHANTUNG

Tsingtao (Ger.)

Lanchow

Sian

Kaifeng

HONAN

KIANGSU

Nanking

Shanghai

ANHWEI

HUPEH

Chengtu

Yangtze River

Hankow

Anking

SZECHWAN

Wuchang

Hangchow

Chungking

Nanchang

CHEKIANG

Changsha

KIANGSI

HUNAN

Kweiyang

KWEICHOW

FUKIEN

Kunming

Foochow

YUNNAN

Kweilin

KWANGTUNG

KWANGSI

Canton

TAIWAN (J.)

Hanoi

Hongkong (Br.)

INDOCHINA
(Fr.)

Revolutionary Provinces in 1911

establishment of the first republican regime in Wuchang in October, to the triumph of revolutionary power in fourteen provinces, to the final abdication of the Manchu monarch in February, 1912. The excitement continued into the first year of the republic. But retrospectively we can observe that there was no major redirection of energies but rather a continuation of tendencies set in motion before the revolution.

The course of the revolution did serve to accentuate or underline some of the themes of the last ten to fifteen years of the Ch'ing. Four in particular are worth elaborating in their revolutionary context: the prominence of the military, the political importance of the provincial unit, the growing power of the gentry, and the continuing foreign encroachment on China's sovereignty.

The Military

During the course of the revolution military men assumed roles of broad leadership. In the first phase of seizure of power, the New Army units in or near most provincial capitals were not just the possessors of the greatest concentration of force but also the best organized centers of revolutionary disposition. Outside northern areas near Peking, the New Army did not need to be won over to the revolution; elements from within it led or cooperated with the revolution from the beginning. Especially in the last three or four years before the revolution, as modern military units were organized in the provinces, the army was fertile ground for revolutionary activity. (Even Peiyang units in north China were not exempt, though with difficulty their disaffection was contained.) Military leadership came easily once the challenge to Manchu rule was under way. In the second phase of consolidation within the provinces and of interprovincial coordination for the projected assault on remaining Ch'ing authority, military tasks were primary: enlisting and training soldiers to resist and attack imperial forces. In the third phase of postrevolutionary republican rule, when military tasks were no longer primary, military men continued in most provinces to lead. The reasons were more complicated than the sheer momentum of the power accumulated in the two previous phases, though this contributed. Let us examine them.

The military profession had, in the years before the revolution, acquired high prestige. In the latter half of the nineteenth century, military achievements were an avenue to high civil positions. After 1900, the ultimate destination changed from civil rank to advancement in the military itself. One trained to be an officer in the army to defend one's nation, whose precariousness was generally recognized by the elite, and to participate in the dignity and perquisites of being an officer. Some of the ablest of the privileged youth, who in other eras would have sought civil position exclusively, began to turn to a military career as a possible first choice. Aspiration toward positions in the civil government was still strong, of course, and other professions than the military had also entered the competition as elite careers—journalism, the law, political organization, business. The army and to a lesser extent the navy, however, for a time offered the greatest glory. Hence, officers were natural candidates for governorship.

With its officers recruited heavily from the gentry, the New Army was in the social complexion of its leadership an appendage of the gentry class (though like the old civil service, it might serve a variety of political functions, not always related to its social complexion). During the 1911 Revolution and its immediate aftermath, the gentry concern for the maintenance or reimposition of "law and order," that is, the enforcement of the social status quo, found its ultimate recourse in the modern military units. Their performance as guardians of the social status quo (even as they were overturning the old political order) was, then, a further reason that military men exercised more than military leadership. In provinces where there was considerable mass violence (that is, not fully mediated by organizations controlled by the elite), notably Szechwan, Shensi, and Kwangtung, the socially repressive role of the New Army was particularly apparent. In any case, the title for provincial chief that became standard during the revolution—*tu-tu*—was a military one and in the majority of instances (eventually eleven out of fourteen) was held by a military man. The predominance of civil officials in the provinces, eroded since the mid-nineteenth century, was overturned in the 1911 Revolution.

Provincialism in the Revolution

Another way in which the 1911 Revolution gave release and expression to movements that had been building pressure in the preceding years was its giving vent to a boisterous provincialism. As described in the previous chapter, the provincial unit increasingly became a focus of nongovernmental political action and sentiment during the first decade of the century. When the revolution came, the combination of self-interested and idealistic concerns that had nurtured provincialism was provided new scope.

When the Ch'ing system of authority came tumbling down, all levels of government were affected, but the province was from the beginning the main focus of reconstruction. In many places, the revolution began in the form of a province declaring its independence of the central government. These declarations were in anticipation of joining some new republican federation, but effective administrative independence was retained. Lesser localities often declared a separate independence (sometimes with their own military governors or *tu-tu*) but, with a very few exceptions, these localities were soon absorbed administratively into the provincial political framework. Nanking as a central revolutionary government from January, 1912, or later Peking as a national republican government could not compete with provincial administrative authority.

Autonomous provinces (making only minor concessions to concepts of formal Chinese unity, once contributions had been made in troops to the joint military effort during the revolution) were not only an accident of power balances. They also rested upon a strong assertion of rightness: provinces *should* run their own affairs. There was no embarrassment among many Chinese nationalists about their provincialism. Its expression was open and principled.

A dramatic expression of provincialism during the revolution was widespread dismissal from office of men from outside the province concerned. The Ch'ing administrative principle of avoidance—forbidding service in the province of one's origin—which had been occasionally compromised before 1911, was turned on its head. Not long after the revolution took hold, eleven of the home provinces had military governors who were natives (not all military men). The nonnative chiefs in the revolutionary provinces from October, 1911, until February, 1912 (mostly New Army officers), were installed by local decisions rather than central revolutionary appointment.

The issue was not confined to provincial chiefs. Thorough purges swept provincial governments and nonprovincials were sent packing. In the capital of Szechwan, for example, the process was almost complete by January, 1912.[1] Even where the revolution had not triumphed, community pressure (that is, from the gentry or merchant elite) was applied in order to effect the same pattern. In Shantung, the provincial assembly pressed for officials native to the province, and by the summer most of the new county magistrates were Shantung men. The military governor, Chou Tzu-ch'i, though appointed in the spring of 1912 by President Yuan, was also Shantungese.[2] In July, 1912, Chihli gentry petitioned the provincial chief (who was not of the province but was replaced in September by someone who was) that preference should be given to fellow provincials in filling official vacancies.[3] The provinces tolerated some nonprovincials in official position, but in the revolutionary provinces, at least, they were soon a minority. The question was not rejection of imperial appointees. Extraprovincial revolutionaries were also disfavored in provincial offices. Provincialism as a principle of political identification was triumphant.

One measure of the strength of the ideology of provincialism—the belief in the propriety of provincial autonomy—was the formal deference paid provincial sovereignty. Provinces which had gone over to the revolution sent troops to the common front against the Ch'ing armies. One major achievement was the taking of Nanking. But otherwise the revolution was not carried from one provincial capital to another by military force. There were only minor cases of "restoration" across provincial boundaries (for example, in eastern Shantung), and they did not reach the point of investing the provincial seat of government. The revolutionary provincial governments banded together against the common enemy of the central Ch'ing government, but on a voluntary basis only.

The major successful exception to nonintervention by one province in the affairs of another is the activities of Ts'ai O's revolutionary Yunnanese government. Ts'ai, a Hunanese military officer ruling Yunnan, was an outspoken opponent of provincial autonomy.[4] His dispatch of troops into both Kweichow and southern Szechwan, however, did not spread the revolution. In Kweichow, it brought postrevolutionary "law and order" in a counterrevolutionary, though still republican, style. In Szechwan, it was preceded by a local Szechwanese revolution and stayed to secure financial advantage. Much resentment was stirred up as a consequence. These cases were untypical. In Sun Yat-sen's Nanking revolutionary government respect for autonomy was briefly taken to the extent of asserting that China would have no dependencies (viz., Mongolia, Tibet) but only federated provinces.[5] In Kwangtung, Cantonese became the spoken language of government.[6] The sentiment favoring provincial autonomy was not universal but it was dominant in the provinces.

In the face of all this provincial assertion and exclusivity, must we conclude that nationalism was after all only a minor aspect of the 1911 Revolution? In general treatments of the period either we are spared any discussion of the provincialist structure and spirit of the revolution, or these aspects are pointed to as evidence that the revolution lacked a progressive, nationalist character. But the dichotomy is false. Provincialism in early twentieth-century China was imbued with nationalist purposes. There is no reason to believe that its practitioners were more (or less) self-seeking and tolerant of foreign imperialism than those opposing provincial autonomy. Proposals to transform a provincial government into a sovereign nation-state did not appear, though the opportunities to try were abundant. The provincialist aim was neither separatism nor, as with warlords later on, conquest of the whole. It was to achieve political integration at the provincial level and to join with other provinces in a high-energy federation that would obviate the need for autocracy in Peking. The theoretical position had already been developed in the last years of the Ch'ing. In chapter 4 we shall observe the reformist zeal that sometimes accompanied its political realization as a result of the 1911 Revolution.

Certain important revolutionaries were not sympathetic to the provincialist tide of politics. But its current inundated them, and they learned to swim with it. Indeed, some of them were able to ride it some distance in their early contests with Yuan Shih-k'ai after the revolution.

Gentry Power

A third manner in which the 1911 Revolution fulfilled the expectations that emerged in the late Ch'ing was the granting of greater power and influence to all levels of the gentry, shared to some extent with wealthy merchants. The prominence of New Army officers was an assurance against an abrupt displacement of gentry influence. But in this respect the New Army was only a replacement or supplement to the old assurances provided by the social complexion of the civil service. There were other developments that were more than assurances of social continuity in a turbulent period; they promised altogether new heights of wealth and power for China's social elite.

Gentry pursuit of self-interest was restrained or challenged in the old system by the dynastic administrative structure above and peasant resistance below. The Ch'ing government had in its last years attempted to purchase increased gentry support for itself by granting the gentry greater privileges and participation. A prime example was representative councils and assemblies. So appetites were already whetted when the revolution came. In the space of a few weeks the remaining restraints exercised by imperial authority were demolished. Institutions which the Ch'ing government had designed in order to use the gentry more effectively for the state became, even before the revolution, instruments of increased gentry dominance. During and after the revolution, this effect broadened. It was public and obvious in the role played by the provincial assemblies, everywhere constituted primarily of gentry. In most revolutionary provinces, the provincial assembly (or its leading members) provided legitimation for the new order.[7] The degree of actual power subsequently wielded by the provincial assembly of any particular province varied widely. For example, in Yunnan it carried little weight.[8] In Kwangtung, Kiangsi, and several northern provinces its role was limited. At the other extreme, when threatened with dissolution by the first revolutionary military governor, the Hunan provincial assembly managed to split the local New Army forces and stage a coup d'etat in its own favor.[9] In the country as a whole, the political importance of the provincial assemblies was increased by the revolution.

The critical political unit during the revolution was the province. Hence gentry influence at that level was vital to the enhancement of gentry fortunes. Much effort and intrigue were invested in securing this influence. The social orientation of the provincial army leaders, however, was often as important as the social complexion of the provincial assembly. And the actual economic payoff for the largest number came with the expansion of the incidence and power of lesser representative bodies—all sorts of local councils and assemblies.

Because the completion of the late Ch'ing program for establishing self-government organs at the local level had been planned for 1914, their existence at the time of the revolution was widespread but spotty. With a lower priority in the Ch'ing plan, assemblies at the county or prefectural level were rarer than the subcounty councils. By their relative obscurity, these various local bodies are not subject to comprehensive scrutiny. There are sufficient indications from the revolutionary period, however, to suggest a common pattern of development. First, the incidence of local self-government organs increased rapidly at all levels. Second, their control of local finances expanded enormously. Third, they aspired to control the appointment of local officials, with some limited success.

In Hunan, for example, local self-government organs extended their activity during the revolution in the collection of major fees and taxes, including the land tax. In most major Hunanese cities, the duties of the prefect in the old administration were taken over by the local assemblies.[10] As a reputed reform measure in Kwangsi, gentry participated in the audit of the land tax, and other taxes formerly collected by officials were farmed out after the revolution to contractors or to local self-government councils.[11] In at least one county of Shantung where there had been no revolutionary occupation, the magistrate came to be selected by the county assembly.[12] In postrevolutionary Chekiang, local self-government bodies widely challenged the power of the county magistrates, who were not uncommonly elected locally in 1912 and 1913.[13] County assemblies were introduced in Kwangtung only with the revolution, and some acquired the power to choose their magistrate.[14] Kweichow's first revolutionary government proposed and partially put into effect a system whereby a respectable gentryman, chosen by local groups, could veto the local application of provincial government orders.[15] As a practical matter of finances and bureaucratic order, most provincial governments were not so solicitous. The Yunnan government, in firm military hands at the provincial level, expressed outright hostility toward what it saw as usurpation of official functions by local self-government bodies and their "evil gentry," but, in parts of the province where the army was absent, local gentry and the self-government councils probably augmented their power.[16] In general this remarkable flourishing of local representative bodies and their privileges was tolerated. The gentry surge was not easily turned back, and there seemed little desire in the governments of most revolutionary provinces to do so.

These advances in political power, with attendant economic benefits, secured at the expense of formal governmental authority, would have been worthless unless threats from below had been contained. To have reduced government controls coming from above would have profited the gentry nothing—indeed would have been a disastrous act of suicide—if they had lost their elite status and their social control locally. There was considerable nonelite, popular activity during the revolution in some provinces. For us to ignore it would not do justice to the amount of turmoil nor to the hint of the potential for more profound social change than occurred.[17] It was necessary for the gentry and their allies to contain or repress mass movement wherever it threatened to develop. They did so, and this is the other side of the gentry triumph during the 1911 Revolution.

In most provinces, a substantial independent movement of the non-elite—independent of socially elite leadership and control and therefore socially threatening—did not occur. Peasants, rootless rural poor, and urban poor were recruited into the revolutionary provincial armies, amounting in the country as a whole to hundreds of thousands. But, despite difficulties experienced in containing these mass armies, they did not turn in any determined way against their socially elite leadership. Mutinies occurred and were rapidly put down. Banditry was widespread, particularly as the army recruits of the revolution were demobilized and frequently turned to local outlawry, whence some had come. But this too was either successfully suppressed or kept at a level that did not disturb the social order. Sometimes the socially disruptive potential of the revolution was contained preventively. This occurred in the case of the young returned student, Ting Wen-chiang, in a Kiangsu rural area, recounted in the previous chapter; or in the case of the Hanlin compiler, Hsu Chao-wei, who upon Kiangsu's declaration of independence left Peking and helped form local militia (funded by the local self-government assembly and officials) to suppress popular movements against taxes and food shortages in his native Ch'ang-shou county.[18] Sometimes gentry-led militia regained control after lower class elements had temporarily seized power, as in Yenan in the northern province of Shensi.[19] In other cases, where the local gentry seemed unable to reestablish the settled conditions whereby they were in charge, military forces attached to the provincial government were dispatched to redress the balance.[20]

In three provinces secret society organizations were major participants in the new order, perhaps even contenders for province-wide leadership, but proved incapable of sustaining their power.

In Kweichow, a revolutionary provincial government was established in early November, 1911, with participation from a broad range of social classes. The dominant civilian leadership, drawn from the lower reaches of the gentry, had allied closely with secret societies in planning revolution and relied on secret society muscle for its military strength after the revolution. A competing high gentry group, though participants, conspired against the new government and spoke in alarm about the breakdown of order. At the invitation of this second group, troops from neighboring

Yunnan invested the capital city without serious resistance on March 3, 1912. They imposed a military government under T'ang Chi-yao of Yunnan. A violent purge of original revolutionaries followed.[21]

In Szechwan the Society of Brothers and Elders (Ko-lao hui) played an important part in the agitation against the nationalization of the Szechwan railway company in the summer of 1911. It contributed to the formation of a primitively armed wing of the Railway Protection League, under whose aegis the agitation was conducted. The resulting irregular troops helped topple Ch'ing power in the province. When Szechwan declared its independence and joined the republican revolution, the prominence of the Society of Brothers and Elders continued. Men associated with it occupied high provincial posts. Its leaders were incorporated into the postrevolutionary army. In Chungking there was even a daily newspaper (one of six in that city by the spring of 1912) which served as the Society's organ.

The social meaning of the apparent success of a group usually considered nonelite was modified, however, by the participation in the Society of socially elite elements. Two of the most prominent and respectable leaders of the Railway Protection League (Lo Lun and Teng Hsiao-k'o) apparently had secret society connections of long standing. The Society's most important leader in Szechwan was the possessor of the first military degree (*wu hsiu-ts'ai*) and a reader of Liang Ch'i-ch'ao's writings. As its power became public during the disturbances of 1911, prominent gentry and even Ch'ing officials asked to join. The social threat of the Society was mediated and softened by its layered social constituency. Even so, as authority in the province gradually centralized again at the provincial level (after its dispersion during the revolution), the Society was eased out of the government by military men and revolutionary party representatives, or given innocuous posts. Its military forces were dispersed without offering resistance. The heights of power in the province were firmly returned to socially elite elements, from whom they had never seriously escaped, within a couple of months after the revolution.[22]

A broadsheet, printed in Chengtu in mid-December, 1911, expressed the way in which maintenance of the social status quo could be grafted onto the aims of the revolution. Its tone was antiforeign, appealing to the nationalist atmosphere of the period. "Are you aware that China is about to perish? Are you aware that we shall sooner or later become the cattle and slaves of foreigners?" The reader is invited to consider the fate of India, where children are prevented from getting an education, where Englishmen use Indians as footstools, where assembly is forbidden and where the penalty for not paying a fee for the birth of a child is death. To avoid this fate, social order in Szechwan must be restored. "My brethren, rather than wait till then to repent, would it not be better for us all now to unite, each attending to his own business, each doing his particular duty, but all guarding the common peace, and supporting the military government? Then foreign countries would not dare to move. . . ." In particular, the populace is warned against a repetition of the rioting of early December, when New Army leadership intervened to restore order and take power from provincial assembly leaders. "You must know that . . . wealth is a matter of predestination. . . . If you have got wealth through this robbery, how can you tell that the men you have driven to crime will not in turn rob you? What is more, when foreign countries hear of it, and that our brethren are despoiling one another, they are certain to proceed to carve the melon." In this view, to abstain from "wrongfully coveting wealth and honor" was necessary to preserve the country.[23]

All over the country, the revolution was reined in by its leaders at an early stage. The reasons for doing so were fear of powerful foreign intervention and fear of social upheaval. It is difficult to know how much social upheaval was feared only as an opening for foreign intervention and how much the horrific vision of foreign intervention was used to legitimate repression of popular activity.[24] Szechwan was about as remote from foreign power as any part of China. On the other hand, remoteness was not immunity, as Szechwan had previously experienced in cases of foreign retribution for attacks on missionaries and in the establishment of treaty ports. The Chengtu broadsheet spoke of British troops *only* a month's march away in India. Whatever the primary motive, the effect was to forestall any profound social change.

In the third province where secret society organization could bid for provincial leadership—Shensi—the bid was more successful in acquiring autonomous administrative authority but did not lead to social changes. The Society of Brothers and Elders in Shensi was from the beginning of the revolution a leading element. In the capital of Sian, the Society led the greatest outpouring of personal violence that the revolution witnessed anywhere the massacre of Manchus, some ten to twenty thousand. A few foreigners were killed in the general breakdown of order surrounding the early days of the revolution. The Society's chief in Shensi, Chang Yun-shan, occupied buildings formerly belonging to the imperial provincial government. Armed groups under secret society orders were established in a loose network in various parts of the province. The resulting administration existed in tandem with another consisting of revolutionary intellectuals and the New Army in Shensi. A missionary witness to the revolution in Sian perceived the T'ung-meng hui as "the anti-dynastic society of the upper class" and representative of "the more humane and orderly element," but far outnumbered by secret society men.[25] Although the revolutionary military governor was a member of the military elite—like his counterpart in several other provinces, a graduate of Japan's Army Officers' Academy— he was weak. His New Army soldiers were recruited in large numbers into the Society of Brothers and Elders. Nowhere else did secret society participation in government remain so conspicuous. And in contrast to Szechwan, the leaders were typically from society's lower orders.

Despite the apparent opportunities offered by the situation, however, the leadership of the Society of Brothers and Elders refrained from social revolution and worked to contain the disruption which might feed it. It was as if the letting of Manchu blood, about which Chang Yun-shan remained proud, exhausted the Society's imagination. Chang was described by one foreigner who knew him as "the Robin Hood type of freebooter," but he was also sufficiently limited in his conception of possibilities so that he brought in as his councillor one of Shensi's leading Confucian scholars. He repressed disorder in Sian with summary justice, even against his friends.[26] And he cooperated in restraining secret society power outside the capital in ways that earned gentry (and foreign) gratitude. In Shensi, as elsewhere, political revolution was achieved without changes in the social structure. Social revolution, which seemed for a fleeting moment to threaten, faded even before asserting itself.[27]

The behavior of secret societies during the 1911 Revolution (and they played roles in other provinces more modest than those described above) was consistent with their previous history. Whether their leadership was diluted with gentry participation (as in Szechwan and Chekiang) or not, their outbursts had in the past expressed discontent without offering ways of resolving it. Plans for a new social order had generally not been part of the secret society message, nor were they in 1911.[28] For social vision, we have to look in the nineteenth century to the Taiping revolutionaries, or in the early twentieth century, to reformers and revolutionaries drawing inspiration from Western conceptions of the good society. In 1911–12, the most radical vision was entertained by the provincial government of Kwangtung, where adherents of Sun Yat-sen's T'ung-meng hui were in charge.

In much of Kwangtung, the revolution arrived under some combination of gentry and merchant leadership. This differed from the common pattern elsewhere in the country only in that the merchant role was more pronounced in several Kwangtung cities. But Canton, the provincial capital, fell to the republican revolutionaries with the help of pressure from a countryside in revolt. A People's Army (*min-chün*)—a federation of Triad secret society groups, bandits, peasants, and revolutionaries—was put together in the market towns of the East River delta. It took Waichow and precipitated the emergence of a T'ung-meng hui provincial leadership in Canton. Its numbers grew to well over one hundred thousand. If the vision of social equality, which had been a secondary feature of prerevolutionary propaganda, were to become a serious objective now that Manchu power was falling, then here were the makings of a power base for radical change. But instead, the Canton leaders took an early opportunity to isolate and destroy this socially threatening force—starting in February, 1912, with a violent climax in March, and continuing for several months.[29]

The reasons touch upon the social background of the T'ung-meng hui revolutionaries, which was shared with the threatened rather than with those threatening, and upon their failure to free themselves by emotional and intellectual effort from these social links with the elite. Their vision had not been sharpened into a critique of the existing social order in China. The emphasis, with few exceptions, was on avoiding future social distortions arising from industrial development. The implication was that China's existing social structure was benign, even if ameliorating reforms were desirable. Though all the Canton revolutionary leaders surely did not accept the moderate view—which did not differ in substance from an outlook widely held elsewhere in China by reformers and revolutionaries alike—the Cantonese government acted on its assumptions. It behaved as if keeping order was more important than designing a new one. The gentry and wealthy merchants of Kwangtung might be troubled by the reforming enthusiasms of the new Canton government, but had no need to fear for their elite status under those revolutionaries. It was roughly the same story in other places where members of republican revolutionary organizations were in charge.[30]

In the 1911 Revolution, China's social elite, especially its dominant gentry component, enjoyed a lightening of controls from above and contained challenges from below. Their adaptation to this new crisis was doubly successful.

Imperialist Encroachment

Conceived out of a growing nationalism, the 1911 Revolution nevertheless left China further diminished in her sovereign authority. Racial or ethnic anti-Manchuism contributed to the unanimity of the Chinese in their overthrow of the Ch'ing dynasty. A more important thread joining the social and political elite of the country during the revolution was the conviction that the Manchu rulers, while increasing their interference in local affairs, had failed to reverse the tide of Western imperialism. The revolutionaries who took Chungking proclaimed as they established their government: "If we do not seize the country from the Manchus now, it will be divided in the future like a melon."[31] The theme was repeated in all parts of China. But, as some, like Liang Ch'i-ch'ao, had warned, the disruption of government occasioned by the revolution provided opportunities for renewed encroachment.

While the Ch'ing government had not managed to stop the tide of Western encroachment, it had, in its last years, been able partially to check it and at certain points to turn it back. Some concessions extorted from China in the 1890s were cancelled before 1911. The German concessions in Shantung were whittled down. The Peking-Hankow trunk line was brought under Chinese management. A forward, aggressive policy was adopted with respect to Peking's authority in the inner Asian dependencies and at certain sensitive and disputed border points.[32] But the critics of the Ch'ing regime were surely right in asserting that it had not worked out any solid basis for real Chinese independence from Western imperialism. Ironically, the revolution itself then precipitated a reversal in the trend of recovering rights.

The institutional forms that Western and Japanese presence and privilege had taken in China by the early twentieth century have often been described. They included personal immunity from Chinese law, portions of territory removed by treaty or custom from Chinese jurisdiction, guaranteed rights to travel, trade and residence (depending on the place and one's business), importation of goods untrammeled at entry by more than a nominal tariff, a customs-collecting agency staffed at key points by foreigners, the right to invest in the so-called treaty ports, concessions to build, manage, and exploit certain mines and railways, and so forth. The foreign imperialist position in China was more than the sum of its parts. It was a whole system of special privilege and dominance, limited only by the effort that the foreigners and their governments were willing to put into it, by the size of China, and by the willingness of the Chinese people and government to risk confrontation with the combined forces of the industrialized world. In 1911, despite some adjustment since 1901, the momentum of foreign imperialist institutions was still very powerful and their financial resources more plentiful than ever.

The additional losses to imperialism that China incurred in the 1911 Revolution were not new in kind, but they were a special humiliation for those who saw the overthrow of the Ch'ing dynasty as a great step into the modern world and hoped that the Western response would be benevolent. They were an unpleasant reminder that the issue between China and the West was not her backwardness or cultural differences, but rather the combination of her weakness and the sheer presence in China of foreigners and their accumulated interests.

The losses of the four brief months of the revolution occurred in both territory and rights. The territorial losses were the effective detachment of outer Mongolia and Tibet from Peking and, especially in the case of outer Mongolia, their slipping into the orbit of European powers. The revolution cannot be held solely responsible for setting the stage. British and Russian interest in these areas had been mounting for some time. Ch'ing efforts to increase control just before the revolution had already precipitated a crisis in Tibet and were brewing another in Mongolia. The Dalai Lama had fled to India in 1910, and a princely Mongolian delegation had gone to St. Petersburg in the summer of 1911 to seek Russian protection against the heavy-handed Manchu resident in Urga. From the point of view of Tibetan and Mongolian leadership, the revolution in China was more an opportunity than a cause for asserting full autonomy from Peking's authority. When revolution spread in the Chinese home provinces, Ch'ing power was also overthrown in Lhasa and Urga by local elites (religious authorities, tribal princes). In Mongolia, Russians, including Russian troops, powerfully assisted the process.[33] The British immediately adopted a protective stance regarding the autonomy of Tibet.

If the military and diplomatic interventions of European power had not accompanied these events, there was the theoretical possibility that the Chinese might have made their peace with Mongolian and Tibetan autonomy, under the same rubric that justified provincial autonomy. For a brief moment this view prevailed in the Nanking assembly of provincial representatives in early 1912. But the possibility of cleaving to this approach was slim. Provincial autonomy had its powerful critics, who were to have their way before two years had passed; even greater was the opposition to abandoning the grip over the dependencies that the Ch'ing government had secured. In any case, circumstances and anti-imperialist sentiment decided how Chinese would react: the real option for Mongolia and Tibet was not escape from greater Han chauvinism into independence, but a transfer from one form of external control to another. This was obviously an arguable option for the Tibetan and Mongolian elites, but it foreclosed tolerance on the part of nationalist Chinese for Tibetan or Mongolian autonomy. China was already surrounded closely enough with European, American, and Japanese colonies. The sense of loss, and of the increase in danger for China that the loss entailed, was great. Outer Mongolia in particular, where the Russian role was large and obvious, was a leading issue in the first years of the republic.

With respect to affairs that were unambiguously internal and Chinese, the most dramatic erosion of rights during the revolution occurred in the handling of the Chinese customs revenue. Prior to October, 1911, the foreign staff of the Imperial Maritime Customs Service only supervised and audited the collection of revenues but did not actually handle the proceeds. It assessed the proper duties and accounted to the government what should have been received through purely Chinese channels of remittance. Most of the proceeds after the expenses of collection went ultimately to foreign banks and governments for debts and indemnities. But the profits from remittance charges, exchange manipulations, and the many ways in which large short-term deposits can be used to advantage fell to Chinese and Manchu. And, in a pinch, the government was in a position to refuse payment on its debts. This system was made possible by the presence of a Chinese customs superintendent at each port of entry, an official who was appointed by and accountable to Peking.

During the revolution, the revolutionary provinces tried to claim all locally collected revenue as their own, and the Chinese superintendents of customs no longer provided a network of remittance to Peking (or to

Shanghai, where foreign debts were paid by the Shanghai taotai). The foreign inspector general of the Maritime Customs Service responded by ordering his foreign commissioners (there was one in most major cities and in some minor ones) to take over the actual collection of duties in the revolutionary provinces and to deposit the proceeds in foreign banks. This emergency measure was then extended to the whole country, including provinces where there had been no upheaval, and was ratified by the foreign powers and the Peking government. Both sides could agree on preserving the centralizing character of the Service against the centrifugal forces of the revolution. The final arrangements, approved in Peking on January 21, 1912, included an International Commission of Bankers (foreign) to manage payment of customs revenues for the foreign debt—thereby usurping the former functions of the Shanghai taotai. Not only had China further lost control over a sizable portion of her own revenues, but the banking profits derived from handling them had largely been transferred from Chinese to foreign hands.[34]

In the name of preserving national unity, the regular payment of foreign debts was insured. The smoothness with which this feat was accomplished owed everything to the presence of foreigners at critical nodes within the government of China. These foreigners told themselves, and perhaps believed, that they were saving China by preserving her international credit. The price was a reduction of sovereignty and resources and an offense to Chinese pride. Concerning these changes the British minister remarked: "The Customs has been immensely strengthened. . . . But the Chinese detest the arrangement and will do their utmost to reinstate the native Superintendents. . . ."[35] They did not succeed for quite a few years.

Less significant for concrete Chinese interests but still humiliating was the foreign takeover of the Shanghai Mixed Court. Before the 1911 Revolution, the so-called Mixed Court was presided over by Chinese judges appointed by the Ch'ing government. With a foreign assessor present and able to intervene when foreigners or foreign interests were at issue, it handled cases arising within the International Settlement when the defendant was Chinese. From its founding in 1864, the Mixed Court and its appurtenances such as jails and police powers were objects of struggle between foreign assertions of authority and Chinese efforts to retain control over their own land and people in Shanghai.[36] During November and December, 1911, the Shanghai Consular Body—that is, the foreign governmental agents in that city—with the permission of their superiors in Peking, unilaterally removed all operations of the court from Chinese governmental authority. The usurpation was innocent of any basis in treaty provisions. In a major section of Shanghai, Chinese on China's soil were subject to a judicial system under full foreign control.[37] Foreigners in China were persuaded that they had thereby choked off judicial corruption in the Shanghai Settlement and prevented criminals from buying their way out of punishment and back into the Settlement. But, somehow, many Chinese did not properly appreciate the by-products of the loss of jurisdiction. Its recovery became an aim of Chinese governments, achieved only in January, 1927, through the momentum of the revolutionary nationalist movement of the mid-twenties.[38]

Although the foreign encroachments so far discussed are the most prominent, in the sense that they immediately became objects of contention, they by no means exhaust the list of losses incurred during the revolution. The Lanchow Mining Company, an effort to recapture the coal market in north China from the British, gave up the fight during the revolution. The negotiations for amalgamation with the Kaiping Mining Company (itself a Chinese property acquired illegally by the British during the Boxer affair) had begun before the revolution, but were consummated on British terms in January, 1912.[39] Absurd claims for indemnification of foreign losses arising from the revolution were registered. For example, a group of German, French, and Japanese speculators in Tientsin who took over some bad debts in 1909 and proved unable to collect them, pronounced their uncollected assets destroyed by rioting in March, 1912, and managed to get the Chinese government to underwrite their alleged losses.[40] And so on. If Western imperialism was about to recede, it was not evident in China in 1912. Doing something to save the situation remained the most demanding task of government.

Less obvious than the continuing vitality of the institutional forms of late nineteenth-century imperialism was the persistence of its attitudes. These attitudes were demonstrated in at least three categories: racist contempt for the Chinese, ambition for profit and domination, and a more subtle paternalistic urge to guide and control Chinese destinies, ostensibly for the good of the Chinese, but in a manner which served the interests of one's own country. These categories are of course interrelated and mutually reinforcing. It is the third—the urge to guide and control Chinese destinies in a manner conceived of as benevolent, for the good of the Chinese themselves—that requires explication.

This attitude had a special force to it, since those adopting it seemed successfully to hide from themselves the self-serving character of their benevolence. It gained strength from its self-righteousness. Because it presented itself as disinterested—concerned only for the uplift of the Chinese— it could mobilize almost all foreign power behind it at once, rendering maneuver among the quarreling imperialists more difficult for the Chinese government. Indeed, one of the ironies of the first year of the republic is that money from lenders operating on motives of profit was acquired at comparable cost and fewer conditions than money from lenders professing benevolence.

With the settlement of the revolution in February, 1912, it was noted in the foreign office in London that "the Banks have gradually relaxed the conditions on which they have been willing to conclude loans to the Chinese Government," but the British government should work to prevent such transactions unless they provide for "adequate guarantees for proper and useful expenditure of the proceeds. . . ." as well as foreign-supervised security for repayment.[41] As John Jordan, the British minister, noted in Peking, "it seems to be our duty to take all the measures we can to prevent China from becoming another Egypt."[42] The powers were called, in this view, to save China from themselves. The method to avoid the tragedy of China's absorption and loss of independence was to diminish some of that independence and to carry on with absorption.

After all, who in 1912 knew what was best for the Chinese? The British minister: ". . . we know more in this Legation about the present state of affairs in China than the Chinese themselves. The proof is that they continually turn to us for information about conditions in the provinces."[43] The inspector general of the Maritime Customs Service (a foreigner in the employ of the Chinese government): ". . . the Powers ought to treat China with severity: it is their only chance for forcing the Chinese with setting things in order [*sic*]."[44] The recently retired president of Harvard University: two measures were necessary for China to establish her credit in the world financial markets, namely (1) to secure a sufficient government revenue "by methods of taxation that have approved themselves to Western economists and statesmen" and (2) to spend it "honestly and effectively on objects and in methods which have proved good in Western administrations." In his recommendations to the Chinese government President Emeritus Charles W. Eliot went on to say, "foreign advisors must be procured and given enough authority to convince Western capitalists and governments" that these measures would be effected. In fact, Eliot knew just the agency to nominate disinterested advisers to the Chinese government—the Carnegie Endowment for International Peace, of which he was a trustee.[45] The first adviser that this procedure turned up was Professor Frank J. Goodnow, who later played a supporting role in establishing Yuan Shih-k'ai's dictatorship and in attempting to abolish the republic.

Intentions were of course honorable. Who could oppose a "useful expenditure" of funds? Or a good credit rating with the "Western capitalists?" Or China "setting things in order?" Who was more vociferous than the Chinese themselves in warning against repeating the late nineteenth-century fate of Egypt? The situation suggests the familiar one accompanying foreign aid programs in the 1950s and 1960s. Westerners thought it reasonable in matters of modernization to require conformity to Western models.[46] They believed they had a special role to play in applying the models. The recipient perceived that the institutionalization of assistance, where power was grossly unequal, threatened the domination of the donor over the recipient. How much help the recipient would take depended on the urgency of his need and the degree to which he could fight off the "strings." The donor, meanwhile, had to explain to himself why the well-intentioned terms of his generous assistance were resisted. He was inclined to attribute it to the natural or culturally derived inferiority of the recipient.

The picture was not uniform. There were Chinese more ready than others to accept humiliating terms for loans. And there were Western critics of a united front of Western capital exacting controls over Chinese finances as an extra price of loans. They included some of the capitalists not invited into the united front. Woodrow Wilson, who was invited, also spoke in this vein. A British diplomat wrote in 1912: "It is high time we cease to treat Oriental countries as children to dance to our bidding. . . . we have no divine right to dictate to her [China] whether she shall spend the money in this way or that."[47] And, in the last analysis, China was too big and complex (the foreigners of course did *not* know more about China than the Chinese), and Western imperialism was not strong enough for controls to be very effective. The attempt was made, however, and, with racism and the open seeking of power and profit, marked the imperialist posture as the Chinese republic was born. The 1911 Revolution had done nothing to diminish the pressure on this front.

Among the many features of the 1911 Revolution, I have chosen to emphasize the importance of four: the part played by military men, the prominence of the province as a field of politics, the growth of gentry power, and foreign encroachment. None was new in 1911, but each achieved a special importance in the revolution. Along with the revolution also went a general expectation among the Chinese elite that things would improve and that China was becoming a modern nation. There was the hope, at first confident but soon desperate, that the revolution would somehow bring the fulfillment of the dreams of progress and international justice that had accumulated in the last years of the empire. Politics was a matter of intense excitement, which expressed itself in party organization, study groups, the publication of newspapers, reform societies, and fervent declamation in the many representative assemblies all over the country. Unity, progress, self-government, militant resistance to foreign encroachment—these were the slogans, the programs. As one Chinese writer expressed it a year later: there was at the bottom this hope, "that by reason of the overthrow of despotism, there was no powerful obstacle to making firm the political order and planning energetically for [China's] wealth and strength."[48]

The presidency of Yuan Shih-k'ai began in the context of these trends. Its response to them was more interesting, more reasoned than has been said. But in the end, it proved quite incapable of fulfilling Chinese hopes.

Chapter 3

The Presidential Team

The primary aim of the revolution—replacing the Ch'ing dynasty with a Chinese republic—was virtually assured within two months of the uprising at Wuchang on October 10, 1911. In forced retirement since January, 1909, Yuan Shih-k'ai was installed by the court as prime minister in November, 1911. Though sponsoring a military drive against the revolutionaries, he promptly turned to the task of negotiating a settlement. It was soon evident to him that Manchu rule was beyond saving. A truce was arranged. Several more months were required to overcome mutual distrust, to arrange the abdication with as little violence as possible, and to find some common description of the postrevolutionary order. The imperial abdication was achieved on February 12, 1912. By April the main lines of an agreed political order had emerged. The revolutionaries accepted Yuan Shih-k'ai as president, while Yuan undertook to honor the republic and a constitution written by the revolutionaries.

As the man who later betrayed the republic, Yuan Shih-k'ai (1859–1916) has been despised by historians of all political colorations. As the "father of the warlords," he has been placed in the category of the reactionary, antimodern, militaristic, feudalistic obstacles to Chinese progress. His behavior has been seen as a fortuitous combination of the worst in both the corrupt Ch'ing official and the antinationalistic, power-seeking warlord.

His career did prove a disaster for China, but the dismissal has been too easy. Interpretations of his presidency that concentrate on flaws in his character or the style of his political relationships neglect the problem of understanding the intended and unintended import of his policies. Much of this book is devoted to filling that gap. Further, such interpretations fail to convey the weight and texture of Yuan's political presence as his presidency began. After all, Yuan was widely acclaimed as he undertook this new office. At an early stage in negotiations for a settlement of the revolution, prominent revolutionaries had called for his leadership over the new order. Although they did this with some misgivings, it is fair to say that, on condition he cooperated in deposing the Ch'ing, he was invited to undertake the presidency and was not foisted upon an unwilling revolutionary camp.[1]

And the chorus of Western approval of Yuan was almost unanimous. We might do well to reflect on the probability that, if a person of Yuan's type and attainments had emerged as leader of an Asian country during the last couple of decades, assistance from the Western world would have been bounteous. In any case, so it was in the early republic, with the difference that Western imperialism then operated more cautiously and on a slimmer budget than in the third quarter of the century.

Yuan Shih-k'ai

In calculating the sources of Yuan's power as the republic began, we can immediately eliminate charisma or any extraordinary aura about him. He was cut more in the bureaucratic than the heroic mold. His political durability surely owed nothing to a commanding physical presence. A witness of his inauguration as provisional president in March, 1912, recorded that Yuan "came in wobbling like a duck, looking fat and unhealthy, in Marshal's uniform, the loose flesh of his neck hanging down over his collar."[2] Short and stocky, Yuan nevertheless communicated authority and intelligence. The American minister Paul Reinsch made these comments after his first interview with Yuan in late 1913: "The President is very cordial and genial in his manner. He speaks fluently and to the point, and loves to give a humorous turn to his thought. . . . Nothing escapes his eye; and while, as in the case of most Chinese, his expressions take on a very general form, he evidently has a grasp and mastery of details."[3] These characteristics— geniality in personal and working relationships, keen powers of observation and memory, close attention to organization and detail, as well as an enormous capacity for work—were also noted by close Chinese associates.[4]

So, too, was there agreement regarding the darker side. He appeared to one foreign diplomat as "more of an opportunist than a statesman, more of an intriguer than a leader. . . ."[5] He was known to be "not overscrupulous, and when occasion requires he can strike swiftly and mercilessly. . . . "[6] Although one Chinese leader of the period could recall Yuan as "a highly intelligent man who invariably accomplished whatever he set out to do,"[7] he was judged by some of those who worked with him as old-fashioned in the post-1911 environment and out of touch with the new moods.[8] His enemies had harsher things to say. Yuan's preeminence as the Ch'ing fell was founded not on a reputation for moral excellence or widespread popularity but on his administrative and political achievements as an official— and on the power accruing from these achievements.

Yuan was a reforming prodigy of the late Ch'ing. By the time of his forced retirement in 1909, he had assembled around him the preponderance of the reforming talent possessed by the imperial bureaucracy and had brought to some degree of fruition a wide range of institutional innovations touching all conventional aspects of Westernization.

Yuan's achievements in wide-ranging reform have been obscured by two clichés concerning his role: that he was a militarist (the echoes are warlordism) and that his inclinations were reactionary. We shall have occasion to return to the partial truths contained in these characterizations. But the point here is how inadequate they are for understanding his part in the early republic.

When we call a man a militarist, we may mean one of several things. We may refer simply to the pattern of his career: he seeks his life's achievements within the confines of military organization. Or we refer to his attitudes: a predisposition toward military solutions to nonmilitary problems, or the advocacy of the expansion of military influence in society. Or, finally, we may mean that his power is based on the support given him by military forces.

From the pattern of Yuan's career, we may infer that he contemplated a military life only for brief intervals. Although acquainted with the military in his childhood through relatives serving the gentry-led regional armies of the mid-nineteenth century, he was educated in proper gentry fashion to take the civil service examinations. Only after two failures, at ages seventeen and twenty, did he give up the high road to office and exploit his family connections to become a military officer of special status in Shantung. Between 1880 and 1885 (age twenty-one to twenty-six) and again from 1895 to 1899 (age thirty-six to forty), Yuan was fully engaged in military training and command—a total of approximately nine years. For the rest of his adult life, either he was altogether removed from military activity (during his ten years as Chinese Commissioner for Trade in Korea, age twenty-six to thirty-five, when all Chinese forces and military advisers were removed from Korea by treaty), or supervising military organizations was only a part, albeit usually an important part, of his responsibilities (while governor of Shantung, governor-general of Chihli, grand councillor, prime minister of the empire, president of the republic, from age forty until his death at fifty-six). Before he was thirty, his career had extended beyond the military, and there is no reason to believe Yuan subsequently contemplated returning permanently to its confines. Like several other prominent Chinese in the last half of the nineteenth century, contributions to military organization and training figured largely in his rise to high posts. The desired destination, however, was civil position. The military quotient in Yuan's success was larger than most, and the top civil posts in the provinces included degrees of military authority, especially in the last decades of the Ch'ing, and more especially in Yuan's case. But Yuan's calling was government service broadly conceived. He was by no means content to rest his claim to prominence on his expertise in military administration.

Similarly, Yuan cannot, I think, be judged to have had exceptionally militaristic attitudes. In international affairs, he was involved more than once in the use of force in Korea where the primary opposition was the Japanese (in the early 1880s and during the Sino-Japanese War). The modernized military units which he later created were a deterrent to a casual use of military threats by Western powers in China, and occasionally this use was quite specific and effective.[9] But overall, he was reluctant to resort to military counterforce against foreign power, even when there was considerable popular support for doing so. By contrast, he did not shrink from the use of military power at home, against his domestic opposition. The contrast was noted by contemporaries. But even in this respect, Yuan does not seem to be exceptional for his time. He had a taste for terror, but no special lust for the use of military force. Nor did he desire an expansion of military influence in the society beyond what the 1911 Revolution introduced. As we shall see, his concerns as president pointed in the opposite direction.

The third sense of the term militarist—dependence on a military base of power—has greater application to Yuan's case. Yuan's career without the Peiyang army divisions is unimaginable, just as Li Hung-chang's would be without the Anhwei Army. A prominent career would still have been probable, only a quite different one. But, as with Li, it was as a reforming official in all areas, not just in the military sphere, that Yuan attained his full eminence.

If we think of Yuan in 1912 as a reactionary who had stumbled on military organization as a key to power but otherwise compared unfavorably to his contemporaries in reforming vision, then we have missed the essence of his achievement and the secret of his power. In 1895, he was an early member of and contributor to the reform society of K'ang Yu-wei and Liang Ch'i-ch'ao, even though he opportunistically abandoned them later. During his second predominantly military stint between 1895 and 1899 (training troops at Hsiao-chan in Chihli which were known as the Newly Created Army), Yuan began addressing the throne on such subjects as tax reform, coal mining, and foreign relations.[10] As governor of Shantung, 1899 to 1901, his tenure was notable, not only for the suppression of the Boxer movement in that province, but also for designing the diplomatic techniques whereby German power in Shantung was in a few years successfully reduced.[11] He had already become a political and diplomatic figure of national stature before his appointment in November, 1901, to succeed Li Hung-chang in the country's most prestigious regional post.

During his five years and ten months as governor-general of Chihli (1901–7), Yuan expressed the full range of his reforming energies. In the wake of the devastation to life and institutions inflicted by Western armies on Chihli in 1900 and 1901, his programs broadened out beyond military administration into all areas: currency, banking, agriculture, industrial development, railways, the police, education, the handling of justice, local self-government, the recruitment and appointment of bureaucrats, the recovery of concessions from foreign hands. While the number of troops trained in Western fashion under his supervision increased from twenty thousand in 1901 to sixty thousand in 1906, his stake in all sorts of non-military innovative programs grew in like measure. The momentum of these reforms carried them on beyond Yuan's partial loss of power after 1906, and even beyond his dismissal from government in January, 1909.

Those were the days of his greatest glory. Yuan as Chihli governor-general and commissioner of the northern ports (a function effectively attached to the governor-generalship, which allowed for activity throughout north China and Manchuria and gave the description "Peiyang" to his group) was the very picture of dynamism, of official nationalism on the march, and of dedication to reform and the gradual rolling back of foreign encroachment. Chihli was a model for the country. Delegations actually came to learn from its example. All this, not just the army, was building power for Yuan. His promise as a reform leader within the bureaucracy (as well as his loyalty to the Empress Dowager) had led to his appointment in 1901. His fulfillment of this promise made him the logical leader of the new China that seemed to be emerging.

In the late Ch'ing, power was the product of reform. Official attention and government revenues were increasingly flowing in reformist directions. Those most successful at it reaped the greatest rewards. Just as the gentry saw both ideals and self-interest in representative government and local reform programs, so too Yuan benefited as he turned with the country toward reform. It was not a grab bag that turned up Yuan for the presidency in 1912, nor was it conspiratorial maneuvering or a simple counting of rifles.

Yuan's Entourage–The Military

Projecting our knowledge of warlord and later Kuomintang (KMT) politics into the early twentieth century, we are accustomed to think of Yuan as the center of a faction (the Peiyang clique) and to understand his successes as the mastery of factional politics. Like the cliché that portrays Yuan as a reactionary militarist, this view conveys a partial truth. But it obscures more than it illuminates.

Presumably no bureaucratic or political structure is free of factions. The bureaucracy of the late Ch'ing was certainly not an exception. Yuan's entourage looked like a well-knit group to contemporaries observing Peking politics. But during the period of Yuan's ascent to preeminence in the late Ch'ing, factions were not determinative. The static structural conditions that favor the predominance of factions were absent.[12] That is, the political system did not lack the ability to carry out innovative programs, and the government was able to act decisively to alter the political environment. The greatest rewards lay not in factional maneuver but in achievement in reform. The dominant mode of political behavior was not personalistic in the manner that we associate with later factionalism. Political liaisons did not grow out of previous personal ties so much as out of common tasks and common purposes, far broader than any factional interests. The Yuan Shih-k'ai political machine developed in tandem with

the expanding enterprises for which he was responsible. It was not assembled together on a personal basis and then assigned to capture already
existing citadels of power. Its leading members very often were specialists
and were important as such to Yuan's political advance.

The military members of Yuan's group, though not his oldest associates,
are the best known, since they went on after Yuan's death to dominate
Chinese politics for a few years. Most, but not all, of those important during the presidency were first associated with him in his efforts to organize
a fully Western-style military unit at Hsiao-chan, near Tientsin, between
1895 and 1899. They were not old cronies from Yuan's first military experience in Shantung or Korea. Of those prominent at Hsiao-chan, only
Hsu Shih-ch'ang and T'ang Shao-i had previously developed significant ties
with Yuan. After Hsiao-chan both pursued primarily civilian rather than
military careers. Yuan's connection with the military men was conceived
in a project of military reform, and those who were in his inner circle
when the republic began were those who had persevered in the project's
subsequent phases.

A recent study of the four-year effort at Hsiao-chan singles out thirty
leading military participants for their subsequent prominence in the early
republic. Of these, twenty-five had attended the Tientsin Military Preparatory School (Wu-pei hsueh-t'ang) before joining Yuan at Hsiao-chan.[13] This
school had been established by Li Hung-chang in 1885 to provide military
instruction according to Western methods with German teachers. Its graduates were among the handful of Chinese who were trained in Western military science in 1895, when Yuan was assembling assistants for his reform
experiment. They included Tuan Ch'i-jui, Feng Kuo-chang, Tuan Chih-kuei,
Lu Chien-chang, Chang Huai-chih, Ts'ao K'un, Li Ch'un (often rendered
Li Shun)–the core of Yuan's military coterie in the early republic.

These senior elements of Yuan's military entourage were men whose
educational experience occurred before strong nationalist sentiments
swept the country's elite. They had embarked on military careers before it
became fashionable to do so. Hence, they were probably less politicized
and on the average less privileged socially than the new wave of military
aspirants of the early twentieth century. But they participated in the great
expansion of fully modernized military units under Yuan after the Boxer
Rebellion. Their careers were grounded in change: their qualifying education and their prominence were owed to reform.

Of the remaining five military officers at Hsiao-chan destined for prominence during Yuan's presidency—that is, those of the thirty who had not attended the Tientsin Military Preparatory School—one, Chang Shu-yuan, was too young to have attended and in fact was to graduate later from the Japanese Army Officers' Academy. Four emerged from the ranks of older regional armies formed in the 1850s and 1860s. Of the four products of the old armies, the two most prominent, Chiang Kuei-t'i and Chang Hsun, returned to old-style units before the 1911 Revolution. In effect, they left the reform movement. And they were correspondingly distant from Yuan's inner councils in the early republic, though they remained important allies. (The relationship was not unlike Chiang Kai-shek's to semi-independent military figures outside the core units of the KMT army in the 1930s.)[14]

The senior men of Yuan's military entourage, then, were not illiterate ex-bandits, as in the warlord caricature, whose sense of self-respect was due to their rescue from ignominy by Yuan Shih-k'ai. Tuan Ch'i-jui (1865–1936), for example, came from a prominent family of modest means with a tradition of military leadership.[15] The family of Feng Kuo-chang (1859–1919) had been well-to-do and had launched him on a course of classical literary training. He turned to a military career only after his family's fortunes declined. In any case, after entering the Tientsin Military Preparatory School, he took time out to win the first-level literary degree (*hsiu-ts'ai*)—an exceptional feat among professional military men of his generation.[16] Both Tuan and Feng studied military science abroad before working under Yuan: Tuan in Germany, 1889–90, and Feng in Japan as part of the Chinese legation immediately after the Sino-Japanese War. Even those of very humble origins had overcome that handicap before serving Yuan. Ts'ao K'un (1862–1938), a cloth-goods peddler for a time in his youth, had become an instructor at the Tientsin Military Preparatory School by 1890, five years before the Hsiao-chan effort.[17] Chang Hsun (1854–1923), an impoverished orphan at age ten, emerged from service in the Sino-French war of 1884–85 as a major.[18] Gratitude for patronage must certainly have been a part of Yuan's influence over his military aides and allies, but in most cases they were not men without rewarding alternatives in the society of their day. Nor, in most cases, did their recruitment or promotion depend on personal ties.[19] When Yuan was governor-general of Chihli, no occasion arose to test seriously his hold over these men. As president and still later as aspiring emperor, he learned its limits.

In discussions of the Peiyang army—those divisions nurtured by Yuan as governor-general in a continuation and immense enlargement between

1901 and 1906 of his work at Hsiao-chan—emphasis is generally laid upon its personal character.[20] The meaning of the assertion that the Peiyang army was a personal one is often unclear. Yuan was the main initiator, sustainer, and decision maker with respect to these divisions as they developed from five thousand troops to some sixty thousand between 1895 and 1907. This fact certainly conferred on him much influence with them even after 1906 when he began to lose direct administrative control. One can imagine a self-effacing servant of reform who would have discouraged the personal loyalties accruing to successful organizational leadership. Yuan was not at all that sort. He was a highly political man, who was extremely conscious of power, of personal relations, and of the advantage of cultivating loyalty among his subordinates. Yuan's weight with the Peiyang army was great, as would be that of any man in any society who had registered similar achievements. And Chinese social norms lent Yuan's personal influence a special, even if limited, strength.

But this sort of personal influence is different from the elevation of personal ties to the status of a primary principle of organization—a characteristic implied when describing these forces as a personal army. An army based on personal relations would presumably be cemented together in a chain of personal ties. The commander would recruit, train, and fund his generals, who in turn would recruit, train, and pay their respective subordinate officers, who would have a similar relationship to their common soldiers. The regional armies of the mid-nineteenth century and the warlord armies of the late 1910s and the 1920s approximated this model.[21] The core divisions of the Peiyang army, as well as other units of the modernized New Army network of the late Ch'ing, while not free of personal influences, were pointed in the opposite direction.

A prominent characteristic of the personally oriented army was the difficulty experienced in attempting to transfer commanding officers, without their subordinates, from one unit to another. In this connection, it is interesting to note the two prominent veterans of Yuan's Hsiao-chan group who later left the modernizing effort became indissolubly linked with the old-style units under their command. Chang Hsun operated as personal and sole authority over his ten to twenty thousand man army throughout Yuan's presidency. Chiang Kuei-t'i (1838–1922), who in 1908 inherited the Resolute Army (*I-chün*), one of the lesser regional armies spawned during the mid-nineteenth century, was only the third commander in the history of the army and maintained his command until his death.[22] The pattern of the Peiyang army under Yuan was quite different. The pay-master system was carefully differentiated from the chain of command. And officers of a given rank and training were interchangeable in theory and were interchanged in practice.

Intensive research might produce a calculation of rates of transfer for different ranks in different years. The indications are that they were sufficiently high at junior as well as senior officer ranks in the modernized units of the Peiyang army before the 1911 Revolution so that resistance to centralized control of personnel on a merit basis did not develop.[23] The momentum of this policy carried over into the early republic, although erosion set in. The phenomenon of personal control over military units by their officers emerged gradually after Yuan's death.[24] Before 1916, despite erosion, the principle of interchangeable commanders remained dominant in the primary Peiyang units.[25] If the actions of the military under Yuan had a bad effect, the problem in most cases was the tasks they were assigned, not some fatal anti- or premodern flaw in their organization.

Allegations of the intrinsically reactionary style of the Peiyang army include the charge of a closed, clannish quality. It has been said, for example, that Yuan rarely recruited military students returned from study abroad, since their contrasting training and background would make them more independent.[26] The picture is overdrawn, however. As builders together of the best of China's modern army, the senior officers of the Hsiao-chan group who persisted in the effort did occupy a special position in the military establishment and in relations with Yuan. The result was what may loosely be called a clique. But only loosely. The modernized army—the basis for their prominence and power—quickly became too large an enterprise to be contained by the Hsiao-chan group. The demand of the army for more military talent forced a degree of openness even on the Peiyang leadership. Yuan never stopped trying to recruit promising new military men into top positions.

By the early republic, the divisions known as the Peiyang army were in fact of heterogeneous composition. Segments of two divisions were derived, not from Yuan's first efforts at Hsiao-chan, but from Chang Chih-tung's comparable achievements in Nanking in initiating the modernized Self-Strengthening Army. Stephen R. MacKinnon in a study of the forces built up by Yuan in the late Ch'ing estimates that one half of the Peiyang officer corps was trained outside the Peiyang military schools.[27] The Peiyang authorities participated in the general move in the first years of the twentieth century to send students abroad, among other things for military training. And the Peiyang military establishment, contrary to common assertions, made good use in their officer corps of the returned military students.

A statistical impression can be derived from the relatively well-recorded careers of Chinese graduates of the Japanese Army Officers' Academy (Nihon rikugun shikan gakkō). This elite Japanese school admitted the first contingent of Chinese students in 1901. The standards for selection and the rigor of the training combined to confer on the Chinese graduates (630 by 1911) a special mark of excellence. Among military men whose training came after the Boxer Rebellion, these were considered the cream. Their rate of advancement upon returning home was often breathtaking. Of those graduating from the first three classes, entering between 1901 and 1904, 38 percent were sponsored by Peiyang authorities, that is to say, Yuan Shih-k'ai's establishment.[28]

The return from this early investment, in the form of Japanese Army Officers' Academy graduates in prominent military posts, needed time to mature. The effect came only after direct administrative control over the Peiyang divisions had already been removed from Yuan's hands (1907). But it did come, and such returnees continued to form a large contingent among high ranking officers after Yuan's return to power as prime minister and president. In March, 1913, of the 275 Chinese officers of the rank of major-general (*shao-chiang*) and above with active military posts, 88, or 32 percent, had been trained at the Japanese Academy. Twenty-seven, or 31 percent of these 88, occupied posts subject to the real appointive power of the Peking government. This number was almost exactly proportional to the number of modern-style divisions subject to Peking's authority at that time. In other words, the modern military organization under Yuan's control in the spring of 1913 contained at high rank the same proportion of graduates of the Japanese Academy as did modern-style military organizations not subject to his appointive powers. (See tables 1 and 2.)

This proportion is less impressive than at first it seems, when the distinction between line and staff officers is introduced. Of the twenty-seven high-ranking graduates of the Japanese Academy appointed under Yuan, only between one-quarter and one-third held line or command posts in the spring of 1913, whereas the rest were scattered in the advisory, planning, administrative and instructional institutions of the military in Peking and elsewhere in the north. On the other hand, the Peiyang divisions were generally older than other modern-style units and experienced their greatest

TABLE 1

Chinese Generals as of March, 1913, with Training at
Japan's Army Officers' Academy

	Total	Number with Japanese Academy Training	Percentage with Japanese Academy Training
Officers with rank of major general and above, active and inactive	530	163	30.8
Officers with rank of major general and above with active military posts (including provincial military governors)	275	88	32.0

Compiled from: Sambō hombu [General Staff], *Shina rikukaigun shōkan meibo* [Register of general-rank officers of the Chinese army and navy], March 10, 1913, microfilms of the Japanese Foreign Ministry, MT5.1.10.5–1, pp. 310–416. Officers with only the brevet rank of major general are not included.

TABLE 2

Japanese-Trained Chinese Generals, March, 1913, in Positions
Appointed by the Peking Government

	Total	Number Subject to Appointive Powers of Peking Government[a]	Percentage Subject to Appointive Powers of Peking Government
"New Army" or modern divisions[b]	56	17.5	31.3
General-rank officers with Japan's Army Officers' Academy training occupying active military posts[c]	88	27	30.7

[a] For purposes of these estimates, it is assumed that all New Army military posts or units in the Peking government or in the provinces of Chihli, Shantung, Honan, Fengtien, Kirin, Heilungkiang, Kansu, and Inner Mongolia were subject to the appointment of the Peking government in March, 1913, and that military posts elsewhere were not. Reality was more complex, but the distinction is useful for a rough, quantitative impression.

[b] Figures in this column are derived from: Sambō hombu [General Staff], *Kakumei-go ni okeru Shina kakushō heiryoku zōgen ichi ranbyō* [A table of the increase and decline of military strength in the various provinces after the revolution], March 10, 1913, microfilms of the Japanese Foreign Ministry, MT5.1.10.5–1, pp. 420–21. The figures exclude an estimated 600 battalions of old-style troops.

[c] For source, see Table 1. Posts in the president's office and the army ministry are included.

growth in the period before many military students had returned from abroad. These circumstances would tend to slow the advancement of their Japanese academy graduates in comparison to those in other military organizations, quite apart from problems of exclusivity and distrust. On balance, the point remains that Yuan's military organization was not particularly closed to entry by those with contrasting backgrounds.

Individual cases of continuing recruitment into the Peiyang military operation illustrate the varieties of channels of entry. Ch'en I was one of the military men on whom Yuan as president most depended. He successfully carried out the sensitive assignment of bringing Szechwan under Peking's administrative authority in the spring of 1915. He had not been at Hsiao-chan nor had he participated in the construction of the Peiyang divisions when Yuan was Chihli governor-general. His military education was received at the Hupeh Military Preparatory School and, at Hupeh's expense, in Japan. Though not a graduate of the prestigious Japanese Army Officers' Academy, he was given major responsibilities upon his return in training Hupeh's New Army units, and engaged in the same sort of work in both Szechwan and Fengtien before the 1911 Revolution. After the revolution, he became army vice-chief of staff in Peking on the recommendation of Li Yuan-hung and remained in that post until his assignment to Szechwan in 1915.[29] His defection from Yuan did not become open until May, 1916, after some Peiyang veterans had already withdrawn their support.

Liu Kuan-hsiung, a high naval officer under the Ch'ing, was active on the revolutionary side in 1911 and was a member of the negotiating team that Sun Yat-sen's revolutionary government sent to Peking in late February, 1912. He was appointed navy minister in the first national republican cabinet under T'ang Shao-i's premiership. He remained for the duration of Yuan's presidency. Yuan entrusted him with sensitive tasks. He was dispatched with about three thousand Peking troops to his native Fukien in October, 1913, to establish Yuan's authority there in the wake of the Second Revolution. He was recalled to Peking in March, 1914, but returned to Fukien in April, 1916, in support of Yuan's influence in the southeast as it was disintegrating in consequence of the monarchical effort of that year.[30]

Yuan also recruited two of the most brilliant young military men of the period, Chiang Fang-chen (also known as Chiang Pai-li, 1882–1938) and Ts'ai O (often referred to as Ts'ai Ao, 1882–1916). Both were graduates of the Japanese Army Officers' Academy—Chiang with a superlative academic record, which he augmented in Germany before the 1911 Revolution. Both had ties with Liang Ch'i-ch'ao. Neither had any experience of service with Peiyang units.

Chiang was appointed director of the Paoting Military Academy in December, 1912, just as it was getting underway. Yuan no doubt had various reasons for the appointment. Chiang came highly recommended from Yuan's close Manchu military associate, Yin-ch'ang, who had become acquainted with Chiang in Germany. He had forcefully urged on Yuan and Tuan Ch'i-jui the importance of officer training as the republic opened. And Yuan had begun to woo Liang Ch'i-ch'ao's group at the end of 1912. Whatever Yuan's reasons, no one could ignore the importance of a post which made the occupant forever the "teacher" (with the durability that such relationships had in Chinese culture) of students who would become China's officer corps. Indeed, Chiang Fang-chen later parlayed his reputation for military brilliance and his brief tenure as Paoting director into a lifetime of military advising, for Yuan Shih-k'ai, for various warlords, and ultimately for Chiang Kai-shek. But his relationship with Yuan did not deepen. In protest over insufficient funding for the school, Chiang dramatically attempted suicide before the Paoting student body in June, 1913. He survived, but subsequently served Yuan in only honorific capacities and split with him over the monarchical issue.[31]

Ts'ai O ruled Yunnan after the 1911 Revolution for two years, but then was induced to work for Yuan in Peking. He played a key public role in laying the institutional groundwork for Yuan Shih-k'ai's dictatorship—the details of which we shall return to. Yuan was clearly interested in finding scope for Ts'ai talents, praised him in private conversations, and later claimed to have offered him the job of chief of the general staff.[32] That Ts'ai, more than anyone else, was the agent of Yuan's final degradation should not obscure Yuan's interest and initial success in enlisting Ts'ai for the presidential team.

When we consider all the military men who served Yuan in one way or another during his presidency, then, we find not one type but a range of them. At one extreme, they included young Chinese graduates of the Japanese Army Officers' Academy, several of whom at the time of the revolution were regimental or divisional commanders at only about thirty years of age. At the other extreme one could find old-timers like Chiang Kuei-t'i, in his seventies, who had fought against the Taipings and the Nien, and who, though loyal to Yuan, had left the New Army for an old-style unit before the revolution. The center of gravity was somewhere in between, both in age and experience. Yuan himself was fifty-two when the republic began. Both the median and mean age of the thirty prominent military participants in the 1890s Hsiao-chan project whose birth year is known (twenty of them) was fifty years in 1912. The careers of most of them were already pointed toward military modernization before they worked for Yuan. Their first war as officers had been for almost all the traumatic Sino-Japanese War of 1894—95. And in most cases, their prominence under Yuan's general leadership before the republic was owed to their role in military reform.

The quality also varied. Tuan Ch'i-jui was widely considered an honest and talented military bureaucrat—before he slowly sank in the quagmire of warlord politics after Yuan's death. As the republic was launched, Japan's leading military China-watcher expressed the view that Tuan Ch'i-jui was the ablest officer in the Chinese army.[33] Yet some of Yuan's most loyal military adherents had odorous reputations, a fact which no doubt kept them loyal longer. Tuan Chih-kuei, for example, had been caught red-handed in a notorious bribery case in the last years of the Ch'ing. Yuan Shih-k'ai recognized his deficiencies but valued his loyalty.[34]

As Yuan's presidency proceeded, especially in its last year, there was an observable shift from reliance on the more reform-oriented military men to greater use of the personally devoted and the politically retrograde. When the ultimate test of loyalty came over the monarchical issue in 1915 and 1916, only a pitiful remnant supported him. It did not include the stars of his late Ch'ing military reform efforts, Tuan Ch'i-jui and Feng Kuo-chang. A record by Yuan's military entourage of what was, in 1912, considered progressive movement by foreigners and many Chinese was no insurance of fulfillment of the expectations invested in it, or even of the cohesion of the group. The group had been assembled around certain programs and policies. It fell apart by reason of other programs and policies. Insofar as there was a Peiyang faction based on personal ties and apart from political orientation, then it showed itself in 1916 to be quite shallow and cannot account for Yuan's prominence and power.

Yuan's Entourage—The Civilians

Most formal photographs of Yuan as president show him in a Western-style military uniform. This visual image reinforces the conception of Yuan as a man of the military, father of warlords. It also marks a shift from traditional mandarin dress, which Yuan generally wore when governor-general of Chihli, to contemporary Western. A leading official of the foreign ministry during the presidency, Ts'ao Ju-lin, tells us that he understood the military costume to represent Yuan's discomfort in the high stiff collar of Western civilian formal dress, owing to an unusually short neck.[35] Although the contemporary military officer's style also sported a high collar, perhaps it did allow the tailor more flexibility and Yuan's chin more room. In any case, Ts'ao's remark reminds us not to accept unquestioningly the received military image as the whole man.

Yuan's self-evaluation, at least in public, certainly stressed his nonmilitary accomplishments. While president, he was forever reminding people of his role in abolishing the old examination system and inaugurating a national network of new schools, in instituting local self-government in Tientsin, in constructing an independent judiciary in Chihli, in encouraging industry, in building railways, as well as in modernizing the army. His remarks in an interview in October, 1915, were characteristic: "My policy in the future will be the same as in the past, that is, progressive reform. From the very beginning of my official career, I have had three objects in view: *a*) the adoption of an efficient educational system in order to disseminate education throughout the land; *b*) development of the country's natural resources and the promotion of industrial enterprises; and *c*) efficient reorganization of the country's military forces."[36] The order in which Yuan stated the objectives, though not original, was habitual.

It is likely that Yuan was embarrassed by the degree of his dependence on military power for maintaining his authority—a motive, therefore, for playing up his nonmilitary achievements. But he had a basis in his record on which to build a civilian reforming image. The extent of his power is inconceivable without the civilian portion of his political machine. By the time of the revolution, he had formed the nuclei of several specialized civilian teams. The three major ones were concerned respectively with railways, industry, and foreign affairs. Over them all, there stood next to Yuan two generalists.

The two generalists, T'ang Shao-i and Hsu Shih-ch'ang, who had the longest association with Yuan of any of his politically important aides, were, like Yuan, above any division between military and civilian spheres. They are considered here with the civilians because even less than Yuan were they products of military careers and, more than Yuan, they were thought of as primarily civilian officials.

T'ang Shao-i (1860–1938) was a nephew of the famous comprador and industrial entrepreneur, Tong King Sing (T'ang T'ing-shu). He spent the years from ages fourteen to twenty-one in American schools (including Columbia and New York University) as part of Yung Wing's China Educational Mission. Soon after his return, on assignment in Korea for the Chinese customs service, he met Yuan Shih-k'ai, who employed T'ang as his deputy in Seoul. From 1885 until 1912, T'ang worked either in close association with Yuan or under his general guidance. After Korea, he served Yuan at Hsiao-chan, and thus participated in the formation of the military units which were antecedents of the Peiyang army divisions. But his main tasks were in finances, railways, and diplomacy. Staying with Yuan through his governorship in Shantung and his governor-generalship in Chihli, T'ang recruited some of the officials who were to become most important in Yuan's presidency. But T'ang himself—Yuan's lieutenant of longest standing who rose to provincial governor and minister of posts and communications under the Manchus and prime minister in the republic—broke with Yuan in 1912 and thenceforth found greater common ground with Yuan's revolutionary enemies.

Hsu Shih-ch'ang (1855–1939) was a scholar whose acquaintance with Yuan in Honan in the 1870s led to being funded by Yuan for the civil service exams and to a close association over much of Yuan's career. Hsu won the top degree (*chin-shih*) in 1886 and Hanlin honors in 1889. Yuan took him on at Hsiao-chan to head the judge advocate's office. When Yuan became governor-general of Chihli, Hsu continued for a time his association with Yuan's military organization. This led to important jobs in Peking's board of war, but Hsu soon expanded his area of activity. He participated in the inauguration of a national police and was first minister of internal affairs in 1905. In 1907 he became Manchuria's first governor-general, overseeing administrative reorganization as well as a range of other reforms in that region. After two years in Manchuria, Hsu like T'ang Shao-i persisted in high offices despite Yuan's dismissal: minister of posts and communications, director of the Tientsin-Pukow railway, grand councillor, and associate prime minister in the new cabinet system of May 1911. He was both an imperial tutor and a member of the commission on constitutional government.[37] He retired from public life when the revolution came. Out of respect for the fallen dynasty that he had served, he resisted Yuan's invitation to reemerge—until 1914, when he became the equivalent of prime minister. A patron as well as a practitioner of traditional scholarship,

Hsu was considered an old-fashioned and unforceful member of Yuan's inner circle. But his rise to prominence and his usefulness to Yuan had been, before the revolution, as an entrepreneur of reform. Like T'ang Shao-i, he had introduced Yuan to several men important in the early republic.

Yuan's loss of his two oldest comrades, the most prominent of his protégés, before the revolution was a year old, highlights the problems of leadership in the early republic. One departed out of his commitment to the republic; the other over his distaste for it. Their behavior also reminds us that personal ties were not the primary determinant of political action.

Below T'ang's and Hsu's level much of the talent that Yuan had recruited in the late Ch'ing conveniently reassembled for the presidency and stayed on. The best known group is the railway specialists, some of whom later constituted the communications clique. The central political figure was Liang Shih-i (1869–1933).

Liang was recruited into Yuan's orbit by T'ang Shao-i in 1903. Like the military men Yuan had recruited almost a decade earlier, Liang was already a man of considerable attainments, insured a respectable career even without the laying on of hands by Yuan. He had won the highest degree (*chin-shih*) in 1894. He gained T'ang's attention because of his outstanding performance in an examination (the *ching-chi t'e-k'o* or special examination in economics) given one time only in July, 1903, in order to search out talent to deal with the crisis facing China from the last years of the nineteenth century.[38] As aide to T'ang, Liang engaged briefly in diplomacy, but he soon specialized in another aspect of T'ang's work, railway management. The last years of the Ch'ing were China's greatest years of railway construction before 1949, and Liang's contributions to railway management, financing, and diplomacy were considerable. He established the Communications Bank in 1907 to handle railway funds, and in 1908 participated importantly in the recovery from foreign hands of China's main completed truckline, the 814-mile Peking-Hankow railway. Liang, then, was a leader in the official wing of the movement for the recovery of rights from foreign hands. Because of the special importance of railways in this period, far surpassing all other forms of official investment, Liang and his cohorts were managers of large sums of money. His managerial and fiscal expertise, combined with his political talents, made Liang a highly valued assistant during the presidency, characterized as it was by fiscal desperation and political turmoil. [39]

Chou Tzu-ch'i (1871–1923), who also played a leading political role during Yuan's presidency, became allied with Liang Shih-i and hence is considered a member of the communications clique, but his career before 1912 was quite removed from Liang Shih-i's. After successfully advancing through the lower stages of the civil service examinations in his native Shantung (though his childhood had been spent in Kwangtung), he turned to foreign studies, first in Canton and Peking (the T'ung-wen kuan) and then at Columbia University. Between 1896 and 1908, he served as a diplomat in New York, Havana, San Francisco, and Washington. Upon his return to China, he worked in the foreign ministry, the government's office for instituting a constitution, and the ministry of education, where he participated in the founding of Tsing-hua University. Although in no sense a railway man, he occupied the post of minister of communications during Yuan's presidency, as well as Shantung military governor and minister of finance.[40]

Liang Shih-i's group, with the addition of Chou Tzu-ch'i and Chu Ch'i-ch'ien (a protégé of Hsu Shih-ch'ang and director general of the Tientsin-Pukow Railway project before the revolution), are generally thought of as a single faction—the Kwangtung or communications clique. By 1915, they seem indeed to have forged a bureaucratic alliance, serving Yuan. But Yuan was not exclusively dependent upon them for expertise in economic reform. Through Chou Hsueh-hsi (1866–1947), finance minister and minister of agriculture and commerce at various times during Yuan's presidency, Yuan could tap an entirely separate collection of bureaucratic entrepreneurs, adept in fashioning reforms and manipulating finances in the manner that produced results.

Chou Hsueh-hsi's special contribution to Yuan's reform machine of the late Ch'ing was resource and industrial development. He ranks, along with Chang Chien, as one of the most energetic and successful industrial entrepreneurs of the early twentieth century. Although Chang Chien's political affiliations were more restrained and retrospectively less odorous, Chou Hsueh-hsi's were more powerful and he accomplished more. The result was small as a proportion of the total economy, but it contained promise and provided another dimension to Yuan's power and to what he could offer the country.

Chou was the son of a leading Ch'ing official, Chou Fu, who had served Li Hung-chang in various capacities, including military and communications development, and who had connections with Yuan Shih-k'ai. Chou Hsueh-hsi followed the conventional route of advancement as far as the *chü-jen* degree, won in 1895, but then turned, more fully than his father ever had, toward reform. Occupying an official post under Yuan Shih-k'ai in Shantung during the Boxer episode, Chou henceforth operated under Yuan's protective umbrella.

The need to revive the economy and society of Chihli after the destruction of the Boxer suppression, much of it by foreign troops, was fashioned into an opportunity for relatively unhampered institutional innovation and economic development. Chou's first achievement was rapidly to organize the minting of copper coinage, thereby greasing rusty economic wheels in north China and accumulating a kitty for investment. By the time the central government prohibited this inflationary practice in 1908, Chou had an investment bank in Tientsin, which handled Chihli's official funds, and a number of industrial projects underway. The projects were stimulated by the tone in Peking (calling for "new policies") and a consciousness of the general backwardness of the north, causing an unfavorable balance of trade and silver export from Tientsin. Chou's program included industrial and agricultural schools, a provincial network of official industrial bureaus as well as semiofficial commercial and agricultural societies to implement general policy guidelines, and pilot factories and agricultural experimental stations. As a consequence, wealthy gentry and merchants were moved to pool their resources in starting their own factories, using the technology and skilled workers provided by the institutions of the province. By 1906 there were sixty factories, and in 1908 industrial investment in Chihli reached an annual peak of over nine million taels. Many of these efforts later failed, but there was presumably some residue. One is left with the impression of an energetic beginning in industrial development.[41]

Aside from creating some of the economic infrastructure necessary for development (though railways, unusually extensive in Chihli, were not in Chou's jurisdiction) and encouraging investment, Chou personally took the lead in a few particular enterprises. The results were mixed. He recovered a cement plant from the British, and with official help and favorable economic circumstances built it into a profitable supplier for all north China, with a subsidiary in Hupeh acquired in 1914.[42] Against this success must be weighed the failure of the Peiyang Lanchow Mining Company, founded in 1907 by Chou and others with funds from Chou's Tientsin bank and, in subsequent years, official and merchant investment. The purpose was to force out of business the Kaiping coal mining company, a Chinese project of the 1870s which had been effectively purloined by the British and

Herbert Hoover during the Boxer Rebellion. However, Ch'ing government temporizing, superior British capital resources and the disruptions of the 1911 Revolution produced the opposite result. As was noted in the previous chapter, it was agreed in January, 1912, that the Kaiping company would absorb the Lanchow company. The Kailan Mining Company, which emerged from this deal, was in practice controlled by British management, although 40 percent or more of the considerable profits went to the Chinese.[43] Happier results for Chou issued from a privately run coal mining company in Shantung, recovered from the Germans; from Peking's modern water works, inaugurated in 1909; and, in the early republic, from the ambitious schemes for the Hua-hsin Spinning and Weaving Company, involving a network of cotton mills in north China. Between 1906 and 1922, Chou personally launched fifteen companies.[44]

Through men like Liang Shih-i and Chou Hsueh-hsi, Yuan connected with some of the most advanced economic activities China had witnessed before 1911. Profits were enjoyed by all—for example Yuan was alleged to be the Lanchow Mining Company's largest shareholder[45]—but not to the point of economic dysfunction. Yuan's economic teams had a formidable appearance as the republic began.

The diplomatic team in 1912, both inherited and newly recruited, was equipped with impressive amounts of foreign education and experience. Yuan prided himself on the recognition he gave to returned students in the form of important appointments. They could be found in all parts of the government. After all, there were few important posts of any kind in semicolonial China that did not include an element of foreign relations. But they were naturally most conspicuous in specifically foreign affairs.

T'ang Shao-i, whom I have discussed as a generalist, had high posts in the foreign ministry and was assigned important diplomatic missions before the revolution, though his highest position in Peking under the Ch'ing was minister of posts and communications. His experience as a youngster in America through Yung Wing's China Educational Mission was shared by others serving in the cabinet during the presidency, including Liang Tun-yen and Liang Ju-hao. Another graduate of Yung Wing's program, Ts'ai T'ing-kan (1861–1935), pursued a naval career upon his return to China. He entered Yuan's entourage, courtesy of T'ang Shao-i. Unlike T'ang but like most of the other American-educated Peking bureaucrats, Ts'ai stayed with Yuan to the bitter end, working as his personal liaison with important foreigners in Peking and in salt and customs posts.

There were younger men, whose foreign experience was more conventional than the fussily chaperoned and nervously interrupted Yung Wing mission. Wellington Koo (Ku Wei-chün, b. 1887) acquired a Ph.D. degree from Columbia University in 1912 and married T'ang Shao-i's eldest daughter. His familial tie with T'ang did not impede his service to the Peking government after T'ang's break with Yuan. Koo played a prominent role in Yuan's diplomacy despite his youth—twenty-five years old in 1912. Not all Yuan's diplomats were American educated. Ts'ao Ju-lin (1876–1966), who attended Waseda and Chūō universities in Tokyo, became Yuan's leading diplomatic expert on Japan and was vice-minister for foreign affairs during much of the presidency. Lu Cheng-hsiang (1871–1949) had no formal foreign education but went directly from late nineteenth-century Chinese foreign language schools into two decades of diplomatic work abroad, mainly in Russia and the Netherlands, where he acquired a Belgian wife and Catholicism. Briefly acquainted with Yuan before the revolution, Lu returned to China in May, 1912, and over the next four years served President Yuan as foreign minister and prime minister.

Some of Yuan's specialists in foreign affairs fell with him in 1916 or were casualties of the May Fourth Movement. Several went on to celebrated diplomatic careers in the 1920s and 1930s. Wellington Koo's career reached into the 1960s, with a seat on the International Court of Justice. If their diplomatic record during the Yuan presidency was a series of humiliations, where achievement consisted of avoiding even greater humiliations, the fault did not lie in ignorance of foreign ways, or a fixation on "Middle Kingdom" ideology, or lack of sophistication. In terms of technical virtuosity, Yuan employed superior talent in the diplomatic as in other fields.

Yuan's own prerevolutionary record in diplomacy was mixed. He had scored some successes in defense of China's sovereignty but, in contrast to some other nationalist officials of his time, was disinclined to allow popular anti-imperialist agitation to be mobilized in support. The skills of his diplomatic entourage had not been enough to compensate for abjuring this increment of bargaining muscle. His fall from power in January, 1909, seems to have been attributable in part to the failure of his strategy to regain the initiative in Manchuria by winning American help against a solidifying Russo-Japanese hegemony.[46] During the presidency, his augmented collection of experts in foreign affairs, minus T'ang Shao-i, worked under the same restriction regarding anti-imperialist mobilization. The results were similar, both in frequently failing to check foreign encroachment and in their fatal effect on Yuan's political career.

There were still others areas where Yuan as president could draw upon specialists who had already worked under him before the revolution: education, the police, the judiciary. Similarly, more were recruited as the republic got underway. The gaps were not in the available stores of expertise, but in the emphasis and priorities assigned to different sorts of programs. For example, although some of his group had special knowledge about constitutional government and representative assemblies (Ts'ao Ju-lin, Chou Tzu-ch'i and others), this expertise was not put to use. Insufficient training or high-level "manpower" deficiency was not where the problems began.

Nor were factional divisions within Yuan's government a major burden on its functioning. Bureaucratic groups formed and reformed in the jockeying for positions of power that marks any large political structure. But such factional infighting was a sideshow, not the main event. The record of Yuan's presidency was determined, not by its factional makeup, but by the interaction between its policies and China's situation in the aftermath of the revolution.

Yuan's Group Faces the Republic

After nearly three years of exile from Peking, Yuan returned to office under the Manchus in November, 1911, as prime minister. Ostensibly his task was to save the dynasty from the gathering revolutionary forces. As the situation developed, it was apparent that this would be impossible. Revolutionary sentiment was too catching. Revolutionary military force was formidable. Foreign help for the Ch'ing was not forthcoming. And Yuan's own entourage, as it reassembled, was not immune to the revolutionary spirit. By mid-November, 1911, close foreign observers concluded that almost all Yuan's civilian associates sympathized with the republican revolution.[47] Yuan himself turned his energies to arranging the termination of the Ch'ing monarchy. By the end of January, 1912, his generals were working to hasten the republic—some eagerly, some reluctantly.[48] Although standing hard by the pinnacle of formal authority in China, Yuan's political machine stealthily but very effectively joined the revolution.

Why? Some combination of opportunism and pragmatism figured largely.

As observed at the beginning of the chapter, the revolutionaries extended an invitation early on. In any case, Yuan's group had no real choice, if China were to remain unified and avoid a prolonged civil war. Further civil war would damage the social order. Foreign intervention would probably ensue. The revolutionary leadership faced a similar dilemma: should the unity of the country and the stability of the society be jeopardized in pursuit of complete victory? Sun Yat-sen's concession of the presidency to Yuan was partly determined by a negative answer to that question. But the least defensible position of all, once the revolution showed some strength, was defense of the Ch'ing dynasty. Manchu legitimacy had eroded to the point where, once seriously challenged, it was doomed. There were progressive politicians, like Liang Ch'i-ch'ao, who advocated the perpetuation of the Manchu monarchy in a watered down, constitutional version, but their voices were drowned out in the spreading acclaim for republicanism. Yuan was enough in touch with opinion to realize this. And the diminution of elite allegiance to the court was in any case a condition far advanced within his own operation. He might not have been able to carry with him his lieutenants—only yesterday ministers of state for the throne—if he had tried to save the Ch'ing.

If we reflect on the characteristics of Yuan's group, their acceptance of the dynasty's overthrow does not seem extraordinary. They had initially been drawn together under the banner of reform. In most cases their rise to prominence, and therefore presumably some of their self-esteem, was linked to achievement in programs infused with nationalist ideology. Training military units designed to be on a par with the best foreign ones; recovering foreign options on railways and mines and striving for Chinese management of those already operating; launching industrial enterprises in an effort to keep profits at home—these had been the activities of Yuan's lieutenants. Like others engaged in or advocating reforms, Yuan's group, too, could not escape the sense of discouragement with the court's leadership. The discouragement was compounded by the court's dismissal of Yuan in 1909 and its mounting suspicion of Chinese in its last couple of years.

On its side, the revolution did not make extravagant demands. The revolutionary leadership did not threaten the social pyramid with inversion. Only a stone or two from the pinnacle need be removed. Those Chinese remaining near the top after the Manchu princes and Manchu officials were discarded were invited to remain more or less where they were. As for the other issues—constitutionalism, nationalism, reform—Yuan and his cohorts had already identified themselves with these notions. Differences there were, but not sufficiently wide or apparent to prevent a shared rhetoric.

Nor was Yuan's group separated from the leaders of the emerging revolutionary regimes in the South by a social chasm. It would be difficult to imagine a more privileged social position than that of Chou Hsueh-hsi, the industrial promoter, whose father reached the post of governor-general and owned over six hundred acres of land in Anhwei. The son had four hundred thousand taels of his own invested in salt trading privileges.[49] On the other hand, the revolutionary leadership contained almost no men of more humble origins than Ts'ao K'un, who journeyed from cloth peddler to general. The typical member of Yuan's group, like the typical revolutionary leader, came from a middle or low position in the gentry. As the revolutionary provinces stabilized, their administrations were infused with quantities of high gentry converts to republicanism, bringing to the revolutionary camp a social tone unsurpassed in Peking. There was no need for Yuan's entourage to feel that their privileged social status was threatened by the revolution, despite a history of socialist rhetoric among some of its early advocates.

Yuan and the revolutionaries were hardly enthralled with each other. Distrust cropped up continuously. Yuan was determined to limit their national influence as far as circumstances would let him. The revolutionaries contemplated expeditions to sweep Yuan's military power out of the north. Attempts to assassinate him recurred periodically. But such impulses were largely restrained and compromises were reached. People seemed to want to be optimistic. Let us listen again to China's young apostle of Western science, Ting Wen-chiang, writing in English from Shanghai in May, 1912:

> I think the most wonderful thing in our Revolution is the complete predominance of Yuan Shih-k'ai's personality. As soon as it became known in the later stages of the peace negotiations that he also regarded the interest of [the] Manchu dynasty as subordinate to that of the nation, the press stopped to attack him. . . .
>
> Every serious thinking man in the country of course realizes the very serious financial trouble we are in, but there is a general hope that now we have a real leader at our head, we will get through somehow. We understand that the work of reform is not less important nor less difficult than before, but with the fountain head cleared

once for all, the efforts made will be immeasurably more real and have less chance to be misdirected or wasted.[50]

Ting, the returned student who had helped preserve social order in his home area during the revolution, was determined to believe that the republic was good. This meant supporting Yuan. In this Ting was not different from most of the vocal portions of the elite, nor from much of the revolutionary leadership in 1912, despite misgivings. The intense sense of contradiction which so many have retrospectively felt in Yuan's emergence as president of the republic was confined to a very few in 1912. Foreign powers and Chinese leaders, with few exceptions, hailed him.

But what would his policy be? How was the great official reformer, thwarted in his prime by the Manchus, going to respond to the new demands on his leadership? How would his government relate to the surge of political participation that the revolution dramatized? How would it deal with the military, with provincial autonomy, with gentry power, with foreign encroachment? As the answers to these questions became clear over the next four years, the disillusionment among Chinese (including Ting) was profound.

Chapter 4

The Liberal Republic

The political premises underlying the arrangements for the national republican government of 1912 were liberal. The influence of the contemporary
West was obvious and openly acknowledged. Not until the 1950s would
China again go so far in modeling her formal political institutions on a
foreign example. In the early republic, the imported Western political
forms failed to take root. Very little of substance survived the decline of
the institutional features that were introduced. But for more than a year,
the appurtenances and some of the spirit of liberal republican government
flourished in postrevolutionary China.

The Liberal Tide

It has not been customary to use the term "liberal" to describe early republican politics. In discussing twentieth-century developments in China, the
attribution has been reserved until recently for the systematic advocacy of
Western liberal principles during the May Fourth Movement later in the
decade. The ideas of liberal May Fourth spokesmen like Hu Shih, however,
had little effect in the realm of practical politics and its institutions. The
political institutions historically associated with Western liberalism enjoyed
their nearest Chinese approximation earlier, during the first and second
years of the republic. The 1911 Revolution released a rush of interest in
new political forms, as well as a short period of tolerance toward new
social attitudes. Thanks to this mood, representative government and
competitive elections among autonomous political parties came closer to
dominating political process in 1912 and 1913 than at any other point in
Chinese history. In many ways the experiment stopped short of a compre-

hensive reproduction of the most advanced Western liberal politics. For example, participation in these new institutions was largely confined to the already privileged (hence the period is better characterized as liberal than as democratic). And the philosophical lineaments of Western liberalism were much more fully articulated in later years. But at no other time was the liberal political style given so much leeway.

The architects of the new national government in 1912 assumed the propriety of representative government. The constitution, drafted in Nanking by Sung Chiao-jen, a leading revolutionary moderate, was a cross between French and American models. Much was left ill defined: for example, the powers of the central government over the provincial governments. But, in contrast to official pronouncements on self-government in the late Ch'ing, the stress was on popular sovereignty, the rights of citizens, and the ultimate supremacy of the legislature. Presidential powers were also broad, and Yuan Shih-k'ai undertook to rule by them.

Political activity among the elite was remarkably boisterous in the new atmosphere of liberation from Manchu autocracy. One study asserts that over three hundred political parties were formed in the wake of the revolution and finds that fifteen are worth some discussion.[1] Even among the weightier fifteen, some were not dedicated to winning political power and many of the others were only supporting clubs for ambitious individuals. But interest in political organization and proselytizing, which had been banned under the monarchy, was high.

Newspapers also burgeoned prolifically. Calculations for the incidence of both magazines and newspapers record totals of 60 in 1898 and 487 in 1913.[2] By the late spring of 1912, Szechwan's capital, Chengtu, had 7 daily newspapers. The province's leading commercial city, Chungking, had 6 (in contrast to only 2 before the revolution). Canton was reported in October, 1912, to have 24,[3] and so on. As with most of the political activity, the clientele was restricted by educational attainment. Newspapers were many, but as a proportion of population, readers were few. A knowledgeable foreigner estimated that the Chinese-language newspaper in central China with the largest circulation published only twenty thousand copies a day.[4] The point is that, by comparison with even the recent past, the level of communication and political organization among the gentry and merchant elite rose dramatically in 1912 and early 1913. The mass of the population remained politically untouched and unorganized, but the elite were brought into provincial and national networks of communication and committees as never before. The resulting political energy enjoyed as its field of action a profusion of representative assemblies and new executive governing bodies at all levels, down to the county and even smaller units.

The first year of the republic was also marked by a conspicuous social liberality and loosening of old ways among the elite. The cutting of queues was undertaken as a republican project throughout the country—a gesture marking the overthrow of Manchu domination, since the queue was a male hairstyle imposed by the fallen dynasty. In Shantung, for instance, Chou Tzu-ch'i, the military governor, who owed his appointment to Yuan Shih-k'ai, made the absence of the queue a condition of voting franchise (though he was later overruled from Peking).[5] In several cities, police or volunteer republican zealots waylaid pigtailed passersby with barber's tools. There were holdouts. Chang Hsun's personal army astride the Tientsin-Pukow Railway militantly retained the queue in declared defiance of the republicans, though Chang accepted the hegemony if not always the orders of Yuan, his old commander from Hsiao-chan days. In general, the common people except in a few urban centers were not caught up in the enthusiasm for the new day dawning for their "betters." Feng Yü-hsiang, later a leading warlord, then a middle-level officer in Chihli, recounts in his autobiography how some of his men wept uncontrollably when their queues were cut on orders from Yuan Shih-k'ai and that it was felt necessary to give each man a dollar to overcome resistance to the shearing.[6] In Szechwan, there were reports of a pro-Ch'ing uprising in the spring of 1912, which had the object of restoring the Manchus, exterminating the foreigners, and killing queueless Chinese men.[7] The results of the national campaign for new hair styles were mixed. But for those who took this step, whether freely or forced, a public break with the past had been accomplished. It was a symbol of liberation.

Simultaneously with the change in male hair styles went a decline in the force of old attitudes and customs. Western-style clothes became fashionable among the urban elite. The kotow on official occasions was discarded. The new president in Peking had himself called *hsien-sheng* (mister).[8] Everyone remarked on the diminishing awe in which government representatives were seen by their constituencies. A prefect under the revolutionary regime in Hupeh was criticized for riding a sedan chair in the style of his predecessor under the empire.[9] A national conference on education, held in the summer of 1912, split evenly on the question of whether Confucius's birthday should be commemorated in the schools.[10] Chinese New Year's Day in 1913, which came on February 6, passed without the customary signs of celebration in Peking, in contrast to January 1, when the city was decked out in flags in honor of the first anniversary of the republic.[11] Peking's participation in these changes, despite its relative conservatism, suggests how widespread they were in the urban centers.

Students in the Western-style schools continued and perhaps augmented a tendency, dating from the spread of such schools before the revolution, to assert their voice in school affairs. A Chinese newspaper complained that the students at Peking University, as elsewhere, were "trying to dictate who shall be appointed their directors or teachers and say to them how they shall behave themselves."[12] Yuan Shih-k'ai was moved to assert that "the most important principle in a school is obedience" and to deplore the students' slighting of teachers and ignoring regulations. He said: "The staffs and students of the schools must realize that the republican polity must be nurtured and the people's excellence heightened before freedom and equality can operate normally within the limits of the law."[13] The cracks in old social attitudes were not enough to threaten the whole order but were nonetheless noticeable.

A new social development at this time with much meaning for the future was the women's movement. In the 1880s a group of men convened by K'ang Yu-wei in his home district began a society to end footbinding, and then nervously disbanded for fear of official disfavor of political organization of any kind outside the government. Even this pale glimmer of female emancipation could not survive before the 1890s, when K'ang tried again and antifootbinding societies began to spread to other parts of the country.[14] By the close of the century, some few women began to take their own measures against their hobbled physical and social condition. During the first decade of the new century, small but growing numbers of women sought personal liberation through Western-style education, in China and abroad. In the revolution of 1911, women constituted uniformed military units in the lower Yangtze areas, Canton, and Foochow. A Female Citizens' Army attached to the Chekiang army numbered forty-five women when it was disbanded by Huang Hsing in January, 1912.[15] In the first year of the republic, groups of suffragists raised the issue of women's right to vote. The T'ung-meng hui, the leading revolutionary organization, advocated equal rights for women (though not universal adult suffrage). Nonetheless, agitation for the vote and the right to sit in the provisional revolutionary assembly was rebuffed by the Nanking government of Sun Yat-sen. The women responded with threats of bombing.[16] A suffrage bill was then passed but pronounced inoperative until reconsidered by the full national deliberative assembly that was to gather shortly in Peking. This time, a dozen women entered the hall and smashed windows.[17] The influence of the contemporary militant suffragist movement in England is apparent in these tactics. A bill providing for female suffrage was later introduced in the provincial assembly of Kwangtung, a province where the executive was dominated by T'ung-meng hui stalwarts. But the assembly voted down the bill, over the objections of ten appointed women members. "The vote or death" became the cry of the Cantonese suffragists, who continued their agitation.[18]

As in the case of other profoundly disturbing social issues, the revolutionary leaders preferred to temporize. Sun Yat-sen, though pressed by women's delegations urging equality, felt he must postpone the issue. He declared in Peking in August, 1912, that, although equal rights for women were an altogether fitting principle, the nation was in danger and a firm government must first be established.[19] A newspaper in Shanghai on the left wing of the political spectrum declared at the end of 1912 that women were as yet insufficiently educated to vote.[20] This argument did not explain why women who could pass the restrictive educational and property qualifications should not be allowed to vote on the same footing as men.

Obviously, more force than the small contingent of socially privileged women that activists could muster was required to register major legal gains. But a preliminary bout had been fought and the ground laid for renewed efforts later. A returned student (male) commented on the Shanghai scene in the spring of 1912: ". . . one cannot help feeling delighted in seeing our girls with natural feet walking about the street, getting into tram cars, dining in restaurants. It seems an entirely new life to me who have known the terribly strict rules of ten years ago. . . ."[21] In the fall of 1912, a student society in Shanghai debated the desirability of China adopting the "free marriage" system of the West. Women joined in the argument.[22] These stirrings were a beginning, even if very limited. And they bore witness to the gradual unraveling of the old social fabric in the liberal aftermath of the revolution.

Limits of Liberalism

The interest in representative government, political parties and the new social styles in 1912 was not based on widespread commitment to liberal principles. The supreme value of the rights of the individual, the tolerance of varieties of thought and behavior, and belief in electoral control over executive and legislative government—these ideas claimed only a very limited acceptance even from the elite portions of the population and were quite irrelevant to the mass of the Chinese people. Such liberalism as did prosper in the first year of the republic owed more to a pragmatic adoption of liberal political forms, an uncertainty of direction with foreign models temporarily filling the void, and a degree of disintegration of social and political controls.

Nowhere was the superficiality of liberalism more apparent than in the republic's president, Yuan Shih-k'ai. As part of the settlement with the revolutionaries, Yuan cabled to the revolutionary assembly in Nanking the oath that had been prescribed. He would devote himself to "enhancing the republican spirit, to cleansing the marring stains of despotism, and to assiduously maintaining the constitution. . . ."[23] In his April speech to the newly constituted national deliberative assembly (*ts'an-i yuan*), he cautiously welcomed the sudden leap from despotism into a republic and cited his record of a keen progressive stand against conservatism.[24] Two months later, in protesting the injustice of suspicions of Bonapartism, he claimed that before the revolution he had come to see a correspondence of the republican order of France and America with the ancient teaching, "the world belongs to all" (*t'ien-hsia wei-kung*).[25] But none of this amounted to an enthusiastic endorsement of the liberal republican message. Nor could many have mistaken him for a liberal leader. His record lay in bureaucratically based reform, not in any sort of political theorizing. And his scepticism about the applicability of the full range of Western republican institutions to Chinese conditions was scarcely concealed. He publicly qualified his welcome of the republic with fears about the backwardness of the country.[26] He confided at this time to the British minister his view that "a republic meant a deal of useless talking and very little work."[27] Later, when reviewing the turbulence of the second year of the republic in the course of preparing the institutions of his dictatorship, he described the Nanking-made constitution as "a disaster."[28] Yuan's foreign and domestic support did not derive from his embodiment of liberal republican values.

Full-fledged adherents of liberal republican values, whether as political groups or as individuals, were rare. Republican institutions enjoyed a rather strong constituency among the social elite, but often for reasons that only tangentially connected with liberal values. Spokesmen for self-government dwelt as much on its value in nourishing state power as on its capacity to check it.[29] But in neither the late Ch'ing nor the early republic did the mobilization of extragovernmental energies through wider participation produce sufficient results in national power to satisfy nationalist expectations. Representative assemblies at different levels in the society turned out to be convenient vehicles for legitimizing the expression of gentry concerns and augmenting gentry strength, against both the state and the peasantry. But the society as a whole, including many leaders of gentry background, ultimately demanded justification also in terms of national solidarity and the creation of social wealth and power.

Here is where the contemporary foreign model ran into trouble. What had come to seem so admirable about the new, Westernizing policies to a socially privileged Chinese nationalist was the conjunction of a vigorous reform movement with his class interests. If the Western achievement could be reproduced in China, then his country could be reformed, foreign encroachments could be rolled back, and he could participate honorably without diminution (or perhaps even with an increase) in his social and economic position. But by 1912, this foreign model when applied to China was rent with contradictions. Let us examine them.

First, the power necessary to dislodge the well entrenched foreign presence (backed, as it was in any showdown, by the combined weight of the industrial nations of the world) was more than could be raised by elite mobilization only. Who knows what might have been accomplished by these means if China, like Japan, had rallied soon after the first warning bell. But by 1900 it was already too late for easy victories. In the last few years of the Ch'ing a remarkable performance along these lines occurred but proved unsatisfactory to nationalistic Chinese.

Second, once having adopted the goal of national independence, the central government's response to its inability to dislodge foreign power was to seek a greater centralization of power, the better to achieve the reforms that might help regain full national sovereignty. This was true both of the Ch'ing court in its last years and of Yuan Shih-k'ai as president. But once on the road toward centralization, there could be no natural resting place. Given the disproportion of power between the Chinese government and the imperialist nations, one act of centralization on behalf of reform and national independence could only be a step on the road to the next. At some point—sooner rather than later—this course would produce conflict between the center and liberal institutions, between a bureaucratic administration and widespread elite participation in politics, between Peking and local self-government. The liberal foreign model provided no resolution. It contained the assumption that the growth of power in the nation-state and increased elite participation in politics were fundamentally compatible. Under Chinese conditions in the early twentieth century, including the special demands that imperialist pressure put on political performance, the assumption was subject to doubt.

Third, by 1912 the provincial unit had become an alternate focus for concentrations of reformist power and anti-imperialist aspirations. In other words, it was not entirely clear where the center was, or whether the center at Peking would ever be an adequate vehicle for nationalism and reform. No Chinese was ready to say that there should *not* be a single government for all of China (including Mongolia and Tibet), but in practice the province became a "second center," justified in terms of local self-government and central government failures. Thus the conflict between centralization of power and liberal institutions became intermingled with the conflict between Peking and the provinces. Yuan Shih-k'ai's disposition to assert strongly the powers of the center and to see liberal institutions as diversions, even impertinent obstructions, aggravated the conflict.

Revolutionaries in the Liberal Republic: The National Leaders

The revolutionaries were not free from these same contradictory pressures. Their best prospects for exercising leadership after the revolution seemed to lie in formal accumulations of state power or in the political organization of the elite. The alternative of involving the masses in politics was never consistently pursued. Taken as a whole, revolutionary leaders were more active in repressing than in stimulating mass movement, once the revolution was well under way. But there were problems in reliance on state power or elite party politics. How could Yuan Shih-k'ai's national authority be resisted without undermining overall Chinese strength? How could one build party power without seeming to pursue partisan interests at the expense of the general polity? If one asserted provincial autonomy against central power, arguing theories of self-government, then on what grounds could one resist the encroachments of lesser political units and political groups that cut into the power of provincial government?

The subject of the revolutionary movement in the early republic is a complicated one, which has been treated in specialized studies with a degree of detail impossible here.[30] In one sense, almost all politically active Chinese had been revolutionaries in December, 1911, and January, 1912, since they were working in different ways toward the end of the Ch'ing dynasty. Even the longest holdouts, Liang Ch'i-ch'ao and his immediate entourage, later claimed (not too convincingly) to have been more responsible than any other group for the demise of the Manchu monarchy. Similarly, virtually no one was a revolutionary after February, 1912, in the sense that for some months there was general acceptance of the legitimacy of the newly created political order. Primacy of place belongs to those who were plotters and revolutionary theorists before the uprising in October, 1911, though they did not constitute a single cohesive organization. But one cannot totally exclude from the general category some of those who rallied to the cause and helped build the revolutionary provincial governments after the first shots had been fired.

However one defines them, revolutionaries were divided on the question of their relation to Peking and on the prospects for representative government. One effort to manage the dilemmas emphasized the maintenance of national unity and the use of a national parliament and a national party to take power at the center on behalf of the spirit of 1911. Sung Chiao-jen, one of the young founding fathers of the T'ung-meng hui, soon emerged as the leader of this tendency. Another approach was to consolidate power at the provincial level and to proceed with reforms within that framework, at the expense of central authority and often of lesser local autonomies. This was a pattern common to several provinces, but found its most radical version in Kwangtung under Hu Han-min, another young veteran of the T'ung-meng hui inner group. A third response was to work through self-government at all levels. This line was characteristic of the formerly non-revolutionary, constitutionalist leadership of the provincial assemblies who transferred their loyalties to the revolution once it came. It marked the politics of Hunan between November, 1911, and the summer of 1913. None of these three approaches was held to the complete exclusion of the others, and several prominent revolutionaries wandered ambiguously among various possibilities, borrowing bits from each. Among them was Sun Yat-sen. And all groups vacillated in their attitude toward Yuan Shih-k'ai's rule.

From the time that the possibility of an accommodation between Yuan and the revolutionaries first became a prospect in November, 1911, opinion about Yuan in the revolutionary South ranged from murderous to respectful and admiring. But the averaging of this range of views produced in practice a collective decision to rely on his cooperation and accept his leadership at the national level, at least temporarily. The way was smoothed by T'ang Shao-i, who had been Yuan's chief formal negotiator with the South during the revolution and was by late February, 1912, his nominee for the prime ministership.[31] Toward the end of March, T'ang traveled to Nanking to negotiate a coalition cabinet and to sweeten the bitter pill of resignation for Sun Yat-sen, president of the revolutionary government, by assisting him financially.

Almost a month earlier at Yuan's request (the purpose was to forestall a Japanese loan being negotiated directly with Nanking), a consortium of foreign banks had put 2,000,000 taels at the disposal of the Nanking revolutionary government. Now T'ang arrived with a personal fund for Sun, which Sun had requested for recompensing his staff. T'ang had in fact negotiated a foreign loan outside the consortium, with no strings attached to disbursement, just before his journey to Nanking, thereby providing the wherewithal for this transaction.[32] Official fiscal legacies of the Nanking government were also assumed by Peking, such as Ch$10,000,000 of bonds.[33] Though these actions did not resolve the fiscal difficulties of the revolutionary provinces and their armies—far from it—they bespoke in financial terms the new government's acceptance of its origins in the revolution.

Agreement on a cabinet was reached within a week of T'ang's arrival in Nanking but not without difficulties. The chief of them was the South's desire to see Huang Hsing as army minister, and Yuan Shih-k'ai's decision to insist upon Tuan Ch'i-jui. Huang Hsing's personal reluctance to assume office in Peking and the underlying unease about the prospect of his departure on the part of those very military commanders who were most emphatic in urging his candidacy facilitated a compromise.[34] Huang Hsing was appointed chief of staff, although he refused the post. More important, he was declared Nanking resident general (*liu-shou*), sharing civil power in Nanking with the Kiangsu military governor and assuming responsibility for the "reorganization" of all military forces in the South. A further element in the compromise was that T'ang Shao-i, the premier-designate and longtime aide to Yuan, joined the T'ung-meng hui, which on March 3 had reconstituted itself as an open political party. Liu Kuang-hsiung, the navy minister, and Yuan's henchman Chao Ping-chün, minister of internal affairs, also joined the T'ung-meng hui, so that the party had a formal majority of seven to four in the new cabinet.[35] T'ang also undertook to secure the appointment of Nanking nominees for the military governorships of Chihli and Shantung. Although T'ang soon dropped his efforts on behalf of Nanking's choice for Shantung (not being Shantungese, the nominee aroused immediate opposition in Shantung), he persisted in urging Nanking's choice of Wang Chih-hsiang for Chihli, where the provincial assembly wanted this native son.[36] These were the main elements of the arrangements preceding the actual formation of a unified government in Peking in April, 1912.

As it turned out, this compromise contained more form than substance for the T'ung-meng hui. Yuan later rejected Nanking's nomination for the military governorship of Chihli. To do otherwise would have been to diminish his authority in the metropolitan province at a time when it was a large part of the area he controlled. But T'ang's inability to deliver on his commitment was one of the reasons for his growing distance from Yuan and his precipitate resignation in June, 1912. Further, despite the formal majority in the cabinet, reliable veterans of the old T'ung-meng hui when it was a revolutionary society were only four at best, and in less powerful cabinet posts. Since the T'ung-meng hui stalwarts followed T'ang Shao-i out of the cabinet, serious T'ung-meng hui participation in the national government was confined by mid-July to the national deliberative assembly.[37] Meanwhile, Huang Hsing's post as supreme commander of the large southern armies contained the potential for building an alternative in the south to Peking. But Huang Hsing, against the advice of some comrades, used the position to keep order in the Nanking area while beginning the job of dispersing and disbanding the large numbers of soldiers drawn from various places to Nanking by the revolution. When he thought he had accomplished what demobilization he could on the limited resources available from Peking, he asked that the position be abolished, so that unity might be fostered.[38]

At the national level, the approach of the former revolutionaries toward Yuan soon took the form of an ideologically liberal drive for parliamentary supremacy, legal procedure, and a cabinet dominated by a political party. Yuan at first adapted to the liberal and party-oriented mood. The interior minister, a Yuan man, announced in April that, since the Ch'ing regulations of newspapers were repressive and the era of free speech had arrived, all press laws were abolished.[39] The evidence suggests that during the first year of the republic, the press had greater latitude in areas under Peking's administration, despite instances of repression, than in most of the formerly revolutionary provinces. Nor was Yuan overtly hostile to party activity. He reportedly urged in May, 1912, that the new justice minister, Wang Ch'ung-hui of the T'ung-meng hui, draw his subordinates from his own party. Many bureaucrats were in fact displaced at this time, producing thereby a community in Peking of ousted officials, furious at the interruption in their careers.[40] Yuan was even quoted as having told one party delegation that "in a free government parties play a necessary part" and that "there should be two powerful parties—one to administer the affairs of state and the other to watch its action and oppose its methods. A party so strong as to crush out all opposition is likely to give way to its own worst elements and becomes corrupt in its practices."[41] The leader of an only mildly political Chinese Socialist Party, Chiang K'ang-hu, was cordially received in Peking by Yuan Shih-k'ai (under whom Chiang had served in the first years of the century) and was even asked for ideas at the interior ministry. By contrast, before this visit, the party's Hunan branches had been harassed by the military governor there. Shortly after leaving Peking, Chiang was arrested at Hankow, where Li Yuan-hung was in charge.[42] Yuan's "low posture" in his initial months as president contributed to a period of good feeling and a delay in contests of power.

Equally important were the efforts of some of the leading revolutionaries to make the compromise settlement work. Huang Hsing refrained from building the Nanking residency general into a center of opposition to Peking. The approval of Yuan's nominees for an interim cabinet to succeed T'ang Shao-i's was obtained only after the national deliberative assembly members (of whom about a third were affiliated with the T'ung-meng hui) were subjected to bribes and threats.[43] But a degree of voluntary assent was required to produce the overwhelming vote of approval on July 26, when only two members withheld their support. When Yuan in mid-August ignored all legal procedures and arranged the summary execution of two high-ranking officers from Hupeh, merely on the basis of a cabled request from Li Yuan-hung that he do so, the outrage in the national deliberative assembly was vigorous, but brief.

Grievances were accumulating from these incidents and shaped the terms of the emerging debate with Yuan. But they did not prevent Sun Yat-sen and Huang Hsing from coming to Peking at the end of the summer in a grand demonstration of national unity. Sun had thirteen interviews with

Yuan, some going on for hours, between August 24 and September 20. He, Huang Hsing, Li Yuan-hung, and Yuan all subscribed to a communiqué calling for unified government and reconciliation, among other things. Yuan proclaimed Sun "an honest and righteous man" who was "wide-awake in his ideas" and whom Yuan regretted not knowing before.[44] Sun announced that he believed in Yuan's sincerity, that Yuan combined new ideas, experience, and old methods in proper proportions, that he was "just the right man" and should be president for ten years.[45] The Kuomintang (KMT) was formed in August by Sung Chiao-jen by the amalgamation of the national T'ung-meng hui with several lesser parties. It significantly moderated the T'ung-meng hui platform. It endorsed a new cabinet under Chao Ping-chün, Yuan's police specialist. The new Kuomintang now commanded a two-thirds majority of the national deliberative assembly. In a scheme advocated by Huang Hsing, the cabinet became a party one, not by selecting its ministers from Kuomintang leaders, but by most of the ministers joining the Kuomintang.[46]

How could leaders from opposite sides of the prevailing political spectrum, soon to become blood enemies, find so much to agree about? Even if one interprets the initial settlement of the revolution as a desperate lurch to achieve the primary objective (the end of Manchu rule) without inviting foreign intervention, the problem of understanding the celebration of national harmony in the late summer and fall of 1912 remains. Among the possible lines of explanation are the continuing dangers of foreign intervention (including conditions for loans); the principled nationalistic belief in unity held by both sides; the weakness of all parties during a period of disintegration of formal government powers and stringent finances; and the maneuverings of those merely biding their time before the moment to strike.

To these I would add another consideration: that the reach of the spectrum defined by Sun and Yuan was not as wide as one might suppose. After the Second Revolution (1913), when the Kuomintang was outlawed and Sun in exile, Yuan accused Sun and his followers of inciting robbery and social disorder under the name of socialism and equality. But Sun in 1912 was careful to assure the public that his notions of "land equalization" aimed at *preventing* the development of social and economic distortions and the emergence of "trusts" and uneconomic investments. In contrast to the West, Sun said in Nanking at the end of March, "social revolution" would be easy and nonviolent in China, because "Chinese civilization has not progressed and industry and commerce are not yet developed." Capitalists, who might obstruct social progress, had not yet emerged in China.[47] Present landlords would not be hurt; the rich as well as the poor would benefit. His principle of the people's livelihood, or Chinese socialism, was not a method for taking from the rich to help the poor, he declared in Peking on August 25, but a way of guarding against capitalist oppression imposed by international monopolies.[48] Indeed, along with female equality, the idea was altogether absent from the formal platform of the newly founded Kuomintang.

Sun need not have been surprised that Yuan agreed with his exposition of the land question in China.[49] He was a man searching for concepts and programs which would lead to a just society while building Chinese strength. In these efforts he and some of his associates were opening paths that Yuan did not comprehend. But in the early republic, Sun's application of his ideas to China was at most a very mild threat to the status quo. Even later, when Yuan used distortions of Sun's social ideas as propaganda against him, it was a propagandistic, not a substantive question. Though some were exercised by it, socialism was not a major divisive issue in these years. It had yet to be presented forcefully in a form that spelled structural social change.[50]

By the end of 1912, the strategy of participation in the new order at the national level had passed through several phases. The coalition cabinet under T'ang Shao-i had collapsed through resignations and had been replaced by others (two in quick succession) more purely of Yuan's concoction, though in each case the approval of the parliamentary T'ung-meng hui or Kuomintang was ultimately secured. By their visit to Peking, Sun and Huang Hsing reaffirmed the commitment to working out the new China through the national government. A broadly based political party, the Kuomintang, had been built around the old T'ung-meng hui. Its political center of gravity had shifted by comparison away from radicalism, and it set out to win control of the constitutional implements of national government. By December, the main focus of this effort was the national elections, from which the Kuomintang emerged triumphant.

Revolutionaries in the Liberal Republic: Provincial Strategies

While the stage was being set for a Kuomintang bid for power at the national level, a second struggle was developing between Peking and the provinces.

While liberalism and nationalism were, with difficulty, adjusting to each other in the national government, liberalism and provincialism were attempting a coalescence at the level of provincial government, with a comparable amount of complication.

The first political fact of the revolution was the devolution of authority. Even as provinces declared their independence, lesser units were asserting theirs. Sometimes this took the form of two or more formidably autonomous military governments in a single province, notably in Szechwan and Kiangsu. Sometimes self-government councils or other groups at the prefectural or county level assumed effective governmental powers. The pattern varied.

By mid-summer, 1912, most provinces had been pieced together again. However, the centripetal movement stopped there. The political provincialism of the late Ch'ing (see chapter 1) found a full measure of institutional expression in the provinces of the first two years of the republic. In contrast to the prerevolutionary situation, where provincialism pressed against a centralized bureaucratic administration present and operating in the provinces, now the heights of provincial power were generally in local hands.

Among the most militant provincial governments in their assertion of independence from Peking (though retaining a commitment to unity in the long run) were those headed by revolutionary nationalists, like Hu Han-min. He and others of similar bent were not any the less nationalists. Their attitudes were a reasonable consequence of their situations and the influence of the endemic provincial nationalism of the early twentieth century in China. The province could, in this view, do the work of the nation largely by itself. It could do it better than the central government and by insisting on its autonomy would contribute all the more to ultimate national strength. The theory had much merit, given the low state of communications development and popular mobilization. It was, in fact, a strategy for the rapid mobilization of those portions of the local population already politicized. It also set its adherents, much more powerful than before the revolution, on a collision course with the Peking government, which pursued national strength through centralization.

The issue was never drawn in absolutes. Yuan tempered his centralizing schemes with concessions to continuing provincial identity and pride. His concessions had more to do with the extent of his power at any particular time than with acceptance of the theories of provincial autonomy. But even at the peak of his power he drew back from some of the more extreme suggestions emanating from his government. For their part, the autonomous provincial governments (they were a healthy majority of the whole in 1912) took up national liberal issues and slogans as well as strictly provincial ones. The national assembly represented provincial interests at the national capital, where its presence prevented Yuan from using legislation and constitutions to diminish provincial autonomy.

On some issues, the internal politics of the province produced apparent departures from a consistent espousal of elective local self-government. A radical newspaper in Shanghai was articulating one common view in 1912 when it said: "The province, taken by itself, is a self-sufficient state. It is natural that the management of its affairs should best be left entirely to its people. Hence, we advocate popular election of its chief executive."[51] But the Kuomintang military governor of Anhwei joined fifteen of his fellow provincial chief executives in November, 1912, in opposing their own popular election, preferring appointment (in effect, confirmation of a fait accompli in most cases) by the central government.[52] A proposal in the national deliberative assembly granting provincial assemblies the power to impeach the province's chief was protested by most of the military governors, including Hu Han-min.[53] Hu joined with the military governors of Honan and Kirin (both Yuan appointees) in opposition to the separation of military and civilian powers in provincial governments. It was more than coincidental that, like Hu Han-min, the Honan and Kirin governors had been under attack by the assemblies in their provinces.[54] There were moments, in other words, when political challenges from within the province were a greater threat to the authority of a military governor, even if a revolutionary veteran, than was Peking. But these moments were rare after the first year of the republic, as Yuan increased the pressure from Peking.

The province of Kwangtung in 1912 and early 1913 illustrates the intersection of revolutionary nationalism and reformist provincialism, as well as the fate of liberalism. As in several other provinces but with particular determination and direction, the postrevolutionary executive leadership in Canton pursued in an authoritarian manner a program of radical Westernizing but nonrevolutionary reform. The range was wide. Plans for universal elementary education were launched. Government schools were prohibited from teaching the classics or from conducting traditional rites in Confucius's honor. A newly formed sanitation board initiated an attack on epidemics, using vaccination, lessons in hygiene, controls on the sale of meat, and campaigns to collect dead rats. Local industry was encouraged and people were told to "buy Cantonese." The access of a foreign cement company in Hongkong to essential resources in Kwangtung was cut off in favor of a local government-owned company—over foreign protests. In Canton, the provincial police commissioner forcibly emancipated women illegally detained as domestic slaves in wealthy households. He provided a school and refuge for them and runaway concubines, child wives, and child prostitutes. Physicians of Western medicine were favored over practitioners of traditional medicine. The police prohibited traditional religious festivals. Prostitution, gambling, and the sale and consumption of opium were outlawed, and so on. The participation in the government of the foreign-educated was conspicuous, as elsewhere. More unusual was the proportion of those with Western (as opposed to Japanese) experience and the prominence of Chinese Christians.[55]

Most Westerners who were officially concerned about Kwangtung were not flattered by reforms so clearly inspired by a contemporary Western outlook. Irritation was more common. When Hu Han-min with his commissioners of police and internal affairs visited the British governor of Hongkong in August, 1912, the colonial rather than the domestic Western model was held up for imitation. "I reminded Mr. Wu [Hu Han-min] . . . that when the Hong Kong Government took over the new territories their first and only concern was to establish an honest Government and to preserve peace and good order, and that even now after more than twelve years of occupation we did not bother the people with sanitation, building laws, compulsory education, and other innovations not of fundamental importance."[56]

The Kwangtung reform program faltered, but not simply because of British disfavor. The government in Canton did not have the power—political, administrative, financial—to sustain the effort. Canton's reach into the rest of Kwangtung was limited, especially outside a few major cities. Gentry power was left uncontested. The popular military forces of the revolution were suppressed. Hu Han-min in November, 1912, was ready to fall back on rural military training bands—characteristic forms of gentry domination—to pacify the countryside in the absence of a police force large enough to do the job.[57] In preparing for the elections in the winter of 1912–13, the Kwangtung T'ung-meng hui, like the Kuomintang elsewhere, tried to conscript the structure of gentry authority in the rural areas, including local self-government leaders, to press its campaign.[58] Though the enforcement of reform in some cities, especially Canton, evoked antipathy from certain entrenched interests, the government left the larger social fabric alone and did not pursue a program of popular mobilization below the elite level. By the end of 1912, financial stringency had in any case caused the abortion of the bulk of Canton's schemes for education, sanitation, industry, and public works.[59]

The failure of the Kwangtung reform program, which contained so many borrowings from the West, was not due to any squeamishness about forceful methods. After the revolution succeeded in Canton, the provincial government conducted a ruthless campaign of suppression of constitutional monarchists, whose movement had some support in Kwangtung, the province of K'ang Yu-wei and Liang Ch'i-ch'ao.[60] Soon after the conclusion of the revolution, when Hu Han-min was away, a newspaper editor was executed for his attacks on Ch'en Chiung-ming, the military governor at the time. This was not the only instance in Canton of repression of newspapers.[61] The commissioner of police, Ch'en Ching-hua, a former county magistrate and Hongkong comprador, enforced reforms and kept order with much spilling of blood. Executions, reported to be occurring at the rate of twenty a day in the summer of 1912, were ordered even for trivial offenses. Police Chief Ch'en once prefaced an announcement with the intimidating confession: "My fame lies in killing people."[62] This law-and-order aspect of the Canton government, "... what practically amounts to martial law," was generally acclaimed by foreign officials.[63] Meanwhile, Hu Han-min, reinstated as military governor at the instance of Sun Yat-sen in April, 1912, ruled without much regard for the powers of the provincial assembly, even as he verbally attacked bureaucratism and defended self-government.

The authoritarian tendency in the Canton government did not dispose its leaders to accept more central authority from Peking. Hu Han-min, besieged at home by various political forces, sometimes played the role of delegate or ally of Yuan Shih-k'ai,[64] but left no doubt that his deference to Yuan was formal and his government's autonomy substantive.[65]

Among the skillful attempts at theoretical defense of Kwangtung's autonomy was that offered by Yeh Hsia-sheng, who had been chief of the political affairs section of the Cantonese T'ung-meng hui. The time was early 1913, when Yuan's desire to assert central authority was becoming more apparent. Yeh saw Yuan's moves as identical to the interventionism of the Ch'ing. Centralization of authority, Yeh conceded, was defended on the grounds of maintaining Chinese strength against the outside world. He would allow a central military jurisdiction and local contributions to its expenses, but all efforts would be worth nothing if there were no spirit, no will to win, no popular feeling for politics, no patriotism. A policy of centralization, Yeh argued, caused divisions and disruptions at home and was no way to meet foreign aggression. He doubted that China should seek confrontation with the foreign powers when she was weakened by the revolution and military preparations were insufficient. But in any case, China would more surely become powerful by delegating rule at home to local self-government.[66] These views were no doubt a deeply felt basis for Kwangtung's policy toward Peking and endowed provincialism with a persuasive nationalist rationale. Even with respect to the national revolutionary leadership, Hu Han-min's group asserted their militancy and autonomy by refusing for a few months to join the new national party, the Kuomintang. The inheritors of the 1911 Revolution in Kwangtung, then, strove to build a new China with a reformist provincialism.

The political ingredients found in Kwangtung in 1912 and early 1913 could be discovered in varying proportions in other provinces. Hunan, for example, experienced an extraordinary burst of reformist energy, very sensitive to interference from the central government. I shall briefly characterize programs in the judiciary, industry, and education.

Extending the network of independent courts to each county—an inheritance of Ch'ing judicial policy—was actively pursued in Hunan, with arrangements actually made for about one-third of the counties, as well as the prefectural and provincial capitals. With some of the new county courts went modern-style prisons, and ambitious plans for a model prison in Changsha. Chinese-owned industries were promoted, partly through a Hunan Industrial Association. Beginnings were made in the organization of several mining companies (one with Huang Hsing as director), four paper mills, four cotton spinning and weaving factories, two flour and rice mills, factories to produce cement, cigarettes, and glass, and several banks. Some of these actually got underway by mid-1913. The primary consideration was not economic rationality (and most efforts soon failed) but the retention of Chinese markets in Chinese hands. The province's industrial commissioner was granted a one million tael budget for agricultural and industrial experimental programs, a model silk filature, a model cotton spinning factory, an afforestation bureau, an industrial gazetteer, and so forth. By the spring of 1913, the province had authorized ten million taels for industrial subsidies for that year. The spirit was one of exuberant economic nationalism rather than fiscal realism.

A provincial educational program took as its aim universal compulsory four-year education for all boys and girls, in a curriculum largely unburdened with the classics. Violent popular resistance to confiscation of temple property for schools impeded the speed of the program. But by the summer, 1913, the achievement, though partial, was considerable. By a very rough estimate, the lower elementary schools listed in table 3, which seem to have been mostly one-room schoolhouses, would provide for one-fifth to one-third of Hunanese children.[67] (We cannot assume that new schools were immediately filled; so the proportion was emergent rather than actual.) In 1913, ninety-four men and four women were dispatched abroad (selected for service to the Kuomintang or performance in competitive examinations) for an education at provincial expense, bringing to six hundred the number of Hunanese on government stipends abroad. In contrast to the previous decade when, for example, Chihli and Szechwan were much more active in establishing primary schools, Hunan was probably unsurpassed in the attainments of its reforms in these years.[68] (Apparently much ground was lost by the early twenties, when lower elementary schools

TABLE 3

Inventory of Public and Private Schools in Hunan, Mid-1913

Type	Number
Lower elementary schools	21,744
Upper elementary schools	3,281
Combined upper and lower elementary schools	143
Elementary schools for girls only	59
Middle schools	41
Training schools for lower elementary school teachers	16
Normal schools (various types)	35
Higher normal school	1
Handicraft schools	10
Industrial schools (various types)	22
Higher police school	1
Railway and telegraph schools	2
Medical school	1
Law schools	22
Universities (probably converted traditional academies)	4
Schools for officials connected with agriculture and industry	4
Miscellaneous	46

Source: Citing a recent census of schools in Hunan, Bertram Giles, British consul in Changsha, to John Jordan, British minister in Peking, August 9, 1913. FO 228/1869. I have combined in common categories some of the figures.

in Hunan had declined to less than half their number in 1913, if the statistics can be trusted.)[69]

These accomplishments were accompanied and no doubt made possible by a drastic military demobilization after the revolution. Hunan had provided large numbers of troops to the battle but then reduced her forces more radically than any other province. In 1913, the proportion of Hunan's modest total provincial expenditure that was budgeted for the army was the least in the country. The military governor, T'an Yen-k'ai, was not a military man: the son of an imperial governor-general and himself the holder of the highest literary degree, he was transformed by the revolution from a prominent agitator for a parliament under the monarchy to the head of the Kuomintang in Hunan. (He also played a leading role in the KMT in the 1920s and early 1930s.) A powerful military, particularly one with the strong revolutionary proclivities of the Hunan army, would have been a threat to T'an's position. Whatever the motivation, there were reformist benefits in the form of more funds accruing to a government where military elements played a relatively minor role.[70]

Hunan's military weakness did not imply deference to central authority. Peking's several attempts at intervention in Hunan's affairs, including her educational arrangements, were firmly turned back. When in the spring of 1913 the central government tried to assert its rights to control part of Hunan's revenue, the response was particularly vociferous. A close foreign observer of Hunan in these years wrote in the summer of 1913: "Indeed the principal reason for all the bitterness against Yuan Shih-k'ai in Hunan really arises out of his policy of centralizing financial control and thus taking away from local administrators what they consider their fair share of the spoils. This is the rock on which any strong central administration seems destined to split sooner or later."[71] This judgment was surely an oversimplification. Liberal and provincial ideologies were important ingredients of politics in Hunan after the revolution and worked against Yuan. But, however one analyzes the content, the inheritance of the revolution in Hunan as in Kwangtung was received into an emphatically provincial framework.

Nor did a reduced military establishment mean unblemished liberal toleration or greater social justice. In Hunan, too, a newspaper might be closed for criticizing a government program, and a reporter might be threatened.[72] And the various strata of the gentry in Hunan were hardly in retreat. There was probably no other province where veteran members of the provincial assembly had more to do with shaping the postrevolutionary government. In the counties evidence of a gentry assertion of authority continued. Local gentry aspirations were perhaps stimulated by an official apportionment directly to the county of about one-third of a newly consolidated land tax. Whether the apportionment actually increased the amount of taxes retained locally or not, it legitimized substantial retention and local control. It was reported that everywhere the new law courts were subservient to gentry influence. The city, town, and rural self-government offices, along with local magistrates, were told to develop police forces and militia (*t'uan-lien*) to keep down the discontented (*ch'ing-hsiang*, purging the countryside of banditry, an expression also used in a similar context by Hu Han-min).[73] Although self-government councils and assemblies were operating in much of China, their scope below the provincial level in Hunan was given more than the usual leeway. In this connection, a report from southeast Hunan in 1913 asserted that people were calling the new order, not a republic (*min-kuo*, or country of the people), but a "gentry-dom" (*shen-shih kuo*, or country of the gentry).[74] Reform was not meant to challenge the social structure. In fact it tended to reinforce the strength of the already privileged. The interacting mixture of reform, self-government, and gentry power which was discussed in the first chapter was particularly prominent in Hunan in the liberal republic.

The variations from province to province were considerable, and intensive studies of individual provinces may produce as many patterns as provinces. At this stage of knowledge, however, I wish to postulate the regular appearance in varying proportions of the same elements in most of the formerly revolutionary provinces. These elements are: reform programs; either a gentry orientation to the reforms or an abstention from applying them where gentry power might be threatened; a consequent increase or maintenance of the social power of this predominant elite group; a degree of repression roughly corresponding to the social and political challenges facing the new government; an important political role for the army (Hunan was an exception and Yunnan the extreme case); and an assertion of provincial autonomy as the basic ingredient of all policies.[75]

For the former leaders of the revolution, a provincial orientation filled what we can retrospectively identify as a debilitating gap in their programs. Like national parliamentary politics, it functioned as a substitute for digging deeper into China's social problems and serving a broader segment of the population. It was another version of elite politics. By borrowing energy from a swelling provincial sentiment already enjoying organizational forms among the social elite, the leaders could hope to consolidate their authority rapidly. And they could hope to secure a defense against Yuan Shih-k'ai and the central government. This is not to say that the posture was cynical. Provincial ideology—the assertion that provincial autonomy was a crucial ingredient of Chinese strength—had been associated with revolutionary enthusiasm since the first years of the century. But we can observe analytically how this theoretical belief in provincial autonomy was reinforced in political circles by the choice of a certain strategy of leadership, that is, one that built on a socially elite base with its preexisting disposition toward provincialist politics. We may also note that this strategy embodied a rejection of the possibility of the broader social base for republicanism that the participation of secret societies and mass armies had represented in the 1911 Revolution. We cannot know what forms a more broadly based politics might have taken. The several moves in that direction—for example, in Szechwan, Kweichow, Kwangtung, and perhaps Hunan for nine days in October, 1911—were all nipped in the bud. In any case, the result of the prevailing strategies was that part of the opposition to Yuan was in a provincial mode. For all its weaknesses, this opposition was much the most powerful threat to Yuan's own conception of how China should be ruled.

The View from the Presidency

The country had to wait until Yuan's power was consolidated to a degree more to his liking before his program became apparent. Perhaps it would be more accurate to say that his program was tailored to what he thought he could accomplish, and for over a year his weakness spelled an absence of much program. He accommodated. He moved gradually and retreated frequently. He did have advantages. There was his mandate to maintain national unity and therefore a presumption of legitimacy. There were the Peiyang army divisions, not predominant in numbers but well trained and linked to Yuan historically. There was the administrative expertise in his staff. And there was a generally favorable foreign attitude toward his rule. Yuan drew on these advantages to build his authority but waited over a year before testing his strength.

While he waited, we may be sure, his impatience mounted. From Yuan's point of view, the situation impeded him from fulfilling his responsibilities as president and his ambitions as first Chinese leader. The liberal republic had placed one obstacle after another in the way of national strength, as he would measure it. After the wraps were off, in mid-summer of 1913, he vented his accumulated grievances. Party prejudices (that is, the refusal of the national deliberative assembly to confirm certain ministerial nominations) had prevented good men from serving in high office and had frightened off others. Military governors, products of the revolution against the Manchus, persisted in disregarding the authority of the central government, he declared. They rejected the separation of civil and military jurisdictions. Yuan claimed to have long refrained from forcing the issue against this self-seeking local sentiment, for fear of provoking an upheaval like Saigō's 1877 rebellion in Japan. But insubordination spread down to the counties. Revenues were retained locally. Efforts to collect national taxes had been opposed, even as the expenses of recovery mounted and payments on old foreign debts were being pressed. Yuan vowed that "the sacred, ancient country of five thousand years should not be overthrown on my responsibility." The way of rescue, he asserted, "lies in reviving the official discipline of government ordinance and in building the prestige of the nation."[76]

Yuan's early attempts to impose "official discipline" on the provinces will be described in chapter 5. For the moment, I shall leave aside Yuan's ideas about the solutions, whose appropriateness is highly debatable, and instead explore the most urgent of the problems he identified, which were real. In particular, the reality of the fiscal crisis and its relationship to military demands are worth underlining. Although many provincial governments were financially strained, none was worse off in proportion to its responsibilities than was the Peking government.

Several provincial governments suffered fiscal difficulties. The autonomy of subprovincial regions was only part of the problem, since, even after most provinces had reestablished their unity, revenue often remained below Ch'ing levels. Various explanations were offered at the time. It was asserted that many took the republic as meaning freedom from taxation, an idea that was encouraged by revolutionary governments as they came to power. The success of the antiopium campaign, which was revived with zeal in most provinces after a brief lapse during the revolution itself, deepened the loss of revenue from that opulent source. Various local campaigns against other vices had similar effects on revenue. In many places, tax lists were destroyed and the men who knew most about collection fled. The new officials had little or no experience in such matters. If locally chosen, perhaps they had little enthusiasm for reimposing tax discipline.

To these explanations might be added the hypothesis, relating more to social autonomy than to the formal administrative independence of localities, that augmented gentry power in the wake of the revolution increased land tax resistance or, once the tax was collected locally, impeded its remission to the provincial capital. A decree by the Kiangsu provincial government in April, 1913, blamed gentry obstruction for the shortages in the land tax. In November, 1913, another order noted that it was the wealthy who were the primary defaulters in grain tax (i.e., former grain tribute) payments.[77]

Financial stringency in the provinces was not owing just to a decline in revenue from already inadequate late Ch'ing levels. While income was down, military expenditure had soared. The problem was generally recognized. As Tai Chi-t'ao, then a radical journalist in Shanghai, wrote: "Everywhere [the provincial armies] seek funds and everywhere they say they lack funds. As soon as they have some, they consume it."[78]

The exact dimensions of the problem of bloated provincial military establishments were impenetrable: too many people had an interest in statistical falsification, not so much for reasons of security (though there was that) as in anticipation of central or foreign financial assistance in demobilization. Military units came in all kinds and sizes, and soldiers in all degrees of training and equipment. During the revolution, the number of troops conscripted may have mounted to well over a million. Disbandment began even before the revolution formally ended, though recruitment continued in places. In the early months of 1913, the Peking government claimed eight hundred fifty thousand soldiers were still enrolled in China's many armies, and proposed in its foreign loan negotiations that about half of these be disbanded at a cost of over Ch$10,600,000 exclusive of back pay.[79] Many contemporary observers, Chinese and foreign, doubted that men under arms numbered so many. They could point to particular cases of exaggeration, though no one, no matter how well informed, could speak confidently about the country as a whole.

Table 4 is adapted from a Japanese military intelligence report, which attempts to measure at two points in time the number of military units organized along modern lines. The basis of comparability is the roughly similar size of full-strength units organized as Western-style divisions (10,000 to 12,500). Divisional units below full strength and brigades seem to have been translated in this report into fractions (rounded off by halves of a division) for tabulation. Actual training and equipment varied enormously. In addition to the units tabulated here, the Japanese estimated 600 battalions (*ying*) of old-style troops surviving into 1913 in various parts of the country. Despite these failings in comprehensiveness and the discrepancies easily found with local reports, these Japanese figures are helpful in giving a rough sense of the distribution of military strength and its fiscal burden. The one universal distinction of the so-called modern units was their relatively high cost. The large size of forces in Kiangsu and Hupeh was an inheritance of Nanking and Wuchang as centers of military mobilization for the revolution. In Chihli, the inheritance was that of a national army, and Yuan was determined to keep that inheritance alive, and under his control.

TABLE 4

Modern-Style Divisions in the Early Republic by Province

Province	Number of Divisions February, 1912	Number Increased or Disbanded	Number of Divisions March, 1913
Chihli	8	−1.5[a]	6.5
Shantung	2.5	−0.5	2
Honan	2.5	+0.5	3
Fengtien	1.5	+2[b]	3.5
Kirin	1	+0.5[b]	1.5
Heilungkiang	0.5	−	0.5
Kansu	0.5	−	0.5[c]
Shinkiang	0.5	−	0.5[c]
Shansi	2	−	2
Shensi	4	−	4
Kiangsu	15	−7	8
Anhwei	3	−1	2
Kiangsi	3.5	−1	2.5
Hupeh	8	−2	6
Hunan	5	−4	1
Szechwan	5	−3	2
Chekiang	2	−	2
Fukien	1	−	1
Kwangtung	3	−0.5	2.5
Kwangsi	1.5	+0.5	2.0
Kweichow	0.5	−	0.5[c]
Yunnan	2.5	−	2.5
Total	73	−17	56

Source: Japanese General Staff, *Kakumei-go ni okeru Shina kakushō heiryoku zōgen ichi-ranbyō,* March 10, 1913. Microfilms of the Japanese Foreign Ministry, MT5.1.10.5−1 reel 463, pp. 420−21. I have adjusted inconsistencies in the figures.

[a]The reduction represents diminished divisional size, not fewer divisions.

[b]The increase represents the reorganization of old-style troops.

[c]No details since the revolution. The prerevolutionary figure is merely repeated.

Toward these ends, Yuan combined recruitment with disbandment among the troops under his authority. Whether or not he had stimulated the rioting of troops in Chihli in late February and early March, 1912, he had been shaken by the extent of it (Paoting in ruins, the Tientsin mint destroyed). Lu Chien-chang, from the Hsiao-chan group of officers, who had kept his soldiers out of the looting, was charged with Peking's security and mandated to recruit and train new units to replace in terms of overall strength those being weeded out. This continuing recruitment was one of T'ang Shao-i's complaints against Yuan when he resigned from the premiership, although the Japanese figures suggest that discharges surpassed conscriptions.[80]

As a provincial army, Yuan's troops were overblown, a drain on Chihli's finances, and a challenge to other provincial armies. As the core of a national army financed by China's central government, they were a modest continuation of the military programs of the Ch'ing. Given the growth of the military in several other parts of the country during the revolution, their relative weight had greatly declined, despite their superior training and equipment. Together with all other old and new armies, they were a burdensome charge on a decrepit fiscal system. The recurrence of mutinies in protest of nonpayment of wages in all parts of the country (one count finds fifteen mutinies between August, 1912, and February, 1913) was evidence that the charge was not being met.[81]

From the point of view of Peking, provincial autonomy and unbalanced provincial budgets meant receiving virtually no disposable revenue from the provinces. Provincial and local administrations, which under the empire exerted themselves to keep funds flowing to Peking, no longer did so. Some provinces continued to honor their allotted payments on the Boxer indemnity, but others did not. The proceeds from the maritime customs—since the revolution, under the direct control of highly independent foreign employees of the Chinese government—were collected in all relevant provinces and accounted for to Peking but disappeared into foreign banks in payment of old debts and indemnities. They did not serve Peking's current expenses. A patriotic campaign of subscription to obviate the need for compromising foreign loans attracted much enthusiasm and many promises over the summer of 1912 but fizzled without substantial result. Salt revenues were commonly retained locally or by the province. The Peking government alleged that in the first two years of the republic the provinces contributed only Ch$2,600,000 toward its domestic expenses.[82] The actual figure depended upon what principles of accounting one used. Single provinces had claimed greater remissions. But the point remained that the flow of revenue from the provinces to Peking was only a small fraction of what it had been.

The temptation for the provinces, especially the productive ones, was obvious. In 1910 Szechwan's contributions to Peking (exclusive of Boxer payments) and to neighboring provinces (exclusive of Tibet) was about 6 million taels, or Ch\$9 million. This was over one-third of Szechwan's normal provincial revenue. Retaining these 6 million taels, if they could still be collected, instead of remitting them out of the province, was a dividend of declaring independence during the revolution and holding on to autonomy after it.[83] As late as June, 1913, the Chengtu government of Szechwan was not even budgeting any remissions to Peking.[84] It was more common for provincial governments to request financial assistance from Peking for demobilizations, currency reforms, and so forth, than it was for them to contribute to the national capital in the old pattern. When G. E. Morrison, presidential adviser, proposed at a cabinet meeting in October, 1912, that Szechwan was prepared to remit 15 million taels, the finance minister laughed and retorted that the previous day Szechwan had cabled asking for 5 million taels from Peking.[85] A 1914 report to the cabinet attributed this state of affairs throughout the country to: (1) the expenses of the swollen military establishment; (2) the dissipation of revenues below the provincial level; (3) the excessive power of self-government organs, which retained public funds and spent them freely; and (4) the superabundance of expensive reform programs.[86] The analysis reflected the mood of a government that felt at last it had a new program and the means to effect it. But the basic problem had long been recognized. In the summer of 1912, Sung Chiao-jen, a national politician with a national orientation, deplored a situation where the provinces were asking the center, which was without funds or plans, for large sums of money.[87] The requests came from provincial chiefs all along the political spectrum.

The Peking government survived fiscally through 1912 by various ad hoc devices: small doles from a consortium of foreign bankers, who hoped thereby to commit China to themselves for a big loan; one moderately large and controversial foreign loan outside the consortium toward the end of the year (the Crisp loan); proceeds from nationally owned enterprises such as banks and railways; and walking along the edge of bankruptcy. Liang Shih-i, the railway administrator of the late Ch'ing, proved to be the most adept in Yuan's entourage at uncovering domestic assets for the government. His great influence, which was widely noted, owed much to this timely talent. Through his authority in the Communications Bank and its participation in railway revenues and railway loans, he was said to dispose of a liquid strength of Ch$500,000 to Ch$1,000,000.[88] But this sort of patchwork did not satisfy Yuan.

The view from the presidency, then, was no cause for complacency to someone with Yuan's cast of mind. One did not have to be in Yuan's entourage to see the situation in the same light as he did. K'ang Yu-wei, who had been agitating for Yuan's execution only four years previously, wrote in 1912: "Under the present threatening circumstances, China's great cause for concern lies particularly in the independence [*tzu-li*] of the military governors." Their baronialism evoked the T'ang commanderies and the states of the Chou period, he argued, and the provincial assemblies were pursuing independence under the guise of self-government. The orders of the central government were, he felt, rendered ineffectual by all this.[89]

About three months after Yuan assumed the presidency, a study by the Japanese general staff summed up its judgment of his position in several stark assertions. His administration was interfered with by the national deliberative assembly (whose "puppet" Yuan had allegedly become). His powers of appointment were uncertain even in Chihli, Honan, and Shantung (with Kansu, the only home provinces that did not go over to the revolution in 1911). The Peking mutiny threw doubt on the value of his troops and his control over his subordinates. Some of his old followers, like T'ang Shao-i, were joining political parties and could not be relied upon. Unification would not be easy. Yuan's powers, the study predicted, were destined to diminish.[90]

In the Japanese general staff, where no love was lost on Yuan Shih-k'ai, the wish may have been father to the prediction, but the description of the predicament was one that Yuan shared. The liberal mood, the liberating social attitudes emerging among the elite, the legal restrictions on his power, the substantial impact on policy of elective assemblies, the political and fiscal autonomy of the provinces—these were not to Yuan's taste. Even as he accommodated or compromised with them, he began work toward a new definition of the problems, a changed balance of forces, a political context in which he was more at home. Supported by significant sectors of Chinese leadership and of foreign interests, he succeeded in the first showdown. The liberal republic fell, not to rise again.

Chapter 5

Yuan's Confrontation with Liberal Government and the Provinces

A year after the revolution, a sense of failure was already infecting the country. The removal of the Manchus had not been the regenerating act that many had hoped it would be. The republic had not brought greater foreign respect for Chinese sovereignty. Reforms, though energetically pursued, had with few exceptions stalled.

At the end of December, a leading Kuomintang journal reflected that 1912 had not been a bright year. Events that tended to retard the formation of a strong government, like party struggle, military mutinies, and the loss of Mongolia and Tibet, were too numerous to count. The government should be contrite, the editorialist went on, "for having no great policy or plan to strengthen and stabilize the country, for leaving finances unorganized, order unrestored, and the economy unhealthy." The bureaucrats, it was charged, had both presumed on their power and neglected their duties, without initiating programs. Assembly members had induced crises through their intemperate struggle, had forsaken their responsibilities in a scramble to win elections, and had forgotten the gravity of the people's trust. Political parties were admonished for "engaging in private disputes instead of political debate, . . . for being caught up in dark designs or perverse behavior, without regard for the nation's benefit or the people's fortune." The people at large lacked patriotism, had shirked responsibilities, had indulged in dreams, had despised foreign learning, and had helped neither the government nor the society. Even newspapermen were charged, in this year-end editorial, with a list of failings.[1] The luster on all sides was dimmed. Thoughts began to turn to what one's next move might be.

Yuan's thoughts apparently focused increasingly on steps toward centralization. He understood the dispersal of administrative authority as dissipation of national power. Although he recognized limits and drew back from some extremes, the thread linking all his policies was the recovery

105

and augmentation of the authority of the central government. Centralization, necessary to keep China from succumbing to foreign rule, required means. His efforts to meddle in the politics of the provinces and tap their resources largely failed. To supplement those rather meager means already at his disposal, Yuan sought foreign loans. So armed, he could tackle the provinces from a position of strength. Sizable foreign funds, it turned out, were not available without compromising conditions. Accordingly, he fell into a strategy of selling out some part of his country's sovereignty in order, ultimately, to defend that same sovereignty. The arrangements were not made lightly. But once he was committed to the idea of centralization as the route to national power (like the court of the last years of the Ch'ing), there seemed to be no other resource to draw upon, paradoxical though it was.

Yuan's strategy of centralization found considerable domestic political support among those already committed to the idea or disillusioned with the performance of the provinces. It also meshed conveniently with prevailing foreign conceptions of what China should do. The Peking government was observably weak and ought to extend its authority, leading foreign officials felt, if only to make the handling of foreign concerns more convenient and to protect foreign commerce. So interested were the foreign powers in their definition of Chinese unity and stability that they would insist on supervising those parts of the process where their money was used. The ends pursued by Yuan and the powers were different, but the routes were parallel. At any particular point, the question could be raised: who was using whom, or who had a better bead on his destination? What was certain was that China's brief history of representative government ended shortly thereafter. The financiers and their governments did not desire this precise result. But by their actions they contributed to it.

Yuan's Campaign to Extend Peking's Authority

A central government was nothing without the provinces. The nature of the proper relationship Yuan saw as one of command, from the top down. Beginning soon after assuming the presidency and reaching a high pitch by November, 1912, he attempted to assert his prerogatives by appointing officials in the provinces. These early efforts were spotted with successes but on the whole failed in changing the balance of forces.

It was difficult for the provinces to argue that the president was without rights in this area. The provisional constitution, largely the work of Sung Chiao-jen at Nanking, provided: "The provisional president appoints and dismisses civil and military officials . . ." with only cabinet ministers and top diplomats subject to parliamentary confirmation. The constitution was eloquently silent about relations between the central and provincial governments, but there was nothing in the text barring the application of this article to local offices. The objection was raised that enabling legislation, to be passed by the national assembly, was a logical precondition to the exercise of constitutional powers, but Yuan proceeded without it.

More important to Yuan than a legal rationale was his conviction that he knew what made for good local administration. As his camgaign of intervention in the provinces accelerated, he disparaged the practice of appointing a magistrate for meritorious deeds not related to administration (that is, for revolutionary service or party loyalty). Rather, he held, qualification lay in education in the science of government or experience in administration.[2] The implied rebuke to the revolutionary provinces was obvious. In a confidential setting, he was more blunt. He told the British minister that "the *tutus* [military governors] were a lot of unruly children. . . ."[3]

In Honan, Chihli, and to a degree in Shantung and Manchuria, Yuan's will prevailed, though not without challenge. For example, in May, 1912, the Honan provincial assembly, which had toyed with the idea of declaring independence during the revolution, elected a civil governor of its own nomination. Yuan quashed the move by cabling his opinion that the assembly had exceeded its rights.[4] Later in the year, when the Chihli provincial assembly and military governor (Feng Kuo-chang) adopted regulations for a local official system, they were told that their act was an unconstitutional usurpation of the functions of the central government.[5] Yuan's control of the choice of the provincial chief executive – the military governor – in these areas allowed him to keep other forces in check.

Circumstances provided him openings elsewhere, which he exploited with mixed results. In Fukien, where Tso Tsung-t'ang's assignment in the Sino-French War of the 1880s had left an inheritance of Hunanese soldiers, both the military governor and the provincial police commissioner after the revolution were Fukien-raised Hunanese. Fukienese hostility focused particularly on the police commissioner, P'eng Shou-sung, not only for his origins, but for the arbitrary and bloodthirsty use of his considerable power. Fukienese associations in Shanghai and Peking asked that Yuan Shih-k'ai send the eminent official of the Ch'ing, Ts'en Ch'un-hsuan, to oust P'eng. Ts'en was a logical choice, since he had immense national prestige, was respected by the revolutionaries, and had once been P'eng's boss. The episode presented Yuan with an obvious opportunity.

Ts'en arrived near Foochow, the provincial capital, on October 5, 1912, with some fifteen hundred soldiers. The noxious police chief, who had been instrumental in Fukien's revolution, acceded to these pressures and to locally raised farewell donations by departing. Yuan Shih-k'ai seized the occasion to appoint Fukien's first civil governor since the revolution, to share powers with the existing military governor. The appointee was from Fukien, a concession to postrevolutionary provincialism. He was also a Hanlin compiler and a prefect under the Ch'ing, who, though a participant in Manchuria's revolution, had played no part in Fukien's break with the Manchus. Consequently, his authority would not grow out of Fukien's politics but out of Peking's support. But on November 18, two days after the new appointment had been announced, Ts'en, Yuan's emissary, decamped precipitately, perhaps because of growing resistance to his presence in Fukien. In these altered circumstances, the new civil governor made no attempt to take up his post for over two months. Shortly after he did arrive, he barely escaped from a bombing attempt on his life. Apparently, injecting a national presence into the provinces was not easy.[6]

The appointment of civil governors was a convenient opening for Yuan. In most provinces, the *tutu* or military governor was also the chief executive for civil affairs, although he would appoint subordinates to administer them. The preeminence of military tasks during the revolution excused this arrangement. As the revolution receded in time, the issue of separating civil from military administration was raised, most ostentatiously by Li Yuan-hung, military governor in Hupeh and national vice-president and chief of the general staff. Li widely advertised Hupeh's theoretically coequal civil governorship and pretended to reserve for himself only military powers in his province.

Shansi was another province enjoying a civil governor's post. As in Hupeh, the influence of the military governor was probably decisive in all important questions within the provincial government. But there was the further question of whether the civil governor would be chosen locally or named from Peking. The question arose with special force in Shansi because Yen Hsi-shan, who was to rule the province for more than two and one-half decades, began his tenure in weakness. A New Army officer schooled in Japan, Yen (1883–1960) was chosen military governor by arrangement with the leaders of the provincial assembly after Ch'ing authority was overthrown early in the revolution. But Shansi was the only revolutionary province where the capital subsequently fell to imperial troops. Yen fled north and did not return until after the Manchu abdication. The result was more than the customary weakness of provincial governments and a policy on Yen's part to borrow strength from Yuan Shih-k'ai.

Perhaps Yuan's interventions began in March, 1912, with the imposition of a civil governor's post in Shansi alongside the military governor and the selection of the first occupant, although Yuan withdrew his first nomination in the face of Sun Yat-sen's protest. The finally successful nominee did not take up his post until May and was eased out in favor of a local politician by September. Provincial autonomy seemed to prevail. In a national debate conducted through public telegrams, Yen declared his opposition to both centralization of authority and any immediate diminution of the general administrative power of the provincial military governors.

In late 1912, however, Yen, a national officer of the Kuomintang, egregiously violated the provincialist's code in order to bolster his power. Southern Shansi, which during Yen's flight north had registered its own revolutionary gains (with help from Shensi), was the rich part of the province and refused to send revenues to Yen's government in Taiyuan. First Yen sent an aide to establish a "national" tax bureau in the area (Yuan's blessing was secured for this maneuver) and negotiate a sharing of tax proceeds. On suspicion of subverting the local leadership, the aide was locally arrested and charged. After an interval, Yen called for help from Peking, which sent in troops and secured the area for the first time on Yen's behalf. As the episode came to a climax in January, 1913, Yuan appointed a new civil governor for Shansi. The new official was, however, from Shansi and probably not a check on Yen's power. Although Yuan sent a national tax official to Shansi, the control of revenues apparently remained in the hands of the provincial government until 1914. In general, the affair ran roughly parallel to the Fukien case just described. There were some differences, however. Yen, more than his counterpart in Fukien, needed Yuan's help and, owing to proximity, feared his wrath. Hence, in the showdown of the summer of 1913, Shansi stayed with Yuan, while Fukien tentatively dissented.[7]

From November, 1912, Yuan made bids all over the country for a share of local power, particularly in the form of revenues. Since he made a point of confirming local appointees where he could not control them, it is not easy to discern what represented real extensions of Peking's authority and what were mere pious rituals of national unity. Moreover, some positions, such as local foreign affairs posts and judgeships, were divorced from sources of real power and were thus uncontroversial. When revenues were at stake, however, controversy was the rule. In the fall of 1912, the finance minister revived the late Ch'ing effort to separate national from local taxes close to the source and to inject a special national fiscal bureaucracy into the local scene. There followed a wave of appointments of centrally appointed financial commissioners for the provinces, much juggling of provincial budget figures, and very little result for Peking except heightened tension. Outside the immediate area of Peking's authority, the financial commissioners were mostly rejected or ignored. Centrally designated salt commissioners met the same treatment. The division between national and local revenues remained a paper reform. Even the Kiangsu provincial government, which was friendly to Peking and cooperated in the appointment of a mutually satisfactory civil governor, managed to remit nothing at all to Peking. Similarly, Szechwan dutifully divided revenues under provincial and national heads, but remitted none to the central government.[8]

The one tax structure that, owing to its predominantly foreign management, had retained a centralized character, was the maritime customs service. Even here, the local Chinese customs commissioners had become provincial appointees during the revolution. Yuan successfully revived central control over these posts, which had lost much of their importance since the foreign staff had usurped some of their functions in 1911. Even so, the local response was hostile. The foreign inspector general of the customs was moved to complain that Peking's men were causing "inevitable friction and provoking indignation among the Tutus."[9] Since customs revenue paid for old foreign debts, not present administrative needs, it may be said that in general Yuan's appointive campaign in the provinces won no power and considerable resentment.

All the while, a debate raged about the proper relationship between center and province. In July, 1912, the government proposed to the national deliberative assembly a provincial administrative system where the chief executive would be a civil official (*hsing-cheng tsung-chien*) appointed by the president and empowered to veto bills passed by the provincial assembly and to oversee troops in his province. The protest from the military governors persuaded the government to withdraw the proposal. In October a proposal originating in the national deliberative assembly, whose members were generally selected by their respective provincial assemblies, called for the supremacy of the provincial assembly over the provincial chief executive, through self-convening and impeachment powers. This met the same fate as the previous one—decisive opposition from the military governors.[10] Opinions and proposals and protests were exchanged thick and fast.

Yuan then tried to bypass the organized opposition to his campaign. In January, 1913, he took advantage of the lack of a quorum in the national deliberative assembly (many members went home for the elections) to promulgate without benefit of a legislature a set of regulations concerning organization within the province. Explicitly, the order was aimed only at a uniformity of organization within the provinces as a preliminary step toward designing a full system of provincial powers. In other words, although names were to be changed, the distribution of power would not yet be affected. But implicitly Yuan was asserting his right to decide provincial matters unilaterally. In this case, the constitution was clearly against him. As was observed in the press, a legal submission of the proposal to the national deliberative assembly would most likely have killed it. Although some provinces adopted the forms required by Yuan's regulations, there was no change in the substantive relations between Peking and the provinces. There was only more resentment.[11]

Nowhere did the tension become more acute than in the contest between Yuan and Li Lieh-chün, military governor of Kiangsi. Li (1882–1946) was a graduate of Japan's Army Officers' Academy and a member of the T'ung-meng hui before the revolution. He was active in three provinces during the revolution, including his native Kiangsi, where he was chosen military governor by the provincial assembly after the republic had begun. His regime was mildly reformist and repressive at the same time, sending students abroad and fighting opium while dissolving subversive political associations and executing large numbers of mutineers. Like Hu Han-min and Yen Hsi-shan, he took up the debate against Yuan's centralization and opposed the separation of civil from military authority that seemed to be part of Peking's effort to reenter the provinces.[12]

One sees from the arguments of Li and others with his background and position that the original T'ung-meng hui conception of a three-stage revolution, beginning with military rule and followed by periods of political tutelage and eventual constitutional government, was not actually abandoned with the success of the revolution. It was transposed with some amendments to a provincial setting.[13] It did not sit well in this form with Yuan's desire to impose his own version of the stage of political tutelage on the country as a whole.

The issue was openly joined over Yuan's appointment of a civil governor for Kiangsi in December, 1912—a post previously lacking there. Wang Jui-k'ai, the man appointed, was at first glance an acceptable colleague for Li Lieh-chün, who had been a student of Wang's at the Kiangsi military academy and subsequently a protégé. Despite Wang's Anhwei origins, Li had invited him the previous summer to employ his experience as a Ch'ing official in assisting in local Kiangsi administration.[14] But Yuan's action was objectionable in Li's eyes: Yuan had no right to appoint provincial officials. Wang arrived in Kiangsi in a manner underlining Peking's role. Resistance to Wang's presence was quickly organized. He was told his life was in danger and, like some other Yuan appointees in the provinces, beat a hasty retreat shortly after his arrival. Negotiations by mediators were unable to produce a candidate mutually acceptable to Kiangsi and Peking.[15]

Meanwhile the issues accumulated. Li Lieh-chün began to reorganize the disposition of his troops. An order for foreign arms and ammunition, which had secured all the necessary clearances from customs and Peking the previous April but had been declined at Shanghai because of inferior quality, was reactivated. Peking, using among other communications systems the foreign customs inspectorate, ordered that the shipment be confiscated, no matter what documents it might carry. Li's man at Kiukiang, Kiangsi's port along the Yangtze, unexpectedly cooperated with Peking on the matter, and the shipment was detained in mid-January, 1913. Fighting seemed imminent, as Li moved to assert his authority over the shipment and over the military situation in Kiukiang. By a series of compromises, amounting to a tactical withdrawal on Yuan's part, shooting was avoided. But illusions about the prospects for continuing peaceful coexistence between provincial power and central ambitions had greatly diminished.[16]

It would be wrong to say that Yuan's campaign to extend Peking's authority had no effect before the Second Revolution of July and August, 1913. Yuan could play upon a habit of deference to Peking, which inclined provincial leaders to accept a central order when it made no substantive difference. Local leaders had not only to satisfy provincial sentiment; they also had to avoid appearing to be willfully and selfishly subverting Chinese unity. And leaders in a particularly weak or exposed position, such as Yen Hsi-shan, or dissident groups unhappy with those holding power in a province, provided openings for Yuan. On the whole, however, Yuan's campaign of persuasion and presumption failed to alter the effective independence of most provinces. They chose their own leadership where it mattered and kept their revenues.

Yuan's failure did not lead him to seek some mode of permanent accommodation to this situation. He stepped up his own military preparation.

The National Challenge to Yuan

Nothing could have more convinced Yuan of the basically inhospitable character of the liberal republic than the national elections of December, 1912, and January, 1913. He had some inkling of their importance but seemed not to know how to do anything about it. He tried, unsuccessfully, to get a £400,000 advance from the international bankers' consortium with which to influence the results.[17] And he orated against being guided in one's voting by party prejudices. If those elected, he warned, "are under the influence of a single faction or under the control of a private person, the effect upon the building of our sacred and august Chinese republic would be unspeakable."[18] But money, when there was not enough of it, and distant exhortation were not a winning combination in the liberal republic. By contrast, the Kuomintang invested in local political organization, a program responsive to provincial interests, and some energetic campaigning. It did remarkably well.

These winter elections stand out as the only time in Chinese history when a sizable proportion of the population chose its national representatives in a manner we associate with liberal representative government. At stake were seats in the two houses of the new national assembly (*kuo-hui*) and in the provincial assemblies. Elections for local councils took place shortly thereafter in most places.

The process was far short of popular democracy. The election for the national assembly was indirect: qualified voters cast their ballot for electors, who assembled by electoral districts to choose lower house members; and members of the upper house were selected by the new provincial assemblies, often with much controversy. The electorate was restricted to literate males over twenty-one years old with either the equivalent of an elementary school education or property (over Ch$500 of immovable property or an annual direct tax bill of over Ch$2). In contrast to the provincial elections of the late Ch'ing, when well under 1 percent of the population qualified, this time those registered to vote ranged from about 1 or 2 percent to 8 percent, with the statistically most reliable instances hovering at 4 to 6 percent. Scattered reports indicate that from one-third to four-fifths of those registered actually voted. The vote seems to have been fairly evenly distributed, in terms of proportions of the population, over urban and rural or small town settings. Merchants were leery of participating, and special efforts were made to reach beyond the main cities. For example, a report from Chinkiang in Kiangsu noted that canvassing in country districts had been very active, especially by agents of the Kuomintang, and these districts were "very largely reflected in the results" of the election.[19] Although the elected representatives were young and more likely to have experienced Western styles of education at home or abroad than their predecessors in the late Ch'ing, it is reasonable to assume that the results reflected the will of the social elite, especially its dominant gentry component. Where the electorate was broadened beyond the elite element, control of political parties, procedures, and electoral colleges remained in its hands.

Corruption was alleged in some areas, and no doubt there was not only that but also pressure from the ruling political group in the province. What is more surprising is the number of cases where the results bore no relation to the political position of the provincial chiefs. In Fengtien, for example, where administrative power was shared by Yuan Shih-k'ai's appointees and local military leaders, particularly Chang Tso-lin, the Kuomintang made a clean sweep of the sixteen representatives to the national lower house and won 50 of the 64 seats in the provincial assembly.[20] It did well in Hupeh, Chihli, Szechwan, and Shantung, where the provincial governments were hostile. There was no comparable incursion by other parties into administratively Kuomintang areas. KMT leaders justifiably claimed a victory. Of 596 seats in the lower house, 269 were won by the Kuomintang, and there was in addition a large number of members with multiple or no party affiliations. Similar proportions obtained in the upper house. This was a mandate.

A mandate for what? Sung Chiao-jen, the revolutionary leader who had turned to national parliamentary politics, had guided the performance, just as he had organized the party itself the previous August. He was an aggregator of interests and a pursuer of coalitions. His views bore the marks of conflicting conceptions of how China should be organized. In his effort to straddle several possibilities, he offered only a blurred vision of the Kuomintang's national policy, where there was something for everyone. His party, as he authoritatively interpreted it, stood for mild reform, a nationalistic but cautious foreign policy (like Yeh Hsia-sheng in Canton, he felt militancy in this area should be postponed), and the division of powers between central and local government in the context of a unified state system. Perhaps the ambiguity of Sung's formulations reflected the tension between his own favoring of centralized power and the unpopularity of that position with his constituency. It may also have been an accurate distillation of the preferences of the politically responsive gentry, who sought both provincial autonomy and at least the appearance of national unity. The contrast with other parties, however, was clear. All parties advocated some version of national unity. The distinctive features of the Kuomintang were its emphasis on provincial autonomy with elected governors, on local self-government, and on a prime minister chosen by the majority party in the national assembly. The first two of these positions in particular were supported enthusiastically by provincial and local gentry, the center of gravity in the electoral process. As a recent study of Sung concludes, he was aware that the gentry were the most powerful group in domestic politics and proceeded to act on that basis.[21]

Although many could stand under the large umbrella that Sung had constructed—and this included most prominent revolutionary leaders, eventually even the Kwangtung contingent—differences on policies and strategies remained. Sung's elaborate exposition of local autonomy within a unitary, centralizing state did not close the gap between those turned toward national politics and those based in the provinces. For Sung, the national assembly was the legitimating heart of republicanism. Li Lieh-chün was so unwilling to accept it as representing the will of the people that he proposed the military governors and the provincial assemblies should have an equal and direct voice in the drafting of the permanent constitution.[22] Attitudes toward Yuan Shih-k'ai also differed. Sun Yat-sen continued to endorse Yuan's general leadership even as the scope of the KMT electoral victory was becoming evident.[23] Sung Chiao-jen, who had disliked Sun's warm endorsement of Yuan the previous summer, was now determined either to oust Yuan or reduce him to a figurehead.

Most accounts of the background of the Second Revolution have asserted that Sung was content to have Yuan remain president and sought only a cabinet organized by the Kuomintang. In his formal pronouncements, it is true, Sung appeared resigned to Yuan's presidency. Beginning in January, 1913, his public remarks grew increasingly critical of Yuan's policies, but emphasized the demand for a party cabinet. He did not insist on a different president, even as he hinted that it was an open question who it should be. About the premiership, he was quite direct. Disclaiming any interest in it for himself, he endorsed Huang Hsing or T'ang Shao-i. During the Nanking revolutionary government of early 1912, Sung had been accused of lusting after the premiership, and the charge was periodically renewed.[24] But Sung's secret goal, though not personal, was more challenging: to deprive Yuan of power by legal, constitutional means.

A regular, as opposed to provisional, president was to be elected by the new, KMT-dominated national assembly. Sung and his secret collaborators decided to back Li Yuan-hung as the most believable candidate for contesting the presidency, if he could be recruited. Li proved to be unwilling. Huang Hsing, who unlike Sun Yat-sen joined Sung in his conspiracy, was another possible candidate. At the least, if Yuan were to remain, he was to be constitutionally shorn of all powers, or "responsibilities," as Sung put it publicly. American diplomats in the lower Yangtze region heard something of these intentions among a portion of the Kuomintang leadership by the end of January, 1913, and the evidence mounted over the next two months. Yuan's intelligence could not have been any slower.[25]

At about the same time a committee was formed by another group of Kuomintang activists to induce the new national assembly to convene in Nanking, after gathering first in preparation at Shanghai. The purpose was stated to be the adoption of a permanent constitution and the election of a president without the interference of Peking's military police. As the previous summer had suggested and later events showed, this was an eminently reasonable concern. But the proposal was attacked by Sun Yat-sen, who argued that it would divide the country, perhaps even lead to partition.[26] Naturally, other more conservative voices joined in the criticism. Although the full plan did not materialize, Yuan had apparently taken it seriously.

These contemplated challenges to Yuan's power were based on the legitimacy of the national assembly and were fully "within the system" of the liberal republic—certainly its values, and to a great extent its legal forms (only the convening of the national assembly in Nanking was constitution-ally dubious). They were also radical, in that they aspired to redesign the national balance of power and to renege on the implied commitments Sun Yat-sen and Huang Hsing had made to Yuan the previous summer. There is a note of paradox in Sung Chiao-jen, the moderate liberal, tacti-cally outflanking on the left Sun Yat-sen, the advocate of what he called social revolution. But Sung had constructed significant organizational con-nections with the gentry, a major social class, albeit a minority elite, and was accordingly stimulated to realize its political potential in national terms. Sung had a style and a message which meshed with the major social force of the moment, a force which had been girding itself for political action for several years. Sun Yat-sen, whose day would come later, was oddly out of phase, a condition his colleagues sometimes remarked on.

The bureaucratic organization centered around Yuan Shih-k'ai was not yet through, however. It acted forcefully and gained a tactical victory, while gravely compromising its legitimacy and its long-run viability. Sung Chiao-jen was assassinated, and the national assembly was subverted, abused, and ignored. If these had turned out to be quick defensive strokes, followed by conciliation and an effort to enlist the gentry movement on Yuan's side, they might have been scars that healed. But as we shall see in the next chapter, they were part of a pattern of attack on obstacles to greater centralization of power in Peking.

Sung was mortally wounded in Shanghai on March 20, 1913, as he boarded the train on his way to Peking where he would have led the major-ity party in the national assembly. Ying Kuei-hsing, the man who organized the killing by recruiting the gunman, was soon apprehended and proved to have been in regular communication with Peking. It appears that Ying's original assignment by Yuan's government had been to check the move-ment to convene the national assembly in Nanking. Selected, presumably, for his combination of unscrupulousness and a history of close association with a number of revolutionary leaders, Ying had seen Yuan Shih-k'ai in Peking in January, 1913, and had been given funds for his subversive mis-sion in central China. Yuan's initiative at that stage is incontestable. Sub-sequently, Ying's communications with the Peking government were handled by a secretary of Chao Ping-chün, the prime minister. Ying's tele-graphic instructions broadened, first to include an effort to discredit Sung Chiao-jen with documents about alleged misbehavior in Japan. Then, with references to Sung's Nanking speech of March 8, in which he harshly attacked Yuan's administration, the subject of the telegraphic traffic between Ying and the prime minister's secretary became Sung's "destruction."[27]

At about the same time, Yuan apparently began to consider the possibility of contracting a large foreign loan without the approval of the national assembly, in defiance of constitutional requirements.[28] The coincidence hardly seems accidental. We can speculate either that the planned defiance of the national assembly was thought to require the liquidation of its natural leader, or that the decision to assassinate Sung as a dangerous challenger was seen as leading to the hopeless alienation of the national assembly from any loan agreement serving Yuan's policies. Whatever the conscious linkages in conception, the combined effects proved to be enormous. It did not matter whether, as one version claims, Yuan had not sought Sung's assassination and was displeased with it.[29] The responsibility of his organization was inescapable. The charge against him was not only a murder; he had callously attacked the symbol of party politics.

Although political killings had not been rare in the first year of the republic, the shock from Sung's death precipitated a changed political climate. In the capital of Szechwan, where the military governor supported the Republican Party (Kung-ho tang), the KMT organized a three-day wake, with a life-sized waxen image of Sung Chiao-jen and speeches against the government. In Wuchang, also under a non-KMT government, a memorial ceremony was reportedly attended by ten thousand people, and a local newspaper warned: "Yuan Shih-k'ai! The measure of your iniquity is full, and the time has come to answer for it." Assassins were reported to be on their way to Peking to exact revenge. A speaker at a commemoration in Shanghai argued: Yuan "feared that if Sung's efforts to secure freedom and equality for the people were successful it would be greatly to his own disadvantage, and it was for this reason that he sent the assassin down here. For this crime I would willingly eat Yuan's flesh."[30] Dislike of Yuan and suspicion of his Napoleonic aspirations were not new, but they reached a new level of intensity and openness after the Sung killing.

Within the national KMT leadership, the rage was accompanied by two policy shifts. Those like Sun Yat-sen who had held back from opposing Yuan now adopted this part of Sung Chiao-jen's policy. And the content of the opposition shifted from Sung's legal emphasis to the active contemplation of an armed assault on Yuan's power. The effect of these shifts was to bring the veteran national leadership closer together (differences remained, of course) and to bring them all as a group closer tactically to provincially based leaders, such as Li Lieh-chün, who were inclined toward the use of force.

This did not happen at once or without twists and turns and retreats. Sun Yat-sen and Huang Hsing, who were talking easily at the end of March about a military showdown with Yuan, became discouraged about the possibilities.[31] But the seriousness with which they were contemplating confrontation is suggested by the variety of lines they put out and the breadth of the coalition toward which they moved—urged on by those younger and more militant. An aide to Huang Hsing recalls Huang and Sun asking military support, shortly after Sung's death, from T'an Yen-k'ai, the military governor of Hunan, Ch'en Chiung-ming, the leading revolutionary commander in Kwangtung, and the Eighth Division in Nanking, which had been formed under Huang Hsing the previous year.[32] Li Yuan-hung was again unsuccessfully wooed and an effort was made, most improbably, to blame Yuan Shih-k'ai for the agitations of a newly formed Hupeh conspiratorial group, the Kai-chin t'uan, suppressed by Li in late March and early April.[33] Ts'en Ch'un-hsuan, the former high Ch'ing official who had purged one of Fukien's revolutionary leaders the previous fall, allied with the plotters of Yuan's overthrow. Fancying himself an independent force with a base of support in Kwangtung and Kwangsi, Ts'en was slated to be generalissimo of the provincial armies against Yuan or president of the new republic which would be formed in the south.[34] Emissaries from Huang Hsing apparently even approached Chang Hsun, the former Hsiao-chan associate of Yuan Shih-k'ai, who occupied in independent warlord fashion an area along the Tientsin-Pukow Railway with over ten thousand queue-wearing troops.[35] From seeking cooperation from Chang Hsun, a notorious opponent of the revolution, it was but a short step to including the Manchu royalist party (Tsung-she tang) in the anti-Yuan united front—a step attempted during the Second Revolution.[36]

Meanwhile, the cooperation of foreigners was also sought. A large British arms manufacturing company was asked in April to supply millions of pounds worth of guns and munitions, apparently on credit.[37] In his inimitable way, Sun Yat-sen enticed Japanese backing by promising the adoption of Japanese currency in China and the consequent expansion of trade and general closeness between the two countries. Sun asked the Japanese government either to suggest to Yuan that he withdraw or to be prepared quickly to recognize a separate southern government. As precedent, he cited America's recognition of Panama![38] The theme of Japanese participation against Yuan was renewed in mid-May by Wang Chih-hsiang, Nanking's unsuccessful candidate for Chihli military governor in the spring of 1912, who had mediated the winter dispute between Yuan and Li Lieh-chün and more recently had served as facilitator of the revolutionary alliance with Ts'en Ch'un-hsuan. He proposed to a Japanese diplomat that in exchange for Japanese help against Yuan a Sino-Japanese bank be established to arrange for the joint management of railways, mines, and other enterprises in Kiangsi, Anhwei, Hunan, Kwangtung, and Kwangsi.[39] The list of provinces apparently combined areas of KMT strength along the Yangtze with Ts'en Ch'un-hsuan's presumed base further south.

The range of Chinese associates being wooed and the rashness of the approaches to foreigners reflected both the urgency and the desperation of the movement to topple Yuan. Galvanized by Sung's assassination into opposing Yuan, as Sung had wished, the T'ung-meng hui founding fathers pursued means that Sung in his zeal for unity and constitutionalism had not contemplated. Discouraged by the poor response to their secret call to arms, some reverted temporarily to legal forms of opposition. Huang Hsing was most conspicuous in this. But the disposition to remove Yuan by any means necessary remained, and efforts to mobilize the resources continued. Yuan was aware of most, if not all, of this activity.

Yuan's Break with the Liberal Republic

By his contest with Li Lieh-chün and with the assassination of Sung Chiao-jen, Yuan had in effect embarked on a course that demanded submission or war from those who still retained substantial power of their own. He more than kept pace with the reaction to these deeds. From the end of March, Yuan was busily clearing the decks for battle with national and provincial opponents. In the process, he consolidated support or benevolent neutrality in the places he needed it.

Yuan's spring program in 1913 had three main features: the disposition of military forces at critical points along the Yangtze, the emasculation of the national assembly, and the conclusion of a foreign loan to finance the program.

The first opportunity to garrison the probable front came with Li Yuan-hung's call for help in early April. Whether the Kai-chin t'uan, a military society that emerged in Hupeh after Sung Chiao-jen's assassination and during an effort at disbandment, was actually directed at Yuan or at Li, Li was frightened by it. His response was to invite northern troops (that is, under Yuan's authority—some were of southern origin) into Hupeh.

We must recall that China was by this time equipped with two railway trunk lines linking Peking with the Yangtze. One, the Tientsin-Pukow line, completed in 1912, reached the northern bank of the Yangtze opposite Nanking only by traversing Anhwei, where a KMT military governor was installed. The other touched the Yangtze at Hankow, without crossing any territory not controlled by Yuan until it entered Hupeh. Hence this early April opening in Hupeh gave Yuan a perch on the whole Yangtze basin, where he had previously had no military presence. By July, in fact, fifteen thousand northern troops were spread widely in the province, and half of them had established themselves near the Kiangsi border.[40]

At the same time that Yuan was reaching the Yangtze at Hankow, he instructed the military governor of Shantung and Chang Hsun, both with troops along the Tientsin-Pukow line some distance north of Nanking, to prepare for war. Chang Hsun, whose first loyalties were to the abdicated emperor, nonetheless preferred Yuan to the revolutionaries and enjoyed Yuan's subsidies for his private troops.[41] Although still impeded in Anhwei along the second trunk line, Yuan seized the occasion of a local attack on the Shanghai arsenal at the end of May for the introduction of northern troops there. He thus acquired a second perch on the Yangtze, though a more tenuous one of about fifteen hundred soldiers. With the cooperation of Kiangsu's military governor (a former Ch'ing governor), Yuan had made some appointments in the province, but this was the first infusion of northern military power.[42] As a consequence of Yuan's careful preparations, his military position in June was much stronger than it had been in March. His chief weakness was along the Tientsin-Pukow Railway.

As he was laying the military groundwork, Yuan also tried to undermine the political instruments of his opponents. One approach was the formation of a progovernment party. The results were not impressive.

Before the national elections, his support for parties which might challenge the Kuomintang had been minimal. Of prominent Chinese, probably none was more hated by the veteran revolutionaries than Liang Ch'i-ch'ao. When Liang returned to China in October, 1912 (after fourteen years of exile), Yuan extended this distinguished intellectual and political leader a generous monthly allowance and offered a subsidy of Ch$200,000 to an amalgamated non-KMT party.[43] But the planned amalgamation did not take place at that time. Yuan actually had no need of it, since his relations with the Kuomintang were good in the fall of 1912. Partly for the same reason, perhaps, he neglected to turn his bureaucratic machine to the task of electoral politics.

A new urgency emerged after the elections. And then with Sung's assassination, the mood in the president's office was closer to panic. For a moment in March, the proposed union of non-KMT parties, still under negotiation, was to be headed by Yuan himself. Finally, Li Yuan-hung, far from Peking, was made the titular chief director of the new organization, the Progressive Party (Chin-pu tang), which emerged only at the end of May, 1913.[44] The new party soon disintegrated. The whole effort had been characterized by endless bickering among factions, the ambiguous attitude of the parties toward the government (one of which had led the attack on the government's Mongolian policy and had joined with the KMT in criticizing Yuan's provincial regulations),[45] and Liang's moody vacillations. Yuan can only have been confirmed in his dislike of party politics.

To prevent the KMT from using the legitimizing power of the National Assembly, Yuan did not confine himself to these more or less legal but ineffective maneuvers. He tried bribery and physical coercion.

If many of those elected to the national assembly imbibed from the culture a degree of self-hate as partisan politicians, they had ample opportunity to indulge it in the atmosphere of corruption as the delegates gathered in Peking in early spring, 1913. There were widespread reports of deputies selling their votes. The price ranged from $100 to $10,000 per vote, and a life of conspicuous consumption and dissipation marked the national assembly.[46] Later one of Yuan's cabinet ministers confessed that a considerable proportion of the government's proceeds from the foreign consortium's Reorganization Loan went to bribing members of parliament.[47] As the bribes took effect and morale deteriorated with the approach of civil war, small groups split off from the KMT to form independent parties. With the outbreak of the Second Revolution, Yuan's tactics turned to intimidation: he arrested some deputies under emergency powers.

Yuan's attack at this time on the integrity of the national assembly was only partially effective. Opposition plans to oust or impeach Yuan were aborted, but the KMT dominated the assembly's committee for drafting a permanent constitution. Important votes continued to go against the government, notably in the rejection of a Sino-Russian agreement over Mongolia. Yuan still required the national assembly to legitimize his office by electing him to a regular term of the presidency. General foreign recognition was waiting on that act (though United States recognition came with the organization of the national assembly). But his outrageous treatment of the assembly was creating anti-Yuan bonds among its members across party differences. Liang Ch'i-ch'ao was by early August taking the deputies' case directly to Yuan and arguing that Yuan must respect them because he needed them.[48]

Attack on the national assembly did not work well for Yuan before his reelection as president, but indifference did. T'ang Hua-lung, a constitutionalist leader from Hupeh, had written the previous summer: "We have learned that what gives strength to a constitutional national assembly is that the government operates within the limits [imposed by the constitution]. If the government does not operate within these limits, the assembly is of no use and there is no way for it to use its capacity and influence."[49] The most grievous blow to the dignity of the assembly was the discovery that its members were unable to make Yuan submit the Reorganization Loan agreement for their ratification, according to constitutional procedures.

Yuan and the Imperialists

There was no more consuming a subject for the central government nor more convoluted a tale than the foreign loan negotiations of the liberal republic. As confrontation between Yuan and KMT leaders developed in 1913, it became the third major object of Yuan's preparatory program. The central government, in Yuan's conception of it, could not survive without fiscal authority in the country as a whole. But the forceful measures being contemplated by March or April, 1913, for attaining that authority required advance funding beyond Peking's domestic capacity. A large foreign loan became a necessity to Yuan's scheme.

Given the need for a loan, Yuan's area of maneuver in getting one was narrow. There had been a series of smaller foreign loans contracted both by Peking and the provinces since the revolution. Although there was much unhappiness with borrowing from foreign sources, by the fall of 1912 public resignation to its inevitability had set in. In this atmosphere, the Peking government sought and obtained legislative ratification for its lesser foreign loans, as it negotiated conditions for the large loan with the foreign banking consortium. While negotiations continued, Chinese freedom to pick and choose among lenders was largely limited to the degree that the consortium of foreign banks and their governments saw fit to tolerate it. China was the object of a united front of the world's leading powers, who assiduously checked her efforts to escape the conditions for loans that they chose to impose. They also rejected a proposal of the Chinese government in the late summer of 1912 to negotiate an upward revision of the treaty tarriff, which might have eased the need for a large foreign loan.[50]

The international consortium had been formed in the last years of the Ch'ing. With Peking fiscally weaker after the revolution, the consortium was more able to tighten the conditions under which China might borrow money on the main international markets. Britain maintained a general leadership over the consortium. France and Germany participated throughout. Japan and Russia joined after the revolution. America dropped out after Woodrow Wilson assumed the presidency in March, 1913, but agreed not to interfere. Formally, the consortium was an ad hoc body of representatives of a particular bank or group of banks from each of the member countries. In practice, policy was largely determined by their respective governments.

The object of negotiations between the consortium and the Peking government in the early republic soon became a so-called Reorganization Loan, at first to be £60,000,000, then reduced to £25,000,000. The loan would help China meet her current accumulated foreign obligations (central and provincial), would reserve a fund for indemnities for damages incurred by foreigners during the revolution (the claims were outrageously exaggerated), would set aside a sum for the reorganization of the salt gabelle, would finance troop demobilization, and would serve certain specified administrative expenses of the government (including the pensions of the retired Manchu emperor and the surviving Ch'ing bannermen). Of these, only the last two categories—demobilizing and administrative expenses—would generate funds that the Peking government would manage itself. Together they provided about £8,500,000, though the disbursement was theoretically subject to detailed controls. The sum amounted to perhaps two or three times the annual revenue of the richest province. Granted that Yuan could freely use only a portion of the £8,500,000, access to it at the moment of crisis gave him a marked advantage over his opponents.

For this advantage, Yuan had to pay a price beyond the promised re-payment over forty-seven years of £67,850,000, principal and interest. The direction toward which the consortium negotiators continually pushed was control: control over Chinese revenues, control over Chinese expendi-tures, and as an inevitable corollary control over Chinese politics. The fact that there were limits intrinsic to the situation preventing the full realiza-tion of this tendency did not stop the consortium from pressing on nor the Peking government from resisting.

The desire of the consortium for control and its practical limitations had already been illustrated during the summer of 1912. By early June, the consortium banks had advanced to Peking just over £1,000,000, mostly for troop demobilization. The condition, aside from an option on the large loan, was supervision of the disbursement of the money, to insure its proper use. A formula was negotiated by T'ang Shao-i's cabinet. Jordan, the British minister, reported to his government that the agreement, justi-fied by "the anomaly of the political situation" and the "unproductive nature" of the uses, "guarantees a stricter measure of supervision than has ever been exercised over the expenditure of foreign money in the past. . . ."[51] Taking the arrangements at face value, local military com-manders at first refused to cooperate, for example in Nanking. But it was soon discovered that the foreign inspector (a deputized customs commis-sioner) could do no more than check the arithmetic of the tabulations submitted to him. The existence of the soldiers for whom the money was disbursed had in no way to be verified. As a result, many statistical coinci-dences occurred, figures were juggled, and old debts were repaid out of the new funds. That any demobilization also took place had more to do with local needs than foreign supervision.[52]

In the aftermath of the summer's effort, Jordan noted that London in its instructions attached more importance to supervision of expenditures than to security for repayment—Edward Grey, the foreign secretary, was particularly insistent—but warned that "even at the ports supervision proved a mockery. . . ."[53] The concerted response of the foreign powers, however, was to seek out ways to tighten the control. With interruptions caused by breakdowns in the negotiations, the consortium pursued this chimera for fourteen months. The last sticking points, which Yuan con-ceded in April, 1913, were requirements, introduced into the negotiations in February, 1913, concerning the foreign (rather than Chinese) selection of the foreign supervisors of disbursement and their contractual powers. The subsequent presence of these foreigners in the Chinese government was a humiliation and an expensive nuisance. But they had only a limited influence over the course of events or the use of funds—nowhere in proportion to the investment of diplomatic muscle that forced their appointments.

The same motive of control dominated the question of the salt gabelle, with a more substantial result. The consortium pressed for a "reorganization" of the complex network of government participation and control in the production, transportation, and sale of salt. By "reorganization," the foreign negotiators meant no specific plan but rather the injection of a foreign associate chief inspector and his staff into the salt administration, in a manner roughly similar to the maritime customs service. The issue was not, contrary to surface appearance, the security of the loan. The British bankers, who should have been most concerned about repayment, were ever ready to relax conditions for the loan and had to be brought into line by the foreign office.[54] Loans contracted outside the consortium, without supervisors or a reorganized salt administration, did well on the market so long as the European governments refrained from subverting them. The general manager of Lloyds Bank wrote G. E. Morrison, chief foreign advisor to Yuan Shih-k'ai, that he was one of many people interested in lending to China but that he was blocked by the foreign office, which opposed any loan outside the consortium.[55] It was recognized inside the foreign office that even the limited salt revenues that Peking was able to collect in the fall of 1912, without "reorganization," were sufficient to finance loans up to £20,000,000 to £30,000,000.[56] The sums that China was seeking were, after all, paltry by comparison with the international flow of capital on the eve of World War I. China's credit was limited but, despite her defaults on some foreign obligations, was quite sufficient for the loan envisaged.

But a foreign foothold in the salt administration would offer a different reward: another lever on Chinese decision making. It was not fully apparent in advance how the lever might be used, but it was not hard to imagine the possibilities. The foreign inspector general of the customs had learned that the most effective instrument for working his will on the Chinese government was the control of considerable funds and their withholding until acquiescence. As it turned out, the salt administration offered the same opportunity. The foreign chief inspector came into his job with £2,000,000 from the consortium loan. The sum was slated for the reorganization of the salt administration but was in fact not needed for that purpose and could be released to the Chinese government only with the foreign chief inspector's permission. He used the power to get his way. Salt revenues in excess of the annual servicing of the attached foreign debt could be and were administratively blocked by the foreign chief or the foreign banks for political purposes.[57]

The motives underlying the urge to control and intervene in Chinese affairs expressed themselves in various ways. Let us explore three ways commonly found among the British. There was the desire to show the Chinese their place and to punish them when they stepped out of line. For example, when T'ang Shao-i contracted a loan on Yuan's behalf outside the consortium in March, 1912, a comment in the London foreign office was: "We ought not to let this opportunity pass for impressing on the Chinese Government that the time for borrowing money on their own terms has gone past. . . ."[58] Jordan in Peking saw the act as one of "carelessness and conceit," and complained that T'ang Shao-i "will not take the trouble to make himself acquainted with any question and acts with all the independence and assurance of a Minister of a first-class Power."[59] The revelation of another loan outside the consortium as the final agreement was reached in the spring of 1913 came close to aborting it. In view of the "grave political situation," it was decided not to withhold funds, but Jordan urged that the Chinese government be made to "atone" by a speedy agreement on a railway concession.[60] Sentiments like these became dangerous when entertained by those with sufficient power to try to implement them. Implementation meant greater control.

Control was also sought to bring Western ideas of proper government to China. There was confusion as to whether foreign experts in the Chinese government would be of intrinsic value to Chinese society or that they would make foreign banks and governments more favorably disposed and thereby indirectly assist China. But there was great confidence that foreigners would make some important difference of benefit to the Chinese. The British consortium representative in a communication to the chief Chinese negotiator attached the description "efficient" to the term "foreign auditor" in the manner of a Homeric epithet.[61] The message seemed to be that efficiency was what China needed and only foreigners could provide it. Even the seriousness of Chinese resistance to foreign controls was more believable if foreigners were associated with it. In September, 1912, when the British government came close to abandoning the consortium in the

face of the early success of the £10,000,000 Crisp loan (contracted outside the consortium by British financiers), one of the reasons given in the
foreign office for giving way was that the determination of the Chinese
government to resist was now backed by its new political adviser, George
Ernest Morrison.[62] Later, foreign officials proudly took credit for the
increased amounts of salt revenue available to the Peking government,
although the contribution of the foreign salt inspectorate to this effect was
blown up out of all proportion and other more profound factors ignored.[63]
Representative government was also felt to be nice if done with dignity
and restraint, but efficiency brought to China in foreign hands was the
great gift of the Western world. Chinese resistance merely confirmed the
belief in their need of it, since the last citadel against foreign control was
intentional inefficiency.

A third British motive in seeking control—and the most openly articulated—was the achievement of a stable environment for trade. The pursuit
of stability meant constant calculations about Chinese politics, in order to
determine what might best contribute to order. In the 1911 Revolution,
the British had maintained a passable neutrality, on the grounds that they
could not influence the result and would do better to stand aside. In 1912
and 1913, they supported Yuan. In the Second Revolution they definitely
contributed to the ease of Yuan's triumph—through the loan and through
specific services undertaken partly on the initiative of the Peking legation,
in Jordan's absence. Yuan frequently tested how far British support could
be stretched, how far he could insist on China's or his government's interests without damaging the British conviction that he was essential to regaining or keeping order. There were limits, as when London almost suspended
the Reorganization Loan after its signature on grounds of Yuan's having
secretly signed another, earlier loan agreement in violation of an understanding. In general, British investment in Yuan's centrality to Chinese
order remained great.[64] The other powers, with the erratic and partial exception of Japan, followed roughly the same course.

The imperialist powers, therefore, supported Yuan in his effort to
extend his fiscal and political authority over the country. In doing so, they
accepted Yuan's schemes. The evidence suggests that Yuan decided by
March 11, 1913, that if he accepted the Reorganization Loan, he would
not submit it to the national assembly for ratification.[65] In early April the
foreign negotiators became aware of Yuan's unconstitutional plans and,
despite some reluctance among the banks in Europe, decided to accept an
irregular validation of the loan.[66]

Not taking Chinese forms of representative government quite seriously, the foreigners involved seemed unaware of the gravity of what was taking place. For those in Yuan's government, however, it was a different matter. Trying to avoid an agreement that would be objectionable to the national assembly, Yuan contracted with only partial success three major loans in opposition to the consortium monopoly after the beginning of the negotiations in February, 1912. As late as April 9, 1913, he was still attempting to secure a £25,000,000 loan outside the consortium, as an escape from its conditions.[67] Chou Hsueh-hsi, the industrial entrepreneur, was the chief Chinese negotiator when the Reorganization Loan was signed on the night of April 26. He conducted the final maneuvers in a state of terror before the wrath of the national assembly. "They want to eat my flesh," he said four days before the signing. He emerged from the trauma a sick man—a nervous wreck, threatened with paralysis, according to a foreign doctor who treated him—and shortly left his post.[68] The confrontation between the assembly and Yuan over loan ratification was not a minor matter. The issue, along with Sung Chiao-jen's murder, quickly acquired symbolic meaning. The authority and dignity of electoral politics and representative government were at stake. Yuan by his behavior had asserted that he would not be bound by these principles.[69]

Encouraged by the assistance of foreign governments and their indifference to his arbitrary use of executive power, Yuan indulged in the pursuit of his maximum objectives. Though not in itself a sufficient explanation of his victories, the backing of foreign governments nonetheless gave him a special margin of advantage over his enemies.

The Second Revolution

From April, 1913, Yuan spoke more frankly about his intention to force the issue of the president's powers in the provinces. At the same time the anti-Yuan coalition, formed in the wake of Sung Chiao-jen's assassination, secretly worked at marshaling sufficient power to oust Yuan. Desperate efforts to mediate the widening gulf, for example by Chang Chien, produced no result.[70]

In June, within a period of three weeks, Yuan dismissed the three leading KMT military governors: Li Lieh-chün of Kiangsi, Hu Han-min of Kwangtung, and Po Wen-wei of Anhwei. Not yet ready to act, they stepped down. But in early July the top veteran revolutionary leaders gathered in

Shanghai and decided to take the field against Yuan.[71] Meanwhile, using the excuses of reported revolutionary activity and a confidential request of July 2 for help from a local Kiangsi military official, northern troops under Li Ch'un entered Kiangsi from Hupeh on the orders of Yuan Shih-k'ai. On July 8, General Li Ch'un reached Kiangsi's Yangtze port of Kiukiang, whence came the invitation, and proceeded to expand his position in the area.[72] In accordance with the earlier decision in Shanghai, Li Lieh-chün surreptitiously returned to Kiangsi on July 7 and started organizing Kiangsi's military forces.

Nothing could now stop a collision. Hostilities began on July 11. On the twelfth, Li Lieh-chün publicly announced the movement to throw Yuan out, and the Kiangsi provincial assembly declared the province's independence of Peking.[73]

The outlook was not good for the revolutionaries. Several of them embarked only with half a will on the campaign to overthrow Yuan militarily. Li Yuan-hung in Wuchang predicted the general outline of events in early May. He had rejected revolutionary overtures to lead the south against Yuan, he told a Japanese diplomat, and had warned them he would personally head an expedition against any revolt. (He was in fact later appointed Li Lieh-chün's temporary replacement in Kiangsi, while retaining his Hupeh post.) The conspirators, he said, could not compare with Peking in finances or arms (Yuan claimed to dispose of eighty thousand reliable troops), and had the participation of the military governors of only three provinces. The Kiangsu military governor was opposed, said Li, and would leave his post rather than cooperate (as indeed he subsequently did). Li was aware of the strength of radicals in Hunan but was confident of the military governor's "peaceful political views." Kweichow, Yunnan, and Kwangsi were firmly on Yuan's side, thought Li, and even in Kwangtung, Hu Han-min's position was weak, and so on.[74] Li's crystal ball had a few cracks, but his general picture was accurate enough. Yuan presumably was receiving similar reports.

Yuan was ready for the Kiangsi revolt, which he had done so much to precipitate. He had been accumulating strength nearby since early April. Li Lieh-chün and other Kiangsi military officers rallied the troops and fought with persistence until overwhelmed in mid-August. Li fled into Hunan and thence to Japan, courtesy of the Japanese army and navy in China.

Yuan was less prepared in Shanghai, though hardly taken unawares.

Shanghai's Chinese elite split in Yuan's favor, but the Woosung forts were in revolutionary hands. Ch'en Ch'i-mei with about thirty-five hundred soldiers organized a vigorous and bloody series of attacks on Shanghai's large arsenal, which Yuan's men had invested since May. The arsenal held, thanks to the British chargé d'affaires in Peking, who, against the advice of the British acting consul general in Shanghai, authorized the disbursement of Reorganization Loan funds on Chinese ships at Shanghai to secure their loyalty to Peking. In Shanghai, too, it was all over in August, even at the Woosung forts.

The greatest military and strategic strength of the anti-Yuan movement lay in Nanking and Anhwei and in the possibility of striking north along the Tientsin-Pukow Railway. If the revolt was not to be merely defensive (as in the Kiangsi campaign) but would press on to Peking, the only conceivable route where the rebels had a foothold was from Nanking through Anhwei. In early May, Anhwei and Nanking soldiers had already begun to move north along the railway with field guns to prepare positions at Hsuchow, in north Kiangsu.[75] It seems to have been the presidential dismissal of Po Wen-wei as Anhwei military governor on June 30 which forced the decision to strike. After shooting started in Kiangsi, Huang Hsing, still doubtful about the wisdom of it all, went to Nanking to secure the southern terminus for the revolution.

The coup in Nanking on July 14 went smoothly. It was based on the strong KMT sympathies of the crack Eighth Division in Nanking, which had been formed under Huang Hsing while resident general there the previous year.[76] The military governor, Ch'eng Te-ch'üan, unwilling to join, departed after a brief confinement. Recalcitrant senior officers were shot. The attack into Shantung began July 16, with some initial successes for the southern revolutionaries, who, with seven thousand troops, outnumbered the local northern defenders and had superior artillery. But the attack was pressed neither far nor long, and by July 22 pro-Yuan forces (including Chang Hsun's troops, which the revolutionary leaders had unsuccessfully wooed before the shooting) took Hsuchow without encountering resistance. It was a defeat for the rebels but not a rout. They retained substantial forces along the railway in Anhwei at Lin-huai-kuan about 140 kilometers north of Nanking and had dispatched troops west to meet an attack from Honan.[77]

At this point, after setbacks on the three fronts of Kiangsi, Shanghai, and the North Kiangsu-Shantung frontier, Huang Hsing decided to close down the Nanking headquarters. On July 29, he left Nanking through arrangements made the by Japanese navy. As he was leaving, he gave his reasons to the Japanese consul. He feared the local military were becoming untrustworthy; the fall of Shanghai was a big blow; the military preparations at Nanking had always been unsatisfactory; and, since he was the symbol of opposition to Yuan, his departure would bring the revolt to an end and save the people from suffering.[78] The short-run strength of the revolution in Nanking was greater than Huang thought; the revolt there was revived by Ho Hai-ming, a revolutionary journalist and organizer of the earlier movement to have the national assembly meet in Nanking. As the Japanese consul had predicted, Nanking held out against Peking's forces for more than a month after Huang's flight. But as Huang had predicted, the suffering in Nanking as a consequence was severe: Chang Hsun's troops cruelly pillaged the city after it finally fell on September 1, 1913.

The main events of the Second Revolution concluded shortly after Nanking's capitulation. There had been sympathetic responses in the governments of three more provinces—unambiguous but distant support from Ch'en Chiung-ming, Hu Han-min's successor in Kwangtung; reluctant support from Hunan's T'an Yen-k'ai, who was being carried along by radicals around him; and a tepid severance of relations with Yuan (but not with the Peking government) in Fukien. Although Szechwan's provincial government at Chengtu stayed with Yuan, troops in Chungking declared war simultaneously on Yuan and the province's military governor.[79] Of these other moves against Yuan, all but that in Szechwan were rescinded without large-scale military efforts: bribes or a new perception of the odds changed the political balance before any fighting. The Chungking rebels—ten thousand soldiers under T'ung-meng hui veteran Hsiung K'o-wu, with favorable responses in other parts of the province—were not so easily intimidated. But they disintegrated when Chengtu's uncertain powers of suppression were supplemented by troops from other provinces, especially Yunnan, Kweichow, and Shensi. Hsiung fled Chungking on September 11. Wanhsien, lower down the Yangtze, resisted until October 2.[80] Four days later, Yuan was reelected president—no longer "provisional"—by a reluctant, coerced national assembly in Peking. He began arrangements for the new order, a centralized dictatorship.

Yuan's success requires an explanation. The revolt against him touched off responses in nine provinces (in addition to those mentioned so far, Hupeh, despite the northern occupation, continued to seethe with anti-

Yuan and anti-Li Yuan-hung conspiracies, and parts of Chekiang fleetingly declared their adherence to the movement). Yet Yuan, with a firm administrative grip on only three provinces at the start, never seemed seriously threatened.

Imperialist intervention was a factor. The foreign powers had proved their support of Yuan and their tolerance of the direction of his domestic policy by accepting an unconstitutional validation of the Reorganization Loan. Yuan was not explicitly asked to centralize authority over the country by force, and the British minister urged peaceful methods as far as possible. But the situation Yuan faced was one of low central revenues, a huge foreign debt, and exclusion by the consortium from the money markets except with "strings" that looked like chains. Someone of Yuan's outlook would feel compelled by this combination of circumstances to seek unification by force if necessary. He told the British minister of his determination. There was no attempt to dissuade him.[81] From Yuan's success the British hoped to gain the settlement of "cases" in the provinces, the winning of concessions, and the appropriate environment for trade.[82] Once the Second Revolution was underway, the British legation, despite the foreign secretary's admonitions to the contrary, consciously departed from the neutrality observed during the 1911 Revolution.[83] Yuan was helped in securing the navy's loyalty, in impeding Ch'en Ch'i-mei's movements in Shanghai, in putting government commercial ships temporarily under the British flag to keep them out of rebel hands, and so on. The support was not unstinting. Some Peking requests were refused; support could not include compromising British rights and interests in China. But Britain and most of the other foreign countries remained passive or extended helping hands to Yuan. It was important to him.

Foreign support was not the whole reason for Yuan's success. In the first place, the revolutionaries were also attended by foreign admirers. Katō Kōmei, between bouts as Japanese foreign minister, had visited China shortly before the Second Revolution and had told Sun Yat-sen and Huang Hsing that Japan would give any future rebels no sympathy whatsoever and warned them to be cautious.[84] However, Japanese were not united behind this approach. Though the foreign ministry agreed with Katō, it did not set policy for other branches of the Japanese government, nor did it control the activities of private Japanese adventurers and businessmen in China. A considerable portion of Japan's various ruling groups wished for their country a greater role in Chinese affairs, disliked Japan's subordination to British policy toward China, and, out of a distrust of Yuan Shih-k'ai and opposition to the emergence of a strong Chinese government, feared a China administratively unified under Yuan. Japanese adherents of these views readily supported movements of opposition to Yuan's presidency, whether from the left or the right.

Despite Japanese participation in the Reorganization Loan and formal neutrality in the Second Revolution, incidents of Japanese intervention against Yuan were common. Japanese firms served as purchasing agents in the supply of arms to the anti-Yuan forces—in one reported case, ¥65,000 worth, without payment.[85] The presence of Japanese troops and gunboats along the Yangtze had increased markedly since the 1911 Revolution, and the resulting network of communications served as an inviolate transportation system for the revolutionaries. Most of the leaders escaped the final debacle by using it. In addition, Japanese military men, sometimes retired, perhaps for the purpose, served the rebels as advisers. Li Lieh-chün in Kiangsi had fifteen at an early stage, including seven noncommissioned officers, a reserve lieutenant colonel and an interpreter detached from the Japanese garrison in Hankow.[86] When Nanking fell in September, eleven Japanese were in active service with the anti-Yuan army there.[87] These figures come from Japanese consular reports. Other foreign observers put the numbers much higher. They also observed tactical interventions, such as a Japanese ship playing its searchlight on a northern army position at Wuhu, thereby enabling a rebel gunboat to shell its opponents and stave off an attack.[88] All this Japanese activity was some counterweight to the more solemn governmental endorsement by the leading powers that Yuan enjoyed. It had the practical effect of making the Second Revolution a remarkably safe one for most leading rebels, even in failure and amidst casualties in the thousands. Though scattered over central, western, and southeastern China, not one of the prominent instigators was killed or captured. Most gathered in Japan, against the wishes of the Japanese foreign ministry, to renew the battle in a better season.

The importance of foreign intervention and foreign money in determining the result must also be qualified by a consideration of the domestic weaknesses of the rebellion. The essence of Yuan's success was that he split China's social elite and their regional and local leaders. Frequently the division was in his favor. Even when it was not, the minority supporting him was sufficient to weaken gravely the revolutionary majority. This was especially true in those provinces where the pro-Yuan minority was in possession of formal administrative power. In 1911, politically active Chinese were almost unanimous in their support of the revolution and Yuan had no choice but to become republican. In 1916, amidst a great deal of indifference or withdrawal, Yuan had few advocates and the rebels easily filled the vacuum. But in 1913, the Peking government could win with many people on the issues. Even bribes and large military subsidies, which Yuan used liberally, required an atmosphere of proper purpose, if they were to work effectively. They worked for Yuan extraordinarily well.

The discouragement with the first year of the republic, whose expression in a Kuomintang journal I noted at the start of this chapter, could be turned to Yuan's advantage. The issues of self-government and provincial autonomy, with which the Kuomintang organizers had won the election, could not bear the weight of a rebellion in their name. Liberalism had shallow roots and the performance of the national assembly had not deepened them. Autonomous provinces had had enough difficulty meeting the payroll, let alone contributing to a surge of national strength, as they were supposed to do in the ideology of provincialism. The advocates of a centralized unity were regaining their self-confidence. Yuan was actually subject to criticism for his dilatoriness in bringing the divided country together.[89]

Yuan declared in the midst of the Second Revolution that cohesion was essential when the nation was struggling for its existence against external forces. In a public justification of his policy, he argued that nations harmonious within were impregnable without, that countries with internal quarrels between classes, religions, races, or regions failed, that China's tradition of centralized unity went back to the Ch'in and Han dynasties and must be protected. "If the idea of regional divisions takes hold in people's minds," he went on, "how would one draw the line at the separation of south from north?" Regions would dissolve into their constituent provinces, county would give way to village, and China would split into thousands of feuding parts. All capability of defending the frontiers would be lost. Such was the harm threatened, Yuan held, by those resorting to arms while mouthing slogans of righteous retribution.[90]

He had a considerable audience for these thoughts. There was a widespread belief that the issues of Sung's assassination and the Reorganization Loan could be settled short of civil war. In this light, the critical question of the Second Revolution was: which side had more egregiously violated the broad gentry consensus that had emerged from the 1911 Revolution?

Albeit with some straining, the consensus embraced both local self-government, including provincial autonomy, and national unity. Although the proper balance between these two goals was infinitely debatable, they were reconcilable through parliamentary federalism. Sung Chiao-jen in 1912 and early 1913 prospered as a political leader by papering over the contradictions and espousing both principles. Yuan had also straddled them. Through 1912 and up to the eve of the Second Revolution, he had refrained from persistently forcing his will against strong provincial interests and had veiled his authoritarian leanings. He had acquiesced in only paper appointments by Peking in the provinces and had demonstrated an ability to compromise. Hence, the uprising of July, 1913, was persuasively portrayed as an attack on national unity. When the gentry as a whole learned the full import of Yuan's centralizing policies, including a cessation of local self-government, many who supported him in 1913 would turn against him.

It has often been noted that merchants opposed the revolutionary recourse to arms in 1913. It is quite true, but they were not the only group, nor the most important. It was more than a calculation of self-interest, presumably, that induced Ts'ai O, ruler in Yunnan and confirmed believer in administrative unity, to stay with Yuan and help to suppress the revolution in Szechwan.[91] Lan T'ien-wei, a young graduate of Japan's Army Officers' Academy, who worked for the 1911 Revolution in Manchuria and Shantung, cabled from Europe his view that the Second Revolution was a "perverse course," since the republic could not afford another convulsion.[92]

Li Ta-chao, a student in Tientsin and later a major figure in the early years of the Chinese Communist Party, wrote articles before and after the Second Revolution that had the effect of supporting Yuan. While mourning Sung Chiao-jen's murder and conceding Yuan's unconstitutional behavior and the political interventions of Peking's military police, Li nonetheless saved his harshest criticism for the provincial military governors. Their "despotic power" was greater than that of the former emperors, he said, and was responsible for the ineffectiveness of central orders, the failure to serve the people's welfare, the parlousness of finances, and the conflicts among Chinese brethren. On the eve of the Second Revolution, Li wrote:

> How could the former brilliance of those heroes who recovered our rivers and mountains [from the Manchus] have become such stu-

pidity? The danger in which the nation finds itself is now twice that facing the former Ch'ing. Mongolia and Tibet have been separated. External troubles are ever more pressing. Finances are exhausted; the cupboard is bare. If each considers himself the man of the moment, without immediate plans for a common rescue effort, then we shall be disregarding the warning of the Balkans and shall eventually follow the path of Egypt.[93]

Li favored the return of military power to Peking and the appointment of civil provincial administrators by the center. It would be even better, he argued, to abolish the provincial unit altogether.

Li Ta-chao reflects in these writings the views of the Progressive Party, formed in the spring of 1913 in opposition to the KMT. The point is that a young man—twenty-four years old in 1913—of Li's talents could be persuaded of them. Yuan was not popular, but the question remained, how to measure his crimes against his usefulness, even his indispensibility.

All might have been otherwise if the revolutionaries had broken out of the confines of elite politics. One is struck by the small scale of the military forces involved, on both sides. In a civil war in a country of over four hundred million, opposing concentrations of soldiers probably did not total fifty thousand at any one point. Money was lacking, but so was the political appeal to substitute for it among the masses of the population in the rebel-held areas. Even anti-imperialism, which might have served as a replacement for the anti-Manchu slogans of the 1911 Revolution, was eschewed or severely muted. The conclusion of a Chinese historian of Hupeh and Hunan in this period applies generally to the Second Revolution: the revolutionaries had no overall program or direction; they were separated from the peasantry; their vision was confined to terroristic assassination and new political plots to change the government; and there was no future in this.[94]

There was even less promise for the Chinese people in Yuan's policy of administrative centralization. But the idea died hard.

Chapter 6

Establishing the Dictatorship

In 1913, China was weak and beset by dangers. To deal with this situation and to hold the country together, Yuan Shih-k'ai chose to construct administrative bonds linking the provinces to Peking and then to draw them tight. In beginning the process, he had run up against the institutions of representative government and provincial autonomy and had been challenged by them. With his victory over the Second Revolution, he was in a position to dispose of these countervailing accumulations of power and legitimacy as he thought best. He proceeded to destroy them. Aborting these alternative approaches to rectifying China's weakness before foreign imperialism and maintaining the social order, he pursued instead an ever greater degree of centralized power.

In this effort, he used familiar methods of control, like the manipulation of official appointments, censorial surveillance of personnel, overlapping administrative responsibilities, official examination systems, the revival of the *pao-chia* system of local control, the exploitation of old symbols of authority. He also adapted new instrumentalities to his purposes. He encouraged the enormous growth of plainclothes investigators or detectives: the result was a crudely developed secret police, though the military also played a large repressive role. A new newspaper censorship law was introduced (there had been none nationally since the Ch'ing fell), and the mails were read. The railways in particular enabled the Peking government to attain, or to aspire to attain, new levels of authority. The existence of trunk lines to the middle and lower Yangtze valley (the second was finished only in 1912) opened these areas to a greater flow of power out of Peking. While Peking was on the defensive, as in 1912 and early 1913, the potential was unrealized. Once Peking had the advantage, it was in a position to dominate central China more than ever before. (Correspondingly, the extreme southern provinces, especially the inland ones, were subject to only a diluted form of the new controls.)

Measured against its immediate goal of administrative centralization, Yuan's dictatorship was impressive. When Chiang Kai-shek tried it after 1928 in much the same style (the addition of a political party to the dictatorship of Chiang's Nanking government turned out to be only a formal and not a substantive difference), the reach of central authority was less. However, although no other national government between 1911 and 1949 could match Yuan's in the extent of its authority, the costs were excessive. Yuan's achievement in administrative power was built on terror and on the suppression of participatory politics. As a result, it could not persuade the population of its virtue, and it alienated the gentry elite.

The Spread of Peking's Power

The most obvious and immediate result of the defeat of the Second Revolution was that the Peking government could appoint officials of its own choosing all over the country and could make its choices stick. The need for political maneuver had not vanished. In some instances Yuan proceeded slowly (as in the removal of Chang Hsun from Nanking in the fall of 1913). Sometimes he preferred not to take on a local power figure who, though possessing independent sources of strength, nonetheless followed orders and accepted a wide range of central intervention (as with Chu Jui in Chekiang, Yen Hsi-shan in Shansi, or the military commanders in the extreme southern tier of provinces). Most of Mongolia, Tibet, and Sinkiang remained beyond the reach of Peking's dictates. Other qualifications could be added, but the contrast with 1912 or with the three decades following Yuan's death is stark. By the standards of the time, Yuan exercised a firm rule over the home provinces of China.

The changes were clearest along the Yangtze. By the beginning of 1914, Yuan's two most prominent military associates were installed at the Yangtze termini of the railway trunklines to Peking: Tuan Ch'i-jui at Wuchang in Hupeh and Feng Kuo-chang at Nanking in Kiangsu. Although the former military governors of these two provinces had remained loyal to Peking during the Second Revolution, loyalty was not enough for such strategic posts. Yuan sought full administrative integration through the installation of his own political machine. In Anhwei and Kiangsi, where the previous military governors had opposed Yuan, the replacements (Ni Ssu-ch'ung and Li Ch'un) were also Peiyang veterans. Peking's authority in Hunan was introduced by one of Yuan's post-1911 recruits, T'ang Hsiang-ming. T'ang, still in his mid-thirties, was a naval officer, trained at the Fukien naval academy and in France, who had helped bring the navy over to the revolution in 1911. A younger brother of T'ang Hua-lung, the prominent Hupeh politician, he became vice-minister of the navy in Peking after the revolution and fought for Yuan during the Second Revolution. He was sent to Hunan in early October, 1913, with three to four thousand Peiyang troops, mostly men from Honan and Shantung, and proceeded to disband local soldiers and arrest (sometimes executing) much of the previous provincial government.[1] In this manner, both banks of the Yangtze were secured for Peking from the point the river leaves Szechwan to its mouth on the East China Sea—about nine hundred miles.

Along the coast, the provincial government of Chekiang remained in the same hands, which served Yuan's administrative purposes so well that the province was held up to the others as a model of good behavior. The Fukien government, however, was ousted in the fall of 1913 by Peking's navy minister, Liu Kuan-hsiung. Liu also forced the departure from Foochow of the Hunanese troops that had been the previous military governor's power base. By the following summer, the military commander at Amoy had been eliminated, by execution. A centrally appointed civil administration began to take over the province.

In Kwangtung, the collapse of the revolutionary government in early August, 1913, perhaps owed more to the subversive work of Yuan's agent, Huang Shih-lung, than it did to Lung Chi-kuang's invasion from Kwangsi. But, after a few days of fighting between the two rival counterrevolutionary groups, Lung, a non-Han Yunnanese officer with no historical ties to Yuan, was allowed to prevail. Civil offices were filled from Peking, but altogether Lung's regime was an abomination for the people of Kwangtung and an uncertain quantity from Yuan's point of view. Compromises between central and local power comparable to that in Kwangtung prevailed in Kwangsi, Yunnan and Kweichow, without Lung's extravagant cruelty and corruption. The balance in these provinces in the extreme south, however, had shifted markedly to Peking as compared to 1912.

In the north, a modus vivendi in Yuan's favor had already been worked out in Shansi. By the summer of 1914, Yuan's people had taken over the provincial administrations of Shensi and Kansu from local power holders:

Major railways

Full administrative integration by Peking

Appointive powers by Peking but tenuous control (foreign influence, remote areas, etc.)

Substantial local leadership continuing

Effectively removed from Peking's authority

RUSSIA

MANCHURIA

HEILUNGCHIANG

KIRIN

FENGTIEN

SINKIANG

OUTER MONGOLIA

INNER MONGOLIA

CHIHLI

Peking

Tientsin

Talien (J.)

TSINGHAI

SHANSI

SHENSI

SHANTUNG

Tsingtao (J.)

KANSU

Yellow River

HONAN

Hsuchow

KIANGSU

Nanking

Lin-huai-kuan

Pukow

Shanghai

Chengtu

Wanhsien

HUPEH

ANHWEI

TIBET

SZECHWAN

Hankow

Wuchang

Chungking

Yangtze

Kiukiang

CHEKIANG

HUNAN

KIANGSI

Kunming

KWEICHOW

FUKIEN

YUNNAN

KWANGSI

KWANGTUNG

Canton

INDIA (Br.)

Hanoi

Hongkong (Br.)

TAIWAN (J.)

INDOCHINA (Fr.)

Degrees of Integration into Peking's Administration by Province, July, 1915

in Shensi, from an administration combining New Army leaders and the Brothers and Elders secret society; in Kansu, from Muslim forces under Ma An-liang and Ma Fu-hsiang. Neither intervention survived Yuan's death. But a traveler in Kansu in 1915 was told that the provincial administration was the strongest since that of Tso Tsung-t'ang, the Ch'ing official who had suppressed rebellion and brought mayhem and reform to the area in dramatic expeditions during the 1870s.[2]

Manchuria was much influenced by the large Japanese and Russian presences. But such Chinese power as there was continued to be shared between Peking's appointees and local military men, notably Chang Tso-lin in Fengtien.[3]

Chinese provinces, then, were in two categories by the end of 1914. In the first category were those provinces where Peking's coercive power was physically present and unquestionably dominant and where administrative integration with the center reached a high level: Chihli, Shensi, Kansu, Shantung, Honan, Kiangsu, Anhwei, Kiangsi, Hupeh, Hunan, and Fukien. Provinces in the second category deferred to Peking's orders and accepted Peking's appointments and administrative schemes. But they managed largely to escape the permanent physical presence of Peking military forces and retained in the top military post men originally put there by local politics or by military actions not controlled from Peking. These provinces were Shansi, Chekiang, Kwangtung, Kwangsi, Yunnan, Kweichow, and Szechwan. The Manchurian provinces and Inner Mongolia hovered somewhere between the two categories. In the first half of 1915, Szechwan moved from the second to the first category, completing Peking's grip on the Yangtze River provinces. By mid-1915, then, Yuan had administratively integrated into a centralized system of control twelve of China's home provinces, with a population of some three hundred million.[4] And his influence in the remainder was by no means slight.

The Terror

The consolidation of Yuan's authority in the country after the Second Revolution was accompanied by an orgy of repression and bloodletting. The aim was to destroy the power of the Kuomintang. But the Kuomintang had several aspects to it. Even if the regime had confined its onslaught to those elements irreconcilably opposed to Yuan, many lives would have been lost. Precision, however, has rarely been a feature of political repression. Distinctions were lost, and many Kuomintang moderates fell victim to the waves of executions. The momentum caught up accidental and apolitical unfortunates. Instead of building on the support that a portion of the elite had lent him during the Second Revolution, Yuan turned to brute force, demanding obedience instead of winning loyalty.

According to the provisional constitution of 1912 and enabling legislation of that autumn, the president had the power to declare martial law if military operations were required within the country. Yuan declared martial law on July 21, 1913. It was gradually repealed at different times in different parts of the country over the next year, but in practice legal protections meant little from that date onward, even as Yuan seemed anxious to cloak his behavior with the pretense of law. After executing thousands of people for sedition, the government in July, 1914, issued regulations amending the provisional criminal code to provide death for membership in secret societies devoted to sedition, for assembling crowds of over one hundred men, and so forth.[5] Newspapers were censored, controlled and suspended, and their numbers markedly decreased from their great proliferation after the 1911 Revolution. For example, by the end of the first winter of the dictatorship, only two of ten newspapers survived in the capital of Hupeh; in the capital of Shantung, seven out of fifteen. Twelve newspapers were closed in Canton during November, 1913.[6] The revolutionary provincial governments had sometimes repressed particular newspapers or their editors; now the scope was national and coordinated. In April, 1914, the republic's first press regulations were instituted, very much along the lines of the press law of the late Ch'ing.[7]

Yuan's officially sponsored terror began in Peking, directly after the declaration of martial law, with the arrest of members of parliament. There was a constitutional clause depriving deputies of immunity with respect to crimes involving internal disturbance. Some twenty-one were arrested before the Second Revolution was over, two were shot, and eight were detailed indefinitely in great danger of their lives.[8] In fact, there were no legal protections. Although dispirited by this assault, the parliamentary wing of the Kuomintang held on admirably and did not fully dissolve until Yuan's formal expulsion of them from the national assembly and the mandated dissolution of the party on November 4, 1913, a measure which had been expected since the previous July.[9]

Terror also accompanied the movement of troops, particularly in the taking of Nanking in early September, 1913. The revolutionary forces in Nanking had behaved toward the population in an exemplary manner, keeping discipline and paying for their provisions. By contrast, the counter-revolutionary armies pillaged, raped, and burned for two weeks once in the city. Many residents were rendered destitute. Refugees left in the thousands for Shanghai. Damage was put at Ch$15,000,000 to Ch$22,000,000. The majority of the troops belonged to Chang Hsun, the independent satrap of western Shantung, once a member of Yuan's staff but an opponent of the republic, whose loyalties to the Peking government were dubious. His troops continued to sport the Manchu-style queue and, in their investment of Nanking, marched under Chang's personal flag rather than that of the republic. For Chang, the taking of Nanking was an opportunity to take revenge on the population for his defeat there during the 1911 Revolution.[10]

Although willing to purchase his loyalty and the use of his troops, Yuan from the beginning had no intention of allowing Chang to control Nanking. His departure was accomplished, through threats and funds, about the end of the year. He was replaced by Feng Kuo-chang. Repression in Kiangsu returned to more formal and organized channels.

The way in which the more routine official repression operated can be documented from particular cases in Honan. Both the 1911 and the 1913 revolutions passed by the province, whose government remained under Peking's control throughout, despite some stirrings in the provincial assembly. But when Yuan declared martial law, a commission of the military and the police undertook a campaign of arrests. The Chinese mail was opened and the recipients were held responsible for any imagined seditious content. Accusations from the general population were encouraged by awarding two-fifths of any fine to the accusers. Arrests were occasions for extortion, torture, and frequently execution.

A foreign employee of the Peking-Hankow railway in Chengchow, Honan, reported that two of his Chinese associates were arrested. Though not seriously political, they had joined the Kuomintang as the party of the revolution. Their incarceration was occasioned by a letter from another employee of the same railway in Peking that contained a phrase about deciding not to go south after all but to stay in Peking. The authorities interpreted this to mean that instead of joining the insurgent armies the writer would try to assassinate Yuan Shih-k'ai. This fabricated guilt was projected onto those who received the letter and led to their arrest. Another person was shot for receiving a letter that mentioned local disorder.

A young railway engineer was beaten to death on the orders of a minor police official for a letter from his home speaking of an unspecified "big affair" (*ta-shih*). On one particular day in early September, 1913, twenty-one gentry were executed in the provincial capital. Five of them were first paraded about town. In the same city, the military tribunal was next to the buildings of the China Inland Mission. The shrieks and groans of the tortured kept the foreign missionaries awake at night.[11] From these glimpses, we may gain some sense of life in Yuan's home province under the dictatorship.

Honan was the point of origin and also one of the areas of operation for a remarkable semipolitical bandit group whose leader, Pai Lang, through an alteration in the writing of his name, came to be widely known as White Wolf. Though operating since 1912, White Wolf was not the object of this first wave of severe repression in Honan. The repression was directed at the socially elite revolutionaries and their sympathizers, not at White Wolf's socially outcast constituency. Yuan's campaign of terror is to be distinguished from conventional "bandit suppression," which was pursued by all powerholders in the early republic, whether agents of Yuan or members of the revolutionary movement in office. After the Second Revolution, White Wolf's group grew impressively and for months resisted large-scale military operations against it. It acquired recruits of higher social origins, partly as a result of the forced disbandment of revolutionary military units in neighboring provinces, but also from refugees from Honan's official terror. White Wolf's movement was suppressed in the summer of 1914, but the campaign of political repression continued.[12]

The brutality and random quality of repression in Honan was not unique but lay perhaps on the extreme end of the spectrum. A newspaper reported in May, 1914, that in the course of a year twenty-two thousand people had been killed there. Chang Chen-fang, the military governor—a *chin-shih* of 1892 and a native of the same Honan district as Yuan Shih-k'ai, to whom he was related by marriage—was unusually incompetent as well as cruel, despite his extensive administrative experience. He was eventually sacked for his failure to crush White Wolf. But was it really much better to live in Hunan under T'ang Hsiang-ming, where, according to one estimate, about five thousand people were executed in 1914?[13] Persecution was less intense, though not absent, in some provinces not yet fully integrated into Peking's administration. In the Szechwanese capital, Kuomintang members were given time to dissociate themselves from their old political affiliations. Though the countryside remained unsettled in 1914, political executions in Chengtu were at the comparatively low rate of ten a month.[14] In Chekiang, the dispersion of the formal Kuomintang structure was accomplished without much fuss. But special surveillance measures were still in effect in the summer of 1914. When the province broke with Yuan in 1916, there were 147 political prisoners to be released.[15]

This enthusiasm for what is now called internal security spawned a profusion of secret police. Yuan Shih-k'ai had proposed the development of such a force as early as the summer of 1912.[16] In a remarkably short time, the phenomenon began to feed on itself. For example, the chief of Peking's twelve thousand detectives, a man who had arranged the arrest and summary executions of many, was himself sentenced to death in October, 1913, for conspiring to assassinate the president. Perhaps he was the victim of the jealousy of the military police.[17] In Shanghai, secret agents of the authorities in Soochow thought they were entrapping revolutionaries when they offered to sell arms to men who were in fact secret agents of Chang Hsun. Chang Hsun's men were arrested twice—once adventitiously for possession of opium and then as part of the entrapment scheme—before all the mutual deceptions were exposed.[18] A high Peking official had the experience of finding a social gathering he had attended reported to Yuan Shih-k'ai as a meeting of revolutionary students with Japan's top continental adventurer.[19] These comic contradictions within the system were the predictable by-product of the Chinese elite turning on itself.

Rebellious sentiment remained alive. The nationwide repression probably helped to sustain it through 1914. Uprisings and plots on a small scale (and a rather large scale in the case of White Wolf and some activity in Kwangtung) occurred in most provinces, perhaps all of them. The connection of any particular incident to the veteran revolutionary leadership was more problematical. For example, the temporary seizure of the city of Tali in Yunnan by troops there in December, 1913, was blamed by the provincial government on Li Ken-yuan, among others. Li Ken-yuan had been Yunnan chief of the T'ung-meng hui but was in Tokyo at the time of the Tali uprising and in his memoirs professes to have known nothing of the affair.[20] There were no doubt many similar cases. The authorities sought comfort in attributing all discontent to a single network of "cold-hearted" revolutionary agitators. Torture could always prove it.

The revolutionary leaders were active, though less than was officially

"LOWER CLASS" VIOLENCE AGAINST A MODERN PRIMARY SCHOOL
USING A TEMPLE BUILDING, HUNAN, 1913

From *Chen-hsiang hua-pao,* Shanghai, July 1, 1913.

A WOMEN'S MILITARY DETACHMENT IN THE 1911 REVOLUTION

Courtesy of Mitchell Library, Sydney, Australia.

TUAN CH'I-JUI
*Army Minister, 1912–15, and
Prime Minister Briefly in 1913
and Intermittently during 1916–18*

From Thomas F. Millard, *Our Eastern
Question*, New York, 1916.

YUAN SHIH-K'AI
President, 1912–16

Courtesy of Mitchell Library, Sydney, Australia.

FENG KUO-CHANG
*Military Chief in Chihli, 1912–13,
and in Kiangsu, 1913–17*

From Edwin J. Dingle, *China's Revolution: 1911–12*, Shanghai, 1912.

CHANG HSUN
*Pro-Ch'ing Satrap along
Tientsin-Pukow Railway*

From B. L. Putnam Weale,
The Fight for the Republic in China,
New York, 1917.

WELLINGTON KOO
*Councillor in Foreign Ministry,
1912–15, and Minister to the
United States of America and
Cuba, 1915–18*

Courtesy of Library of
Congress collection.

CHOU HSUEH-HSI
*Intermittently Finance Minister,
1912–16*

From Thomas P. Millard, *Our Eastern
Question*, New York, 1916.

T'ANG SHAO-I
Prime Minister in 1912

From Thomas E. Millard, *Our
Eastern Question,* New York, 1916.

LIANG SHIH-I
*Aide to Yuan in
Finances and Politics*

From B. L. Putnam Weale,
The Fight for the Republic in China,
New York, 1917.

SUNG CHIAO-JEN
Drafter of the Provisional Constitution, 1912, and Organizer of KMT, Assassinated March, 1913

Courtesy of Mitchell Library,
Sydney, Australia.

HU HAN-MIN
Military Governor of Kwangtung, 1911–13, and Revolutionary Activist

Courtesy of Mitchell Library,
Sydney, Australia.

SUN YAT-SEN
Senior Statesman of Revolution and Director of Railway Development, 1912–13

From John Stuart Thomson, *China Revolutionized*, Indianapolis, 1913.

DRAFTERS OF THE "TEMPLE OF HEAVEN" CONSTITUTION, 1913

From B. L. Putnam Weale, *The Fight for the Republic in China*, New York, 1917.

LIANG CH'I-CH'AO
*Progressive Party Organizer,
Minister of Justice, 1913–14,
and Leader in National Protection Movement against Yuan*

From B. L. Putnam Weale, *The
Fight for the Republic in China*,
New York, 1917.

LI YUAN-HUNG
*Hupeh Military Governor,
1911–13, and National Vice-
President, 1912–16*

From Edwin J. Dingle, *China's Revolution: 1911–12*, Shanghai, 1912.

Ts'ai O
Military Governor of Yunnan,
1911–13, and Leader in
National Protection Movement
against Yuan, 1915–16

From B. L. Putnam Weale,
The Fight for the Republic in China,
New York, 1917.

attributed to them and even then often in support of local groups rather than leading them. Sun Yat-sen, upon his arrival in Japan in August, 1913, sought to win Japanese support for another anti-Yuan effort with promises of privilege. And he tried to rally the leading exiled revolutionary cadres in a new organization of greater discipline (the Chinese Revolutionary Party). The material was there: the Japanese foreign office listed 260 important Chinese exiles in Tokyo in May, 1914.[21] Despite only very limited success in acquiring cash and comrades, Sun dispatched agents to keep the fires hot at home. He may have tried to establish links with White Wolf, who might threaten Peking from the west. In January, 1914, he sent Ch'en Ch'i-mei and Tai Chi-t'ao, veterans of the 1911 Revolution in Shanghai, to Talien (in Japanese, Dairen) to organize a revolutionary thrust from the northeast. The arrest of some of his emissaries by the Peking government, the intervention on Yuan's behalf by the Japanese government (which possessed Talien), and the failure of Japanese businessmen to come through with funds doomed the program to failure.[22] In a style and with a doggedness reminiscent of his activities before the 1911 Revolution, he nonetheless persisted, for example in efforts to incite military men to revolution in Chekiang in October, 1914, and in Kiangsi in 1915.[23] Meanwhile, another faction of former Kuomintang revolutionaries organized bandit groups in Kwangtung for an attack on Fo-shan in November, 1914, as part of a general campaign against the atrocious government of Lung Chi-kuang in Canton. Over a hundred casualties ensued, and the effort failed. At the end of the month, military prisons in Kwangtung held sixteen hundred inmates, with daily executions to reduce the number.[24]

Both organized revolutionary activity and systematic repression tapered off with the trauma of the Twenty-One Demands, a startling demarche by Japan that was the focus of political attention from January to May, 1915. Yuan Shih-k'ai's offer of amnesty for the rebels of 1913, first put forward in May, 1914, for those who had not been leaders, was broadened in February, 1915. There was a response. The desire of some Japanese to exploit the Chinese exiles for purely Japanese purposes had perhaps become too obvious. The insult to Chinese dignity and the threat to Chinese autonomy contained in the Japanese government's demands on Peking made cooperation with Japanese purposes intolerable for many exiles. Some one hundred fifty of them, though not Sun Yat-sen or his closest associates, left Japan and rallied to their government, despite its dictatorial character.[25] The time came in the summer of 1915 for a reconsideration of the direction the dictatorship should take. Meanwhile, the political and administrative institutions of the country had been profoundly altered.

Abolition of Representative Assemblies and Local Self-Government

Yuan's appetite for centralization seemed voracious. In his search for strength, he not only risked alienating large sections of the elite by his indiscriminate and bloody campaign against the Kuomintang, which had been the victorious party in the recent national election. He went further and tore down the whole structure of elective councils and assemblies that had grown up since the last years of the Ch'ing. He thereby tampered with the interests of the gentry class, which had taken hold of self-government institutions at all levels and in almost all places and knew how to benefit from them. Official foreign observers, who watched with at most only minor concern the government's slaughter of revolutionaries, were shocked at Yuan's audacity in offending the country's social elite by this measure.[26] Spurred on by his consciousness of China's weakness, Yuan, along with other like-minded political figures of the times, not necessarily in his entourage, saw representative assemblies as obstacles to more efficiency, greater revenues, and more administrative control. Despite his promotion of local representative bodies when Chihli governor-general, Yuan now abolished them in the name of national strength.

If Yuan was ready to antagonize major portions of the gentry, did he have a conception of an alternate base in the society on which to build his policies? There were at least elements of such a conception in both the rhetoric and the programs of the dictatorship. For example, part of the rationale for the suspension of self-government was its misuse by rapacious gentry at the expense of the common people. But if Yuan were to deal seriously with exploitation by gentry, the next step might logically have been the wooing of classes below the gentry. As we shall observe in the next chapter, he did make gestures in this direction. His gestures, however, were completely inadequate for the task. In brief, he was trying to establish absolute rule on the strength of a bureaucratic machine and lacked a social strategy. He was building for a great fall.

The dismantling of representative government occurred rapidly but not all at once. Some bodies were singled out for their special crimes and given individual attention. For example, Yuan ordered the Hunan provincial assembly dissolved on August 17, 1913, four days after its moderate Kuomintang military governor had rescinded the province's break with Peking during the Second Revolution. But the future was as yet undetermined, and the province was invited to elect a new assembly. Yuan still had need of representative government at the national level: most of the foreign countries were waiting for his formal election as president by the national assembly (as well as for assurances regarding their various claims against China's sovereignty) before they would officially recognize the republic. The remaining members, including many Kuomintang deputies, were induced by money and threats to perform this ritual on October 6, 1913. Thenceforth, the survival of the structure of elective assemblies became increasingly doubtful.

Yuan had been considering various schemes for dealing with the national assembly since it convened in the spring of 1913. But he was moved to take decisive action by the shape of the assembly's proposed constitution. Just as the assembly had been commissioned to change the status of the president from provisional to regular, so too was it charged to produce a permanent constitution to replace the provisional one written in Nanking at the end of the 1911 Revolution. The constitution-drafting committee included Kuomintang members. Many of the others had also been offended by Yuan's treatment of deputies over the summer. The resulting document, the Temple of Heaven draft, was designed to reduce presidential powers. Despite Yuan's victory over the Second Revolution, the national assembly, at the end of October, was about to try to impose by committees and votes what the Kuomintang revolutionaries had failed to achieve with arms. Yuan moved swiftly to incapacitate the national assembly (the first step was the expulsion of Kuomintang members on November 4), and eventually followed this up with the dissolution of all elective bodies.

Yuan's instrumentality in this period was the Political Conference (*cheng-chih hui-i*), convened on November 26, 1913, and lasting into the following June. It consisted of representatives appointed by the provincial governments, by the president, the prime minister, and the various departments of the central government. Its charge was to pool knowledge and discuss basic policy for the coming period of administrative reconstruction.[27] Its most active member, presidentially appointed, was the thirty-one-year-old Ts'ai O, recently military governor of Yunnan, whence he had been weaned by the opportunity to choose his successor and by the possibility of other jobs.

At first glance, it seems odd that Ts'ai O, the same man who raised the flag of revolt against Yuan's monarchical attempt in December, 1915, should earlier have been a major figure in establishing the dictatorship. But on the issue of centralization of power, Ts'ai stood with Yuan. When still military governor of Yunnan, he gave this impression of his ideas to a visiting journalist: "A purely parliamentary government will endanger the republican regime and the country itself: President Yuan Shih-k'ai must be invested with much enlarged powers. The political parties should disappear."[28] As were so many others who met him, Yuan was favorably impressed by Ts'ai's abilities, which together with a correspondence of views, presumably led to this and other appointments.[29]

Both general and specific arguments against the representative institutions of the liberal republic were put forward. At the most general level, the critique was one expressed by Liang Ch'i-ch'ao seven years previously in his debate with the T'ung-meng hui: given the size and complexity of China and the low level of education, the country was not ready for representative government. Liang believed in the superiority of republican institutions and contributed to the spread of knowledge about representative government. And he was not always so pessimistic about Chinese potential. But his doubts about what a premature adoption of democracy might actually produce were widely shared, among revolutionaries as well as reformers.[30] A few months after the convening of the national assembly, Liang revived his old theme and noted that the assembly had been formed hurriedly, lacked men of great ability, and was achieving nothing. "Although we highly value the national assembly," he wrote, "our esteem for it cannot compare to our regard for the nation." If such a measure would bring peace and prosperity to the nation, he concluded, the national assembly could be disdained and destroyed.[31] Although clinging to the hope that the national assembly would somehow prove itself according to his lights and privately disapproving of its dissolution when the moment came, Liang as a leading member of the cabinet at the time acquiesced in Yuan's measures.

Li Yuan-hung summed it up in an interview in mid-1914, after he had lost his base of power in Hupeh: "The condition of the people is such . . . that an iron rule is necessary. The people are still in a preparatory state rendering the rule and control of the central government essential. China tried government by the people, for the people, and chaos resulted: government must be by the few for the many."[32]

The specific charges against the national assembly were that it had passed no significant legislation, that its proceedings had been dominated by party struggles, reflecting private interests, that its members had been selected not by the true will of the people but by party machines, that it had neglected to show a strong rejection of rebellion by purging itself of the Kuomintang, and that it had obstructed the executive in its pursuit of the national welfare. On January 9, 1914, the Political Conference recommended that all remaining members be sent home.[33] It was done.

The contamination of partisan strife was charged also against the provincial assemblies. Even as parties blossomed during the liberal republic, anxieties regarding the propriety of open competition for political power were recurrent. Leading Kuomintang spokesmen bravely defended party struggle as a necessary and healthy feature of republican politics.[34] But the preference for the concealed rituals of bureaucratic power-broking was strong among the Chinese political elite. The tensions were sometimes unbearable. One of Liang Ch'i-ch'ao's associates quit in the early stages of party formation in 1912. He argued that party politics was "prejudiced and dissipated," and was leading to the collapse of the country.[35] In an atmosphere where such feelings were common, corruption and the electoral process were irresistibly drawn to each other; or rather, people were disposed to believe it so. A poster in Wuchang in early 1913 said: "Under monarchical despotism, censors are bought and sold. Under the despotism of the very rich, assembly members are bought and sold."[36] The provincial assemblies, like the national assembly, were told to expiate their sin of selfishness by dissolving.[37]

The relevant report of Ts'ai O's committee within the Political Conference, however, had a more elaborate argument. Willing to grant the integrity of most provincial assembly members, it questioned the structure that emphasized the province as the field of political contest. Chinese provinces, the report said, were the size of some European and American nations. If they were allowed to function as self-governing systems within the larger national unit, you would have federalism and worse. National unity would be impossible. The ultimate revival of a national assembly and local self-government organs, suitably purified and reformed, was assumed. The issue was the appropriateness of injecting intermediary elective bodies into the future system. The new national system, if not fully abolishing the provincial unit of administration, would in any case subordinate the provincial chiefs to the ministries in Peking to a degree unknown under the Ch'ing, according to Ts'ai's report. Counterbalancing representative organs would no longer be necessary at that level. So, although provincial administrators in a petition to Yuan had asked only for a temporary suspension of provincial assemblies, the Political Conference, on February 27, 1914, recommended their abolition, at least until final decisions were made about the total administrative system.[38] The assemblies—those that still remained—were ordered dissolved the next day.

For the dissolution of self-governing bodies below the provincial level, Yuan proceeded on his own in early February, 1914. The Political Conference added its support and buttressed the rationale a month later. Here Peking was delving even more deeply into the Chinese social order. The bill of particulars could be divided into two categories. It was charged that first, although basically a good idea, local self-government organs had usurped powers properly belonging to higher levels of government and thereby obstructed administration and siphoned off revenue. Second, by their indiscipline and avarice, they provoked the common people and thereby brewed discontent and rebellion.[39] The finger was pointed at gentry power.

There was no need to manufacture evidence. Lower class protest against these institutions, noted in chapter 1, continued into the republic. Even during the revolution, there were cases in which the populace sided with the imperial officials against the self-government leaders who were joining the revolution.[40] In Chekiang, where revolutionaries had worked closely with local educational and self-government groups in spreading the revolution, there were complaints by the spring of 1912 about the corruption and self-serving schemes perpetrated by self-governing organs at the city, town, and rural community level.[41] On the eve of the Second Revolution, in Chan-hua county in northwest Shantung, popular anger centered on the county self-governing assembly, which was said to be composed of the wealthy and privileged. It was alleged that the assembly members used their position to exploit the poor farmers and fishermen of the area. A large new tax on the fishing fleet provoked 100 villages into sending representatives to the county capital to assault the county assembly and its members. The magistrate, who was chosen locally, intervened to negotiate a settlement.[42] Across the border in Chihli, the assembly of Hsien county was accused of malfeasance in its handling of funds for riparian works and for schools. The local population organized in response, took its charges to the magistrate, proved them, beat up the county's chief education official, and deposited him in the mud outside the city gates.[43] Systematic research is needed to determine the extent to which popular protest was directed against self-government councils and their programs in this period. But at least we can say that, when Yuan's officials charged the self-governing bodies with exploitative behavior, they were identifying something also perceived by those being exploited.

Money taken from the population by the gentry-run self-government organs could also be funds denied higher levels of government. The income of the Shanghai city council nearly tripled between 1905 and 1913.[44] In Chekiang, whose civil governor added his voice to those registering complaints against the self-governing system, the self-governing body of Ningpo dominated the city's appointed officials.[45] In both town and country, local elective organs seemed to the administrators to be out of hand.[46]

By abolishing the whole panoply of local assemblies and councils, however, Peking was touching the sensitive nerves of local elite interest. Regarding the establishment of a local, eighty-man assembly in Soochow in early 1913, of roughly prefectural scope, an American consular official observed: "This republican form of self-government seems to be a continuation and expansion of the activities of the gentry with the infusion of new material in the form of younger men of more aggression and less property."[47] The invigorated self-government movement of the early republic, no matter how self-serving it might appear to the peasant or bureaucrat, could not be cut off without leaving a residue of resentment. Even under the dictatorship, newspapers dared argue against the action. An editorial in an organ of the Progressive Party, a few days after Yuan's order for dissolution, asserted that self-government was a necessity for a constitutional country, and the longevity of the nation and of the constitution depended upon the advance of local self-government.[48] In southern Honan, missionaries noted opposition in mid-February, 1914, among the well educated to "what they call the present reactionary policy of Yuan Shih-kai." The British consul in Shantung observed that, despite the reputation for corruption and extortion that had settled upon the self-government bodies, when they were abolished, the "lettered classes" responded with mistrust.[49]

More readily discernible than the muffled reports of discontent under the dictatorship was the eager return to the forms of local self-government as Yuan's regime crumbled in 1916. The governor in Kiangsu ordered his local magistrates to proceed directly with the reestablishment of local self-government at the moment that Yuan's star was indisputably setting.[50] At about the same time in Wuchow, Kwangsi, great joy was demonstrated at the return of local self-government, a main attraction in the break with Yuan.[51] In Chekiang some local self-government bodies were back in operation by the end of April, 1916.[52] A revolutionary contingent operating in Shantung on behalf of Sun Yat-sen's organization at the time of Yuan's death recognized the appetite for local self-government by facilitating gentry efforts to reorganize it. The significance of the gesture lay in two assumptions: that the issue would win them friends and that local self-government was a gentry function.[53]

Yuan was not entirely insensitive to all these possibilities. He had, after all, launched a representative system in Tientsin during his governor-generalship there (with a broader electorate but fewer powers than the slightly older Shanghai system). As he announced the abolition of the local assemblies in early 1914, he declared that previous legislation had constructed too many levels of assemblies and that the areas served by the assemblies had been too large. He instructed the ministry of internal affairs to devise new procedures for gradually reviving local self-government.[54] Similarly, planning for a new national assembly with a new name (*li-fa yuan*) was ordered.

In 1914 and 1915, however, Yuan was preoccupied with centralizing power. His promises of revived self-government were insufficient salves to the wounds he had inflicted on gentry pride and self-interest. The speed of preparation was unconscionably slow, and the early signs were that the result, even when it came, would not quicken the gentry pulse. Regulations for this or that aspect of the process were churned out regularly in Peking, but in late 1915 the prospect was for a September, 1916, opening of the national assembly. Requests that the revival of local self-government be hastened were rejected, and some official remarks indicated that even the highly controlled form being contemplated would take at least three years to become fully operational. In mid-1915, the minister of internal affairs spoke of the government's need for the assistance of "the gentry and people," but the assistance was asked on the government's terms. In the lengthy preparations for the new national assembly the gentry (for example, in Kiangsu) discovered that in the new dispensation extraprovincial officials, not local gentry, would manage the election and the winners were to be largely prearranged. The new electorate was well under 1 percent of the population, closer to the Ch'ing levels than to those of the liberal republic (when perhaps 4 percent or more of the population was registered). The notables had no interest in these pale imitations of their recent experience.[55]

Apparently undeterred by the rumblings of discontent, Yuan had taken a major step in centralizing authority. He had struck a blow against those people he characterized as "degraded local gentry, who use the management of education as an excuse to poach on public funds."[56] And government operations began to balance their budgets. In 1914, in contrast to the previous two years, provincial governments took in more revenue than they spent. Chia Shih-i, the chronicler of early republican finances, attributes the change to savings realized from the abolition of the local assemblies and their many schemes.[57] With Peking's power reaching firmly into most provinces, the surplus went to strengthen the central government.

The New Administrative System:
What to Do with the Provinces?

If we think of Yuan merely as head of a bureaucratic faction—the Peiyang clique of officials and military officers—then we would expect him to sit back and enjoy the fruits of his victory of 1913. His opposition was routed, the institutions that impeded his rule were destroyed, and he could appoint his own men at will to most parts of the country. But Yuan was not content with having his cohorts staff the inherited structures of authority. His pursuit of national strength through centralization led him further on.

We may assume that Yuan was infected by that endemic human disease, a belief in the intrinsic virtue of one's own power. But we can also recognize the special imperatives of China's international situation. Whatever strategy one adopted to turn back foreign encroachment on Chinese sovereignty, there was a built-in escalatory pressure to carry the strategy one step further, because the discrepancy between Chinese and foreign power remained so great. Yuan chose the strategy of bureaucratic centralization over that of mobilization through widespread opportunities for participation. Although he had smashed his enemies in 1913, he could not rest. He proceeded to enhance the position of Peking by tightening control over the provinces. The effort had two prongs: the reduction of the power of provincial administrations and the reduction of the power of military men, including his own, in those administrations.

Far-reaching proposals issued from the government during the fall of 1913. They were designed by the "cabinet of talents," installed during August and September under Prime Minister Hsiung Hsi-ling, a reforming official of the late Ch'ing and veteran of the 1898 reform movement, who had already served Yuan in other posts after the 1911 Revolution. The cabinet included the eminent gentry reformer and industrialist, Chang Chien, and was dominated by the ideas and energy of Liang Ch'i-ch'ao, also a cabinet minister. Working closely with the president's office, it publicly pressed for the abolition of the province as an administrative unit. As a complementary aspect of this aim, as well as an end in itself, it sought ways to bring the generals in the provinces under civilian control. Liang tied his continuance in the cabinet to achievement in these two areas.[58]

The idea of doing away with the province, in favor of administration directly through the circuit (about one-fourth or one-fifth of a province) or some lesser unit, was not new. K'ang Yu-wei had advocated it from abroad in the last years of the Ch'ing, and the question had been raised inside the Ch'ing bureaucracy. Ts'ai O proposed the measure to Sun Yat-sen's government in Nanking in early 1912. Liang Ch'i-ch'ao's Democratic Party (Min-chu tang), later absorbed into the Progressive Party, urged the measure from its founding in September, 1912. The idea insinuated itself into abortive proposals for administrative reorganization in the liberal republic. It was the subject of much debate.[59] But it had never been proclaimed as the policy of the Peking government.

Prime Minister Hsiung Hsi-ling did so, in November, 1913, in a long policy statement written by Liang Ch'i-ch'ao. The provincial administrative unit was too large, it was argued. Policies did not penetrate, and, with so many layers of administration, officials were divorced from the people. The solution was to pare the structure down to the two levels of the circuit (*tao*) and county (*hsien*).[60] When we consider the special vigor of provincial sentiment in the early twentieth century and the recent history of provincial autonomy, the proposal could hardly have been more radical. Of course, it was precisely the centralizing reformers' hostile response to burgeoning provincialism that inspired the idea to begin with.

But Yuan Shih-k'ai was unwilling to press it against provincial opposition. The new provincial chiefs, who were at first generally military men, were tasting provincial overlordship and presumably liking it. Yuan bluntly violated the interests of China's gentry elite, but, in the case of his own military servitors, he turned to more subtle methods of deflation, which we shall examine presently. Still, the thought did not die. Even as Peking's power was crumbling in 1916, Liang Shih-i prattled on about administering China without provinces.[61]

By early 1914, Yuan had been won over to a less drastic approach to administrative reorganization in the provinces. The results were promulgated by the summer. First, the names changed. The *tu-tu*, or military governor, became the *chiang-chün*, or general-in-chief. The civil governor, who had been known in most provinces possessing one as the *min-cheng-chang*, was renamed the *hsun-an-shih*. Behind the new titles lay a new apportionment of responsibilities. Before the Second Revolution the post of civil governor was limited to a few provinces and was used by Yuan in a generally unsuccessful attempt to insert Peking's power in places dominated by the Kuomintang. After the Second Revolution it was established in all provinces and was assigned formal precedence over the top military post (except in Chihli, where a civilian held both jobs after a short period of divided occupancy). All civil functions were taken from the military governor and given to the civil governor. In addition, over the protests of the army ministry and some provincial military commanders, the command over all old-style troops, still numbering in the many thousands, as well as over subprovincial local forces, went to the civil governor. The military governor, or the provincial general-in-chief in the new system, was to be in charge of the modern troops. He could use old-style troops only with the permission of the civil governor. Further, the generals-in-chief and their troops were to be worked into a national military system, administered by a headquarters directly under the president in Peking, where the attendance of the generals-in-chief would be periodically required. The aims of these reforms were unconcealed: to assert civilian administrative supremacy, to separate civil from military functions (old-style troops were regarded as keepers of local order, a civil job, not defenders of the nation, a military job), and to undermine tendencies toward regional military autonomy among the more powerful military units.[62]

The basic conception was not original. The resemblances to the Ch'ing system, though not perfect, were considerable. The separation of civil and military authority had been advocated, and contested, ever since the 1911 Revolution collapsed the two into one executive in most provinces. The

Peking government had unsuccessfully introduced a bill in the national deliberative assembly in July, 1912, that already contained several features of the 1914 system. Although the Kwangtung T'ung-meng hui and Li Lieh-chün, among others, had opposed the separation of military and civil powers, Sung Chiao-jen had urged it.[63] When Yuan had attempted to reduce the power of military governors during the liberal republic, it was reasonably interpreted as a maneuver against the Kuomintang. When he tried it in 1914 and 1915, the meaning was more general. Presumably he shared some of Liang Ch'i-ch'ao's sentiments, expressed in November, 1913: that the dominance of military men was an "illness," not just in the obvious case of Kwangtung, but also in Kiangsu, Anhwei, and Kiangsi, where Yuan's old associates were in command.[64] The problem was not factional, but national. So too was the effort to deal with it.

Yuan did not succeed in turning back the political weight of the military to its pre-1911 level. He declined to pursue more radical measures against military independence that were in the air: the abolition of provinces, or the creation of military districts apart from the provincial unit (one suggested number was nine), or the posting of the general-in-chief in a city other than the provincial capital.[65] But inroads occurred, evidence of some degree of seriousness. In two provinces, Fukien and Kweichow, the old post of military governor was abolished without any replacement at that level. In Fukien in particular, a strong civil administration was formed under the civil governorship of Hsu Shih-ying (1872–1964), a *chü-jen* from Anhwei, who in a long official career served the Ch'ing, Yuan Shih-k'ai, Tuan Ch'i-jui, and Chiang Kai-shek.[66] Even in Kwangtung, the civil governor managed to divest Lung Chi-kuang of some important responsibilities.[67] That something real had been taken away from the military chiefs in the provinces was indicated by Yuan's tactic of offering the return of civilian administrative authority to his generals when, like Feng Kuo-chang, they began to defect in 1916. And when a province did openly break with Yuan, it promptly returned to the pre-1914 system of a military governor (*tu-tu*, later *tu-chün*) with civil powers.

The final judgment on Yuan's effort to reassert civilian control must be that he did not press hard or far enough and failed, in the remaining two years of his rule, to reverse the military tide. The experience of Han Kuo-chün (1857–1942) illustrates both the reform's direction and its limitations. Han was a Kiangsu *chü-jen* with more than two decades' experience as a Ch'ing official at the county, circuit, and provincial levels. Following the Second Revolution, he was appointed civil governor in his home province, after assurances from Peking that his authority over civil affairs, especially finances, would be independent of the military. In some matters, at least, he successfully fought off military intervention. For example, he blocked Chang Hsun's efforts in October, 1913, to appoint county magistrates and *likin* collectors. A resident foreigner courting government assistance in land development and reforestation schemes at this time discovered that Han Kuo-chün was the man to see. Even where Han proved unable to assert his authority in the province, as in the inauguration of a unified police system, the obstacle seemed to be local interests, not the military governor. But Feng Kuo-chang, who succeeded Chang Hsun in the military post, secured Yuan's help in easing Han out, in the summer of 1914, in favor of a more pliant colleague. One defeat for civil supremacy. Han was then appointed civil governor of Anhwei, after several conferences with Yuan Shih-k'ai in Peking. With Han's arrival in Anhwei, the absolute rule of Ni Ssu-ch'ung, the general-in-chief and one of Yuan's cohorts from his years as Chihli governor-general, came to an end. Han replaced Ni in the senior of the two yamens in the capital and intervened in Ni's patronage system. He even dared to secure the dismissal of local magistrates whom Ni had earlier appointed. The resulting tension was characteristic of relations between the civil governor and the general-in-chief in several provinces. Han was able to hold on, presumably with Yuan's backing, until the launching of the monarchical movement in mid-1915. Ni was a leader in the movement, and Yuan further wooed his favor by transferring Han to Hunan. A second defeat for civil supremacy. Han had had enough and, without taking up the post in Hunan, retired to his home town, as was his habit when trouble was brewing.[68]

Han's case, which reflects reasonably well the pattern in most provinces, shows that Yuan was moving in the direction of checking the growth of independence among his military commanders but that he compromised before the results were decisive. He eschewed the radical measures of Liang Ch'i-ch'ao. The resignation of the Hsiung Hsi-ling cabinet in February, 1914, though linked to a number of issues, was in part an expression of disappointment with Yuan's decision not to override provincial feeling and military pretensions.[69] Still, Yuan continued to pursue lesser versions of centralization and civilian supremacy in the administrative reorganization of 1914, which permitted men like Hsu Shih-ying and Han Kuo-chün brief periods of prominence. The goal was a centralized bureaucratic state, staffed by sober men of experience, knowledgeable about both the modern world and the old established ways of Chinese officialdom.

Bureaucratic and Fiscal Controls

The nature of Yuan's goal, which was the same as that of the Ch'ing government in its last years, led to the revival of a variety of institutions and practices of the Ch'ing. The purpose was to recapture the power and reformist energy of the central government in its post-Boxer mood, and to go further. Yuan's belated participation in the overthrow of the Ch'ing had in no way derived from a rejection of the reforms of the dynasty's last decade. But he was unable, or was not disposed, to separate out those achievements from the political style that accompanied them. Since revived practices tended to embody old attitudes and old constraints, the effect was partly reactionary. Centralization, reform, and reaction became intertwined.

Centralized bureaucratic control was enhanced in a variety of ways. The attempted division of civil and military responsibilities, described above, had this aspect. The emergence of a more powerful civil governor checked military independence. Several generals-in-chief in the provinces were in fact summoned periodically to Peking, thereby underlining the national rather than regional character of military power. Their budgets were cut by Peking fiat. Fairly successful attempts to reintroduce the principle of avoidance in appointments—the rule that one did not serve in one's native province—were made in those areas under Yuan's direct control after the Second Revolution. Han Kuo-chün's transfer out of his native Kiangsu in the summer of 1914, though stimulated by Feng Kuo-chang's desire for local power, had this aspect as well. The purges of nonprovincials that had occurred in most provincial and local governments after the 1911 Revolution were reversed. A version of the censorate was revived, empowered to impeach wayward officials and invited to admonish the president (which, to Yuan's embarrassment, it did).[70] In provincial and local government, the center intervened even more forcefully than in the late Ch'ing. The civil governor was made more directly subordinate to Peking's ministries and was guided from Peking to a degree surpassing the Ch'ing. Under the civil governor the levels of local government were reduced (following a tendency apparent before Yuan's reorganization). The circuit was reintroduced (headed now by a *tao-yin*), a move interpreted at the time as giving Peking greater leverage in the provinces. Other intermediate levels (the *fu* and *chou*) were eliminated, until one reached the *hsien* or county. In general the new system was characterized by an economy-minded bureaucratic neatness.

Much attention was given to improving and monitoring the quality of officials. Although the results are debatable, Yuan's personnel management was nothing if not vigorous and self-confident. He used both carrot and stick. He raised the salaries of county magistrates and approved official pension and disability schemes.[71] On the other hand, in the first year of his dictatorship he pronounced a majority of county magistrates then in office as incompetent and ordered a wholesale review by the civil governors.[72] Dismissals, even executions, of magistrates, as well as special commendations, became familiar items among the orders of the president in 1914 and 1915. In another departure from the Ch'ing structure, an administrative court (*p'ing-cheng yuan*) for official crimes was established, and many cases were referred to it, involving officials at various levels.

A prominent case of punishment served to demonstrate the government's determination. At issue were the crimes of selling offices, accepting bribes, and using law suits to extort money. The accused was Wang Chih-hsing, of Shantung, who had served Yuan at Hsiao-chan and was a protégé of Hsu Shih-ch'ang and Chao Ping-chün, both intimate associates of Yuan (though Chao died suddenly before the case reached its dénouement). He had been a leading police official in Manchuria before the revolution. In October, 1913, he became governor of the Peking capital region. A censorial impeachment and investigation by the special court for officials brought out that he had sold twenty-two of the twenty-four magistracies in the capital area. He had embezzled local tax funds to buy land in Tientsin, and so forth. The evidence appeared conclusive. The case went from the administrative court to the ministry of justice to the supreme court. Yuan, according to ex post facto regulations, but to everyone's surprise, ordered him shot on October 21, 1914. Official corruption did not thereupon cease, but presumably the lesson and others like it in different parts of the country were inhibiting.[73]

Much effort was put into another form of quality control: examinations for official posts. The model was not the old literary examinations, which Yuan had helped to abolish in 1905, but the function-specific civil service examinations of contemporary Western-style bureaucracies. Although the way the examinations were administered tended to favor those with past administrative experience, the purely classical academic training of a literatus was insufficient. In December, 1913, it was ordained that all county magistrates, both those to be appointed and those currently in office, should pass a special qualifying examination (exemptions were sometimes granted). The examination was to test them in Chinese literature, existing laws and foreign treaties, the skills of local administration (judging cases, composing dispatches), and knowledge of popular customs. Using the vacated facilities of the national assembly, thousands began undergoing these tests in February, 1914, and the process was repeated every few months thereafter. The many presidential orders relating to the appointment of particular county magistrates in provinces in most parts of the country and specifying attainment in these exams, as well as occasional foreign observations, indicate that the combination of the examinations and the rule of avoidance had a major impact on staffing local offices. The effects were to loosen the grip of local social and political leaders on local administration and to reduce the number of young returned students in local administration in favor of former officials of the Ch'ing.[74]

Students returning from study abroad were not forgotten. Yuan in fact publicly deplored the lack of recognition given their special skills in the past. After all, he could present himself as a leading patron of foreign-educated Chinese, as we have seen in chapter 3. But it was generally not as local or provincial administrators that he felt them useful. Their usable skills did not apply to controlling the Chinese population but to the specialized needs of central ministries, of schools, banks, industry, hospitals, agricultural schemes, and so forth. As in the last years of the Ch'ing, a special examination served to qualify them for posts, largely in the central government. Although employment opportunities were very restricted in the fiscal retrenchment of the dictatorship, returned students who passed the examinations received appointments in respectable numbers (for example in early May, 1915, nine to the foreign ministry, nine to the ministry of internal affairs, twenty-two to the finance ministry, twenty-one to the ministry of agriculture and commerce, eighteen to the ministry of communications, sixteen to the ministry of education).[75]

There were other elaborations on the effort to improve the quality of officialdom. In September, 1914, Saturday lectures on local administration for the benefit of all officials in Peking were instituted, with grades awarded and the inducement of better appointments for the successful.[76] Plans were laid toward the end of 1915 for an examination qualifying one for the upper reaches of the civil service. The emphasis was on graduation from an institution of higher learning at home or abroad (although there were alternate prerequisites one might meet) and on Western subjects and foreign languages. One's grounding in Chinese literature and history was also tested. Further, special diplomatic and judicial examinations were instituted to qualify for service in the appropriate ministries.[77]

Some of these measures were plans, not accomplishments, and whatever execution that did occur was partial. The contemporary judgment on the results were mixed: some saw only a return to the stiff-necked obscurantism of the Ch'ing mandarinate. Others were impressed. Liang Ch'i-ch'ao, who was not a tradition-bound conservative and who participated in different capacities for two years, gives us the picture of a spare and capable bureaucracy, at least in Peking. As cabinet minister, he found himself compelled by the opinion of his staff to appoint only those qualified by ministerial standards. Even the president, he claimed with some exaggeration in the course of resisting patronage requests, did not dare to interfere in appointments within the ministeries.[78] Some years later he recalled that the staff of the currency bureau that he headed in 1914 had been a small group of hardworking men. That same office in 1917, when Liang was briefly finance minister, had become a home of corruption, he said.[79] Perhaps the best way to consider the administrative side of Yuan's dictatorship is as a respectable continuation of the tendencies of the reforming bureaucracy of the last years of the Ch'ing. It was not a recreation of pre-twentieth-century imperial officialdom, with its Confucian and precedent-bound perspectives. Nor was it even pointed in that direction. On the other hand, it was hardly bursting with energy. And like all reformist bureaucracies, it could perform no better than the tasks it was assigned. Yuan's vision of possibilities was narrow.

One task was clearly assigned to the reorganized bureaucracy: to balance Peking's budget without foreign loans. This meant the reduction of expenses and an increase in the flow of revenue to Peking. The achievement in this area was considerable. The price included setbacks to reform programs.

Retrenchment marked all levels of government. The finance ministry, for example, dismissed over 130 officials at the beginning of Hsiung Hsi-ling's cabinet in 1913. The new judiciary was radically pruned the next year. The modern police forces (though not, it seemed, the hordes of secret agents) suffered similarly. Peking successfully demanded reduced expenditure on the part of provincial governments. The axe fell on both provinces tightly bound to Peking and those still headed by local leaders. Hupeh under Peiyang leadership drastically consolidated offices and reassigned functions to fewer administrators. The Shantung budget was cut Ch$1 million in 1914 by order of the Peking government, and the general-in-chief had to reduce his staff. Peking turned back requests from Chekiang and Fukien to ease the retrenchment in their military budgets.[80] In view of the fact that, next to the foreign debt and indemnities, military expenditures were invariably the single most consuming item, the dip in the size of the military establishment during 1914 and 1915 shown in the estimates on table 5 had great fiscal meaning. Under the circumstances of the early republic, a smaller army could be achieved only by a relatively stronger central government.

TABLE 5

Estimates of the Number of Chinese Soldiers, 1911–28

Year	Number of Soldiers (in thousands)	Year	Number of Soldiers (in thousands)
1911	570	1920	900
1912	649	1921	1,050
1913	572	1922	1,060
1914	457	1923	1,190
1915	520	1924	1,330
1916	700	1925	1,470
1917	690	1926	1,580
1918	850	1927	1,700
1919	914	1928	1,830

Source: Oikawa Tsunetada, *Shina seiji soshiki no kenkyū* (Tokyo, 1933), pp. 758–59, citing materials from "reliable Chinese government sources."

Reducing expenditures was only half the job. The rest of the task was reviving the flow of funds from the provinces to Peking. Four main types of income were stimulated, all with some degree of success: remittances out of provincial funds, special national taxes or charges, revenues from the salt administration, and domestic loans. These were sources either nonexistent or largely denied to Peking between 1911 and the Second Revolution. Together, they provided about three-quarters of Peking's reported income in 1915 (about Ch$130 million, although this did not include certain items, such as government railway revenues).[81] Proceeds from foreign loans, which had played such a large role in 1912 and 1913, were in 1915 only a minor item. Partly this was necessity: the European war absorbed international capital. But it was also design: well before war broke out, Peking had begun to scale down the sums it was seeking to borrow abroad.[82] A kind of fiscal stability was achieved.

With the exception of the maritime customs revenue, which went in its entirety to service the foreign debt, all the main sources of national funds at this time depended upon the extension of central authority into the provinces. This was obviously so in the case of provincial government remittances and special national taxes. It was less obvious but also true of central government proceeds from the salt administration. The foreign salt inspectorate was established at roughly the same time as Yuan's program of centralization and, once established, was much more successful than other fiscal mechanisms in maintaining a flow of funds to Peking after Yuan's death. But the setting in place of the foreign inspectorate and the increases in remittances of salt revenue to the center were inconceivable without the extension of Peking's authority throughout the country from the summer of 1913. Indeed, despite the extraterritorial protection afforded the salt collections through international agreement and foreign staff, the remissions to Peking began to decline the year of Yuan's death, even as local collections tended to increase.[83] Similarly, the 1914 and 1915 domestic loans, engineered by Liang Shih-i and netting the central government substantial revenue, depended for their success not just on Liang's ingenious confidence-producing mechanisms (including foreign sponsors) but also on a cooperative bureaucracy covering the country and a growing network of national bank branches.[84]

Let us look at the fiscal relations between Kiangsu province and Peking during the dictatorship as an example of a common pattern. In 1913 Peking had introduced into the province a preparatory office for a national tax bureau (*kuo-shui t'ing ch'ou-pei ch'u*), with the idea of defining national tax sources, as opposed to those belonging to provincial and local government. The move was an attempt to get some share of local tax collections. It failed to do so and became defunct.[85] After the Second Revolution, the report on finances of the Political Conference (the same body that recommended the dissolution of national and provincial assemblies) urged that all local tax collection be unified under a central agency.[86] Now that Peking had administrative power in the provinces, separating national from local tax sources was no longer meaningful nor sufficiently advantageous to Peking. The goal of direct control over all revenue sources was put forward. It was the other, and more ambitious, side of Peking's assumption of the right to dictate the amounts of expenditure for particular items within the province.

Practice fell short of the goal, but the balance of power in negotiations had shifted to Peking by 1914. A Kiangsu branch of Peking's audit office was opened in January, 1914, but closed by August. It was tainted by its association with foreign controls stemming from the Reorganization Loan and had met local resistance. A provincial finance office (*ts'ai-cheng t'ing*) directly under the central finance ministry, however, struck roots. The civil governor was provisionally assigned functions with respect to this office. Meanwhile, old taxes were consolidated and new taxes were added. The land and grain taxes which had been collected only leniently since the 1911 Revolution but had nominally increased with local surcharges, were in 1914 to be collected in full for accounting to the central government, with the local surcharges absorbed into the centralized accounting. One tael of the prerevolutionary land tax, which was commuted to Ch$1.50 of tax at the time of the revolution, became Ch$2.335 of tax by the end of 1915. Similarly, the grain tribute tax, commuted to Ch$5 per picul after the 1911 Revolution, had grown by 30 to 40 percent in early 1915 and was threatening to grow still more. New national duties included various wine and tobacco taxes, land transfer fees, and fees for the re-registration of land deeds. The proceeds of the domestic loans went to Peking.

The question of how much of these various heads of revenue, formally defined as national, should stay with the province was a matter for negotiation. The amount of provincially collected revenues that General-in-chief Feng Kuo-chang was permitted to keep for military expenses declined from Ch$7.6 million in 1914 to Ch$4.3 million in 1915, to a projected Ch$3.6 million for 1916. Kiangsu's overall requests for funds (in the form of a budget proposal) were reduced in early 1915 by 25 percent. The provincial government managed to bargain the cut down to 15 percent. This translated into a projected expenditure of almost Ch$9 million out of an estimated provincial government revenue of over Ch$13 million. With roughly the same estimated revenue the previous year, the provincial budget had exceeded Ch$11 million. The surpluses went to Peking in frequent remissions throughout the year. Furthermore, Kiangsu as a geographical area was funding Peking's budget in a variety of other ways that formerly fed the provincial government. For example, the large salt revenues in Kiangsu figured nowhere in these estimates, since they were completely removed from local accounting as an item of direct national revenue, in the manner of some of the special fees.[87]

These fiscal measures appeared to be an impressive increase of central intervention over the Ch'ing system, let alone the provincial autonomy of the liberal republic. Roughly similar measures were taken in most provinces. Even in distant and unconquered Yunnan, Peking was able to decree a reduction of almost a fifth in the 1915 army budget as against that of the previous year.[88] Nevertheless, a degree of scepticism about the quality of the achievement is warranted. First, the proliferation of taxes and their steady increase stimulated complaints and unrest. Local gentry, who had happily raised taxes through self-government bodies for local projects, were no longer consulted systematically. Merchants, victims of many special fees and of the reviving *likin,* were outraged. Second, the fiscal result, even discounting the loss of salt revenue from provincial accounting, was still less than the proceeds from late Ch'ing tax collections that were accounted for at the level of provincial government. Third, full centralization remained elusive. A foreign consular student of Kiangsu revenues observed toward the end of 1914: "It seems that the Civil Governor and the Finance authorities at the Provincial Capital must always, no matter how strongly they adhere to the Central Government, take to a large extent the colour of local opinion, or officially perish; and that the control of the Central Government can never be complete or arbitrary, even in the moment of military triumph."[89]

This judgment surely reflected some hard political realities that were bound to frustrate Yuan's program. Centralization by military and administrative means, though pursued with greater success by Yuan than his successors of the next two decades, produced a result incommensurate with its terrible human costs. It did not generate national power adequate to fend off imperialist encroachment. Indeed, the question remains whether the administratively decentralized and fiscally chaotic institutions of the liberal republic would not have done as well or better in generating the overall social energy that might hold foreign power at bay. True, the liberal republic entailed gentry aggrandizement and official suppression of peasant resistance; part of its energy was thereby diverted from reformist and anti-imperialist tasks. Yuan perceived the destabilizing consequences of gentry aggrandizement. But his strategy, instead of successfully tapping the political energy latent in the nonelite portions of the population, had the practical effect of suppressing elite *and* nonelite movement outside the government. In Yuan's politics, both the KMT and White Wolf were enemies who had to be destroyed. We must acknowledge Yuan's achievements, but we cannot ignore the high price, which tended to vitiate the fundamental nationalist objectives of the achievements. The rewards of bureaucratic centralization have often been overestimated and its defects overlooked. Its abuses were amply illustrated in Yuan's dictatorship.

Response of Yuan's Foreign Friends and Helpers

There was, of course, no uniform foreign view of Yuan's abandonment of limited representative government in favor of dictatorship. By some he was excoriated. The British journalist B. Lenox Simpson (known to his readers as Putnam Weale) and many Japanese observers were in this group. Others urged him on. After his assault on the Kuomintang in early November, 1913, the *North China Herald* in Shanghai, which often reflected British business and financial interests, editorialized: ". . . the only real cause of complaint is surely that the resulting dictatorship is not, as yet, absolute enough, while the form of Parliamentary administration, admittedly impracticable in China, still retains sufficient vitality to clog the actions of those who know what ought to be done."[90] After all traces of representative government had been swept away, an editor of the *Times* of London assured Yuan's chief foreign adviser of the paper's general support for Yuan's administration, despite occasional criticisms. The *Times,* he wrote, "does not care a straw about any deviations from the strict 'constitutional' path which the President may have found necessary."[91]

From Yuan's point of view, the practical question was the policies of the governments of the imperialist powers. They could be summarized in two aspects: (1) The governments all supported Yuan's regime, in the sense that they gave no serious consideration to alternative candidates for leadership. Japan was the country least committed to this proposition, especially in its army general staff, but formal cabinet policy departed from it only in 1916. (2) Even as they supported Yuan, the foreign powers all continued to make demands on the Peking government in the pursuit of their own interests, thereby rendering his leadership more difficult. Some were more insistent than others. Germany was removed as an actor in the Far East by the consequences of the outbreak of war in Europe. Japan took advantage of the war to attempt to realize her accumulated desires and unfulfilled dreams regarding China in one grand confrontation. I shall discuss these features of Yuan's environment in the next chapter.

A separate and particularly interesting category are those individual foreigners close enough to Yuan to feel some of the responsibility for what had happened. Though imperfectly informed, they knew the general features of Yuan's policies and their human meaning. In the case of several prominent foreign participants in Peking politics during the dictatorship, we have detailed knowledge of their responses. Their cases present to us the moral problems and intellectual traps of the foreign adviser and technical assistant in a semicolony.

John Newell Jordan (1852–1925), British minister, represented his government and was not an independent agent. Nonetheless, he dispensed his own advice liberally, often without first checking with London. An old acquaintance of Yuan's, he was disposed to sympathize with Yuan's rule. But curiously, Jordan seems to have been more divided in his responses to the dictatorship than many other close Western observers. On the one hand, he was wont to praise Yuan and justify his behavior to London. Like Yuan, he had from the beginning been sceptical about the suitability of republican institutions in China and saw the national assembly as characterized by disorder and the absence of even "a stroke of constructive work." He wrote of Yuan after his death as "a great man and a true patriot," as someone who had an "admiration of British ideals."[92] On the other hand, Jordan was sensitive to some of the more brutal aspects of Yuan's regime, and entertained doubts about the wisdom of Yuan's basic policies.

While the representative assemblies were being dismantled, Jordan wrote disapprovingly that Yuan "is attempting to govern China very much on the British Crown Colony system." Perhaps Jordan did not recall that this was precisely the model recommended to Hu Han-min in 1912 by the governor of Hong Kong. In any case, Jordan did not think it sturdy: "It rests on too small a basis and is becoming more and more a one-man affair."[93] Even before Yuan became president, Jordan had suspected that a military dictatorship was in store for China. Three and one-half years later, he pronounced the military dictatorship a fact, presumably even less desirable for China than the British colonial style: "a despotism which [in contrast to the Manchu regime] I should hesitate to describe as benevolent. . . ."[94] In March, 1914, Jordan was sufficiently disturbed by what he reported as "something in the nature of a 'reign of terror' " to suggest to Yuan (with no immediate effect) a general amnesty.[95] But rectifying a deplorable situation that he had helped to bring into being by crucial support to Yuan on the eve of the Second Revolution was not Jordan's conception of his task. What he described as a wartime policy was generally true: "Personally, I had only one policy and that was to try and keep China intact as a commercial asset during the War."[96] Jordan could feel secure and reduced the personal dilemma by retreating behind the imperative of British policy. Hence, he felt relieved of the need to justify his association with a regime partly built on terror.

Yuan's formal foreign advisors had less to hide behind and were more uncomfortable. Two lines of defense were common. The first was to deny culpability by claiming lack of influence. It was a constant refrain among foreign advisors of the Chinese government, and much exaggerated, that they were not kept informed and were not listened to. The second was to accommodate to Yuan's policies and to justify them to oneself and others. A reason for their initial hiring was the expectation that they would communicate Peking's viewpoint forcefully to their own countries. The expectation was fulfilled in the cases of Yuan's three most prominent advisers: George Ernest Morrison (1862–1920), former Peking correspondent for the *Times* (an Australian who functioned as a Britisher); Ariga Nagao (1860–1921), an eminent Japanese scholar of international law and professor at Waseda University; and Frank Johnson Goodnow (1859–1939), professor of administrative law and municipal science at Columbia University, soon to be appointed president of Johns Hopkins University.

Among Morrison's several functions in the Peking government was that of publicist and press agent. Owing to his reputation as the leading foreign authority on Chinese politics and to his journalistic skills and contacts, he did a superb job of influencing Western opinion and discreetly feeding Chinese official views to international news services, especially Reuters. But he was unhappy with his lot. He periodically resolved to quit, though he stayed on as presidential adviser until his death in 1920. While generally putting the best possible face on Yuan's policies in his public remarks and his active correspondence with notables around the world, especially in Britain, he did not manage to persuade himself and suffered anguish at his association with an unsuccessful enterprise. Though well informed about Yuan's campaign of terror, he apparently did little to check it. He exerted himself in one or two specific instances to try to rescue victims, but let others pass by. More than most other foreigners close to the government, he advocated representative government for China. He was increasingly prone to vent his disgust openly to high officials in the administration, including Yuan Shih-k'ai. But he did not undertake serious agitation until mid-1915, and even then the burden of his complaint was that China bungled everything and was not powerful like Japan.[97]

Ariga Nagao, perhaps the best paid of Yuan's generously salaried advisers, also usefully represented Peking's views to his home government. He took Yuan's part during the negotiations over the Twenty-One Demands. He managed to communicate the seriousness of the matter to the Japanese elder statesmen (*genrō*), who had been left poorly informed by the aggressive foreign minister, Katō Kōmei. The result was a dressing down for Katō, a softening in the Japanese position, and virulent attacks on Ariga by Japanese expansionists.[98]

The job for which Ariga had been hired was to assist in drafting a constitution, but, as in the crisis of the Twenty-One Demands, Yuan sought from him political services. An earlier example was Yuan's request for advice in June, 1913, on how to handle the recalcitrant national assembly. Ariga protested that it was inappropriate for him as a scholar and on his present assignment to give such advice but then immediately suggested a manipulative tactic (that was not adopted).[99]

Ariga was not keen on Western models of representative government, even for the West. What China could learn from France or America, he felt, was quite limited. China was not ready for a "liberal republic" (*jiyū kyōwa*), he wrote.[100] A melding was necessary between the old imperial system and the new republican one, so that national order could accompany progress and so that old and new forces could be harmonized. Almost his first public suggestion was a revival of ceremonies for the worship of heaven.[101] Though surprised upon his arrival at Peking in early March, 1913, at the high degree of both order and general satisfaction with the republic, he was distressed at the indifference he found toward the Chinese political tradition and its replacement by ideas borrowed from the West. "So whenever I see anyone, I urge the necessity of making connections with the old thought." Hardly anyone agreed, he noted.[102] He took the subsequent chaotic performance of the national assembly (its "disorder and incapacity") as validating his view.[103] Ariga and Yuan were on very similar wave lengths in these matters.

Ariga's stance contained in addition the special anxieties of a Japanese conservative in a world of potentially falling dominoes. It was a great defect in representative government, he wrote at the time, that it involved majority rule, since the majority was made up of the poor. Socialist parties might thrive in such a structure, as they seemed to in some parts of Europe. It was from this perspective that he opposed too broad an electorate in the Chinese republic. The vote in the hands of the masses might lead to socialism in China. The infection might spread to Japan, he speculated, which had so far managed to keep the franchise limited.[104] Morrison in early 1916 was urging on Yuan the immediate restoration of the provisional constitution and the national assembly to save a desperate situation for the Peking government. At the same time Ariga argued that as much as possible of the policies of "conservative centralization" of the previous two years be preserved. If a legislative assembly was required for political reasons, Ariga held, then it should be partially appointed and the elections should be indirect and highly restricted in suffrage.[105] In general it might not be unfair to say that Ariga's main influence on Yuan Shih-k'ai was to reinforce his scepticism about the value of vigorous representative institutions.

For a second constitutional adviser, Yuan wanted a republican, since in early 1913 he was concerned about accusations of imperial ambitions and needed a balance to Ariga, who was a monarchical subject. He also wanted someone expert on the French constitution, to which he was attracted by the nonpartisan, magisterial, and arbitrative role of the president and, presumably, by its centralism.[106] When Yuan accepted the recruiting services of the Carnegie Endowment to fill the post, in a manner arranged by Charles W. Eliot, president emeritus of Harvard, he got Frank J. Goodnow. Goodnow, though a generally knowledgeable political scientist, was not an authority on the French constitution. Nor did he prove to be a confirmed republican. But he served Yuan faithfully during his brief tenure.

Goodnow had been the first president of the American Political Science Association, which was not quite ten years old when Goodnow came to China. The new republic in Asia was an object of great interest to some leading members of the association—a place to test theories and offer the special wisdom of Western social science. Another former president of the association, Woodrow Wilson, was entering the White House as Goodnow signed on with Yuan Shih-k'ai. One of Wilson's first initiatives in foreign policy concerned China—the withdrawal from the consortium. Of course his main attentions were directed elsewhere, but others in the association, like Goodnow, became more deeply involved. Wilson appointed as American minister to Peking Paul S. Reinsch, professor at the University of Wisconsin, who had been the association's vice-president in its first year and was a member of the board of editors of the association's journal when he went to Peking. James Bryce, the famous British scholar of the American system, who had served a year as president of the association while British ambassador in Washington, toured China after leaving the ambassadorship and was chairman of the Anglo-Chinese Friendship Bureau in 1914. He freely offered his advice through Jordan and Morrison (and perhaps directly to Yuan) in support of executive absolutism, a carefully planned succession of power, and monarchy.[107] Professor Jeremiah W. Jenks of Cornell and New York University, who had been chairman of the initial organizing committee of the association, established a public relations service in New York (the Far Eastern Information Bureau) for the Chinese government on a Chinese stipend (US$1,500 a month).[108] Goodnow, when he resigned his job in China to accept the presidency at Johns Hopkins, arranged that Westel Woodbury Willoughby, yet another former president of the youthful American Political Science Association and managing editor of its journal, should be his successor.[109] With a sizable proportion of its leading lights concerned, American political science was poised for its first great contribution to the exportation of modernization. Of those residing in Peking, Reinsch was preoccupied with diplomacy. The starring role for assisting China's internal development fell to Goodnow.

Recently, Goodnow's contributions to political thought have been hailed by a leading theorist of political modernization. Between the Federalist Papers and the 1950s, Gabriel A. Almond has written, Goodnow's "systematic and creative leads" were unrivaled insights into the functional theory of politics.[110] The application of these insights to China—an aspect of Goodnow's work to which Almond understandably does not address himself—has not enjoyed such a good reputation.

Like other foreign employees of China who did not directly control large amounts of Chinese revenue, Goodnow was disappointed in the reception accorded his expertise. But he worked with a will. Although excluded from the national assembly's constitutional committee on grounds of his link to the executive, he met regularly with the president's legal experts. He drafted a moderately liberal constitutional proposal, combining the American model of an independent, fixed-term presidential executive with the French supremacy of the center over the provinces, but with a considerable role for the national parliament.[111] Soon after his arrival, however,

the Second Revolution broke out. He reported back to the Carnegie Endowment his sense that the trend was toward dictatorship and that "whatever form of government may be adopted, he [Yuan] will run the show
one way or another. . . ."[112] That he might resign over the gradual demise of representative government seems not to have occurred to him. In
part, he may have accepted the philosophy suggested by a New York friend
that an illiberal and reactionary government cannot dispense with a constitutional adviser "any more than the large corporations here who intend to
disregard the law start out without the best lawyer of the land in their
cabinet."[113] He also began to believe in the necessity of Yuan's policies
and ended up publicly defending them.

By his approach to politics Goodnow was led continually to refashion
his position. He believed that institutions, in their multifunctional complexities, must accord with realities if they were to prosper. He was willing
to work with a definition of reality given him by ingrained Western notions
of Chinese incapacities, by the views passed on by the restricted circle of
his Chinese acquaintances (including Yuan Shih-k'ai), and by the faits
accomplis of the Peking government (his employer). His functionalism
became, in practice, an instrument for justifying a flight from liberalism.

Not long after his arrival in 1913 he became a participant in Yuan's dictatorial moves. When the national assembly proposed a constitution with
clear legislative supremacy and Yuan outlawed the Kuomintang in response, Goodnow took Yuan's side. Just before the crackdown, Goodnow
published an attack on the assembly's draft. Soon after the crackdown he
published an article arguing Yuan's case regarding presidential rights in
constitution making.[114] He had not given up on some sort of representative
government but started proposing highly limited forms. He urged Yuan
not to dissolve the national assembly completely.[115] When that happened
anyway, he developed with Ariga a scheme involving an assembly partly
appointed and partly elected on the basis of the functional representation
of certain classes (literati, merchants, and landowners).

As Goodnow's commitment to representative government for China
attenuated, he became an apologist for the dictatorship. He chimed in with
others in pronouncing the former national assembly unfit.[116] In May,
1914, Yuan's government fashioned and promulgated the so-called Constitutional Compact, in theory a revision of the Nanking provisional
constitution, pending the drafting of a permanent constitution, but in
practice a ratification of Yuan's autocracy. Although Goodnow and Ariga

reasonably disclaimed full responsibility for this document, they probably influenced aspects of it. At any rate they met frequently in subsequent weeks with the president and his staff to discuss its implementation. In a report to the Carnegie Endowment, Goodnow made this comment on the Constitutional Compact: "Most of the ideas which I recommended in the draft I made about a year ago have been adopted, although they have given the President somewhat greater independence of the legislature than I had proposed. I must confess, however, that on the whole I approve of what has been done."[117] In an article published in America that year, Goodnow concluded that "for quite a time to come the function of a Chinese representative body should in large measure be consultative and advisory."[118] In the guise of prescription, Goodnow was describing, and implicitly endorsing, the institutions by which Yuan had decided to rule for the time being, that is, advisory councils.

Goodnow's work in Peking was interrupted by his acceptance of the offer of the presidency of Johns Hopkins University. He left China in the summer of 1914, promising to return the subsequent summer if his services were required.

Appropriately, he reported the findings of his experience, not only to the press, but also to the American Political Science Association at its annual meeting in Chicago, December, 1914. In an address entitled "Reform in China," he described a China, which like the rest of Asia was bound to lose out to Western efficiency in the emerging conflict between East and West. To remedy her lack of the institutional and psychological preconditions for industrial development, China must in these matters "rely very largely on foreign management and submit to foreign control." In the political and social sphere, Goodnow reported, she was without the concept of political authority (but relied instead on ethical and customary notions), without the rule of law, without the idea of individual rights, without discipline, and without the concentrations of property and organized classes characterizing the European societies where parliaments began. He counseled his audience that "a form of government which has many of the earmarks of absolutism must continue until she develops greater submission to political authority, greater powers of social cooperation and greater regard for private rights." "Representative government," he asserted, "certainly in forms in which we find it in the modern European states, may well be impossible of adoption in China until such time as greater capacity for social cooperation has developed."[119]

Goodnow's analysis contained two remarkable assumptions. First, his conception of development postulated a unilinear progress of societies, whose culmination was the contemporary Western model.[120] Given the nature of this scale and China's position on it, China's dependency and her need for tutoring were made to seem natural. The second assumption, flowing partially from the first, was that the route to national independence in China's case lay through greater foreign control. We have also observed this attitude among foreign government officials: China could be saved from the powers only by putting herself more firmly into their hands.

Goodnow's address did not go unchallenged. Professor Charles Beard of Columbia University voiced his disagreement with the proposition that the Chinese were unsuited for representative government. In an extended rebuttal, Professor Sudhindra Bose of India and Iowa University argued strongly that only the practice of self-government prepared a country for self-government and that the cliché of the lack of fitness for it among Asian people did not bear examination. He concluded: "We of the East ask only one thing of the West. It is this—that you of the West stay away from us and our problems: leave us to solve our own problems, to work out our own destinies, while you spend your time looking after yours. The greatest good you can do us, the lasting benefit you can confer on us, is to let us alone."[121]

Bose speaks to us poignantly across the decades. But Goodnow was apparently unmoved. He returned to China the next summer, where he assisted Yuan in his great debacle, the attempt to abolish the republic.

Chapter 7

Yuan's Programs

By mid-1914, Yuan had an extraordinary grip upon the administration of the country and its provinces. Inherited institutional obstacles to the exercise of his dictatorship, such as representative assemblies, had been swept away. The prospects for achieving fiscal solvency on the basis of domestic resources were promising. Although sometimes dubious about the methods Yuan had used to accomplish these things, an important body of Chinese leaders who were not Yuan's close associates had supported the establishment of the dictatorship as a necessary preliminary to reform. Among them were Liang Ch'i-ch'ao and Ts'ai O. But the question remained whether Yuan would convert the painstakingly accumulated administrative power into strength, dignity, and progress for China. Perhaps even among Yuan's old entourage this question hovered in the recesses of an overtly unconditional loyalty to the chief.

Once freed to design his own programs without hindrance from competing centers of power, did Yuan reveal himself as a reformer or a reactionary? The answer has to be that he was both. He was, or fancied himself, a realist. He tried to move China along by careful steps that reflected the limitations of her weakness and backwardness. Programs were designed with these realities standing in judgment over what was desirable. Given her besieged circumstances and the pace of change in the world at large, this sort of realism for China was only one step from defeatism.

Even the modest programs for social and institutional change adopted by the dictatorship tended to falter. Yuan entertained and endorsed many reformist schemes, but "Chinese conditions" seemed, with few exceptions, never to allow for quick enactment or for more than pilot projects. Retrenchment was the keynote. Inherited reform programs were cut back. Among those in power, the handiest explanation for this state of affairs

177

was the lack of responsiveness in the benighted population. How was one to reach the people and enlist their energies? Rather than renewing the movement toward broader participation in politics, Yuan sought to sustain the momentum of his rule by political gadgetry. He turned to old symbols of political authority, refurbished them to suit changing tastes in political imagery, and foisted them upon the country. By the manipulation of symbols, he hoped to recapture the spontaneous response to authority that he recalled from his years as Chihli governor-general. It was, paradoxically, the reactionary road to reform.

Foreign Affairs under the Dictatorship

After the Second Revolution, in an address outlining his ideas about where China was and what had gone wrong, Yuan described the urgency of the situation in these terms:

> Some nations in this world owe their greatness to military efficiency, others to trade or industry. When we turn to China, her state differs scarcely from the brute creation. How can we expect a nation reduced to this condition to escape the fate of dismemberment at the hands of others? . . . what we must remember is that our neighbors are interested spectators and unless we set speedily to work, others may take the task in hand in our stead. When our finances are under alien supervision and our territories apportioned into spheres of influence, the fate of Vietnam and Korea will be upon us, and it will be too late for repentance.[1]

In effect, Yuan in this address was justifying his break with the liberal republic on grounds of its inadequacy in turning the imperialist tide. What might have seemed to be Yuan's own previous failings in this regard, such as the Reorganization Loan and (as we shall see) the Mongolian matter, were attributed to the constraints placed on the president's diplomacy by the "disorder" of the liberal republic. But could the dictatorship do better?

By the summer of 1914, Yuan had centralized much of the country's administration and had increased the power of the state. As Yen Hsi-shan recalled in his memoir, "The years 1914 and 1915 were China's most tranquil period and were also the period when Yuan's influence was at its peak."[2] The time had arrived to demonstrate an improved ability to deal with foreign imperialism. The idea that centralization was the best road to strength had been vigorously contested, but it had been Yuan's. He would now be tested by it. Hence, an examination of his record in foreign relations is important for understanding his domestic political problems. The failings in that record help explain his search for further domestic political remedies beyond those concocted in setting up the dictatorship in late 1913 and early 1914.

To fail in handling foreign encroachment was not a new experience for the government of China. But frustrations with failure were cumulative (as were the actual effects of the failures). The frustration led to ever greater demands on Chinese leadership.

Yuan was faced with an unceasing stream of crises in foreign relations. Regarding them, he was neither traitor nor militant anti-imperialist. He tailored policies to China's strength. Since he perceived China as weak—as indeed she was in conventional terms—his policies had the effect of caving in to foreign pressures. His stance looked less like the militancy of the last few years of the Ch'ing than it did the accommodation of the nineteenth century. There is no doubt that the conceptions and goals of late Ch'ing nationalism remained. Much of the personnel was constant, and Yuan faced dissent to his compromises from within his entourage. But a consciousness of a continuing weakness and an unwillingness to risk all in confrontation produced a highly compromising policy. There were some small diplomatic successes. Taking China's weakness as given, one might conclude that Yuan's government managed an impossible situation with considerable skill. But the temper of the times did not make allowances of this kind. To a Chinese nationalist, the returns on Yuan's dictatorship were negative.

For a guardian of the nation's sovereignty, Yuan was too eager to grant railway and resource concessions in return for short-run liquid assets. The Peking government spent most of the disposable portion of the Reorganization Loan in subverting the national assembly and suppressing the Kuomintang and was thirsty for more funds before the end of 1913. Simultaneously, the consortium countries, previously restrained by mutual agreement from contracting so-called industrial loans, that is, for purposes such as railways and mines, were freed to indulge. While Yuan was organizing his administrative system and its revenue-raising features, the central government was sustained by advances on new railway contracts, chiefly British and Belgian. (The Belgians, not bound to the consortium, had landed their big contract before the Second Revolution.) In addition, all sorts of lesser deals were being offered and sometimes taken. In early 1914, the capital was infested with international loan sharks, offering quick money on easy terms. When challenged on his policy, Yuan pleaded financial stringency.[3]

Even as his government was contracting loans, the Political Conference in Peking was warning of the danger of unchecked foreign borrowing.[4] Soon the pace did slacken. Then, with greater domestic solvency and the termination of foreign lending upon the outbreak of World War I, the short concession-mongering phase ended. Its chief legacies were a more firmly entrenched British sphere in the Yangtze area and parties of prospectors from Standard Oil, fruitlessly puncturing Shensi province with their machines in search of exploitable reserves. In other words, the practical consequences were not major. But it was somehow the wrong foot on which to begin the strengthening of the nation.

Less public was Yuan's deferential attitude toward foreign interference in Chinese governmental prerogatives. The attitude often carried no promise of positive action. Even when it did, the calculation was no doubt to give in on little things so as to build credit for the big issues. The effect, however, was perhaps to confirm foreign agents in their sense of the rectitude of interference.

For example, when Yuan's first nominee for Chinese representative to a conference with the British on Tibet refused to go, the British minister suggested Ch'en I-fan (Ivan Chen), schooled in England and longtime diplomat in London.[5] Ch'en was appointed. During the Second Revolution, as Kwangtung was being secured by counterrevolutionary forces, both the British consul general in Canton and the governor of Hongkong, not to mention the British chargé d'affaires in Peking, shamelessly proferred their choices for provincial military governor. The British-sponsored candidates did not get the job. In fact, although there are indications that Yuan later contemplated replacing Lung Chi-kuang, the local figure initially appointed as part of a battle plan to defeat the Kuomintang in August, 1913, he finally refrained from attempting to impose one of his own men on Kwangtung in that post. But instead of firmly turning the British suggestions aside as unwarranted, the appearance of a cordial reception for advice of this sort was maintained.[6]

With regard to the many disputes over foreign rights and privileges ("cases," they were called by the diplomats who took them up), Yuan's regime was generally accommodating. In return for support during the

Second Revolution, Yuan arranged for the settlement of a number of outstanding British grievances. A notable, though not isolated, case was the renewal of limestone supplies from Kwangtung to a British cement company in Hongkong. The Hu Han-min government had cut off those supplies in favor of a provincially owned cement enterprise. The British company had suffered. British officials in Canton and Hongkong had been furious and had protested vigorously. At the end of October, 1913, Yuan promised satisfaction on this and other cases pressed by the British chargé d'affaires in Peking, to show that "Chinese gratitude was not an empty phrase."[7] Kwangtung limestone export was resumed. There were concrete advantages in having a strong man in Peking who would flex his muscles on your behalf.

One could easily add to the instances of Chinese deference under the dictatorship. Phan Boi Chau, who occupies a position in the development of modern Vietnamese nationalism similar to that of Sun Yat-sen in Chinese nationalism, found refuge in Kwangtung under Hu Han-min but was arrested and held for ransom or other sorts of bargaining by Lung Chi-kuang (the negotiations with the French reached no conclusion).[8] The British consulate general in Hankow found the negotiation of cases much easier after the abolition of the provincial assembly and the stilling of "inexperienced and hotheaded critics."[9] In late 1915, British and Japanese diplomats successfully protested tax and duty exemptions for Chou Hsueh-hsi's large-scale textile project, the Hua-hsin Spinning and Weaving Company.[10]

Yuan, of course, did not enjoy deferring to foreign requests, and foreigners were often frustrated by Chinese resistance. Two successive British consuls in Nanking, in contrast to their colleague in Hankow, complained of the lack of responsiveness in the Kiangsu government after Yuan's reorganization, citing an increasing Chinese desire to curtail foreign rights and privileges, and an inability to make provincial officials settle one case, even a minor one.[11] After the scramble for railway concessions ended with the outbreak of World War I, foreign engineers were alleged to be obstructed at every turn. Sun To-yü, the Chinese director general of a projected line between Nanking and Changsha, who was an engineering graduate of Cornell and younger brother of a close associate of Chou Hsueh-hsi, was described as "arrogant and anti-foreign," taking the view that the foreign role was ended once the money was lent.[12] Yuan himself blatantly tried to subvert the foreign administration of the salt revenues. He successfully ignored his foreign financial advisers and auditors. He believed that the unpopularity of Chou Hsueh-hsi among foreigners in 1915 derived from Chou's resistance to their schemes, and this belief clearly increased his enthusiasm for Chou.[13] Even the reemergence of a former Ch'ing official could be an act of defiance. The British minister was much distressed by the appointment in March, 1915, in western Szechwan (that is, bordering on Tibet) of a former taotai of Yunnan, who had been removed at British insistence in September, 1911, for his "obstruction and rudeness" over the issue of the frontier with Burma.[14] We would be missing the point if we assumed that Yuan's failures in defending his country's sovereignty were owing to a peculiar softheaded trust of imperialist benevolence, or to a reckless rush into the protective arms of foreign guardians.

Yet he did fail. The major crises in foreign affairs during the presidency have been examined in specialized studies and cannot be recreated here in all their complexities. I shall briefly examine three of them—regarding Mongolia, Tibet, and the Twenty-One Demands—with a view to characterizing the temper of Peking's response, in both its external and internal strategies.

During the 1911 Revolution, princely Mongol resistance to growing Ch'ing interventionism blossomed into revolt against all authority coming out of Peking. The opportunity was taken to seize power and declare an independent state. Russian support was immediate. By the time the Peking government was reorganized in its republican form, it faced the accomplished fact of large portions of Mongolia (Outer Mongolia) under a separatist government. Troops from Chihli quickly crushed a revolt in Inner Mongolia in mid-summer 1912, and the further spread of separatism was checked. But the Russian-Outer Mongolian relationship was formalized to the world in an agreement of November 3, 1912, promising Russian protection from Chinese troops and granting Russians special trading privileges. The Peking government was directly warned that the dispatch of Chinese troops to Outer Mongolia would be considered an act of war against the tsar.[15]

The outcry in the Chinese home provinces was enormous. The call for war, particularly after news of the Russo-Mongolian agreement of November, 1912, was widespread. The Shanghai vernacular press seems to have been unanimously favorable to a strong military response.[16] The Kwangtung government made it a major issue and established a bureau for soliciting contributions to the war effort. The Hunan government offered to grant Peking almost Ch$1 million as soon as war was declared against the

Mongolian separatists. Chinese in Singapore remitted Ch$20,000 to Peking
for this purpose. Feelings in the Szechwanese capital were greatly aroused
over the Russian action. In Hupeh, there were public meetings, patriotic
subscription campaigns, bellicose articles in the newspapers, and a call for
volunteers for the front.[17] Curiously, it was Liang Ch'i-ch'ao, just returned
from his long exile, and his Democratic Party (Min-chu tang) who led the
attack on the Peking government for its dilatoriness regarding Mongolia.
The national Kuomintang, having recently endorsed the new cabinet of
Chao Ping-chün, called instead for rallying behind the government, although
it was keenly militant against the Russians.[18] In terms of domestic politics,
the moment could not have been more opportune for Yuan to lead a national crusade to regain lost territories and repulse the imperialist aggressors.

The realistic administrator in him and his sense of China's weakness,
however, foreclosed this option. It is doubtful that he ever seriously considered it. His efforts at centralization had so far not been successful.
Waging a war with the Russian empire on the basis of voluntary donations
from the provincial governments was, to Yuan, not an activity worth contemplating. Would the donations be forthcoming? One might reasonably
doubt it. Aside from the provinces' own fiscal difficulties, there were voices
within the T'ung-meng hui and Kuomintang camp counseling delay in confronting foreign powers (for example, Yeh Hsia-sheng and Sung Chiao-jen,
already cited on this point). Would it not be better to bear the obloquy of
certain security than to run the risks of inspirational leadership of a country
at war?

In any case, Yuan distrusted citizens' movements, no matter how elite
in social complexion. With sarcasm, he described the failed strategy of his
foreign minister of the moment, the American-educated Liang Ju-hao.
Liang had believed that the Russian action would unite the Chinese
—it did, said Yuan, in an attack on Liang.[19] Yuan devoted himself to getting foreign affairs back into the proper channels, that is, the official ones,
and cooling off the public fever, seen as an interference with orderly diplomacy. He tried to puncture bellicose pretensions by offering to head an expedition of five hundred thousand well-trained and well-equipped troops,
provided the provinces would supply them.[20] Checked by admonitions
and bits of repression, popular agitation did fall off by February, 1913.

As it turned out, the Russians were not pressing for a complete detachment of Outer Mongolia from the Chinese republic. In May, 1913, a formal
agreement between St. Petersburg and Peking was negotiated. It confirmed

Russian privileges and the protectorate, and prohibited Chinese coloniza-
tion, but admitted the continuation of Chinese suzerainty and some physical
presence. It was now the turn of the Kuomintang to lead the opposition,
with Liang Ch'i-ch'ao carping on the sidelines. Just as the Second Revolution was beginning, the KMT-dominated upper house of the national assembly rejected the agreement. The Russians thereupon hardened their
position. Yuan's hostility toward popular participation in determining
foreign policy was presumably confirmed, and his commitment to bureaucratic centralization strengthened. An arrangement substantially the same
as that of the previous May but somewhat less favorable to Peking was
declared the day after Yuan's coup against the parliamentary Kuomintang
in November, 1913.[21]

Despite the new powers of the dictatorship, further diplomacy served
only to solidify the effective separation of Outer Mongolia from any real
Chinese authority. After months of negotiations, an agreement (the
Treaty of Kiakhta) was signed in June, 1915, by Russia, China, and Outer
Mongolia. In essence, it merely reaffirmed the arrangements of 1912 and
1913. The process was neat, with low risks for the security of the home
provinces and for Yuan's position. But what patriot would admire such
leadership?

The detachment from Chinese authority of Tibet, the other substantial
Ch'ing dependency, took a similar course but with interesting differences.
A startling heightening of the level of Peking's control in Lhasa in 1910 and
1911 was reversed as a consequence of the disruptions of the 1911 Revolution. The British from their colonial base in India, trying to exert an influence over Tibetan affairs since the 1880s, took advantage of the sudden
decline of Chinese power in Tibet to press on all parties arrangements
more to their liking. The new British position, which was communicated
to Yuan's government in August, 1912, was that China should surrender
the realities of power in central Tibet in exchange for a face-saving retention of Chinese suzerainty. The Tibetan authorities for their part would
have to forgo formal political separation from China and settle for a guarantee of internal autonomy, since too obvious a substitution of British for
Chinese overlordship might provoke Russian demands for compensation in
Afghanistan, Persia, or Sinkiang.[22]

The popular Chinese response to the loss of most of Tibet was, by comparison with the uproar over Mongolia, subdued. An overt foreign physical
intervention in Tibet was lacking. There were no British or Indian soldiers

in or near Lhasa, and the British government was not threatening war. Tibet did not impinge as directly on Chinese security, nor were Chinese historical ties of the same intimacy as with Mongolia. Still, the excision was keenly felt. Troops were dispatched from Szechwan (the Szechwan authorities rejected Yunnanese and Hupeh offers of assistance as a matter of provincial pride and privilege). The Peking government attempted, as it had in the Mongolian case, to woo the separatist leaders through diplomacy. These efforts all failed, and Yuan agreed to negotiate.[23]

What Yuan had accepted in the case of Mongolia, where popular feeling opposed concessions, he resisted in the case of Tibet, where agitation outside the government was minimal. As one who disdained uncontrolled political agitation, Yuan presumably calculated instead the different level of foreign pressure and decided to stand firm on Tibet. The Simla Conference, from October, 1913, to July, 1914, produced draft agreements that would have divided Tibet into "inner" and "outer" regions, with Chinese authority reduced to a nominal suzerainty in the "outer" region (including Lhasa, as well as some territory actually occupied by Chinese troops). The draft agreements also aspired to establish exclusively British trade marts in Tibet. The resemblances to the Mongolian settlement already agreed to were many and not accidental. But, despite conditional acquiescence ("initialing") by the British-nominated Chinese delegate, Ch'en I-fan, the Peking government flatly rejected the arrangements. The British minister attributed the obstinacy to generally wounded pride and to "a number of young men who run the Tibetan policy of the Government" who considered the abandonment of the policies of the late Ch'ing "a national disgrace."[24] Yuan himself referred to the clamor that would ensue and argued that the republic was too young and weak to sustain the shock.[25]

One senses even in Yuan's moments of firmness a lack of militancy, a flexibility that invites further compromise. With the failure of negotiations, Yuan resumed attempts to entice Tibetan leaders back into the Chinese fold. When these efforts came to nothing, he turned again to the British for another round of talks but was rebuffed. After his death, the Chinese position in eastern Tibet deteriorated further. Yuan had formally conceded nothing regarding Tibet, but his dictatorship had not produced the national power that might regain something. Since social reform was not on the Chinese agenda, the reassertion of Peking's power in the old dependencies would simply have laid another layer of authority over the peoples of Mongolia and Tibet. Perhaps these areas suffered no great misfortune in trading off Chinese for Russian and British overlordship. In the Chinese home provinces, however, Yuan's luster was further dimmed. Then, at a time when the expectation that the dictatorship might redress the balance with foreign imperialism was already fading, it received a much more devastating blow.

The Twenty-One Demands

With the outbreak of war in Europe and the consequent absorption of European energies away from Asia, the main theme of Peking's foreign relations became problems with Japan. As the confrontation between the two countries reached a climax in the spring of 1915, Yuan was offered another opportunity to risk war and seize the high ground of nationalism. Again, he took the cautious road and compromised. From this blow to his prestige there was no recovery.

Japanese policy toward China since the 1911 Revolution was poorly coordinated. Different sectors in Japanese society and government had too intense an interest in China for the foreign ministry to retain full control. But the main tendency was apparent: ever greater Japanese intervention in Chinese affairs. Many Japanese who were actively engaged in China carried with them a sense of Japan's special responsibility for their large neighbor, a "responsibility" expressed in superintendence of China on behalf of modern civilization, with appropriate compensation. General Aoki Norizumi, top military representative in Japan's Peking legation at the start of the republic, was reported in Februrary, 1912, to have the view that the powers should give Japan a mandate to preserve order in China.[26] During the Second Revolution, Japan's financial agent in Peking pursued the same theme with the British.[27] Striking a different note but to the same effect for China, General Aoki wrote confidentially in August, 1914: "With the clash over the racial problem that will inevitably emerge in the future, it is an urgent necessity to prepare an impregnable position, in order beneficially to supervise and lead the Chinese."[28] Japan's chief negotiator of the Twenty-One Demands, upon his subsequent departure from Peking, was quoted as telling his diplomatic colleagues that no minister to China "could satisfy the insatiable demands of the Japanese people . . ." and that he was relieved at his release from a thankless post.[29] Illustrations of the Japanese appetite abounded. The Japanese foreign ministry exhausted its ingenuity in attempting, often unsuccessfully, to keep it within bounds that protected Japan's overall international position. But it was a foreign minister, Katō Kōmei, who perpetrated the most flagrant acts of the period.

The relative freedom from the obstruction of other imperialist governments afforded by World War I was an added inducement to Japan's forward policy in China, but not its cause. Katō came into office in April, 1914, prepared to increase Japan's role in China even at the expense of British displeasure. A conflict of claims had already emerged in the Yangtze region during the rush for railway concessions in the winter of 1913—14. Katō complained vigorously against the British pretensions to exclusive rights in the area. And he soon summoned his representative in Peking back for consultations on the future of Japanese policy in China. From these preliminaries and from the views Katō was known to hold on China policy, something like the Twenty-One Demands was bound to be sprung from the Japanese bow, with or without the European war.[30] But the war removed some restraints and widened possibilities.

The first new opportunity was the displacement of German authority in Shantung. Plans to occupy the area were developed simultaneously with Japan's entry into the war against Germany in August, 1914. Despite British uneasiness about it all, London's cooperation was secured. Yuan Shih-k'ai, sensitive to the dangers of the injection of a new and ambitious presence into the modestly stabilized German position, urged on the British minister the internationalization of Germany's ouster. According to his own account, Yuan offered to provide a large body of troops—in effect, joining the war against Germany. He actually began the movement of troops to the Kiaochow frontier but later claimed to have been rebuffed by Jordan.[31] The job was left to the Japanese, with token British participation. The Germans soon capitulated. Despite Chinese declarations of neutrality, definitions of a war zone, and British assurances, Japan proceeded to enlarge on the former German holdings.

As the extent of Japanese pretensions in Shantung became evident, militancy mounted among Chinese. Chang Hsun, the independent military traditionalist in western Shantung and northern Kiangsu, offered to attack the Japanese and managed to harass their supply system in small ways. Liang Ch'i-ch'ao and Ts'ai O rose in the appointive council in Peking (*ts'an-cheng-yuan*) that was serving as an interim legislature and called for an accounting by the president. Feng Kuo-chang, Yuan's most prominent military representative in the lower Yangtze, joined with other generals to urge Yuan to respond. They promised to do their duty in the protection of Chinese territory. Troop movements toward Shantung gave weight to these urgings.[32] But Yuan settled for Britain's promises on behalf of her obstreperous Japanese ally.

Meanwhile Katō was engaged in putting together a package of desiderata, designed to settle at one swoop all the pending issues and accumulated aspirations entertained by Japan regarding China. The result was the Twenty-One Demands, presented to Yuan Shih-k'ai on January 18, 1915. They concerned Shantung; southern Manchuria and eastern Inner Mongolia; the coal and iron complex of the Han-yeh-p'ing Company, centered in Hupeh and much in debt to Japanese; Fukien, from which any American naval base was to be excluded (though the language was more general); and, in the notorious fifth grouping, a miscellany of special privileges, posts, and concessions for Japanese, including a joint Sino-Japanese administration of police forces "where such arrangements are necessary." The total effect was so outrageous that European and American officials were reluctant to believe the Chinese as they began to leak the details.

The saga of the Twenty-One Demands and the Japanese ultimatum in May, 1915, has been told many times. For our purposes, it will suffice to register a few points about the negotiations.

First, the quality and integrity of the Chinese diplomatic bureaucracy was demonstrated. Recent studies, based on close readings of the record, recognize the skill of Peking's diplomats, who conducted the negotiations under the detailed guidance of Yuan Shih-k'ai.[33] A tenacious resistance to Japanese insistence, planned delay, and carefully arranged disclosures served to stimulate the British and American governments into remonstrances directed at Tokyo. The use of Yuan's Japanese legal adviser, Ariga Nagao, who undermined Katō's belligerence from within his own government, was mentioned in the previous chapter. These tactics were more effective than the Chinese government was allowed to know. The governments in London and Washington kept from China the substance of their representations to the Japanese. In the final agreement, which is rightly described as a capitulation by Peking, China lost a great deal. But the original demands had been considerably winnowed. Those losses that were new in kind in the long history of imperialist encroachments on Chinese sovereignty were notably provisions allowing individual Japanese to lease agricultural as well as commercial and industrial land in southern Manchuria and to reside there with extraterritorial legal status. The Japanese position in Manchuria, already well established, was greatly enhanced, and a limited penetration of eastern Inner Mongolia was provided for. Elsewhere, not a great deal was changed by the final product of the Twenty-One Demands. Katō had led his country to believe that much more would be gained. His failure cost him his job.[34] Peking's diplomacy, as conducted by Yuan, Lu Cheng-hsiang, Ts'ao Ju-lin, Wellington Koo, and others, was part of the reason.

Second, the assistance given Peking in the negotiations by foreign governments was primarily motivated by the defense of their own claims on China against the sweep of Japanese ambitions and by the desire to avoid the complications that would ensue from a Sino-Japanese war. The United Kingdom was the most influential third party with both contending sides. It tried to deflate the expectations of success in both Tokyo and Peking. Katō's humiliation was his public abandonment of the fifth group and of demands for railway and mining rights in the Yangtze area that the British felt infringed on their established privileges and position (although Britain accepted the consolidation of Japan's grip on the Han-yeh-p'ing Company). British pressure contributed largely to this effect.[35]

On the other hand, British officials from first to last urged the Peking government to accept the main thrust of the Japanese demands. When Liang Shih-i came to Jordan on the eve of the Japanese ultimatum to pose detailed questions regarding Britain's posture in the event of a Sino-Japanese war, Jordan in effect said no help was likely and China should submit.[36] After the delivery of the ultimatum, Jordan called on Peking's foreign minister and tearfully urged him to endure the insult and accept unconditionally.[37] Jordan's line was approved and reinforced from London. The British posture was a major consideration in Yuan Shih-k'ai's councils. War was eschewed in favor of a humiliating capitulation.

Third, even more sharply than before, Yuan was presented with the choice of leading a popular nationalistic movement at great risk to himself and the country or of settling sensibly for safety. Opinion in that limited part of the population tied into the national communications system was unmistakable. From March, 1915, on into the summer, a variety of anti-Japanese campaigns spread over the country. China had never before experienced this degree of nationwide agitation over imperialist encroachment. Funds were raised for resistance. Manifestoes were written and circulated. Patriotic plays were staged. The most compelling weapon was economic resistance: merchants turning back consignments of Japanese goods, consumer boycotts, campaigns to "encourage home industries," Japanese steamers forced to sail empty, the refusal to accept Japanese bank notes. Yuan issued orders forbidding any boycott, lest it provide an excuse for Japanese intervention. Enforcement of the orders was sporadic and half-hearted.[38]

Meanwhile, many former Chinese enemies of the dictatorship declared a cessation of hostilities toward Peking. Large numbers of exiles returned from Japan under Yuan's amnesty program. Even such prominent opponents as Huang Hsing, Li Lieh-chün, Po Wen-wei, and Ch'en Chiung-ming, though reaffirming their opposition to Yuan's dictatorship and remaining in exile, publicly promised to conduct themselves so that the country would not be harmed. Specifically, they resolved not to be tools of Japanese threats against Peking.[39] The offer of support for Peking was broad. It was also conditional. A pamphlet written by Chinese students returned from Japan and distributed in Hangchow in April, 1915, put it this way: "We must not split into parties, but must be patriotic and support the Government. We must not agree to a single one of Japan's demands. Even if our Government agrees, we cannot do so."[40]

Sun Yat-sen and a much reduced band of personal followers held out against the surge of sympathy for Peking and antagonism toward Japan. This posture deepened Sun's isolation of the moment. Pointed remarks about those few individuals among the revolutionaries who were national traitors or about those irresponsible radicals who threw bombs and fomented trouble in China were attributed during the negotiations to revolutionary veterans like Ho Hai-ming and Po Wen-wei.[41] In April, 1915, H. H. Kung (K'ung Hsiang-hsi, 1881–1967), addressed a confidential report to a friend in the Peking government suggesting stratagems for depriving Japan of "this tool," his wife's brother-in-law, Sun Yat-sen. "The facts in regard to Japanese machinations and their personal manipulation of Dr. Sun are known to the writer through personal investigations and from reliable sources. He feels it his duty to report the situation to those who are in close connection with the government. . . . The name and prestige of Dr. Sun Yat-sen are worth more to Japan than several divisions of an army. Since his arrival in that country from Formosa, to which place he withdrew during the second revolution, Dr. Sun has been flattered, supplied with a house and funds, and guarded as carefully as if he were an emperor. . . . In order to thwart Japan's strategy it is most important that Dr. Sun should leave Japan. . . . "[42] Neither shared experiences of revolution nor marriage ties were sufficient to check the movement of patriotic support toward the Peking government.

Although he encouraged defections from the revolutionary camp, Yuan declined the role of national liberator that was being implicitly proposed by the growing support. He was more impressed by the remaining threat of revolutionary activity under Japanese sponsorship and by the strength of Japanese arms. Sun's resources at the time were in fact negligible. But the Japanese military threat was not, and was flaunted ominously during the negotiations. The buildup of Japanese forces in China began in March, 1915. To appreciate the effect of these moves, we must recall the semicolonial condition of China, that permitted the stationing of Japanese troops not only in Talien and Kiaochow, but in Tientsin and Hankow, Mukden and Tsinan. China had no effective way to check the swelling numbers, which proceeded with ostentatious drama throughout the spring. The Japanese garrison forces in China doubled, amounting to perhaps sixty thousand.[43] If war had come, the Japanese attack on China would have been launched from within the country as well as from Korea and Japan. When the ultimatum was delivered, Japanese nationals in China were evacuated from areas not under Japanese military protection. The message had every aspect of seriousness.

At an early stage of the negotiations, when the fifth group of demands was being pressed by the Japanese, Yuan spoke of unflagging resistance, even if the Japanese army were to enter Peking.[44] But at the end, with Japanese troops in place and the reduced demands accompanied by an ultimatum, Yuan decided to accede. He rejected Tuan Ch'i-jui's advice to defy the ultimatum and face the consequences. He argued that, though a great humiliation and an injury to Chinese interests, acceptance of the final form of the demands, without the fifth group, would not destroy the nation.[45]

It has been alleged that Yuan was pleased with the denouement of the negotiations and considered it a personal triumph.[46] It is true that Yuan took some satisfaction in having played his cards better than Katō. But he knew that skillful play had not overcome an initially poor hand. He repeatedly declared the results to have been a "national humiliation," a "loss of rights," a "great disaster."[47] Although conveying to the Japanese the notion that all was now settled between the two countries, Yuan seemed to G. E. Morrison to be obsessed with the diabolical dangers that Japan continued to pose.[48] An extraordinary month-long conference was called in Peking during the summer, at which Peking officials and representatives

from the Manchurian provincial governments planned methods for minimizing the impact of Japan's new privileges in southern Manchuria and
parts of Inner Mongolia.[49] Neither Yuan nor his government felt triumphant.

Having eschewed the risks of a patriotic war, Peking had to face the
costs of having disappointed patriotic expectations. The West Indian-born
Eugene Ch'en (Ch'en Yu-jen, 1878–1944), editor of the bilingual *Peking
Gazette* in 1915 (and foreign minister in the Kuomintang revolutionary
government, 1926–27), asserted on the eve of the ultimatum that any sign
of weakness on the government's part would be the harbinger of revolution.
Later, like many others, he judged that Yuan had given away too much.[50]
Revolution did not come without further stimulus to disaffection. But the
accumulated record of retreat before foreign pressure and of rejecting
more militant proposals from leading associates, such as Feng Kuo-chang,
Tuan Ch'i-jui, and Liang Ch'i-ch'ao, gravely weakened Yuan politically. Or
at least so we can infer. As we shall see, Yuan evidently believed that some
remedy was required.

Domestic Reforms under the Dictatorship

Even though it was not a total disaster, Yuan's diplomacy fell far short of
the nationalist aspirations of the time. Whether anyone else in his position
could have done better, without first presiding over a major mobilization
of popular energy and the consequent social transformations, is another
question. Certainly his strategy faced the opposite direction: he declined
to lead the widespread sentiment for militant resistance to Japan's pretensions. The relevant political point was that, like his predecessors in Peking,
he had lost the contest with foreign imperialism.

There was another side to the nationalist program where Yuan might
conceivably have regained some of the political legitimacy he lost in the
diplomatic field. This was domestic reform: that is, programs tending to
build national strength and hence promising to provide the tools with which
imperialism could ultimately be stemmed. Investigation reveals markedly
progressive features to some of Peking's reform plans during the dictatorship. But the results were negligible. Yuan's domestic audience, including
some of his supporters in the earlier contest with the Kuomintang, took
greater note of the resurgence of traditional forms, of his retrieval of bits

and pieces out of the past. The judgment of one of his closest aides in June, 1915, was widely held (and often more harshly expressed): "Yuan is more conservative now than he was when Viceroy."[51]

It is doubtful that Yuan would have admitted the justice of the judgment. His self-image seemed to be that of a consistent, gradualist reformer, blending visionary planning with cautious execution in accordance with China's real condition. In the spring of 1914, he proclaimed at length his philosophy of reform. The world, the statement read, no longer allowed a country to stand still and survive. Yuan, as he so often did, adduced his own record of introducing and enforcing reforms, but claimed that since the revolution popular impatience and fiscal collapse had produced a decline. "Generally speaking most of the young men who have just acquired influence are inclined to theories unsuitable for the circumstances of the country, while the more steady and experienced class are not far-sighted and too conservative. Should we desire to utilize the services of both and to amalgamate these two forces, it is necessary that we should be careful and progressive at the same time."[52] The theme of this statement, which often recurred in Yuan's pronouncements, is probably a fair indication of what he thought he was doing throughout the dictatorship.

A factor that reinforced the conservative aspect of Yuan's blend of reform and caution was the policy of retrenchment. In order to balance the budget without foreign loans, a concerted effort to reduce expenditure began at the end of 1913. In March, 1914, the Political Conference, which had recommended the abolition of the national and provincial assemblies, suggested further economies in official funds for the police, for charity, for education, for promoting industry, and so forth.[53] In general, the call for retrenchment of expenditure was sounded throughout the government. Before the Second Revolution, when provincial governments were remitting almost nothing to Peking and the central government survived on infusions from foreign loans, the costs of reform programs were met by provincial funds. In 1914, Peking was using its new authority over the provinces to divert these funds to the central government to keep it solvent without foreign money. Yuan said that, where possible, reforms should be delayed until the country's financial situation had acquired some little surplus. Meanwhile, he cautioned, the basic structure of each reform should be preserved so that forward movement could later be revived and expanded.[54] It was not an illogical position, but the consequences were a national cutback in several reforms.

The fate of the modern judiciary was illustrative of the impact of retrenchment. The republic inherited from the late Ch'ing reforms a blueprint for an independent judicial system, with a skeletal structure of courts already established around the country and a modernized criminal code ready for enactment. The criminal code was promulgated in the first year of the republic. The extension of the new courts proceeded at different rates in different provinces. By the end of 1913, about 10 percent of the counties (*hsien*) of the country possessed the court of first instance provided for in the blueprint. The prefectural (*fu*) courts were more nearly completed, and all but three provinces had the higher courts required for the overall scheme. The supreme court was in operation in Peking.[55] The purpose was not simply to remove the burden of dispensing justice from the administrative structure. It was explicitly a step toward the abolition of extraterritoriality, the immunity from Chinese law enjoyed by foreigners in China. It certainly had nothing to do with humanitarian equity; in fact, the new courts were most unpopular as dispensers of justice. In other words, judicial reform was a part of the nationalism of the early twentieth century.

In terms of its primary purpose, the new judiciary was not working. In Tientsin, some British companies took cases to the new court, and in Shantung the Germans tacitly recognized the jurisdiction of the new system sometime in 1913, presumably for civil cases. But generally the foreign powers and their nationals refused to take even their nonextraterritorial legal cases to the new courts, as a matter of policy and treaty right. They insisted on pressing their claims with Chinese administrative officials in the old manner. There was never any question at this stage of compromising their rights to extraterritorial hearings as defendants. But even in the remaining area of legal questions, efforts to engage foreigners in initial moves toward regaining Chinese legal sovereignty were rebuffed. The Western governments often spoke as if they wished to see China modernize. But the reforms for which they lobbied in Peking regularly took the form of an increased Western role in Chinese affairs. A reform, such as an independent judiciary, which threatened foreign privileges, frequently met foreign hostility.[56]

If the new judiciary was not successfully enticing foreigners along the path of treaty revision, then what good was it? There were people who had answers to that question. Liang Ch'i-ch'ao, who was minister of justice at the beginning of the dictatorship, spoke of the independent judiciary not only as "the essential ingredient to the recovery of legal rights" but also as "the foundation of constitutional government."[57] But the system had no broad constituency. And the president was sceptical. While boasting of his contributions as governor-general to an independent judiciary in Chihli, Yuan saw its operations in the early republic as "a convenient loophole" for evildoers, in need of narrowing.[58] Perhaps the surprising feature of the judiciary is the extent to which it remained active under the dictatorship. The supreme court in particular reached its peak of activity during 1915 and 1916 and managed to fend off some attacks on the modernized penal code.[59] The dictatorship was also marked by a great emphasis on prison reform: on building new prisons, remodeling old ones, establishing work-houses attached to prisons, improving sanitary conditions, and on prison as a place to reform the criminal's character. Most people, however, including those in the government, saw little value in the new judiciary and its ad-juncts.[60]

The most conspicuous feature of the modern judiciary during the dicta-torship was its diminution. Corporal punishment, substantially reduced by its exclusion from the new penal codes, was formally revived for certain crimes in order to relieve the jails (and reduce expenses). Owing, it was said, to a lack of funds and qualified officials, the county-level courts, never generalized throughout the country, were abolished. The exception was courts in the treaty ports. (The purpose of the whole system, that is, the re-covery of rights lost in treaties, was underlined by this exception.) Existing higher level courts were generally retained. While reiterating the desirability of an independent judiciary, the government returned primary jurisdiction to the administrative officer at the county level.[61] As with other reforms, Yuan did not allow the new judiciary to sink completely out of sight, but its prominence was greatly reduced.

Far more sensitive than the comparatively peripheral judiciary was the question of education. Modern nationalist and traditional moralist agreed on its central importance in shaping the society. By the time of the repub-lic, few people seemed disposed to reverse the policies of the late Ch'ing, which aimed at establishing a modern school system. Within that broad consensus, a number of issues remained. How fast and how far should the new educational system go, since it was still quite incomplete when the revolution came? Who should be educated? What level and what types of education should receive priority? What should be the balance between traditional and modern subjects in the curriculum? How much money should be allocated from limited funds? The dictatorship's response to these questions was conspicuously marked by Yuan's inclination to blend the new and the old.

As with the judiciary, Yuan looked for ways to reduce expenses. Hence the elaboration of the overall educational system was bound to be slowed under the dictatorship. But, in contrast to the judiciary, Yuan sought retrenchment at the top and continued growth at the bottom. He favored the spread of lower level elementary education over the further articulation of higher level schools, unless they were concerned with teacher training. As a result, Yuan's educational policies had a curiously antielitist aspect, which requires explanation.

There was no part of his educational policy that Yuan was given to asserting quite so regularly as the aim of "universal education," that is, for all male Chinese children. This was not an original conception: it had been a goal of the Ch'ing reforms in their last years; it was reaffirmed by educational authorities during the liberal republic. Yuan, however, gave it particular stress. In a climate of retrenchment, the stress carried with it the sacrifice of progress in elite education. A four-year primary education, in the plans issuing from Peking, was to be compulsory and free. Advancement beyond that level was to be expensive and less available than formerly. In pursuit of the mass education of the citizenry, Yuan's government planned half-day schools and literacy campaigns in alphabetized Chinese. It proposed to tackle the problem of the reluctance of university and normal school graduates to return to the villages by giving old-style village teachers short courses in the new learning. Its various programs regarding education, which were articulated in the course of 1915, showed a reasonably coherent concern for a major goal, widespread popular education.[62]

Peking's emphasis on this goal did not mean that Yuan was turning social revolutionary. First, there was the ancient Chinese precept that education was the mother of virtue and desirable for all, no matter what their station in life. As Mary C. Wright pointed out, the fear of mass education that has marked Western conservatism is generally absent in Chinese conservatism.[63] In the early twentieth century, the old idea of the moral efficacy of education helped feed a new hope, shared by reformer and revolutionary, that new styles of education, spiced with patriotism, would invigorate the population and strengthen the country. There would have been little disagreement in theory with Yuan's desire to instill in all children morality, practical skills, and a martial spirit. Mass education was seen as spreading nationalism and making better soldiers, not as stoking social discontent. Second, Yuan explicitly acknowledged the socially structured nature of the population by ordering a two-track system, one for the common people emerging from poverty and illiteracy and another for the cultured who aspired to climb the educational ladder to greater heights. On grounds of educational practicality, and perhaps also to make the program more acceptable to the social elite, Yuan offered to the children of literati families a new system of special preparatory schools attached to existing middle schools, while the rest of the primary school system was to be devoted to achieving compulsory education for all. The gentry may have resented the economies in higher education. But the idea was obviously to make the mass of the people more useful to the existing order of things, not to change that order.

Yuan's approach was culturally as well as socially conservative. This was revealed in his insistence upon injecting the whole texts of certain Confucian classics into the curriculum. The intent was not to make the classics the sole or even the primary object of study, which remained theoretically centered on the "new learning." Rather, his aim was to prevent their exclusion, as in some provinces during the liberal republic, or their extreme dilution, as desired by some of Yuan's ministers of education, notably T'ang Hua-lung in 1914 and 1915. As pictures and praise of Sun Yat-sen and Huang Hsing were removed from primary school textbooks, the *Mencius* and the *Analects* were inserted into the elementary school curriculum. Under the new regulations a child in his third and fourth years of primary school, which would complete his compulsory schooling, was to read the *Mencius;* in his fifth, if he went on, he was to begin the *Analects.*[64] Although others, like Huang Hsing, shared Yuan's concern about the lack of moral discipline among the educated youth, Yuan was noticeably on the conservative end of the reformist spectrum when it came to ethics and their instruction.[65]

Yuan was anything but a social revolutionary or a cultural iconoclast. But the conventional portrayal of him as a full-blown reactionary does not convey the peculiarities of his program, in education as in other fields. He resisted efforts to restore preformist styles of education and he persisted in educational experiments. In late 1915, Yeh Te-hui, famous for his attack on the 1898 Reform Movement, urged from his position as chairman of

Hunan's educational society that more classics be added to the school curriculum. The suggestion was dismissed by Yuan and his ministry of education as impractical and not worth consideration.[66]

In December, 1915, Yuan approved a model system for literacy classes, using an alphabet (*chu-yin tzu-mu*) designed in 1913 by a national conference of scholars. A pilot project in the Peking capital region called for a network of learning stations and half-day and open air schools. Later the techniques were to be transferred to the provinces. Yuan had long been interested in the educational potentialities of a Chinese alphabet. In this instance, the anticipated benefits were described as removing the wall separating the government from "the rude illiterates," who would learn patriotism and the government's will; as enabling old peasants and artisans to record their experiences and traditions, and allowing coolies and old women to read, thereby contributing to cultural progress; as facilitating practical education with twice the results for half the cost; and as leading to the union of the written and spoken languages and to the national standardization of the spoken language.[67] When we consider the degree to which these ideas had advanced in the heart of Yuan's bureaucracy, the rapid success of the *pai-hua* movement in the late 1910s and early 1920s is less surprising.

The regime began to implement its educational policies. With exceptions, notably Kwangsi, where the provincial government appears to have drastically reduced its support of education, the provinces seemed to be following Peking's direction. Educational budgets were generally maintained at high levels amidst the retrenchment of 1915 and were scheduled to increase in 1916. While higher level schools were being starved of funds, the primary level schools (renamed *kuo-min hsueh-hsiao*, or citizens' schools) were continuing to grow and preparations were underway for their generalization.[68]

If pursued to completion, these policies might have produced the same effects as did Yen Hsi-shan's educational policies from 1918 in Shansi, which were remarkably similar to those of Yuan's dictatorship. In Shansi, literacy was greatly increased (one estimate puts 57 percent of elementary school-age children in school in 1919); the instruction was low in quality but utilitarian; the gentry felt threatened and sabotaged the program; and no profound change in the society occurred.[69] Yuan's program of mass education was a logical part of his program of national strength through a centralized administration, where all should serve the state to the best of their ability. And it was another interesting example (along with his abolition of representative assemblies) of his willingness to defy gentry preferences. The social base of potential organized opposition to Yuan's rule, we should remember, was the gentry and other privileged urban dwellers, not "the rude illiterates." If consistently implemented over time, the program might have inadvertently laid the basis for lower class demands for participation in the political process. But this effect was hardly Yuan's intention and would have been fiercely resisted. One can imagine the Shansi result on a national scale. Without a larger conception of the needs of Chinese society, educational plans were not the key to national salvation that it was hoped they were.

Economic development was also on Yuan's agenda, but without any grand plan or striking results. The government spoke of increasing crop areas through national irrigation and flood control projects and of improving agricultural techniques through experimental stations. It proposed to encourage Chinese industrial enterprises by low interest loans, reduced railway freight charges, the reduction or abolition of export tariffs in certain commodities, technical assistance, and subsidies.[70]

Special official attention in resource development was granted to sugar production, the breeding of livestock, cotton growing, yarn spinning, the tea trade, mining, and afforestation.[71] Ting Wen-chiang, the young British-trained scientist, was launched in late 1913 on his geological survey of China, though the initial budget for this subsequently famous enterprise was miniscule.[72] By early 1916, his office had been promoted to a special bureau of the ministry of agriculture and commerce.[73]

There was, however, no crash program. The European war was immediately seen as a unique opportunity for the expansion of Chinese industry. And the anti-Japanese boycott of 1915 augmented the opportunity.[74] But in budget plans laid in 1915 for the following year, the allotments under the heading of agriculture and commerce at the national and provincial levels amounted to little more than half that for the judiciary, despite the sharp drop in the judicial budget since 1913, and were less than a third of the educational budget.[75] One is left with the impression that the industrial advances made by Chinese industry on the basis of investments conceived during World War I were due very little to Chinese governmental policy. In any case, the political fact was that the economic impact of the advances were not felt until well after Yuan's death.

Some reforms inaugurated under Yuan's rule clearly depended on his success in establishing a centralized administration over much of the country. One was the greater uniformity and increased revenues in the salt administration, where the foreign inspectorate imposed by the 1913 Reorganization Loan agreement reinforced but by itself could not produce the new arrangements. As Richard Dane, the chief foreign inspector, wrote in October, 1913: "Apparently the Chinese Government intends to try and enforce the centralization of the whole [salt] administration, and if they really do mean to do this they must do it themselves."[76] Similarly, progress toward a national currency rested on Peking's new national authority. Minting was confined to a few designated localities. The long-lived 1914 dollar (called *Yuan ta-t'ou,* or "Yuan's big head," after the visage decorating it) attained a national stature previously unrivaled by any Chinese silver coin. Liang Ch'i-ch'ao, who helped design Yuan's currency reforms, attributed the limits on their success to the noncooperation of the foreign-managed maritime customs service.[77]

A major achievement in monetary stabilization was the retirement, according to Peking plans, of over $31 million depreciated Cantonese notes. These were the accumulation of inflationary printing and counterfeiting in Kwangtung during the liberal republic. In Hunan, a lesser amount was retired by methods similar to those used in Kwangtung.[78] Liang Shih-i, who was instrumental in these various currency programs, was also the key figure in launching two unprecedentedly successful domestic bond issues. Although often tried, domestic borrowing had never before produced such large proceeds as did the 1914 and 1915 government loan subscription campaigns.[79] Nor was it to succeed so well again for a long time. The demise of Yuan's centralized administration, with its expanding central bank branches and a national network of solicitation, was a good part of the reason.

In the suppression of domestic opium production, another achievement of the presidency, the contribution of a centralized administration was more dubious. It is true that, even though he apparently tolerated the habit among some of his entourage, his policy was to press for the extirpation of the domestic and imported product. When county magistrates were undergoing a national campaign of evaluation under the dictatorship, their performance in suppressing the cultivation of the opium poppy was frequently used a measure of merit. And, if we may accept the judgment of contemporary foreign observers, both official and missionary, poppy cultivation markedly declined, to the vanishing point in most areas. One handy index of the seriousness of the official effort against consumption as well as production was the growing concentration of sale and smoking in foreign enclaves, where Chinese authority could not reach. The municipal council of the Shanghai International Settlement, which had issued 87 licenses to opium shops in 1907, issued 663 in 1914 (up over 100 since 1913).[80] In other cities, the buildings of foreign firms (in one case, the Hongkong and Shanghai Bank) and the Chinese employees of foreign offices, because of their relative immunity from Chinese authority, became increasingly active in the remaining opium (and the growing morphine) business.[81] During the presidency, despite foreign sabotage and resistance, the suppression of opium was carried to the point of fulfilling the terms of a late Ch'ing international agreement pointing toward the end of foreign opium importation.

But the achievement was imperfect. Some areas persisted in poppy cultivation. The final arrangement between Peking and the last of the opium importers was colored by compromise over the disposal of stocks and by unbecoming profit sharing. And the role of Yuan's presidency was to bring to a conclusion a campaign that had shown equal energy and effectiveness in the last years of the Ch'ing and, with a brief interruption during the 1911 Revolution, also during the decentralized period of the liberal republic. In other words, credit belonged to many. One might conclude from this particular history that strong popular feeling on the issue in a highly political but administratively decentralized environment could be as effective in reform as a system of centralized command. We may be sure that this was not Yuan's conclusion, but it may have been that of some of those watching and judging his performance.

Yuan's first concern in 1914 and 1915 was to articulate an administrative system and consolidate control over the country and its revenues. In the process, he cut back several reform programs. He was not opposed to the general direction that reform had taken in the late Ch'ing and in the provinces during the liberal republic. He believed in caution but insisted on his commitment to continuing the advance, particularly at a time when the administration would be firmly established and revenues flowing richly. He was still ready to entertain ideas remarkably progressive for the period. But the impression left with his countrymen was of marking time and the restoration to authority of the bureaucracy of the late empire. Yuan in no way made up in domestic dynamism what he lost in setbacks in foreign affairs.

The Traditionalistic Revival

Yuan Shih-k'ai was losing his audience. He demanded much from the country and gave little. The desire for national unity, which had induced the country to offer him the presidency in 1911 and early 1912 and which had kept a sizable proportion of political leaders with him in 1913, was wearing thin as the justification for all policies. Perhaps Yuan sensed the steady erosion of his support among the politically active and the socially dominant—the people who had made the Ch'ing reforms, the 1911 Revolution, and the provincial governments of the liberal republic. In any case, he drew increasingly on symbols out of the past as props for his sagging political appeal. While at every point attempting to win elite assent to his revivals by "modernizing" them, he sought to broaden his base in the population, not by new social policies, but with ceremonial. Strike the right poses, he seemed to think, and the people would show the wonderful reverence for authority that he imagined they had before the revolution. Had it not worked in Meiji Japan?[82]

If not personally attracted to some of the old forms, he would not have had confidence in their political efficacy. We cannot dismiss the elements of belief and choice. For example, he surely believed in the moral effect on young minds of reading Mencius, though he sent some of his sons to England for their schooling. The revolutionary leaders may have been inconstant in their advocacy of equal rights for women: Yuan, with some fifteen or more wives, appeared sincerely committed to the opposite view when he spoke of the idea as destructive of morality, family, and the nation.[83] But in most instances the manipulative intent was conspicuous and probably decisive. The premise underlying the traditionalistic revival was that the mass of the people had no idea of the meaning of republicanism, equal rights, and representative government, and were only confused by it all. In this Yuan was undoubtedly correct. How could they have learned, in a society where these matters belonged only to the privileged? He also seemed confident that the general population would respond to the emission of familiar political signals out of the past and that the sensibilities of the Westernizing, nationalist elite would be unoffended or could be ignored. In this he was disastrously wrong.

The question of the relevance of Confucius to the republic was complex but less contentious than one might suspect. The name of Confucius was used by all sorts of people for all sorts of purposes. There was a nationalist overtone to the late Ch'ing and early republican effort to transform the veneration of Confucius into something it had never been, a formally established state religion. The leaders of the movement were not obscurantist scholars nostalgic for the past, but the idiosyncratic reformer K'ang Yu-wei and Ch'en Huan-chang (1881–1931), a Columbia University Ph.D. degree recipient. In any case, Yuan Shih-k'ai explicitly rejected this tack. He announced that, in order to establish moral standards and in acknowledgment of the reverent regard in which Confucius's doctrines were held by millions of Chinese, officials high and low, including himself, would preside over rites in honor of the sage. "Although one must reform the system of administration according to modern methods, ceremonies and customs should by all means be preserved." The distinctive quality of China should be acknowledged. But this "is not at all the advocacy of a religion," Yuan emphasized.[84]

The honoring of Confucius, particularly on his supposed birthday, was a common custom during the liberal republic. In the fall of 1912 in Canton, for example, the city's schools celebrated the birthday with schoolroom exercises and suspended classes, although more traditional Confucian rites were banned from the schools by the education commissioner of the province. In Soochow in that same year, a school holiday was declared and ceremonies performed.[85] A prorevolutionary English-language journal in Shanghai, under Chinese management, combined extravagant praise of Sun Yat-sen with welcome to the movement for the promotion of Confucianism. It disputed the idea that the study of Confucianism fed reaction: ". . . we shall certainly lament if our people, in aiming to be strong and wealthy, lose our moral greatness."[86] The same committee of the national assembly that in October, 1913, produced a draft constitution reducing the power of the president also ruled that Confucianism should be the basis for national education in ethics.

By ordaining official sponsorship of rites venerating Confucius, Yuan was going further. Though the rites were modernized with newly composed songs and dances (one is reminded of the Meiji refurbishing of *gagaku*) and though in Nanking officials led the ceremonies in Western-style frock coats, Yuan was attempting to draw on old responses for present social and political purposes.[87]

Yuan's revival of the worship of heaven, an ancient ceremony previously performed only by the emperor, served the same purposes. The argument, as it was expressed in early 1914 in the Political Conference (where there was some opposition to the proposal), was that the masses were unenlightened and the revival of old ceremonies was a practical measure designed to check the moral decline evident since the revolution.[88] The worship of the Yellow Emperor, the mythical progenitor of the Han people, was considered as an alternative, but was rejected on the grounds that the other four "races" of China would be excluded (indeed a Mongol delegate sought to inject Chinghis Khan into the act for balance). Further, it was argued, the worship of heaven need not be an imperial prerogative, since, if one pursued the records back far enough, the ceremony was once broadly shared. In fact, what could be more republican than taking what had belonged only to emperors for thousands of years and inviting the whole population to participate? The subcommittee of the Political Conference recommended: "We have now entered upon a new era, an era in which all marks of inequality are obliterated, and therefore the worship of Heaven should be made universal."[89] The president would represent the people, but local authorities in the provinces should follow suit. Every family should be allowed to perform its own little ceremony. What had been a reaffirmation of the cosmological centrality of the emperor was converted into a device for piecing together a dissolving polity, with a manipulative intent openly discussed. In this fashion, using old ideas to make new political patterns, Yuan on December 23, 1914, led a ceremony adapted from China's oldest public cult.[90]

There is no evidence that any of this produced the intended effect. To the progressive element, these ceremonies reeked of reaction and suggested preparations for an imperial restoration. Truly traditional scholars could only be offended by the ersatz quality of these patchwork revivals. And the mass of the people was surely unreached or indifferent.

Yuan's grasping at symbols was at once more catholic and discriminating than is implied by singling out his attention to Confucius and heaven. On October 10,1914, after his first public ceremony for Confucius and shortly before his first trip to the Temple of Heaven, he reviewed troops and received school children at the T'ien-an-men, while Peking was bedecked in honor of the anniversary of the Wuchang revolutionary uprising of 1911. He ordered protection and restoration for the temples of Ch'ing officials who had helped suppress the Taiping Rebellion (some had been destroyed after the 1911 Revolution). His main argument was, not the justice of their cause, but the innocence of their error, since "Euro-American culture" had not yet reached China at that time and the old moral imperatives of ministerial loyalty toward the sovereign still pertained. He also ordered that sacrifices should be offered for those who had given their lives for the 1911 Revolution. In June, 1914, the Peking government embarked upon a queue-cutting campaign. The police removed the queues of anyone arrested, and the minister of internal affairs ordered that all officials and their servants, as well as rickshaw haulers and carriage drivers, must abandon the Ch'ing style or lose their jobs. Merchants were to be exhorted in public lectures to follow suit. An effort was even made to induce Chang Hsun to shear his men.[91] Like Charles de Gaulle, Yuan saw himself as inheritor of both the conservative and the progressive past.

Yuan also exercised selectivity in considering precedents and rejected those that he felt were incompatible with the new age. A censorial suggestion in late 1914 to revive the kotow was rejected by Yuan, who continued to bar the ceremony even when he entered upon his emperorship late the following year. When the discovery of a fossilized dragon was reported from Ichang in Hupeh in early 1915 as an omen favorable to the new imperial era, Yuan dismissed the interpretation as superstition. "Science is steadily advancing," he announced, "and everything must be thoroughly probed for its truth value." He refused to send the object to the Office of History (*shih kuan*) and declared that his only concern was the happiness and well-being of the mass of the people.[92] Yuan had traditional and modern reasons for whatever he did, with arguments drawn from both Chinese circumstance and Western or Japanese precedent. He believed he was making a new, reformist product from a mixture of old and modern elements.

And yet the sense of a growing conservatism was everywhere. While police were cutting queues in Peking in the summer of 1914, Cantonese who had earlier adopted the new style were letting their hair grow in anticipation of a reversion. So it was elsewhere. The traditional scholar's gown, which had been giving way to Western dress among the well-to-do, made a comeback. By the end of 1914 in Kiangsi, officials were reviving the sedan chair as a mode of travel, temporarily abandoned after the 1911 Revolution.[93] As the gentry's participation in reformist politics through representative government and other organizational activity was suppressed by Peking, the more liberal, Westernized styles that accompanied politicization also faded. For all Yuan's eclecticism in theory, the weight of practice helped to reverse the social and cultural liberality of the first two years of the republic. There was no compensating sign of greater happiness and well-being among the mass of the people.

The Dictatorship and the Social Order

The manipulation of symbols proved not to be a satisfactory substitute for a social strategy. Yuan made no sustained effort to offer programs that would serve the interests and aspirations of any major social class or to communicate to it a sense of common purpose and shared fate. He spurned and repressed popular movements, even when they were securely dominated by China's upper class. National strength, he thought, could be constructed out of efficient administration and centralized controls. Participation by the people was desirable, but only in a highly controlled manner that reinforced central government power. The practical consequence of his strategy was a bloody assault on popular politics, the imposition of autocracy, and indefinite delay in the reemergence of representative institutions. People who had suffered that sequence were not likely to be dazzled by traditionalistic, pseudorepublican, or pseudoimperial pomp and circumstance.

I have touched upon several ways in which Yuan's policies tended to alienate the gentry, whose support any government unwilling to sponsor social revolution most needed. He abolished their assemblies, which had been integrated into the exercise of gentry power. He neglected elite education, thereby narrowing the prospects for entry into positions of high status. He generally reduced reform programs, vehicles for gentry aspirations and ideals. He succumbed to foreign imperialist pressure, thus betraying the hopes of nationalism, which had found its most fertile ground up to this time among the gentry. It could be conceded that his government had accepted the job of policing the social status quo and suppressing rebellion among the rootless and the peasantry. But even here Yuan's government had for a long time bungled in the case of White Wolf. Meanwhile new grievances emerged. A program for the surveying of agricultural land (initially under Ts'ai O) was inaugurated in 1915 with a view to improving the efficiency of the land tax. The program met with protests in the provinces. At least some of the protest came from the gentry, whose tax privileges were threatened. Peking called the program off altogether in an effort to retrieve popular support as Yuan's power was slipping away in 1916.[94] True centralization of authority did not easily mix with gentry power, and Yuan did not exert himself to try.

The regulations promulgated in May, 1914, for local protection corps (*ti-fang pao-wei t'uan*) might seem at first glance to be a major concession to gentry power.[95] Within the tradition of local militia, the new system contained elements of compromise with gentry influence. For example, gentry and merchant representatives were to be enlisted as assistants to the county magistrate in planning and management. But what was given with one hand was taken away with the other. The emphasis was on bureaucratic control rather than local military development under gentry leadership. Yuan's militia was to start with the registration of households, proceed with the conscription of one adult male from each household, and result in the grouping of those conscripted in decimal units, along *pao-chia* lines. The first function of this system was the preparation and delivery of census lists to the official bureaucracy rather than coordinated local defense. The weight that Yuan put on control from above resulted, it seems, in a lack of gentry cooperation in the system's purposes.[96]

What large numbers of people actually thought about these matters is of course difficult to know. At this point in research on the problem, we have only occasional glimpses of contemporary impressions. I have referred to a few in chapter 6 in connection with Yuan's abolition of representative assemblies. A report from Hunan in mid-1914 fits the pattern of many reports, though it carries no statistical significance. When the local judge and the chief of police in Chu-chou, both products of modernizing reforms, were dismissed and their duties returned to the county magistrate, the merchants and the "mass of the people" seemed to approve, since these posts were tax burdens and further opportunities for official "squeeze." But, it was observed, some of the students and the gentry mourned the return to old ways.[97] The tolerance or even support that Yuan enjoyed among the social elite in much of the country in mid-1913 seems to have rapidly dissipated under the dictatorship. At the end of 1914, T'ang Shao-i asked the British minister to tell his former patron that "his Government was an autocracy of the worst kind and that his tenure of power would be limited unless he gave the people of China some share in the management of their own affairs."[98] It is reasonable to assume that those who had had substantial shares felt most keenly their loss.

Other segments of the society, even less able to articulate their sentiments than the gentry, seem not to have responded much more favorably to the dictatorship, though without the recent gentry experience of organization and movement it mattered less for the political shortrun. Any benefit to the peasantry accruing from Yuan's check on the gentry would have taken a longer time to mature than was afforded. The benefits were in any case problematical, since Yuan's aim was not to bring power to the peasantry but to absorb it all up for the bureaucratic administration. In any ultimate social contest, his government stood behind the existing order, not behind those who might gain from its overthrow. Yuan's troubles with the gentry should not be mistaken for serious support for lower orders in the society. Nothing had occurred that might induce anyone to believe that it was. Rural and urban worker discontent, expressed in scattered uprisings and strikes, continued, though at a frequency and level of organization that did not disturb the social order.[99]

There remained the merchants. Enthusiastic supporters of the 1911 Revolution, they had not inherited its rewards during the liberal republic and had no special reason to fight Yuan in 1913. The provincial governments of 1911 and 1912 had in many cases reduced or abolished the *likin* commercial transit and sales tax, the bane of the merchant community. But in about as many cases, it was soon reimposed. In Fukien, for example, *likin* was abolished in November, 1911, but reimposed in March, 1912, to liquidate a loan from the local Chinese chamber of commerce.[100] In Hunan, while the land tax remained constant, *likin* receipts rose enormously.[101] The revolutionary government in Chekiang at first abolished the *likin* but quickly reintroduced it under another name. The rate rose steeply.[102] The *likin* in Hupeh was the first tax abolished by the revolutionary government in 1911, but after its revival in the spring of 1912 it was said to be higher than ever.[103] Merchants in most places discovered that the liberal republic was not devoted to their interests.

After the Second Revolution, statements sympathetic toward merchant interests emerged regularly from Peking, but nothing substantial was done, except perhaps to free the Tientsin-Pukow railway of *likin* stations and, in early 1916, to introduce a consolidated transit tax for the twenty-four counties of the Peking metropolitan area on an experimental basis. As Yuan Shih-k'ai explained in late 1915, though an improper tax, *likin* revenues would be needed until the foreign powers agreed to raise the maritime customs rates.[104] Implicit was the proposition that merchant interests must wait upon larger national aims, that merchant welfare was not vital.

Indeed, Yuan, in his urge to strengthen central control and increase revenues, inevitably irritated merchant sensibilities. The great proliferation of little taxes were more likely to attach to merchant trade than to gentry property. Yuan's government even threatened an income tax that was directed chiefly at businesses, bondholders, and bankers. It was budgeted to produce almost $3 million in 1916, but was postponed until midyear as an act of grace by the new emperor.[105] Strict regulations for chambers of commerce, designed to facilitate official control, produced protests from Shanghai and Canton.[106] The dictatorship's policies of industrial and general economic development were insufficient compensation for the neglect of immediate merchant interests. The policies largely remained potentialities, without quick return. Large industrial enterprises were in any case the property of officials and gentry more often than of significant numbers of the merchant class. When Yuan toppled, the merchant community looked on with equanimity.

There is no reason to believe that Yuan nurtured animosity toward any particular social group. He came from the gentry; he believed in commercial and industrial development; he viewed the peasants with the patronizing benevolence characteristic of those far removed from any real dealings with them. Having decided to pursue the aims of Chinese nationalism through administrative centralization of power, however, he had nothing to offer the immediate concerns of any group. All he could urge was sacrifice and trust in himself. His performance inspired neither further sacrifice nor trust. Indeed, it was crippled from the start, since the power that could be readily mobilized by purely bureaucratic means was nowhere near enough to stand down the forces of imperialism. The effort to proceed in this fashion only deepened pessimism and disillusionment. Perhaps the impossibility of the strategy that Yuan adopted helps explain the rashness of his last great decision, to cap his traditionalistic revivals with a monarchical movement.

Chapter 8

The Monarchical Attempt

As the magnitude of Yuan's error in attempting to make himself emperor became apparent in early 1916, his adviser G. E. Morrison was struck by the irony: "He had restored a fair measure of order throughout the whole country, his word was law, he had at least as great control of China as had ever been obtained by any ruler, and yet he goes and sacrifices everything for the sake of an empty bauble."[1] The puzzle posed by the contrast between the extent of Yuan's power, even if we allow for the exaggeration in Morrison's description, and his precipitate fall has resisted easy explanation. But it remains an important question. The monarchical attempt was the conclusion to Yuan's career. He was saved from the full consequences of its failure only by a timely death. The inclination in studies of the man to make it the key to his whole political life is understandable. At the least, any interpretation of the presidency has to take into account his only partially fulfilled monarchical moment.

Decision for Monarchism

As we look back from some distance, the 1911 Revolution seems not only to have unseated the Manchu monarch but to have also mortally wounded the monarchical principle. Republicanism in some form or other decisively triumphed, despite the youth of the idea among Chinese. In the first years of the republic, however, the permanence of the victory was not obvious. The gentry were schooled in millennia of monarchical history and the countless tales of imperial heroes, imperial achievements, and imperial villainies that gave the history substance. The consciousness of the political possibilities of monarchy had not been nullified by the recently acquired knowledge of the Western republican model; it had only been overlaid. Among the nonelite portions of the population, where monarchical song and story were embedded in the culture, even the overlay was absent. As Mao Tse-tung was reported to have said in another context in 1970, "It was hard . . . for people to overcome the habits of 3,000 years of emperor-worshiping tradition."[2] Among republican partisans, the possibility of a monarchical restoration was a source of great anxiety. Except for polemical purposes, few Chinese considered it "an empty bauble."

The prime monarchical candidates during the years of Yuan's presidency were the deposed Manchu court, which continued after the revolution to have some few domestic and foreign supporters, and Yuan Shih-k'ai himself. From the moment that the seriousness of the 1911 Revolution became apparent, agitation by some in Yuan's entourage for his enthronement emerged and recurred intermittently until Yuan adopted their goal as his own in 1915. In November, 1911, Yuan K'o-ting, Yuan Shih-k'ai's eldest son, explored with important foreigners in Peking their reaction to the possibility that, after a transitional republican stage, the revolution might acclaim his father as emperor.[3] Yuan Shih-k'ai himself did not indulge in these explorations; if he had been surreptitiously floating trial balloons, he acknowledged their failure by sending his son home to Honan in early December, 1911.[4] Tuan Chih-kuei, an intimate military associate of Yuan's, and Chang I-lin, a literary secretary, seem also to have favored Yuan's enthronement at the time of the revolution.[5] Although prorepublican sentiment predominated among Yuan's aides during the 1911 Revolution, the obvious alternative of Yuan's own emperorship was present from the beginning and never failed to find its advocates.

The life of the monarchical alternative was best demonstrated, however, by the fear of it among republicans. Much more common than the occasional advocacy of monarchy among a minority of Yuan's entourage was the constant warning against its reemergence among the makers of the revolution. When the 1911 Revolution was not two months old, Ts'ai Yuan-p'ei, a veteran Shanghai revolutionary intellectual, wired from Berlin his suspicion that Yuan Shih-k'ai would use the occasion to make himself emperor.[6] During January, 1912, when the negotiations between Yuan and the revolutionaries seemed bogged down, the thought that Yuan was aspiring to imperial honors was frequently expressed in Nanking. After the abdication, there was worry that Yuan might cooperate in a Manchu restoration.[7] Actually, serious consideration seems to have been given in 1914 in Peking to the possibility of a Manchu figurehead monarch with Yuan as prime minister or regent. The idea was publicly broached, and the American-educated Liang Tun-yen, minister of communications at the time, espoused this course.[8] But the primary fear, and the real possibility, was that Yuan himself might assume the throne. In Kwangtung in late 1912, opposition to policies of centralization was justified partly in terms of thwarting Yuan's presumed imperial pretensions.[9] Huang Hsing in Shanghai, a couple of weeks before Sung Chiao-jen's assassination, understood Yuan to be striving to become emperor.[10] Sun Yat-sen from his exile in Japan in early 1914 was warning Japanese of Yuan's imperial eagerness.[11] Many more instances of this sort could be cited. Monarchy remained a plausible option: feared by many, but very much alive.

Why did Yuan try to exercise that option? The question cannot be answered definitively. Perhaps Yuan himself could not have explained it to our satisfaction. An aide observed that he had never seen Yuan, who was given to quick decisions, so uncertain and "torn with conflicting emotions" as when he was deciding for the monarchy.[12]

Certainly Yuan had ambition. The quality would seem to be inherent in a career that had gone so far. The question remains: why did his ambition assume an openly monarchical form in 1915? We cannot exclude the element of dreams of imperial glory for himself and his progeny. Few people within reach of exploiting the august imperial tradition of China would be entirely indifferent to its temptations. But those who were close to Yuan at the time and have recorded their impressions have not stressed his vainglory or preoccupation with personal fulfillment. Being unable to follow Yuan very far into this intimate psychological area, I can only convey my sense that an infatuation with images of yellow robes and dynastic splendor was at most a minor factor in his decision. Nor have I discovered any premonitions of imminent death that might have inspired a last gamble for dynastic immortality, although Yuan's health was noticeably poor from the summer of 1915 onward.

The public power of China's ruler and his government, however, was very much at issue. In the aftermath of Yuan's submission to the Japanese ultimatum in May, 1915, an aide spoke of the president's concern "at the mess he is making of things" and of his desire to do something "theatrical."[13] As the monarchical movement was launched in August, 1915, Yuan spoke privately of his frustrations as president, of how he had been less beset by restrictions on his authority when he was governor-general under the

Ch'ing.[14] Although the reach of his political power had in fact never been greater than it was in mid-1915, he was dissatisfied with what he had accomplished and feared for the polity's future stability.

The belief that the revival of monarchical forms would succeed where a republican dictatorship had failed rested on assumptions about the "real conditions" of China. Yuan had never been persuaded of the suitability of the republic. Even as he was maneuvering toward a republican posture during the 1911 Revolution, he held that the "masses of the people . . . were intensely conservative and monarchical."[15] Peking officials and old China hands entertained new foreign arrivals with stories of popular ignorance regarding the republic, of how only a few miles from the capital the common folk took the title of president as a new name for the emperor. Monarchical advocates often said that the republican system had not engaged the feelings of ordinary people, that it was premature in China.[16] In expounding the new presidential election law of December, 1914, which reduced the process to a very limited ritual, Yuan asserted: "The fundamental laws of a nation should reflect the country's history and the sentiments of its people. This is definitely not a situation where the people's welfare and the national need can be served merely by legal theories and abstract speculations."[17]

In the formal defense of monarchy inaugurating the movement in August, 1915, the argument was made that the republic, loose talk about freedom and equality, and low levels of education among the people had combined to diminish respect for the state and to dissipate the power of the central government. Even Peiyang soldiers had become disobedient.[18] From this point of view, the republic, with or without representative institutions, spelled instability. The Latin American cases were often cited, particularly the contemporaneous Mexican upheavals. Unwilling fully to face his own failures of leadership and blind to the fundamental flaws in his strategy of bureaucratic centralization, Yuan opted for monarchy as an accommodation to popular psychology and as a means of gaining public order and greater power for the central government.

In effect, Yuan was appealing to the sanction of popular will. How could he reconcile this appeal with his hostile attitude toward assertive representative assemblies? In this aspect of the matter, Yuan was operating in a field of political ideas that shared more with the modern West than the nineteenth-century Chinese empire. Like subsequent Chinese political leaders, Yuan had to pay deference to the theory of popular sovereignty. Both in establishing his dictatorship and in aspiring to emperorship, he was exercising power within a new, "postimperial" political order, where the leader was directly accountable to the popular will. Hence, like other modern politicians, he had to adopt an operational understanding of the popular will that would suit his purposes. In late 1913, for example, he said that ". . . the term 'national will' only possesses value when it represents the will of the majority of law-abiding citizens. The one desire of law-abiding citizens is to pursue their respective avocations in peace and quietness: I am absolutely certain that they have no sympathy with that minority of turbulent demagogues who only delight in making mischief. So too with public opinion. . . ."[19] This was propounded when his government was about to suspend all institutions of representative government and when a campaign of terror against the largest political party was in full swing. Proceeding from these attitudes, Yuan could see his monarchy as an effort both to represent and to reach the "intensely conservative and monarchical" masses. And he could dismiss as self-interested or narrow-minded the swelling opposition.

It is important to note that in one sense Yuan was right. There often exists an inarticulate, politically inert majority, who may not feel represented by the society's active organizations and spokespersons, including its elected officials. But Yuan did not intend to break down hierarchical social and political structures in order to reach mass sentiment, to organize it on its own terms, or to give it power. Rather, the very powerlessness of the unorganized masses, lacking effective voice, seems to have attracted this practitioner of bureaucratic politics. Almost any opinion could be ascribed to the people. Accordingly, claims to legitimacy could be based on such ascribed sentiments and on manipulated elections.

The monarchical movement in China in 1915, then, was an effort designed to express the presumed preferences of the mass of the population and, by appealing to ingrained attitudes, to win greater responsiveness to the government. The result was to be a stronger and more advanced country, with a better chance for stable constitutionalism. Or so the movement's defenders insisted. In October, 1915, Liang Shih-i and Chou Tzu-ch'i argued that a reversion to monarchy would facilitate reforming the land tax, which was the ultimate test of China's ability to survive. They did not envisage simply the revival of Ch'ing levels of taxation; in their view, modernizing programs would require that the agrarian sector bear a heavier burden than ever before. The sanction of national traditions, "a form of authority with which the people are more familiar," was necessary, they said, to meet these new requirements.[20] Wellington Koo, who was appointed minister to the United States in 1915 at age twenty-eight, had worked closely enough to Yuan to be familiar with his thinking. Perhaps he expounded Yuan's views when he explained the new monarchy to the American Academy of Political and Social Science in January, 1916. The Chinese were divided internally, he said, between the old literati and the foreign-educated, leaving "the problem of striking a middle course of action between the conservatives on one side and the radicals on the other. . . ." But only a strong and unified government could handle China's impaired freedom of action under the treaties, he argued. The decision for the monarchy reflected the need for a "government able to hold the country together, develop its wealth and strength, and help realize the intensely patriotic aspirations of its people."[21]

The major weakness of the monarchical argument in 1915 was not the assertion that republican sentiment among the mass of the people was shallow. Ch'en Tu-hsiu, dean at Peking University and later head of the Communist Party, wrote in 1917 that Yuan had been quite right in thinking that "most people still believed in monarchy and had no faith in a republic."[22] His mistake was in thinking that this "belief" meant support, in the absence of any political links with the masses, and in thinking that the educated elite would cooperate.

To win the support of the social elite and to bridge the gap between the "conservatives" and "radicals" of Wellington Koo's analysis, Yuan's monarchical movement stressed the modern character of his projected empire. Although the process was blatantly rigged, Yuan had himself *elected* emperor. He referred frequently to his emperorship as arising from the will of the people (an interpretation that also served as a convenient excuse for violating his republican oath): "Our country's sovereignty is founded upon the whole body of the people. How could I oppose their desire?"[23] The name of the new order was to be the Empire of China (*Chung-hua ti-kuo*, an alteration of one character from the name of the republic, *Chung-hua min-kuo*), rather than a traditional dynastic appellation (such as *Ta-Ch'ing-kuo*).[24] The kotow, certain servile forms of address, the use of eunuchs as palace attendants—"all the worthless features of monarchy"—were rejected.[25]

Most important of all, the monarchy was to be constitutional. Indeed, those who publicly launched the monarchical campaign in August, 1915, argued that a monarchy was an essential precondition to constitutionalism. Because of the disorder attendant upon republicanism under Chinese conditions, the republic led inevitably to despotism, they said. Ironically, they cited the character of the dictatorship to illustrate the need for monarchy. They held that the dictatorship contained merely the forms of constitutionalism (and little enough of them, one might add), but was governed by the spirit of despotism. Only a monarchy could bring true constitutionalism; and only constitutionalism could bring wealth and strength to China.[26] The argument was ingenious and self-serving. Everyone was supposed to be appeased by the blending of traditional and contemporary, Chinese and Western, monarchical and constitutional.

We have seen in chapter 6 how pale in fact were the first practical reflections of the constitutionalist promises. How could it have been otherwise, when the monarchy was being invoked in support of greater power to the state, in pursuance of more effective administrative centralization?

There remains the matter of timing. Advocates of Yuan's monarchy had been in his entourage since the outbreak of the 1911 Revolution. Whether Yuan had always secretly agreed with them or not, we cannot know. But Yuan made their policy unequivocally his own only during 1915. His intentions became public with the formation of the Society to Plan for Peace (Ch'ou-an hui) on August 14, 1915, and the subsequent officially orchestrated agitation. The major possible determinants of the timing were three: the stage reached in the consolidation of his power in the country as a whole; his reading of Japanese intentions; and his feeling of need for a new prop to his political authority.

If Yuan had been waiting for sufficient power to work his will before arrogating the throne, then 1914 would have served almost as well as 1915. By early 1914, his forces were consolidated in most of the northern and central provinces. As he reorganized the country's administrative system, he could have tried to inaugurate his monarchy. Of course there was room for further accretions of power, and Yuan might have been waiting for his to grow before trying for the throne. For example, the replacement of county officials throughout the country took time. The most notable event that might have been a form of preparation was the investment of Szechwan by Peking's forces.

During the Second Revolution, Szechwan had suffered incursions from some northern troops, as well as contingents from Yunnan and Kweichow. But the provincial government, which sided with Yuan, remained the one that had emerged out of local politics after the 1911 Revolution. In 1914,

Szechwan, with her population of some 50 million, continued for a third year to be ruled by Szechwanese. Despite the overt loyalty of the provincial government, Peking was not pleased with the result. True, the provincial assembly was shut down; and the Szechwan railway company, the center of provincial loyalties in the great struggle of the summer of 1911, was quietly nationalized. But restiveness at Yuan's policies and resistance to central interference persisted. A Peking plan for the redemption of depreciated Szechwanese paper currency, such as was effected in Kwangtung and Hunan, was successfully deflected in 1914 by the local authorities. Yuan complained that Szechwan was not doing its share in remitting funds to the central government. A British consular report in April, 1914, summarized the province's response to the dictatorship in this way:

> The refusal . . . to remit to Peking may legitimately be considered as a symptom of lack of sympathy with the centralizing policy of Yuan Shih Kai and a sign of widening breach between Peking and the Provinces as a direct outcome of recent Presidential action in abolishing Parliament and the Assemblies and so flouting the wishes of the gentry for representation in the Government of their country. The substitution of the bureaucratic for the democratic ideal is by no means popular in Szechwan.[27]

To root out any lingering traces of "gentry democracy" and overcome resistance to centralized rule in this populous and comparatively wealthy province, Yuan sent his own men and troops to take over the provincial and local administration. By early January, 1915, Yuan had decided to appoint Ch'en I, the army's vice-chief of staff, to replace both the Szechwanese civil governor and the Szechwanese general-in-chief. Ch'en I, a native of Hupeh, brought with him two airplanes and twelve to fifteen thousand Peiyang troops, including a unit commanded by Feng Yü-hsiang. He arrested more than a dozen high provincial officials, among whom was the financial commissioner, later reported to have committed suicide in prison. Within three months of his arrival in April, 60 percent of the province's county magistrates had been replaced. The rest were slated for imminent removal. All over the province, Szechwanese officials, civil and military, were being replaced or edged aside by extraprovincial bureaucrats and officers. Tension was high, but there was no physical resistance. By July, 1915, Szechwan was integrated into Yuan's centralized administrative system.[28] In August, 1915, the monarchical movement was formally launched.

Other plans for a greater concentration of central power, such as a new elite military force based in Peking, were in too preliminary a stage to tip the balance in favor of some new risky move. But the apparent absorption of Szechwan—the note redemption scheme was quickly put into effect, an illustration of Peking's new power in this province—may have been considered a major enabling factor. Only later did Yuan discover the fragility of his bureaucratic style of control over the country-sized province of Szechwan.

A second possible influence on the timing of Yuan's decision for the monarchy was his concern about Japan. It has been argued that Japan systematically led Yuan to believe she would support his monarchical movement and then, when it was too late for retreat, showed her true colors of opposition, thereby toppling Yuan's rule. In its extreme form, the argument includes the charge that Yuan arranged to exchange submission to Japan's Twenty-One Demands for acceptance of his monarchy.[29] Suspicions of a Japanese conspiracy are not only latter-day reconstructions. Some contemporary observers had the same thoughts.

Monarchical advocates in Yuan's entourage had quietly renewed their agitation in December, 1914, or January, 1915. Such agitation had occurred before, and it was not until the end of July, 1915, that well-informed observers became convinced that Yuan Shih-k'ai was endorsing the idea. But the suspicion that he might was common. At one stage of the negotiations over the Twenty-One Demands, Liang Ch'i-ch'ao feared that Yuan had secretly agreed to the Japanese demands in return for their support for his emperorship.[30] Indeed, some Japanese were trying to create that impression.[31] Yuan's extended resistance to the demands and the embarrassingly ambivalent quality of Japan's victory in May removed much of the credibility from the specific charge of collusion. But after the monarchical movement went public in mid-August, 1915, the early Japanese response was notably receptive. The prime minister and acting foreign minister, Ōkuma Shigenobu, announced in early September that Japan would not interfere in this Chinese affair, unless Japanese interests were affected. The impression given was one of support for Yuan's monarchy. Then, in late October, the Japanese government publicly and threateningly expressed its doubts about the advisability of the abandonment of the republic. Jordan, the British minister in Peking, interpreted the move as a sudden shift that had surprised the Chinese government and betrayed its expectations.[32] Even after Japan's formal declaration of opposition, certain Japanese continued to bear reassuring messages to Yuan, to the effect that the opposition was not unalterable and a delay in inaugurating the monarchy would meet Japanese objections.[33] G. E. Morrison later came to believe that the Japanese, by convincing Yuan that they supported his monarchical movement, had "lured him to his destruction."[34] In this view, then, the timing of the monarchical effort was largely determined by Japanese manipulation of Yuan.

No Japanese blueprint for enticing Yuan into this political trap has been discovered. If there was one, it was not followed by the Japanese government as a whole. Japan spoke with several voices. Yuan certainly hoped that Japanese power would not be used against his monarchical project. But any deception in the matter was at least in part self-induced. Yuan chose to believe those Japanese voices that said what he wanted to hear, and closed his ears to others or ignored them. Toward the end of August, 1915, Hioki Eki, the Japanese minister in Peking, warned of possible Japanese opposition to Yuan's monarchy and expounded to Yuan's top Japan expert, Ts'ao Ju-lin, the causes of Japanese hostility.[35] Shortly thereafter, Ts'ao was reported in the Shanghai press as saying that Japan opposed the abandonment of the republic.[36] Ariga Nagao, who had proved his ties to the *genrō* during the negotiations earlier in the year, spoke to Yuan in late August or early September regarding the illegality and dangers of any change to monarchy.[37] Along with occasional reassurances, Yuan's diplomatic representative in Tokyo also reported the open hostility in early September of the Japanese military and the newspapers.[38] Even Ōkuma's friendly remarks contained the important qualification that Japanese interests must not be disturbed by the consequences of the proposed changes. At the very time that Ōkuma was making his statement of benevolent neutrality toward Yuan's assumption of the throne, the Japanese legation in Peking was accumulating impressive evidence of high-level opposition in China to the monarchical movement. The likelihood of domestic upheaval and the consequent endangering of foreign interests seemed great to official Japanese observers. Japan's new foreign minister, Ishii Kikujirō, confirmed this state of affairs for himself by a trip through China before taking office in Tokyo in October.[39]

At the end of October, 1915, Japan and England joined in a public warning to Peking, urging postponement of the monarchy. Yuan need not have been surprised. With London's approval, the British minister had several times expressed to Yuan and his lieutenants his disagreement with the monarchical effort.[40] Only an obstinate pursuit of his goal could have caused Yuan to miss the more subtle Japanese warnings and then flout the public foreign challenge to his plans.

Yuan's refusal to disavow the monarchical movement, despite the rapid accumulation of danger signals in the fall of 1915, underlines the importance of the third possible determinant of his timing: his sense of political need for the monarchy. His plan to ascend a throne of his own making was not understood as a reward granted by the Chinese public or foreign powers for services rendered. He knew he was not being elevated to the monarchy by irresistible popular demand. He also realized that he had neither appeased Japanese aspirations in China nor won their gratitude. The monarchy was not a reward; it was a weapon, to fend off external threats and build domestic strength.

We have already noted the arguments for the monarchy as an antidote to domestic difficulties, such as sluggishness in reform programs—difficulties that were increasingly remarked upon by Yuan's erstwhile supporters by early 1915.[41] In foreign affairs, the failure was if anything starker. Yuan continued to live in terror of further Japanese actions after he signed the treaty in May, 1915. The aftermath of the Twenty-One Demands produced, not a confidence that the Japanese would support him in whatever he did, but a desperate lunge at an institutional alteration that might help to protect him against them. As Liang Shih-i explained it when he was working toward the monarchy, the Japanese would be more sympathetic if a monarch reigned in China. Or as Chang I-lin, former chief of Yuan's secretariat and his newly appointed minister of education, described the strategy at the end of 1915, the monarchical movement would act as a diversion, delaying any Japanese attempts to impose further demands on China. Whether Japan welcomed the change or not, time would be won, perhaps until the European war ended and a balance of power would return to the Far East to check Japanese ambitions. At least so Chang described Yuan's reasoning.[42] Jordan had noted ". . . the foolish belief amongst the Chinese that they will be in a better position to withstand Japanese aggression under a Monarchy than under a Republican form of Government. . ." and hence would discount Japanese warnings against the monarchy.[43] Yuan did discount the warnings. He exaggerated every sign that well-placed Japanese remained favorably disposed. But he was driven to press on in any case, because the idea was ultimately to confound Japanese ambitions. In this peculiar fashion, the trauma of the Twenty-One Demands contributed to the decision to reach for the monarchy. The depth of the feeling in mid-1915 that domestic and foreign affairs both were in serious trouble may have been the most compelling factor in determining the timing of Yuan's move.

Yuan's most conspicuous foreign advocate in this enterprise was Frank J. Goodnow, an assistant in the first year of the dictatorship, who returned to Peking from his presidency at Johns Hopkins University for six weeks during the summer of 1915. One of Goodnow's closest associates during his previous tour had been Yuan K'o-ting, who in 1915 was a leading agitator on behalf of the monarchy.[44] Goodnow was a known quantity to the monarchists. He was asked soon after his arrival in July, 1915, to write an essay on the suitability of a Chinese monarchy. He agreed and came out privately and publicly for a monarchical restoration.[45]

Goodnow's intervention on this issue demonstrated an extraordinary cultural and academic arrogance. But he meant what he said. Some have seen Goodnow as an unwitting dupe, or worse, an intellectual mercenary, consciously prostituting his scholarship.[46] It is true that he soon regretted his temerity and began to emphasize the conditions (foreign and domestic toleration, arrangements for the succession, and plans for a constitution) that he had attached to his monarchical prescription. On the other hand, he believed that the conditions would be readily met.[47] Generally, his monarchical advocacy was quite consistent with the approach toward Chinese problems that he had taken in supporting the dictatorship in 1913 and 1914.

His famous essay began with the thought that ". . . the form of government which a country usually possesses is for the most part determined by the necessities of practical life." His analysis, as in the earlier years, stressed the uneducated state of the people, their low political capacity, and, because of the global character of European capital and its enterprises, the growing Western intolerance of disorder anywhere. His weighing of these factors led him to this conclusion: "It is of course not susceptible of doubt that a monarchy is better suited than a republic to China. China's history and traditions, her social and economic conditions, her relations with foreign powers all make it probable that the country would develop that constitutional government which it must develop if it is to preserve its independence as a state, more easily as a monarchy than as a republic."[48]

With the formal launching of the monarchical movement in mid-August, much was made of the scientific basis provided the movement by Goodnow, a distinguished scholar of a leading republic. A translation of his essay was widely circulated. But neither Goodnow's support nor the rest of the elaborate rigmarole that attended the monarchical movement proved persuasive to Yuan's domestic audience.

Yuan accepted his "election" as emperor on December 11, 1915, and ignoring further formal warnings from England and Japan, proceeded with plans for his full investiture. Blending old imperial styles with the Western calendar and an implied promise of constitutional government, on January 1, 1916, official documents began using Yuan's chosen reign title, Hung-hsien, or era of the grand constitution. Actual enthronement was scheduled to occur within a few weeks. Meanwhile dissent had been building up at home. It emerged as a full-blown, armed challenge on December 25, 1915. Yuan never recovered.

The Government Divided

Yuan's fall presents a picture of the disintegration of apparently well-established dictatorial power. His government had successfully crushed the only energetic political party of national scope, the Kuomintang. Even the KMT's exiled leaders had failed to remain together. Exercising administrative authority throughout the country, in most places to a high degree, Yuan was able to compel almost unanimous public approval among provincial chiefs for launching his new order. Many foreign observers concluded that serious opposition to Yuan's enthronement was totally lacking. It is true that there was no ready-made organizational focus for dissent and that political apathy had taken hold among large portions of the elite. But outward appearances were deceiving. They often are, where a regime is built on large doses of repression. The resulting apathy may be real, but unstable, ready to give way to new possibilities if given a chance. This condition obtained in China in late 1915 and did not go unnoticed; to the penetrating investigator, an enormous disaffection from Yuan's plans revealed itself.

The disaffection could be found next to the top of the political pyramid. Yuan's Peking government divided over the issue. The weightiest and most prestigious participants in Yuan's political and military machine did not support the monarchy, with very few exceptions. The active proponents were as a group not Yuan's finest.

The initiators of the movement before Yuan Shih-k'ai made it his own were his eldest son, Yuan K'o-ting, and Yang Tu. His son was not an impressive physical or intellectual specimen, a fact that the father seemed ready to acknowledge as a weakness for the new dynasty. He had done nothing to win general respect and was not a leader in the overall governmental operation.

Yang Tu, at age forty, was a veteran of several political movements and affiliations. A student of the conservative Hunanese scholar Wang K'ai-yun, he was an early participant in the experience of study in Japan and attended Waseda University. He did well in the same special examinations in economics of 1903 that brought prominence to Liang Shih-i and Chang I-lin. He worked briefly with Huang Hsing's revolutionary group in 1904, but did not join the T'ung-meng hui and associated himself for a period with Liang Ch'i-ch'ao. He participated in the constitutionalist movement of the late Ch'ing both in and out of the government. He served Yuan in Peking during the 1911 Revolution but found no place in the new republican government for over a year—blocked, apparently, by T'ang Shao-i and Liang Shih-i. Even after he was officially employed, his jobs were of secondary importance, until he became the key figure in agitation for Yuan's enthronement.[49] The suggestion of ambition emerges strongly from this career, although he seemed too ready to take risks to be characterized as a mere opportunist. When the monarchical experiment came crashing down in utter failure, Yang Tu stuck to his position, asserting in May, 1916, his continuing belief in the desirability for China of constitutional monarchy and adding: "I was mainly responsible for the bringing about of the movement, and . . . I do not intend, neither have I any desire to shirk my responsibility for so doing."[50] Yang Tu, like Goodnow, may have been a sincere advocate, but he was not a heavyweight in Chinese politics.

Early in their campaign Yuan K'o-ting and Yang Tu tried to win support among leading military men. They fared poorly. Tuan Chih-kuei, who is said to have advocated Yuan's enthronement during the 1911 Revolution, became a leader in the 1915 movement. Tuan Chih-kuei was among the least reputable of Yuan's longtime military associates. Ni Ssu-ch'ung, general-in-chief in Anhwei, soon became a second military leader in the movement, engaging in persuasion and threats to bring others around. These two were the only men with substantial military and administrative authority in 1915 who took an active part. As rebellion against the monarchy began in Yunnan, its well-informed leadership cited four authors of Yuan's monarchical effort: Yuan K'o-ting, Tuan Chih-kuei, Yang Tu, and Ku Ao (a Japanese-educated politician and legislative aide to Yuan Shih-k'ai).[51]

In later revolutionary lists of monarchical criminals, Tuan Chih-kuei and Ni Ssu-ch'ung led the names of implicated generals. Other military men were lesser figures, occupying desk jobs or honorary posts in Peking at the time of the monarchical movement.[52]

Although failing to win the committed cooperation of most of the country's leading military figures, the monarchical movement did secure the active engagement of one important segment of the Peking government. Liang Shih-i had not joined in the early agitation. His place in Yuan's operation had already declined in importance, since a degree of fiscal regularity and financial solvency had rendered his manipulative skills less necessary. Beginning in June, 1915, a number of his close associates (the core of the "communications clique") were impeached for embezzlement. In fact, a major upheaval was underway within the bureaucracy, with charges and countercharges flying in all directions. How much of this was an aspect of the campaign to marshal support for the monarchical movement is uncertain. In any case, by the beginning of September, 1915, Liang Shih-i was working energetically for Yuan's imperial effort. Chu Ch'i-ch'ien and Chou Tzu-ch'i, by this time close to Liang Shih-i, also joined up.[53]

The organizers and leading spokesmen of the monarchical movement of 1915 were, then, only a portion of those who had formed the basis of Yuan's political strength over the years. They were not the most traditionally oriented nor the oldest. Several had spent time abroad. They were generally under fifty years of age. But, with the exception of Liang Shih-i and Chou Tzu-ch'i, they did not include the leading lights of Yuan's administration.

The response of the rest of the government ranged widely, from begrudging submission to outspoken opposition. Overt acts of opposition were of course less common than confidentially expressed dissent, either to Yuan Shih-k'ai himself, to the outriders of the monarchical movement, or to inquiring diplomats. But if Yuan's plans were considered a mistake from their inception by a considerable number of old associates and leaders in his government, the prospects for acceptance in the population at large were impossibly slim.

The moment and motives as well as the manner of opposition varied greatly. Tuan Ch'i-jui was Yuan's most valued military associate and had served him in a variety of top posts, including army minister, prime minister, and provincial chief. He was not, however, a lackey without a will of his own, and tension between Tuan and Yuan had emerged over other issues than Yuan's possible enthronement. Tuan had objected, for example, to the manner in which Yuan had planned the development of an elite army contingent in Peking, the so-called Model Army, putting nonmilitary men in command (and thereby both compromising its professional quality and reducing any influence Tuan might have regarding it).[54] A reorganization of the chief military agencies in 1914 had impaired the independence of the army minister, who Tuan was, and added another irritant to the relationship.[55] According to one contemporary story, Tuan's negative response to a question by Yuan at a banquet in February, 1915, about the possibility of dissolving the republic further widened the gap. In early May, on the grounds that China was militarily unprepared, Yuan declined Tuan's advice to reject the Japanese ultimatum. Shortly thereafter Tuan resigned as army minister (in the form of sick leave, which turned into a formal resignation at the end of August). Tuan's differences with Yuan had more than one dimension. But his particular opposition to the monarchical movement became widely known. As Yuan's troubles accumulated, Tuan resisted urgent pleas to rally to Yuan's side. He returned only after the monarchical effort was abandoned and he could write his own terms.[56]

A summary in early September, 1915, of Japanese intelligence on opposition to Yuan's monarchy in the Peking government painted an advanced state of disaffection.[57] Hsu Shih-ch'ang, Yuan's oldest ally and friend, who in 1914 had joined the government as secretary of state in the president's office or the equivalent of prime minister, was reported to be secretly opposed. And, indeed, he left the government about a month and a half later. Hsu's two deputies were also reported opposed (mistakenly, in the case of one of them), as was the chief of the president's secretariat, Chang I-lin. Although Chang I-lin stayed in the government, Yuan soon transferred him out of the secretariat on account of his opposition, which stood firm in the face of threats by Tuan Chih-kuei and Ni Ssu-ch'ung.[58] Three other members of the president's office were identified by the Japanese as being against Yuan's enthronement. Among cabinet ministers, T'ang Hua-lung, the minister of education, had already left his office on the pretext of illness. Both the foreign minister, Lu Cheng-hsiang, and the new army minister, Wang Shih-chen, were said to be opposed.[59] Chou Hsueh-hsi, the finance minister, had advised Yuan against the monarchy and was being urged by his illustrious father, Chou Fu, to resign. In the *ts'an-cheng-yuan*, Yuan's appointed pseudolegislature, twenty out of the full membership of seventy were known to be "clearly opposed," including the chairman, Li

Yuan-hung, who was also national vice-president. Further, half of a ten-man committee to draft a permanent constitution—an integral feature of Yuan's plan to establish a constitutional monarchy—was opposed to a monarchical system under Yuan Shih-k'ai. The Japanese tally of early opposition is largely confirmed by other reports and by later events—further resignations, requests for leave (sometimes denied), open resistance. It is worth remembering that these were men appointed directly by Yuan, who lived immediately under the shadow of his retributive power. In an ancient tradition, the censorate, which Yuan had revived in 1913, risked his retaliation by calling in September, 1915, for the suppression of the monarchical movement.

The leadership that Yuan had installed in the provinces proved in several important cases to be equally reluctant to welcome the new order. The key figure within Yuan's own establishment was Feng Kuo-chang, both for his record of service and leadership within the Peiyang army and for his strategic position in 1915 as general-in-chief at Nanking. His opposition to Yuan's monarchical scheme was the most public and the most consistent of Yuan's inner group. When Liang Ch'i-ch'ao visited Nanking in June, 1915, bearing tales of monarchical agitation, Feng responded by traveling to Peking and confronting Yuan face-to-face on the issue. He was assured that Yuan had no interest in being emperor and would never accept the honor. The whole exchange was actually recounted in the press, apparently committing Yuan firmly to republican abstinence from any monarchical flirtations. The public launching of the monarchical movement with Yuan's implied blessing less than two months later was naturally displeasing to Feng. In early September, he expressed his opposition through the local newspapers in Nanking, in a letter to Peking, and in statements by his staff to foreign officials.[60]

Feng did not sustain this overt opposition through the fall. In communications with the representatives of the rebellion in December, 1915, he temporized, expressing sympathy but arguing temporary weakness. But, when G. E. Morrison visited him in January, 1916, he spoke vigorously and in the hearing of many of his attendants about his opposition to Yuan's monarchy, which was already underway. He told Morrison that the formal telegrams of support that had been sent over his name in the fall were compelled by Peking and, in one instance, had actually been sent without his knowledge by an official from Peking who came all the way to Nanking for the purpose. As Feng had requested, Morrison reported this conversation in full to Yuan upon his return to Peking in early February. Knowledge of its content and of Yuan's angry reaction spread.[61] On March 20, 1916, Feng joined with others in a direct request to Yuan to cancel the monarchy. Although the cancellation was announced two days later, Feng was only partly mollified and adopted an ambiguous attitude toward Yuan's continuation in the revived presidency. He maintained his contacts with the revolutionaries, as well as with anti-Yuan Manchu royalists.[62]

Feng stopped short of outright defiance of Yuan and claimed a continuing friendship with him. Kiangsu province still remitted money to Peking. But his pressure against the monarchy was persistent. Even though he declined to join the open rebellion against Yuan, and thus disappointed the maximum hopes of its leaders, his opposition went beyond Tuan Ch'i-jui's silent withdrawal. It greatly encouraged others in their resistance to the monarchy. It revealed the hollowness of Yuan's scheme of imposing on the country a bureaucratically centralized administration. If Feng Kuo-chang would not automatically follow the direction of the center, who of importance could be trusted to do so?

In Chihli, where the posts of civil governor and general-in-chief were held concurrently by the same man, the occupant was Chu Chia-pao. Chu possessed in full measure the quality that Yuan so favored: administrative experience. A *chin-shih* of 1892, he had served in the board of rites, had been district magistrate in four different places and prefect in two (including Paoting), and had risen to provincial judge, provincial treasurer, and provincial governor before the revolution. But this impeccable mandarin background did not dispose him favorably to Yuan's monarchical attempt. He was reported opposed in September, 1915. He succumbed to the signature campaign and was induced to stay in office only after successive warnings and personal visits from Tuan Chih-kuei and Ni Ssu-ch'ung.[63]

It was said in Canton in October, 1915, that the civil governor, Chang Ming-ch'i, who had also been governor there under the Ch'ing in 1911, was opposed to a new dynasty.[64] In Peking the story was told in the fall of 1915 that General Chang Hsun, when prodded by the monarchical agitators, responded: "I very much agree with the imperial system, but who is to be emperor?"[65] In 1917, he was to lead an attempt to restore the Manchus to their throne. In 1915 and 1916, he remained cool to Yuan's own monarchical hopes. In a conversation with G. E. Morrison in January, 1916, the military chief of Shanghai bemoaned with tears in his eyes Yuan's "blunder."[66] Lu Jung-t'ing, general-in-chief in Kwangsi, who later joined the armed revolt against Yuan, was reported opposed as early as October, 1915. Like the other provincial executives, military and civilian, he gave his name in the fall of 1915 to petitions calling for the monarchy. He later justified himself on the grounds that the president dealt in falsehoods with his subordinates, so it was natural that he should receive lies in return.[67] Many cloaked their real feelings with the same prudential camouflage. We cannot know in what proportion of the whole they did so. Open opponents of the monarchical scheme, and even of Yuan as president, became numerous within Yuan's own operation as it became safer to take that position. The point needs to be registered, however, that much of it was not mere opportunism: disaffection had already been apparent, if one cared to look, when it could be quite dangerous and the ultimate outcome was unpredictable. Yuan's failure owed much to this condition.

Sentiment among the gentry and other parts of the social elite eludes measurement. Heavy repression, numerous informers, and a controlled press contributed to an appearance of apathy. For the population as a whole, indifference certainly prevailed. But reports of popular opposition were frequent, and signs of a positive response (the essential postulate of Yuan's scheme) virtually absent.

In Hunan, intelligence reports from missionary stations around the province collated by the American consul in December, 1915, and January, 1916, showed widespread objection to Yuan's emperorship, despite a muzzled press and a fear of expressing political opinions. The "thinking class" of Changteh, for example, while admitting that Yuan's departure might cause difficulties, was said to favor the continuation of the republic. Even those who did not oppose the monarchy noted unfavorably that Yuan was being abandoned by "all good statesmen."[68] A missionary in northern Hupeh wrote in mid-January, 1916: "Talk about the 'will of the people,' if they had their way in this district, I am afraid there would not be anything left of 'Yuan-shi-kai.' "[69] In the capital of Chekiang in the fall of 1915, the British consul described popular sentiment as favoring the republic.[70] Reports from Hankow and Tientsin emphasized the desire for stability and peace.[71] More characteristic were the reports from Shantung: efforts to arouse enthusiasm for the monarchical movement in the fall of 1915 were failing and subscriptions to the patriotic fund to resist Japanese encroachment abruptly ceased with the news of the movement; people could not bring themselves to see Yuan as more than an ordinary man and hence opposed his imperial pretensions; the gentry entertained a great deal of concealed opposition from the beginning of the movement, and once the revolutionary flag was raised in Shantung, pressed the officials of the province to declare the province's independence and join the rebellion.[72] In a moment of wit, shopkeepers in Kaifeng, the capital of Yuan's native province, declared that the decorations they were forced to display in late December, 1915, in honor of Yuan's accession were for Christmas.[73] In most provinces the scramble to dissociate oneself from Yuan's unpopular movement gathered momentum through the winter of 1915–16.

Despite the disposition of elite portions of the population outside the government to oppose Yuan's monarchy, popular sentiment did not become politically organized except in a few instances. The instrument of Yuan's downfall was not a broad movement in the social elite, such as had occurred in 1911. His ruin was more directly due to a split within his own bureaucratic establishment, a split where the most capable tended to join the opposition or to withdraw. The weight of gentry opinion no doubt encouraged or enabled the defections to occur. But the defectors chose not to reach out systematically into the population for support. They had, after all, been part of Yuan's dictatorship and shared many of his attitudes, including a bureaucratic conception of politics. Yuan's administrative organization retained its bureaucratic attitudes even as it lost its centralized coherence. Feng Kuo-chang in Nanking ruthlessly suppressed all antimonarchical agitation in Kiangsu, on grounds of preserving peace and order, while speaking out against the monarchy himself. Ch'en I, who had taken over Szechwan in the name of Peking's centralized control, proceeded to bargain with the rebellion against Yuan shortly after it broke out. In a few months, his defection from Yuan was complete. But, he cooperated only cautiously with popular Szechwanese movement. At an early stage, he had one student shot and six others arrested for complicity in the antimonarchical movement.[74] In Yunnan itself, where the first base for the rising against Yuan was established, popular enthusiasm for the movement to overthrow Yuan was perhaps less than anywhere in the country. For Yunnanese, it represented only the continuation of a military dominance, established by Ts'ai O in 1911, which had granted little space in the province for broadly based gentry power.

The dispersed KMT leadership, which collectively might have broken through the narrow political habits of the dictatorship, was divided and demoralized. It played a primary role in only a few limited areas.

Sources and Arguments of
the Opposition

The arguments offered by prominent defectors from Yuan's government for their opposition were more complicated than one might at first suppose. Denunciations of tyranny were sufficient only for former leaders of the KMT, who had built an honorable record of resistance to Yuan's authority. The others had been accomplices to Yuan's dictatorship. Furthermore, the monarchical movement could not simply be dismissed as reactionary. It came dressed in ideas of modernization. It made statements about Chinese conditions, about the psychology of the people and their educational level, about programs of gradual reform, about constitutionalism. Some of the arguments for the monarchy had once been in the mouths of its newfound opponents. Younger bureaucrats and the foreign educated were among those playing a major role on behalf of Yuan's enthronement. Frank J. Goodnow was on their side and provided them with a text. Opposition to all this might come from almost anywhere on the political spectrum.

Liang Ch'i-ch'ao led the polemical riposte to the monarchical movement. Despite Yuan's efforts to buy him off, Liang published in late August, 1915, a major statement of his objections to the establishment of a monarchy. As a prerevolutionary opponent of republicanism, Liang presented his postrevolutionary opposition to monarchism as a consistent objection to changing the basic form of the state, whether it happened at the time to be monarchical or republican. Tinkering with fundamentals, as opposed to administrative reforms, was an act that invited trouble. In response to the movement's constitutionalist emphasis (historically his own), Liang both doubted the likelihood of constitutional promises being fulfilled and argued against their present desirability. The dictatorship, he argued, was suitable for China's current circumstances and gave the president quite sufficient power to regulate the succession in a manner that met objections to the destabilizing effects of republican elections. Part of Liang's critique, then, was from a position apparently more conservative than that of the monarchists.

Liang's most telling point, however, was that the revival would not serve its purported ends. Even if the monarchy were restored, he insisted, it would work no magical attraction upon the people. A monarch held sway—and was thereby politically useful—by a kind of "awe-inspiring influence" (*tsun-yen*), conferred by tradition. Once violated, Liang argued, the influence could never be revived. The republican revolution had permanently destroyed awe and respect for the monarch. The usefulness of the monarchy, its legitimizing power, was irretrievable. The monarchical institution had not just been suspended: it was dead.[75] Here Liang touched on the most vulnerable part of the monarchist position. He also was debating in the same language of political modernization used by the monarchists.

Men still under the influence of traditional political ethics found the call to a new imperial sovereign abhorrent in quite a different way. Having been subjects and officials of the Ch'ing, they could not work for a new dynasty without transgressing the prohibition against serving two masters. Yuan's presidency had been an institutional oddity that did not fit the old ethical schemes and hence could be discounted. But Yuan as emperor raised uncomfortable moral questions.[76] Presumably this attitude characterized Hsu Shih-ch'ang's withdrawal. As Chang I-lin expressed it to Yuan, with the raising of the monarchical question, "the pure scholars have retreated into the mountains as deeply as possible."[77] The American consul in Foochow was surprised to discover that the old literary scholars of the city strongly disapproved of Yuan's monarchical efforts.[78] From this perspective, the idea of the monarchy was not dead; on the contrary, it was too much alive to be trifled with.

Trying to win on all sides by mixing the old with the new, Yuan instead lost out with almost all groups. The truth was that any effort to invigorate his rule with institutional gimmicks was bound instead further to sap its strength. People objected to Yuan's policies, the style of his rule, and its failures. I have discussed some of the issues around which objections accumulated: the terror (including Sung Chiao-jen's assassination), the abolition of self-government organs and provincial autonomy, the stagnation of reform, and the capitulations to foreign pressure.[79] The monarchical movement, with its awkward pretensions, was a catalyst to a situation already on the verge of crystallization. For those who had supported Yuan during the dictatorship, it was easier to attack the monarchy than to admit that the policies of the dictatorship had been wrong.

Ts'ai O presents a good instance. By his own testimony, he was a warm supporter of Yuan during the Second Revolution. We have seen his role in helping to establish the dictatorship. He had a variety of appointments from Yuan and the prospect of more.[80] But by January, 1915, he was having doubts about Yuan's leadership. Yuan lacked purpose, Ts'ai recalled, and took up a subject only to drop it. Even as he was organizing the revolt against Yuan in December, 1915, Ts'ai seemed as unrepentant of his role in the dictatorship as was Liang Ch'i-ch'ao. He interpreted his turn to rebellion as serving the wishes of "the educated and influential classes [who in a large proportion] were strongly in favour of a republic."[81] It was presumably also in the service of those classes that the revolt he dominated called for greater freedom for the provinces in a federal system and for representative assemblies at all levels of government.[82] Ts'ai O's rebellion was more than an antimonarchical movement. Althouth Ts'ai seemed reluctant to pursue all the powerful political possibilities in this side to the movement, it was also a repudiation of the policies so recently Ts'ai's own with respect to the organization of the country.

Once the revolt was under way, Liang Ch'i-ch'ao's arguments shifted their focus from the unworkability of a revived monarchy to the undesirability of Yuan Shih-k'ai. His dissatisfaction with Yuan's leadership, Liang wrote from the partial sanctuary of Shanghai in early 1916, developed before the monarchical movement and was the reason for his opposition to it. Dismissing principles as "students' ideals," Yuan's administration had no general, long-term plan; reforms were fragmentary; and his response to problems was extemporaneous. Liang admitted Yuan was very skillful and quick in devising short-run solutions to national problems. One had to admire his energy, his attention to work, and the sharpness of his mind. But, although he talked a great deal about imparting wealth and power to the nation, his mind could not encompass a program extending over decades. Liang made no attempt to deny his former support of Yuan. The minimal basis of his support, he said, had been that without Yuan China would have fallen apart. Even if unsatisfactory, Yuan had seemed better than any likely replacement. Now, Liang argued, not only was Yuan incapable of bringing progress to China; he could not even maintain China as she was and was sowing the seeds of disastrous disruption. Liang confessed not to know who could replace him, but no one, he felt, could be worse.[83]

As a consequence of these deeper roots of opposition to Yuan, the cancellation of the monarchy on March 22, 1916, did not quiet the storm. Feng Kuo-chang, for example, continued to press charges against the centralization of power, the assumption by Peking of control over financial and military affairs, and the continual reductions in provincial military forces.[84] Yuan's whole program was at stake. The goal of opposition to him became his full retirement from political life.

The National Protection Army
and the Defection of the Provinces

The beacon of the armed opposition to Yuan and the best-known event was the military rising based in Yunnan, in which the most prominent figure was Ts'ai O.

The rising was sparked by an ingathering in December, 1915, of military leaders, mostly graduates of the Japanese Army Officers' Academy, who had worked on the development of the Yunnanese New Army division before the 1911 Revolution (over twelve thousand troops). Some, like Ts'ai O, had served Yuan during the dictatorship. Some, like Li Lieh-chün, had been leaders in the KMT. They joined with Yunnanese officers, who had remained in the Yunnan army and had been secretly planning opposition to Yuan's monarchy since the previous September. They were bound together, neither by provincial origin nor by party ties, but by opposition to Yuan and a shared experience as military reformers in Yunnan under the Ch'ing. The incumbent general-in-chief, T'ang Chi-yao, was one of them in these respects.

T'ang was persuaded to send an ultimatum, dispatched in the late evening of December 23 and delivered on December 24, giving Yuan one day to abandon his monarchical plans. As anticipated, Yuan ignored the ultimatum. Expeditions, already planned, were formally launched under the name of the National Protection Army (*Hu-kuo chün*), the core of which was the approximately six thousand soldiers of the modernized Yunnan army of 1915. The war against Yuan was carried by expanded elements of this army first to Szechwan, then to Hunan and Kwangtung.[85] Risings elsewhere in the country often adopted the name of the National Protection Army, which became a generic term in 1916 for opposition to Yuan and his rule.

The test of what the Yunnan military revolt against Yuan could accomplish was the expedition into Szechwan under Ts'ai O's personal command. Starting with little more than three thousand troops (later up to five thousand) and maintained over difficult mountainous routes, Ts'ai's small force reached the Yangtze and by January 22, 1916, took a major Szechwan town on the river after defeating Szechwanese and Peiyang troops in the area. Ts'ai's attack was supplemented by a few thousand troops entering Szechwan from Kweichow, which had joined the rebellion soon after it was announced. But against these elements of the National Protection Army stood as many as twenty thousand Szechwanese troops and twelve to fifteen thousand Peiyang soldiers that had accompanied Ch'en I to Szechwan the previous summer or who were added shortly thereafter. Then, with the Yunnanese attack in January, 1916, Yuan ordered large-scale reinforcements into Szechwan, soon amounting to about twenty-five thousand, under the command of Peiyang general Ts'ao K'un. Ts'ao established his headquarters at Chungking.[86] Despite these formidably adverse odds, the National Protection Army in Szechwan maintained its perch on the Yangtze in a seesaw exchange of towns and positions, absorbing and inflicting heavy casualties. It was a remarkable performance. As long as Yuan could be shown to be less than invincible, unable to repeat the rapid triumphs of 1913, the bravery of the disaffected would grow.

The small Yunnanese expedition was able to score these successes for combinations of military and political reasons. Ts'ai O was a brilliant commander who was able to achieve superb coordination among the different segments of his expeditionary forces.[87] His officer corps was cohesive and his troops were well trained and disciplined. The good behavior of the Yunnanese troops toward the Szechwanese populace reinforced an already favorable disposition toward the cause they served. A missionary at the Szechwanese provincial capital wrote in January, 1916: "It is really pitiable to see how keenly some of the Chinese feel about this monarchical question. At a meeting held not long ago, old men and young were all weeping and in tears for their country, which they felt had been so terribly disgraced before the world, and their Republic made a mock of."[88] In the Szechwanese cities occupied by the Yunnanese, despite a bad record in the area acquired during earlier incursions from Yunnan and Kweichow in 1912 and 1913, the troops were welcomed by the local population.[89] The National Protection Army was more popular in Szechwan than in its home province. One practical consequence of the receptivity of Szechwanese to the Yunnanese invasion (which promised to free them from the recently imposed heavy hand of Peking) was the unreliability of the Szechwanese troops from Peking's point of view. Indeed, Ts'ai O soon benefited from the defection to his side of one of the two Szechwanese divisions, with its Szechwanese commander, although Ts'ai had a poor opinion of its quality.[90]

Ts'ai O was also powerfully assisted by a large guerrilla war, that seriously impeded the effectiveness of the many modern troops sent into southern Szechwan by Yuan Shih-k'ai. The widespread secret society organization in Szechwan, which had provided a primitively armed wing of the movement against railway nationalization in 1911, had been augmented by an accession of relatively upperclass remnants of Hsiung K'o-wu's forces after their defeat in the Second Revolution. In 1915 it had already become difficult to distinguish political agitation from organized brigandage.[91] With the revolt against Yuan, representatives of the National Protection Army were sent to stimulate further activity. For some months in 1916, Szechwanese "brigandage" went political in a grand style. Clandestine mobilization took place in various parts of the province, especially among secret society members, outlaws, and former soldiers. Some recruits were sent south toward the Yunnan and Kweichow frontiers, where lay the formal battle front; others operated in their home districts.

A British diplomat in Szechwan made these observations concerning the resulting popular armed movement: "Its leaders have shown great skill in utilizing their forces to create the widest disturbances possible. Recognizing their inability to face well-armed bodies of troops they have contented themselves with rapid descents on ill-prepared cities denuded of their garrisons. Though in some cases indiscriminate looting has occurred, the procedure of these bands is, generally speaking, confined to seizing all arms and public funds, burning official premises and setting prisoners free." In one particular case near Chengtu, two thousand of them occupied a market town, established an administration, reduced rice and salt prices by one-third, and "were more or less accepted by the people at their own valuation as saviours of the state rather than robbers." They adopted the name of the National Protection Army. "All available evidence," wrote the British official, "goes to show that the movement is political and connected with the events in the South and with the idea dear to the Szechuanese mind of securing self-government for the province."[92]

For Ts'ai, this "brigand" National Protection Army confounded the supply system of Yuan's troops, waylaying shipments of arms and ammunition, while providing Ts'ai with indispensible transportation services.[93] By mid-summer one estimate of their numbers, perhaps inflated, was more than one hundred thousand; their weaponry was said to include thirty thousand modern rifles and large amounts of ammunition, no doubt in part the proceeds of raids on Yuan's supply system.[94] Chu Teh, a Szechwanese and founder with Mao Tse-tung of the Red Army in the late 1920s, was an officer under Ts'ai O on this expedition. He has recalled: " 'We did our first mass work among the peasants during this war against the monarchy. . . . We had the Ko Lao Hui peasants behind us, . . . and they were like the sands of the sea.' "[95] In such ways were Ts'ai O's small numbers compensated for.

If Ts'ai O's forces had integrated politically with this popular movement, in addition to benefiting from its services and helping to finance it, then the rising against Yuan might have taken on a radically different cast, breaking out of its elite military mold. Such was not Ts'ai's way. His alliance with various local forces, like the brigand army, was tactical only. From the beginning of the venture in Szechwan, he seemed more concerned to win over Yuan Shih-k'ai's administration in the province than to overthrow it. In this he was successful. It was not long before Ts'ai O and Yuan's agent, Ch'en I, were exploring a local settlement.

Ts'ai and Ch'en, both high-ranking but young military officers who had worked for Yuan, had been acquaintances in Peking. Ts'ai called on Ch'en to join the revolt as it began. In January, 1916, Ch'en apparently received a code book from Yunnan and forthwith sent a telegram offering to break with Yuan under certain conditions. In early February Ch'en sent an emissary to consider Ts'ai's proposals. Although some bitter fighting ensued between Feng Yü-hsiang's troops and the Yunnanese (Feng later claimed that he tried to avoid it through negotiations of his own), Ch'en I, his commander, told him in early March not to press the battle. The man Yuan had chosen in 1915 to be his proconsul in western China was not prepared to defend the monarchy against its challengers.[96] Ch'en I was not a partisan of revolution or of Ts'ai's movement. He stood in between. But what was at stake was not just the monarchy, but also Yuan's centralized structure of authority. Ch'en's behavior formed a break in the structure. Whatever his intentions, the effect was to assist Ts'ai and help destroy Yuan.

After Yuan announced his abandonment of the monarchy on March 22 and Peking sanctioned a truce in Szechwan, Ch'en I developed closer ties with the Yunnanese invaders, instead of rallying back to Yuan. Among the forces pushing Ch'en toward an open break with Peking, the "brigand" National Protection Army and other sorts of politically inspired "brigand" attacks around Chengtu may have been as significant as the Yunnanese invasion. In early May he called on Yuan to retire, and in late May he declared Szechwan's independence of Peking. In the reorganized provincial government, he appointed Ts'ai O's protégés to high positions. Szechwanese political groups were kept on the periphery by this arrangement. They might have remained excluded if Ts'ai's fatal illness had not forced him to leave soon after succeeding to Ch'en I's position.[97]

In any case, Ts'ai's main task had been accomplished. Yuan's political weakness, despite his fearsome accumulation of formal institutional power, had been exposed in Szechwan. Gentry resentment of the dictatorship was exploitable. The Szechwan army was ripe for defection. The military and civil machine under Ch'en I, which Yuan had sent to possess Szechwan for Peking in 1915, was not ready properly to serve him. And the special expeditionary forces under Ts'ao K'un, dispatched on the occasion of the rising, were rendered ineffective by politicized brigand bands. A decisive blow, and the whole edifice crumbled.

The rot became visible everywhere. Plots against Yuan were discovered within his own secretariat and bodyguard in Peking.[98] In Kwangsi, the general-in-chief Lu Jung-t'ing was counted by the rebels as a certain supporter from the beginning. He delayed until mid-March, 1916, but when he did move into action, it was with great effect. In Fukien, Hsu Shih-ying, the forceful civil governor, arranged for a declaration of independence from Peking in early April, with gentry support. After initial acquiescence on the part of the locally stationed military representative of Peking, the move was killed by his change of mind and by reinforcements from the north. But Fukien, despite the fact that its government had been staffed out of Peking since 1913, could hardly be considered loyal to Yuan. In Chekiang, the civil governor acquiesced in a rupture with Peking in mid-April. The general-in-chief, Chu Jui, withdrew when his forces divided on the issue. The expedition of the National Protection Army into Hunan did rather well there. T'ang Hsiang-ming, who had killed so many suspected revolutionaries for Yuan, did not waver openly until May, when Hunan declared its independence.[99]

In Kwangtung, an immensely complicated situation developed, where the military chief, Lung Chi-kuang, temporarily held out for Yuan and his own dominance against several pressures: a Yunnanese expedition, opposition from within his own government, Japanese insistence, and local uprisings organized by veteran revolutionary leaders. He gave in begrudgingly and piecemeal, but he gave in. There was a coup d'etat in Shensi against Yuan's appointees. Yuan's power in Manchuria faded quickly. In Shantung, Chin Yun-p'eng, the general-in-chief and an exception to Yuan's revival of the principle of avoidance in regional appointments, had let his opposition to the monarchy be known from the beginning of the year. So he was ready to temporize with Japanese-supported revolutionary movements that got underway in April and with gentry desires for a break with Peking. He skirted close to a break with Yuan before throwing in the towel at the end of May in a state of nervous exhaustion. Li Ch'un, general-in-chief in Kiangsi, was thought to be disaffected from Yuan in reaction to the monarchical effort. The steadfast adherents of Yuan's rule in high provincial positions, like Yen Hsi-shan in Shansi and Wang Chan-yuan in Hupeh, were a minority five months after Ts'ai O left Peking for Yunnan.[100]

Yuan's retreat before the disintegration of his domestic support and in face of foreign (chiefly Japanese) pressure was measured but constant. In January, 1916, he postponed indefinitely his formal enthronement. In February he abandoned preparations for it. In March he canceled his acceptance of the monarchy, reverting entirely to republican forms. At that point, some of his old associates, like Hsu Shih-ch'ang and Tuan Ch'i-jui, were willing to return to the Peking government. But in April the retreat continued regardless, with Tuan Ch'i-jui assuming as prime minister a proportion, perhaps most, of Yuan's powers. In May, at a Nanking conference of military representatives from over ten provinces (mostly Peiyang men, but behaving already in independent warlord fashion), sentiment for Yuan's full retirement predominated. The end was in sight, and Yuan was making arrangements with the American legation for his flight from Peking. Before that became necessary, a debilitated physical condition of a few months duration suddenly turned serious. He died on June 6, 1916, of uremia. Eugene Ch'en, editor of the *Peking Gazette,* commented: "Thus Yuan himself has found the best solution of the crisis."[101]

As we have seen, a revolt against Yuan's rule was precipitated by the monarchical movement and destroyed his administrative control over the country. Japanese intervention also contributed to Yuan's collapse in several ways. Indeed, Chang I-lin, one of Yuan's aides unsympathetic to the monarchical movement, has recorded his belief that foreign pressure rather than popular opposition forced Yuan's abandonment of the monarchy.[102] Recent writing on the subject has followed this line of interpretation.[103]

The Japanese role was considerable. There were the formal foreign warnings in October and December, 1915, that the Japanese government organized. Official and semiofficial assistance in transportation was provided various leading rebels by Japanese.[104] Official Japanese used their privileged channels of communication to convey messages among the revolutionaries. Beginning in January, 1916, rebel representatives, notably Sun Yat-sen and Ts'en Ch'un-hsuan, negotiated with the Japanese for money and arms. Between February and April, Sun collected at least ¥1,400,000, which went mostly to the special projects of his group in Shanghai and Shantung. Ts'en, who in contrast to Sun was directly allied with the leaders of the Yunnan uprising, received ¥1,000,000 from the same source on March 22. It is doubtful that any of these funds reached the Yunnanese main forces while the battle for Szechwan was underway. Moreover, distrust of Japanese ambitions in China was pronounced among anti-Yuan elements in both Kunming, Yunnan's capital, and Chengtu. But the prospect of Japanese aid was a useful political weapon in Yunnan and elsewhere in the south.[105] In Shantung, Japanese support for the armed revolutionary groups which launched their campaigns in April, 1916, was open and concrete. Further, Japanese officials, such as the consul general in Canton and General Aoki on special assignment in Shanghai from mid-January, 1916, offered encouragement to the revolutionaries and exerted pressure on provincial leaders to break with Yuan. The Tokyo government, in a flagrantly political use of the 1913 agreement concerning the salt gabelle, prevented the salt revenue surplus, after payment of all charges, from being transferred from foreign banks to the Peking government.[106] Yuan's obsessive fear of Japan, which G. E. Morrison noted in Yuan several times in 1915, proved amply justified.

To suggest that Japanese policy and behavior developed independently, without reference to changes in China, would be inaccurate. The Japanese government did not create the opposition to Yuan; rather, it exploited the opportunities provided by the welling up of Chinese antipathy to Yuan's schemes. The Japanese government followed Chinese opinion with great attention. By the end of September, 1915, the porosity of Yuan's support, even within his own entourage, was apparent from confidential surveys of Chinese views. Japan's policy of opposing Yuan from late 1915 into 1916 arose not simply from dislike of Yuan, though that was there. It was also a response to the knowledge that his was a ship in danger of sinking. The decision of the Japanese government was to gain credit in the right places by helping to sink the ship. Governments, like people, prefer to bet on what they believe are certainties.

As in the Second Revolution, there was a gap between formal Japanese cabinet policy and the undisciplined activities of military men and miscellaneous adventurers, notably in Manchuria and Shantung. But the discrepancy seems less in 1916 than in 1913, partly because the cabinet gradually adopted a fully anti-Yuan position. In January, 1916, a scheduled visit by Chou Tzu-ch'i to Tokyo was canceled by the Japanese prime minister, and through Japanese army channels Yuan was personally warned of the inflexibility of Japan's opposition to the monarchy. The cabinet's policy in that month emphasized nonrecognition and continued warnings but stopped short of concerted support for the rebellion.[107] Then in mid-February, the Japanese minister in Peking concluded that "Yuan's authority has already fallen to the ground" and was bereft of popular support, without present hope of rescue. On March 7, the Japanese cabinet for the first time made the removal of Yuan a formal objective. Yuan, an obstacle to Japan's "preponderant influence in China," was to be removed in ways that corresponded to trends within China, so that Japan would not be responsible for decisions about the future government nor blamed for Yuan's troubles (since this might incite a wave of sympathy for Yuan and inadvertently rescue him from the corner into which he had painted himself). The cabinet also held that Japan should not exceed the limits of tolerance of the European powers and the United States regarding interference in Chinese affairs. But quiet infusion of money into the rebellion, as well as a recognition of the belligerent status of the National Protection Army when the moment was right, were deemed appropriate measures.[108]

Although the right moment for recognizing the south as a belligerent party apparently did not arrive, the Japanese government was henceforth out to get Yuan. But by this time Yuan was already far gone, as indeed the Japanese government calculated in making its decision. So we see that Japanese activity and indigenous Chinese developments underway since the inauguration of the monarchical movement stimulated each other in an intricate interplay. Foreign imperialism was once again intervening in domestic Chinese affairs. In 1916, its efficacy depended on attaching itself to a widespread Chinese disillusionment with Yuan and all his works.

Chapter 9

The Presidency in History

The policies of the presidency did not survive the president. In fact, they began to disintegrate months before his death, both as a price of wooing adherents to his monarchical movement and as a consequence of the alienation from Peking induced by that movement.

Domestic production of opium revived rapidly. The recrudescence of poppy planting was particularly marked in Yunnan, Kweichow, and Szechwan, in what was presumably an effort to finance the sudden augmentation of military forces in the area.[1] Such financial centralization as had been achieved by Yuan's government was in turn rapidly abandoned. Even salt revenue remittances, supposedly protected by foreign staff and an international agreement, suffered an immediate decline. First in Yunnan and then more broadly, provincial authorities, with or without agreement with the national salt administration, withheld large portions of the collections from Peking. By mid-summer, 1916, the foreign chief inspector, Richard Dane, was complaining of little or no returns from remunerative areas of Kwangtung, Hunan, and Szechwan.[2] Despite the erosion of salt revenues reaching Peking, returns from this source were soon the main fiscal prop for the increasingly isolated Peking government.

Provincial sentiment and provincial power asserted themselves, as they had done in the liberal republic. There were strong pressures, in some areas successful, for the return to local staffing of provincial governments. Efforts were made to revive representative assemblies and their former prominence in politics. All these tendencies were repudiations of Yuan's plans for the country.

The most decisive repudiation, with the greatest meaning for the following decade, was the reversal of Yuan's program to subordinate military to civil authority. This program was far from complete, but such progress

241

as had been made was rapidly wiped out. In order to woo the generals in the provinces, Yuan had begun compromising his policy of civilian supremacy from the beginning of the monarchical movement. By early 1916, the generals-in-chief were extorting formal civil administrative powers from the Peking government at an accelerated rate. The revival of the office of military governor with civil authority (*tu-tu*) had been one of the first measures taken by the rising in Yunnan. It spread. Even where civilian authorities took the lead in breaking with Peking, as in Fukien, military dominance was soon asserted. When Yuan died, the separation of military and civil powers had already ended in many provinces. Although the 1911 Revolution had carried many military men to positions of political leadership in the provinces, civilian participation had remained prominent, and some of the men in military posts were civilians. In the wake of Yuan's collapse, indeed, as he was collapsing, military men, without significantly sharing power with civilian politicians, were asserting their predominance and independence in the provinces. The warlord era was underway.

Yuan is frequently referred to as the founder or father of warlordism in modern China.[3] There are elements of truth in this assertion. He was the key figure in building China's modern army in the late Ch'ing. Because he controlled most of the country at the end of 1915, generals associated with his Peiyang divisions were established in strategic positions throughout central and north China as disintegration occurred. They therefore dominated the early years of the warlord period.

It is quite wrong, however, to suggest that the patterns of warlordism were an intended consequence of Yuan's policies. The Ch'ing government at the end of the nineteenth century felt the need for a modern army, and Yuan was given a large share of the responsibility for this effort. There was nothing in the original plan or in the method of creating the army that made warlordism probable. For the military to seize power, usually crudely, when civil authority collapses, is not extraordinary. Yuan's programs during his dictatorship were designed precisely to prevent this eventuality. He worked for the assertion of a civilian administration over regional military power, including that of his generals. He reduced the number of soldiers and tried to reorganize the military as an instrument of national power under central control. Yuan's greatest contribution to the warlord period was his failure to complete his own programs.

Yuan's policies had a way of producing the opposite of their intended effect. A large foreign loan, incurred partly for the purpose of welding the country together to guard against foreign encroachments, brought with it an increased foreign role in the Chinese polity. An elaborate campaign of administrative centralization led, through the hostilities it evoked and the interests it violated, to a greater degree of disunity than China had experienced for centuries. The monarchy, a device to bind the population to the government and to ward off Japanese designs on China, alienated Yuan from his country and provided an opening for Japanese machinations. The efforts to impose civilian supremacy gave way to a period of unparalleled military dominance. When one contemplates the human consequences, failure is too gentle a word for Yuan's presidency.

There were defects in Yuan's character, to be sure, that contributed to these results. He was ruthless and instigated the deaths of thousands as part of the cold calculations of state policy. He was distrustful and manipulative in his administrative methods, preferring to keep for himself the keys to any situation. On the other hand, those who worked with him seem to have been more critical of his lack of achievement than of his personality. He had a retentive mind, was well informed, and generally maintained a genial, good-humored manner in his personal and official relations. Liang Ch'i-ch'ao was reported to have said that "it is like drinking champagne being with [the] President."[4] Those who worked with him objected chiefly to the limitations of his political imagination. A frequent comment was that Yuan had made a good governor-general but lacked the inspiration necessary for supreme national leadership.[5]

The lessons in his presidency lie not so much in the man as in the policies. Put most simply, Yuan's presidency was guided by the proposition that in order to respond adequately to China's modern problems it was necessary to centralize the administration of the country. The chief problem was foreign pressure on China's sovereignty. The best chance for countering foreign pressure without inducing anarchy and disorder in the society, in this view, lay in a gradual enactment of reform programs administered through a centralized chain of command. The population was seen as politically passive, with the exception of a few self-interested agitators. After the necessary education and training, the people would engage in the support of the national government through the mediation of institutions appropriate to their social position and carefully designed for the purpose. Selfish politicians, like the leaders of the Kuomintang, exploited the people's political immaturity to steal power from the central government for their own aggrandizement. Such activities divided the nation, weakened the central government, and tore the social fabric. Once these activities were suppressed and the institutions (such as provincial autonomy and uncontrolled representative assemblies) that allowed them to flourish were destroyed, the Peking government could settle down to serious reformist programs. Of such ideas was the sense of self-righteousness in Yuan's presidency made.

The difficulty with this strategy, apart from its misrepresentation of the motives of its opponents, was that it could not work. The pressure of foreign imperialism was a present problem that required immediate attention. This was true both because imperialist encroachment would not stop of its own accord and because nationalist sentiment among growing numbers of Chinese demanded immediate results. Foreign imperialism had to be dealt with by means then available to China. Gradualistic reform programs that would mature in the form of a new Western-type society at some indefinite time in the future only mocked the nationalistic impulse. Given the weakness of China's polity, even if every ounce of administrative authority had been wrenched from existing local offices and concentrated in Peking, the total accumulation of power would still have been insufficient for ejecting the industrialized nations that presented their imperialist face to China. The confirmed bureaucratic centralizer could respond to this impossible situation only by trying to wrench more authority from the existing administrative structure. Yuan's course lay in this direction. Quite naturally, he began to collide with every vested interest, with every lesser aggregation of political aspirations, with the outlying segments of his own administrative structure, and in general with the country's social elite.

In order better to define the lineaments of Yuan's spectacular failure—spectacular because of the distance of the fall—let us briefly consider his strategy in three contexts: in relation to Chinese society, in comparison with subsequent Chinese political movements, and in comparison with analogous situations in the Third World.

The Presidency and Alternative Social Strategies

I have argued that Yuan as president had no social strategy. That is, his administration and its approach to politics lacked a clear or firm base of support in the social structure. Nor were there plans for acquiring one. Many gentry were reformist nationalists, pushing for participation in the political process. Although they were of his class and cultural style, Yuan ultimately rejected the various deals and political arrangements that would have constituted a solid alliance with this predominant segment of the social elite. And perhaps because of his class and cultural style, he had no conception of throwing in his lot with peasants or other laboring classes. Much of Yuan's strategy might be explained if he had represented merchant or treaty-port interests. But neither his policies nor the merchant response to him suggest that this was the case. As described in chapter 7, Yuan's centralized administration was curiously disconnected from the social order.

Why had Yuan crawled so far out on so slender a limb? I think the explanation lies in the new understanding of China's situation that had been adopted by most leaders in Yuan's time. With the development of a nationalist consciousness around the turn of the century, there was sharp realization of the depth of the difficulty that China faced. A natural response among those in or near authority at the national level was to work for more power at the center. The centralizing policies of the last decade of the Ch'ing were, in this sense, reformist with respect to the relatively decentralized (or loosely centralized) structure of the nineteenth-century empire. Yuan as president aspired to carry these policies even further. If support for such a program were to be found in the population at large, where was the class, organizationally integrated at a national level, that could satisfy its interests in this manner? The gentry, by virtue of education, a tradition of leadership, and growing political organization, came closest to fulfilling these conditions. It was primarily to this class that the reforms of the late Ch'ing made their appeal. But gentry engagement, once evoked, reacted against centralization. Perhaps because country-wide links among the gentry were still in an early stage of development, gentry political movement tended to favor provincial bases of power and to challenge the center. One result was the 1911 Revolution and the politically vigorous but decentralized structure of the liberal republic. The effort to centralize lacked organized support in any broad sector of the society.

Yuan's response to this situation was not to abandon his centralizing strategy but to depend all the more heavily on administrative structures and to look for foreign assistance. As a result, his rule was singularly bureaucratic and repressive, as well as compromising toward foreign demands.

There were at least two major alternatives to Yuan's strategy. One would have been to let gentry participation run its course. This would not have solved all problems; Yuan's reasons for spurning the adjustments that this would have required were not trivial. But we must acknowledge crucial contributions from gentry politics to the major accomplishments of the period: the movement for the recovery of rights, the overthrow of the Ch'ing dynasty, and the political parties and provincial reforms of the liberal republic. Yuan was wrong when he thought he could do without this source of political energy or some substitute. Indeed, it is my view that gentry resentment at Yuan's policies after the Second Revolution created an environment where, with the precipitating event of Yuan's monarchical movement in 1915, disaffected leaders could successfully challenge Yuan.

Lest too much be made of this gentry alternative, I should observe that it had a short life. The return to a decentralized national polity after Yuan's death did not bring back the political and reformist élan of the liberal republic. Perhaps there was the memory of the limitations of the earlier provincial reform movements: their tendency to bog down even before the Second Revolution has been noted. Perhaps Yuan's destruction of institutions that had been vehicles for gentry activity (the representative assemblies, the unfettered press, the Kuomintang) was fatal. In any case, the gentry's political role seems widely to have turned from aggressive political action to the more traditional stance of wielding a veto over local policies and powerholders. As Yuan's centralized administration was crumbling in 1916, gentry could be observed busily striking with local military forces those deals that mark the warlord period.[6]

The golden age of gentry nationalism had passed. In limited times and places, parts of the gentry might be mobilized again, for example, against warlord excesses in the 1920s or against the Japanese in the late 1930s. In the localities, they remained resistant to any centralized administration. The gentry, or their social successors, were well entrenched and difficult to overturn. But they never recaptured the political dynamism demonstrated in the first part of the century. The diverse activities, such as entry into industrial enterprise and the new professions, that accompanied the gentry's mobilization in the late Ch'ing and the liberal republic, came to be expressed in growing social divisions within the elite. After Yuan's presidency, amid the ensuing disorder, the enlarging gap between the urban and rural or small-town worlds tended to divide the elite politically. In comparison to the first years of the republic, the elite became politically weakened. Whatever the prospects might have been in the early republic for nationalist achievement on the basis of gentry movement, they were much dimmed in later years.

The second theoretical alternative to Yuan's bureaucratic centralization was popular mobilization below the elite level. Some hold that popular mobilization is an inappropriate concept in a discussion of Chinese politics before the founding of the Chinese Communist Party. The objection seems to attribute to the Communists the discovery of the idea and to assume that in any case only radicals would contemplate it. Certainly the Communists, particularly Mao Tse-tung, refined it and achieved remarkable results. But the idea cannot be so simply pigeonholed. In the period with which this book is concerned there were, for example, the dramatic cases of mass mobilization occurring in some provinces during the 1911 Revolution—even though the impetus was turned back—and the large guerrilla movement in Szechwan in 1916. As for Yuan, like other conservative leaders seeking to augment the powers of a central state, he seemed sometimes to be looking for a formula to link ruler and commoner and to tap the people's energy to counterbalance the notables. Such occasions include the formulation of his educational policies, stressing mass literacy, and his straining for symbols that would reach the minds of the masses. Yuan did not pursue the logic of these initiatives. Why not?

The answer can only be surmised. Perhaps the most fundamental explanation lies in the balance of power: the state was too weak, despite all the reforms since the late nineteenth century, and the notables—the gentry—still too strong. Yuan lacked the wherewithal to begin reaching out to the peasantry in successful ways. The chauvinist appeal of expanding empire, that worked so well for the Japanese rulers in the early twentieth century, was denied him, as Chinese sovereignty shrank. And to mobilize a militant defense of that sovereignty by taking on the foreign powers directly was too risky. The gentry, meanwhile, were not giving up their swords, as did the samurai after the Meiji Restoration. Rather it would seem that they were continuing to arm themselves, as they had since the mid-nineteenth century. In short, Yuan was not able to get very far in circumventing the social elite, even though he tried. Of course, the idea of abandoning hierarchical social structures altogether and throwing in one's lot with ordinary people was beyond Yuan's ken, as it was that of his opponents.

Two sets of incidents in Shantung in 1916 suggest the distance that both Yuan and his revolutionary enemies were from addressing themselves to the needs of the majority of the population. In a rural district fifty kilometers south of Tsinan, the capital, a serious riot erupted in March. Against a background of rising land taxes—a surcharge for Yellow River dykes and a surcharge for schools and the modern police force, recently increased yet again—a check of land holding was underway. The authorities insisted on including as taxable property small patches of land reclaimed from barren hillsides. After initial complaints produced no satisfaction, a large delegation of peasants went and complained to the county magistrate. It was dispersed by the magistrates' guards, who fired shots killing two and wounding others. In the rioting that ensued, several edifices were reported destroyed, including schools, tax offices, the land survey bureau, and part of the county magistrate's yamen. Resistance in the countryside was not suppressed until troops were dispatched from Tsinan. Villages were burned. Executions followed. About a month later, almost the same sequence, with protestors reportedly numbering twenty thousand, was played out in another rural district sixty kilometers north of Tsinan, unconnected with any revolutionary movement. Repression, military-style, was an unreflecting response in Yuan's administration to social disturbances.[7]

Not long afterward revolutionary forces gained control of several towns in the same province on the railway between Tsingtao and Tsinan. In the name of the National Protection Army and of Sun Yat-sen's Chinese Revolutionary Party, these forces made flagrant use of Japanese protection and pressure to establish themselves in the area, so firmly in the Japanese sphere of influence. After Yuan's death, when the Japanese lost interest and supplies ran low, the revolutionary troops in Shantung turned to exactions from the peasantry to support the operation. (It may only be coincidental that about this time Chiang Kai-shek became the army's chief of staff.) In one district along the railway the burden was so intolerable that there was an uprising against the revolutionary troops. Elements from this army, which had made its political appeal primarily to the gentry of the province, retaliated with the destruction of at least five villages.[8]

It is possible that some disciplinary action was taken within the revolutionary army against the leading perpetrators of the slaughter.[9] And it is true that some on the revolutionary side entertained visions of social reform that included justice for the peasant majority. But to the over-taxed peasant, there was in practice little difference between Yuan and his enemies. As Yuan's era came to a close, the major political movements still found common cause in the retention of the received social order. The response of most of the political elite to peasants who could tolerate no more was bloody repression. They were actually attempting to stifle the greatest reservoir of energy the country possessed. It is no wonder that their strategies were no match for Western and Japanese imperialism. It is no wonder that the period of Yuan's presidency offers us a catalogue of failures and aborted hopes.

Yuan and Chiang Kai-shek

Another context in which we might profitably consider Yuan's strategy is in comparison with subsequent designs for national leadership.

Yuan has not been the only Chinese leader of this century to stress centralization and bureaucratic controls. Yuan himself borrowed much from the programs of the late Ch'ing. After Yuan came a decade of political decomposition and change, often described as an era of warlordism but also marked by a revived and radicalized revolutionary movement. Then, from 1927, Chiang Kai-shek (1887–1975) spurned the revolutionary origins of his national power and tried to build the sort of bureaucratically centralized regime that had served Yuan's presidency so poorly.[10]

A thoroughgoing comparison between the governments of Yuan and Chiang would make another book, in which one important theme would be the contrasts between their situations and responses. But some points of similarity stand out. They both attained national supremacy on the back of revolutionary movements they subsequently turned against in bloody and indiscriminate repression.[11] They shared grandiose reformist ambitions (Chiang's Nanking government had accumulated a longer list). Their reformist accomplishments were, to say the least, disappointing. Both tried to blend ideas and symbols out of the Confucian and imperial past with contemporary concepts of science and politics. They both aspired to exert a finer degree of control over the population than any of their predecessors had achieved. National strength was in both cases the goal, but in neither case was it the result. Both leaders had either contempt or fear of autonomous popular movement, or for that matter of any organization not within the government's purview.

Given these similarities, it is perhaps not surprising to discover that Chiang indirectly inherited specific programs of the Yuan dictatorship.

Yen Hsi-shan's admiration for Yuan extended after 1916 to carrying on in Shansi some of Yuan's programs. This seems to have been true of Yen's educational policy, as was noted earlier. Another program borrowed by Yen was Yuan's scheme for the reconstitution of local self-government. With some modifications, the Nanking government modeled its local administration, below the county level, on Shansi's local self-government system.[12] Neither Yuan nor Chiang actually put into effect the self-governing features of these regulations. Both, as bureaucratic centralizers, seemed loathe to augment in any way the already troublesome power of the unofficial local elite.

The similarity of policies and, in terms of nationalist goals, their common failure suggest certain conclusions about the Yuan presidency. First, interpretations of Yuan's policies that stress personal idiosyncracies or private amibitions seem inadequate. If so much could be shared between Yuan and Chiang, presumably their policies emerge to a great extent from the gross social and political situation to which leaders were responding in the first half of the twentieth century. Second, the importance of Yuan's relationship to the social order, or rather of his lack of a firm relationship, is underlined. In their years of greatest power, both Yuan and Chiang found the entrenched power of local elites to be obstacles to their centralizing schemes. But neither consistently sought to create a counterpoise to those elites through mass organizations. It would seem that Chiang, in contrast to Yuan, established closer links with the world of industry and commerce in the coastal treaty-port cities, particularly Shanghai, until the Japanese took it from him. This social basis for the Nanking government, at least in its early years, helps explain such power as it was able to accumulate. But even with its growth after World War I, the treaty-port world was too slim a base for true national power. Yuan's administration, as a consequence of its policies, had even feebler roots in the social order. In this light, Yuan appears to have gone as far as he did by virtue of the momentum of reform and organization stemming from the late Ch'ing. Deprived after 1913 of the substantial participatory aspect that reform had acquired in the Ch'ing, the momentum gave out shortly.

In the vastly different circumstances of the People's Republic of China, centralization registered its greatest achievements. The aspiration to penetrate the society deeply and administer it broadly was not new, but the degree of attainment has been quite unprecedented. Among the many contrasting features of the Communist movement, perhaps the most important was its relationship to the social order. Mao's strategy involved a high degree of popular participation and mobilization, with special emphasis on those most numerous but previously most ignored—peasants and workers. Mao had available to him on balance no greater material technology in the 1940s than Yuan Shih-k'ai had had in the 1910s. Popular mobilization was not dependent on technical development but was, in terms of generating national power, a substitute for it.

A further point of interest in a comparison with Yuan is that the new heights of centralization in the People's Republic have been accompanied by countervailing movements to decentralize, at least in part to check the bureaucratism that reduces popular participation. The character of Yuan's failure is highlighted by the success of the Communists in attaining the goals of Chinese nationalism through massive participation in a broad-based political movement.

The Early Republic as a "New Nation"

Another elucidating context in which to consider Yuan's presidency is in comparison with the situation of Third World countries after World War II. This comparison, like that with Chiang's Nanking government, is presented here suggestively rather than systematically. It depends on a general view of Third World developments in the 1950s and 1960s that some may not share. But I feel the comparison to be compelling and useful in gaining perspective on the early republic in China.

After her 1911 Revolution, China faced several problems similar to those besetting the colonized countries that gained formal sovereignty without a social revolution after World War II, particularly the problems of the first decade of independence. Much as colonial governors were abruptly recalled from African and Asian outposts beginning in the late 1940s, so in China in 1911 and 1912 a minority ruling group (the Manchus) was suddenly dethroned. It bequeathed to the new order a bureaucratic establishment, including Yuan Shih-k'ai and his associates, that a few years earlier had greatly augmented the scale of its reform schemes. The heritage of the reforms included the beginnings of a Western-style school system, a Western-style army, and some representative assemblies at different levels in the polity. But these products of the reformers, in and outside the government, had struck only shallow roots in Chinese society. The Chinese people as a whole were unaffected, or knew only the costs, not the benefits.

The reforms in China gained as much ground as they did because, since the late 1890s, an increasing proportion of the dominant social elite had discovered in them a congruence between their newly acquired ideals (summed up in nationalism) and their entrenched interests (the benefits derived from local social control). The consequence of their enthusiasm for reform along Western lines was an increased cultural distance between the elite and the mass and a greater disproportion of social rewards, rather than the harmonious social unity promised by the nationalist vision. Yuan Shih-k'ai noted this result, but his methods for dealing with it proved inadequate and self-defeating. Shortly thereafter, profound political disintegration—warlordism—occurred. Other countries in Asia and Africa have more recently experienced some part of this sequence, although, partly because of a tenser and closer international environment, they have usually been denied indulgence in long years of civil war on the warlord pattern. The comparison underlines the possibility that Western-style modernization may have unfortunate social and political effects on non-Western societies. And it suggests that the dilemmas of Yuan's presidency, for all their particularity, were also part of a global pattern.

There is another similarity between the situation of excolonial countries where the people have not been mobilized through social revolution and that of China after the 1911 Revolution. The acquisition of formal national independence can mean, at least in the short run, trading one sort of alien intrusion for another. Real autonomy may remain elusive. In China, Western imperialism was unmoved by the departure of Manchus with their Ch'ing dynasty from the political arena and the inauguration of a republic. Although they did not try to take up the formal instruments of rule laid down by the Manchus, the Western powers nevertheless stepped up their interventions in the domain of the old empire. They protected separatist regimes in Mongolia and Tibet. They wielded financial power, for example, with the Reorganization Loan of 1913, to penetrate more deeply the Chinese body politic. In a roughly analogous manner, the United States after World War II greatly expanded its role in Asia and Africa behind the departing Belgians, French, Dutch, British, and Japanese. The overthrow of the Ch'ing, like the acquisition of formal independence in the Third World, was not a trivial achievement. But, like the end of colonial rule, it did not meet nationalist expectations about turning back foreign interven- tion in domestic affairs. In both cases, sensitivity to the various forms of imperialism was heightened in the aftermath.

Fruitful questions are raised, then, by thinking of early republican China as a harbinger of the Third World phenomenon after World War II. Prominent among them are the issues of the suitability of Westernizing re- forms, their social impact, and the character of foreign pressure on the society. The record of the presidency of Yuan Shih-k'ai lends itself to a comparative discussion of these questions.

In any such discussion, one contrast needs to be emphasized. When at- tempting to understand the politics of the early republic, I think it would be a mistake to assume the same degree of structural dependence on the international network of trade and finance that often characterized Third World countries after World War II. The fact that China had not been a full colony made an important difference. Its inherited productive and marketing structures, though eroded on the edges, were substantially in- tact in the early twentieth century. Those Chinese who did find a place in the international capitalist world—the so-called comprador class—were rather few and did not achieve a predominant position in the society. That a large proportion of the Chinese economy was not recast to serve export markets may have, in one conception, retarded growth. It certainly disap- pointed the foreign traders in their pursuit of the fabled and never satis- factorily realized China market. But it helped preserve large amounts of Chinese autonomy.

The result was that, for all the efforts by foreign powers to manipulate matters in their favor, Chinese politics was still ultimately Chinese. China was far from enjoying full sovereignty, and the foreign role in domestic politics was considerable. An internal balance of forces might be tipped one way or another by foreign intervention. But the balance had first to be established in Chinese political terms. Perhaps this is the context in which to understand the merely peripheral role of foreign power in the resolution of the 1911 Revolution. In the Second Revolution of 1913, foreign inter- vention was much more important, but depended for its effect on Yuan's ability to marshal considerable support domestically, as well as on the poorly prepared base of the revolutionaries. In 1916, Japanese assistance to the movement against Yuan is, in my view, more accurately understood as following along behind a major shift in Chinese opinion than as creating the situation, or even determining its outcome. In some Third World countries after World War II, the United States has been able to create political parties, manipulate whole elections, and covertly design in detail the overthrow of governments, even without any substantial American military presence.[13] The British and the Japanese did not have it so easy in China.

Having noted the limits of foreign control, however, we need to remind ourselves that imperialist pressure on China was a major factor in Chinese politics in the early republic. Although never a colony, China was a semicolony, or a country in constant danger of being divided into colonies. The steady diminution of formal sovereignty over seventy years had made the Chinese state immensely vulnerable. To prevent an occasion for the partition of the country and to establish more advantageous lines of defense had become the first task of politics.

Here the similarity between early republican China and the Third World reemerges. The effort to regain full sovereignty becomes a desperate one. The desperation engenders apparently contradictory or paradoxical behavior. For example, both Yuan Shih-k'ai and Sun Yat-sen (and there were others) were willing to enlist foreign assistance on highly compromising terms in order, in their differing conceptions of this, to work for greater national independence. In so many ways, the pressures under which politics had to operate were most unenviable. Yuan's dictatorship was one sort of response—in my view, a misconceived one, tragic for the Chinese people. Although it did not do the job demanded by the situation or by the nationalist standards of the time, it described a pattern later repeated in China and elsewhere.

Abbreviations

CFKP   *Cheng-fu kung-pao* [Government gazette] (Peking, 1912–28). References to the Taipei reprint edition add "rep." and the appropriate volume and page numbers.

CTSTL   *Chin-tai-shih tzu-liao* [Materials on modern history], comp. Chung-kuo k'o-hsueh-yuan chin-tai-shih yen-chiu-so chin-tai-shih tzu-liao pien-chi tsu [The group for compiling materials on modern history in the institute of modern history of the Chinese academy of sciences], series (Peking, 1954–66).

FO   Great Britain, Foreign Office, Archives, Public Record Office, London.

Gaimushō 1.6.1.75   "En Seigai teisei keikaku no ikken" [The affair of Yuan Shih-k'ai's monarchical scheme], Japanese Ministry of Foreign Affairs, Archives, Gaikō Shiryōkan, Tokyo.

Goodnow Collection   Frank Johnson Goodnow, private papers, Eisenhower Library, Johns Hopkins University, Baltimore, Maryland.

HHKMHIL   *Hsin-hai ko-ming hui-i-lu* [Memoirs of the 1911 Revolution], ed. Chung-kuo jen-min cheng-shih hsieh-shang hui-i ch'üan-kuo wei-yuan-hui wen-shih tzu-liao yen-chiu wei-yuan-hui [Committee on written historical materials of the national committee of the Chinese people's consultative conference], 5 vols. (Peking, 1961–63).

Japan MFA film   Microfilmed archives of the Japanese Ministry of Foreign Affairs, Library of Congress, Washington, D.C. Series and reel identifications follow Cecil H. Uyehara and Edwin G. Beal, *Checklist of Archives in the Japanese Ministry of Foreign Affairs* . . . (Washington, D.C., 1954).

Ko-ming wen-hsien   *Ko-ming wen-hsien* [Documents of the revolution], comps., Chung-kuo Kuo-min-tang chung-yang wei-yuan-hui, tang-

255

shih shih-liao pien-tsuan wei-yuan-hui [Chinese Kuomintang, central executive committee, committee for the compilation of materials on party history], series (Taipei, 1953–).

Liang . . .   Ting Wen-chiang, ed., *Liang Jen-kung hsien-sheng nien-*
nien-p'u   *p'u ch'ang-pien ch'u-kao* [First draft of a chronological biography and sequentially arranged materials of Liang Ch'i-ch'ao] (Taipei, 1958).

MP   George Ernest Morrison, private papers (uncataloged), Mitchell Library, Sydney, New South Wales.

NA 893.00   United States Department of State, "Records Relating to the Internal Affairs of China, 1910–29," National Archives, Washington, D.C.

Nihon gaikō   *Nihon gaikō bunsho* [Documents on Japan's diplomacy],
bunsho   comp. Gaimushō [Ministry of foreign affairs], series (Tokyo, 1936–).

PDN   *Peking Daily News* (Peking, 1909–17).

YPSWC   *Yin-ping-shih wen-chi* [Collected essays from the Ice-Drinker's Studio], Liang Ch'i-ch'ao, 16 vols. (Taipei, 1960).

Notes

Introduction

1. One expression of the involvement of regional officials in foreign affairs (as well as in Western-style reforms) during the latter half of the nineteenth century was the spreading use of specialists in Western studies on provincial-level staffs. Kenneth E. Folsom, *Friends, Guests, and Colleagues: The Mu-fu System in the Late Ch'ing Period* (Berkeley and Los Angeles, 1968), pp. 58–59.
2. Lien-sheng Yang, "Ming Local Administration," in Charles O. Hucker, ed., *Chinese Government in Ming Times: Seven Studies* (New York and London, 1969), pp. 1–10.

Chapter 1

1. CFKP 660: 1 (March 10, 1914).
2. G. E. Morrison to Lady Blake, Peking, August 9, 1911, MP item 172.
3. "Annual General Summary of Medical Reports from His Majesty's Consulates in China, edited by Dr. Douglas Gray, British Legation, Peking. Second Series: For the Year Ending September 1911," FO 369/ 452. The practice that is described here was not new and had been frequently noted in earlier years.
4. Mark Elvin, "The Last Thousand Years of Chinese History: Changing Patterns in Land Tenure," *Modern Asian Studies*, vol. 4, pt. 2 (April 1970), pp. 97–114, presents a stimulating discussion of the degree of change in the situation of gentry over the centuries.
5. Chung-li Chang, *The Chinese Gentry: Studies on Their Role in Nineteenth Century Chinese Society* (Seattle, 1955), pp. 113, 140–41.
6. Frederic Wakeman, Jr., "High Ch'ing: 1683–1839," in James B. Crowley, ed., *Modern East Asia: Essays in Interpretation* (New York, 1970), pp. 12–14; R. Keith Schoppa, "The Composition and Functions of the Local Elite in Szechwan," *Ch'ing-shih wen-t'i*, 2.10: 7–23 (November 1973).

7. Albert Feuerwerker, *The Chinese Economy, 1912–1949* (Center for Chinese Studies, University of Michigan, 1969), pp. 72–73.
8. Biographical details and quotations from Hu Shih and Fu Ssu-nien are taken from D. W. Y. Kwok, *Scientism in Chinese Thought, 1900–1950* (New Haven, 1965), pp. 109–20.
9. V. K. Ting (Ting Wen-chiang) to G. E. Morrison, Shanghai and Soochow, May 5, 1912, MP item 171. "Chao Er Fong" was undoubtedly Chao Erh-feng, the prominent Chinese official, assassinated in 1911 while in the emperor's service.
10. Elvin, "The Last Thousand Years of Chinese History," p. 105, asserts that by the early nineteenth century, five-sixths of landlords in Kiangnan lived either in market towns or in county capitals (or, presumably, in grander cities). Chung-li Chang, *The Chinese Gentry*, p. 52, suggests that a move to a more important town or city often accompanied a rise in gentry status.
11. Marianne Bastid, *Aspects de la réforme de l'enseignement en Chine au début du XXe siècle: d'après des écrits de Zhang Jian* (Paris, 1971), pp. 20–22, succinctly describes the complex shadings and combinations of features that characterized the elite at the end of the Ch'ing. For an analysis of different groups emerging from the gentry, and particularly of a new urban reformist elite, see Joseph W. Esherick, "Reform, Revolution and Reaction: The 1911 Revolution in Hunan and Hupeh" (Ph.D. diss., University of California, Berkeley, 1971). Charles Herman Hedtke, "Reluctant Revolutionaries: Szechwan and the Ch'ing Collapse, 1898–1911" (Ph.D. diss., University of California, Berkeley, 1968), pp. 298–300, defines a "new elite" at this time in terms similar to Esherick's. For an emphasis on the fragmentation of the gentry from an approach different from Esherick's, see John Fincher, "Political Provincialism and the National Revolution," in Mary Clabaugh Wright, ed., *China in Revolution: The First Phase, 1900–1913* (New Haven, 1968), pp. 209, 220.
12. For example, the phenomenon of reading rooms, offering books, magazines and newspapers, was widespread. Edward J. M. Rhoads, *China's Republican Revolution: The Case of Kwangtung, 1895–1913* (Cambridge, Mass., 1975), p. 64, notes that by 1911 reading rooms were "a common feature of many cities and towns . . ." in Kwangtung. Fragmentary evidence suggests that Kwangtung was not atypical in this. On the establishment of reading rooms in Szechwan from 1906, see Hedtke, "Reluctant Revolutionaries," pp. 101, 146. A reading room in a village in southern Honan was reported in early 1914 to be stocked with Peking newspapers and used by local citizens. "Report on Military Situation in South-East Honan," in John Jordan, minister in Peking, to Edward Grey, foreign secretary (February 21, 1914), FO 405/214.
13. These activities are described by John Howard Fincher, "The Chinese Self-Government Movement, 1900–1912" (Ph.D. diss., University of

Washington, 1969), pp. 98–116, and by Hedtke, "Reluctant Revolutionaries," pp. 142–44.

14. The extent and reach of such coordination remains a subject for investigation. Although circumstances varied, we should not assume that an experience of activity at a higher political level meant a severance of local ties and position. Robert Keith Schoppa, "Politics and Society in Chekiang, 1907–1927: Elite Power, Social Control, and the Making of a Province" (Ph.D. diss., University of Michigan, 1975), pp. 137–38, records that, of members of the Chekiang provincial assembly in the late Ch'ing whose subsequent activities are traceable (46), over 70 percent returned after the revolution to positions of leadership in their home areas.

15. Marie-Claire Bergère, "The Role of the Bourgeoisie," in Wright, *China in Revolution*, pp. 229–95. According to a recent study, even in Kwangtung, where the political organization and assertiveness of merchants in the post-Boxer decade were probably greater than anywhere else in the country, merchant predominance was quite limited in time and place, and the gentry were "ultimately the chief gainers from the post-Boxer reforms and the revolution...." Rhoads, *China's Republican Revolution*, p. 276; see also ibid., pp. 130–52, 173–74, 229.

16. Lloyd E. Eastman, *Throne and Mandarins: China's Search for a Policy during the Sino-French Controversy, 1880–1885* (Cambridge, Mass., 1967), pp. 190–93.

17. Philip A. Kuhn, *Rebellion and Its Enemies in Late Imperial China: Militarization and Social Structure, 1796–1864* (Cambridge, Mass., 1970), pp. 89–97, 211–19. In his "Local Self-Government under the Republic: Problems of Control, Autonomy, and Mobilization," in Frederic Wakeman, Jr., and Carolyn Grant, eds., *Conflict and Control in Late Imperial China* (Berkeley, 1975), pp. 277–79, Kuhn has qualified this view. Mark Elvin, "The Administration of Shanghai, 1905–1914," in Mark Elvin and G. William Skinner, eds., *The Chinese City between Two Worlds* (Stanford, 1974), pp. 240–61, discovers antecedents to the development of modern urban self-government in a variety of autonomous gentry and merchant urban organizations that flourished in the eighteenth and nineteenth centuries, but points out the important differences in inspiration and function.

18. John E. Schrecker, *Imperialism and Chinese Nationalism: Germany in Shantung* (Cambridge, Mass., 1971), pp. 251–57. Although it took some time for these ideas to reach remote areas, the sensitivity regarding imperialism that nourished them was not confined to the eastern coast. For example, on the spread from the mid-1890s of Szechwanese concern regarding foreign encroachment, see: Hedtke, "Reluctant Revolutionaries," pp. 59, 78–79, and 81–85; and Roger V. Des Forges, *Hsiliang and the Chinese Revolution* (New Haven and London, 1973), pp. 59–70.

19. Bastid, *Aspects*, pp. 82–85, explains how the new schools served the social elite while burdening ordinary people and widened the gap between rich and poor. Exceptions, such as Mao Tse-tung, illustrate the rule, as in Mao's account of his own oddity among his classmates at this time, who were from landlord families. Edgar Snow, *Red Star Over China* (New York, 1938), pp. 119–20. Mao recorded in 1927 his recollection that in his own student days peasants expressed their dislike of the Western-style schools, which lacked a peasant orientation and were more distant culturally from the peasants than the old style schools had been. Mao Tse-tung, *Selected Works of Mao Tse-tung* (Peking, 1965), vol. 1, p. 54.
20. Cited in Mark Elvin, "The Gentry Democracy in Shanghai, 1905–1914" (Ph.D. diss., University of Cambridge, 1967), p. 90. The date was 1905. The next year, a municipal council was established in Chefoo, "in order to resist the foreigners." Ibid., p. 93. Kuhn, "Local Self-Government," pp. 268–76, discusses some of the theories informing the inauguration of local self-government in the late Ch'ing.
21. Self-governing councils at the local level were neither universal nor uniform in performance. Mark Elvin argues that self-governing organs in Shanghai were neither corrupt nor extortionist, though they were never popular with the common citizenry. Mark Elvin, "The Gentry Democracy in Chinese Shanghai, 1905–14," in Jack Gray, ed., *Modern China's Search for a Political Form* (London, 1969), p. 60; and Elvin, "The Administration of Shanghai, 1905–1914," p. 261. This was in contrast to many other places. In any case, what constitutes corruption or extortion depends on one's point of view. What Elvin describes as "the teething-troubles of a modern and depersonalized system of local administration . . ." can perhaps also be understood as class conflict. Elvin, "The Gentry Democracy in Shanghai, 1905–1914," pp. 109–16.
22. From the *Tung-fang tsa-chih* (January 1911), reprinted in *Hsin-hai ko-ming* [1911 Revolution], Chung-kuo shih-hsueh hui, comp., vol. 3 (Shanghai, 1957), p. 435.
23. Translated in Elvin, "The Gentry Democracy in Shanghai, 1905–1914," pp. 71–72.
24. Nishikawa Masao, "Shisen horo undō—sono zen'ya no shakai jōkyō—" [Social conditions on the eve of the Szechwan railway protection movement], *Tōyō bunka kenkyūjo kiyō*, no. 45 (March 1968), pp. 125–50.
25. Yamashita Yoneko, "Shingai kakumei no jiki no minshū undō—Kō-Setsu chiku no nōmin undō o chūshin to shite" [Mass movement in the period of the 1911 Revolution, with special reference to peasant movements in Kiangsu and Chekiang], *Tōyō bunka kenkyūjo kiyō*, no. 37 (March 1965), pp. 140–48, 151–52. A considerable literature on this late Ch'ing phenomenon now exists in Japanese. Rhoads, *China's Republican Revolution*, pp. 76–77, 175–79, describes similar instances in Kwangtung.

26. Edwin O. Reischauer and John K. Fairbank, *East Asia: The Great Tradition* (Boston, 1960), p. 293.

27. The most elaborate statement asserting late Ch'ing regionalism occurs in Stanley Spector, *Li Hung-chang and the Huai Army: A Study in Nineteenth-Century Chinese Regionalism* (Seattle, 1964), especially Franz Michael's Introduction, pp. xxi–xliii. In exploring the growing literature that challenges the assertion, one might start with Kwang-ching Liu, "The Limits of Regional Power in the Late Ch'ing Period: A Reappraisal," *Tsing Hua Journal of Chinese Studies*, new series 10.2: 176–223 (July 1974).

28. Diana Lary, *Region and Nation: The Kwangsi Clique in Chinese Politics, 1925–1937* (London, 1974), pp. 1–20. In drawing lines of development from the late nineteenth century, Lary perhaps pays too little attention to the critics of the concept of nineteenth-century regionalism and does not take into account the special characteristics of the twentieth century's first two decades.

29. Chūzō Ichiko, "The Role of the Gentry: An Hypothesis," in Wright, *China in Revolution*, p. 300: the participants in the constitutionalist movements, at levels lower than K'ang Yu-wei and Liang Ch'i-ch'ao, "were more deeply concerned with provincial matters and their own businesses than with national interests. Their goal seemed to be, 'Our native province governed by ourselves.'" Charlton Miner Lewis III, "The Opening of Hunan: Reform and Revolution in a Chinese Province, 1895–1907" (Ph.D. diss., University of California, Berkeley, 1965), p. 141: after 1900, gentry leaders "became a shifting alliance of powerful individuals, held together more by their provincial interests than by a transcendent concern for Confucian doctrine or national power." See also Robert A. Scalapino, "Prelude to Marxism: The Chinese Student Movement in Japan, 1900–1910," in Albert Feuerwerker et al., eds., *Approaches to Modern Chinese History* (Los Angeles and Berkeley, 1967), pp. 201, 208. Joseph R. Levenson, "The Province, the Nation, and the World: The Problem of Chinese Identity," in ibid., p. 270, concedes the " 'objectively' nationalist character" of provincialism in this period but emphasizes the subjectively antinationalist tendency of its sources and inner character. While Yoshihiro Hatano and John Fincher see provincialism in this period as part of a new and progressive political movement, they limit it to the role of facilitating the transition to nationalism—that is, to a stage in the development of a full nationalism that was emerging more slowly. Yoshihiro Hatano, "The New Armies," in Wright, *China in Revolution*, p. 382; Fincher, "Political Provincialism," pp. 187, 220, 224, 225. The idea that provincialism was somehow incomplete and less advanced remains. By contrast, I see provincialism as an integral alternative to emphasis on a centralized nation-state and as fully nationalist in its inspiration and goals as the nationalism that

insisted on the complete subordination of provincial movements to the central government.

30. Karl Deutsch has described modern nationalism as "the vast effort to convert the channels of culture into stormladders for masses of individuals to social advancement and economic privilege." *Nationalism and Social Communication: An Inquiry into the Foundations of Nationality* (New York, 1953), p. 76. Some forms of pan-Asianism also stressed cultural similarities as a basis for political cooperation.

31. Noriko Kamachi, "Huang Tsun-hsien (1848–1905): His Response to Meiji Japan and the West" (Ph.D. diss., Harvard University, 1972), pp. 251–63.

32. Ibid., pp. 251–58; Hao Chang, *Liang Ch'i-ch'ao and Intellectual Transition in China, 1890–1907* (Cambridge, Mass., 1971), pp. 126–27; Liang Ch'i-ch'ao, "Lu-su hsueh-an" (Basic ideas of Rousseau), YPSWC, 3.6: 110.

33. *Che-chiang ch'ao* (Tokyo), no. 2 (1903), p. 3. For further quotations in this vein, see Hatano, "The New Armies," p. 366.

34. Feng Tzu-yu, *Ko-ming i-shih* [Fragments of revolutionary history] (Taipei, 1953), vol. 1, p. 98. Li Ken-yuan, *Hsueh-cheng nien-lu* [Annual record of Li Ken-yuan] (reprinted in Taipei, n.d.), p. 30. For a summary of *New Kwangtung*, see Rhoads, *China's Republican Revolution*, pp. 47–49.

35. Hatano, "The New Armies," pp. 375–78, describes a case of local identification in Kwangtung in 1910.

36. For a translation of the relevant entry in Sung Chiao-jen's diary, see Hsueh Chün-tu, *Huang Hsing and the Chinese Revolution* (Stanford, 1961), pp. 40–41.

37. Ch'en T'ien-hua, "Chin-jih ch'i fen-sheng-chieh chih jih yeh" [Is this the time for provincial divisions?], *Min pao* (Tokyo), no. 1 (November 1905), pp. 119–20.

38. Kit Siong Liew, *Struggle for Democracy: Sung Chiao-jen and the 1911 Chinese Revolution* (Berkeley and Los Angeles, 1971), pp. 68–69.

39. *Liang . . . nien-p'u*, p. 339.

40. K'ang Yu-wei's ideas in the first decade of the century on local self-government and its application to the administrative structure can be traced in: Lo Jung-pang, ed., *K'ang Yu-wei: A Biography and a Symposium* (Tucson, 1967), pp. 191–223; K'ang Yu-wei, "Kung-ming tzu-chih" [Citizen self-government], *Hsin-min ts'ung-pao* (Yokohama), 5: 37–46 (April 8, 1902), 6: 17–24 (April 22, 1902), 7: 27–38 (May 8, 1902); K'ang Yu-wei, "Kuan-chih i" [A discussion of the bureaucratic system], especially its sixth section, "Chung-kuo chin kuan-chih ta-pi i kai lun" [On the need to reform the great shortcomings of China's present bureaucratic system], *Hsin-min ts'ung-pao*, 52: 59–67 (September 10, 1904). K'ang Yu-wei, "Fei-sheng lun" [On abolishing the provinces], in *Min-kuo ching-shih wen-pien* [Republican essays on public affairs], eds. Ching-shih wen-she (reprint ed., Taipei, 1962), vol. 2, pp. 509–22,

although written in 1912, reflects the development of his thoughts over the previous decade or more.

Chapter 2

1. W. H. Wilkinson, consul general in Chengtu, to Jordan (January 1, 1912), FO 371/1313.
2. J. L. Smith, consul in Tsinan, to Jordan (May 28, 1912), FO 228/1837.
3. PDN, July 13, 1912, p. 1.
4. William R. Johnson, "China's 1911 Revolution in the Provinces of Yunnan and Kweichow" (Ph.D. diss., University of Washington, 1962), pp. 92–94; Albert Maybon, *La République Chinoise* (Paris, 1914).
5. F. E. Wilkinson, consul in Nanking, to Jordan (January 11, 1912), enclosed in Jordan to Grey (February 9, 1912), FO 371/1314. The idea of ending the category of dependencies was given a different, centralizing interpretation by Yuan Shih-k'ai later in the year. Alistair Lamb, *The McMahon Line: A Study in the Relations between India, China and Tibet, 1904 to 1914* (London, 1966), vol. 2, p. 391.
6. Edward Friedman, "The Center Cannot Hold: The Failure of Parliamentary Democracy in China from the Chinese Revolution of 1911 to the World War in 1914" (Ph.D. diss., Harvard University, 1968), pp. 598–99.
7. John Fincher, "Political Provincialism," pp. 185–226; and Chang P'eng-yuan, *Li-hsien-p'ai yü hsin-hai ko-ming* [Constitutionalists and the Revolution of 1911 in China] (Taipei, 1969).
8. Donald Sinclair Sutton, "The Rise and Decline of the Yunnan Army, 1909–1925" (Ph.D. diss., University of Cambridge, December, 1970), pp. 99–101.
9. Esherick, "Reform," chap. 6; Chang P'eng-yuan, *Li-hsien-p'ai yü hsin-hai ko-ming*, pp. 152–54.
10. Bertram Giles, consul in Changsha, to Jordan (December 29, 1911), enclosed in Jordan to Grey (January 29, 1911), FO 371/1313.
11. Oliver R. Coales, acting consul in Wuchow, to Jordan (October 14, 1912), FO 228/1843.
12. *North China Herald* (Shanghai), July 5, 1913, p. 24.
13. Schoppa, "Politics and Society in Chekiang," pp. 142–44, 146–48, 295–96, 299.
14. Rhoads, *China's Republican Revolution*, p. 250.
15. Johnson, "China's 1911 Revolution," pp. 165–66, 192–93.
16. Ibid., pp. 106, 118–19; Sutton, "Rise and Decline," pp. 103–21.
17. For a useful survey of this aspect of the events of the revolution, see John Lust, "Secret Societies, Popular Movements, and the 1911 Revolution," in Jean Chesneaux, ed., *Popular Movements and Secret Societies in China, 1840–1950* (Stanford, 1972), pp. 165–200.

18. Yamashita, "Shingai kakumei," pp. 124–25. An example of the formation of local militia under gentry leadership during the 1911 Revolution can be examined in a diary account from Hupeh: Chang Yü-heng, "Hsin-hai ko-ming Hsiang-yang chien-wen lu" [A record of experiences in Hsiang-yang during the 1911 Revolution], CTSTL, 1963, no. 2, pp. 6–19. Schoppa, "Politics and Society in Chekiang," pp. 97–98, observes that in almost every Chekiang county for which he has information, militia units were formed during the revolution by those who composed the self-governing organizations.

19. Ernest F. Borst-Smith, *Caught in the Chinese Revolution: A Record of Risks and Rescue* (London, 1912), pp. 48–61.

20. The possible combinations of factors were of course numerous. For example, in the salt-producing center of Yangchow (Kiangsu), revolutionary leadership by a socially radical artisan, Sun T'ien-sheng, was overthrown within a day or two by gentry-merchant appeals to troops in nearby Chinkiang under the former salt smuggler Hsu Pao-shan, who then set up an independent but socially moderate regime of his own in Yangchow. Yamashita, "Shingai kakumei," pp. 198–99.

21. Johnson, "China's 1911 Revolution," pp.138–86; Lust, "Secret Societies," pp. 180, 191–92. Hunan might be added to the list on the grounds that the first military governor, Chiao Ta-feng, had secret society connections and was assassinated in a socially conservative coup. But his government lasted less than two weeks, and the organizational role of secret societies in the government was not developed. In addition to Hunan and the provinces I discuss in this section, Lust, "Secret Societies," pp. 195–96, also finds a secret society role in Honan and Shansi, but the scale and extent were quite limited.

22. The remarks regarding Szechwan are based on: Ichiko Chūzō, "Shisen horo undō no shunōbu" [On the leaders of the railway protection movement in Szechwan], *Ochanomizu Joshi Daigaku kiyō*, 6: 164 (March 1955); HHKMHIL, vol. 3, pp. 174–76; Chang P'eng-yuan, *Li-hsien-p'ai yü hsin-hai ko-ming*, pp. 132–43; British consular reports from Chengtu and Chungking during 1912, FO 228/1838. For a general account of the revolution in Szechwan, see Hedtke, "Reluctant Revolutionaries," pp. 227–50. Ibid., pp. 53 and 268, finds participation in the Ko-lao hui by members of the Szechwanese social elite in the late 1890s.

23. "Anonymous printed poster: Chengtu, December 18, 1911," translated by W. H. Wilkinson (December 20, 1911), FO 371/1312.

24. Sutton, "Rise and Decline," pp. 114–15, describes an incident at Mengtzu in Yunnan in December, 1911, where the suppression of social disturbances by the provincial government was directly related to an actual, not hypothetical, French threat to intervene. But, of course, suppression of popular movement in Yunnan and elsewhere did not wait on the actualization of threats of intervention.

25. Father Hugh Scallan, Sianfu, November 25, 1911, enclosed in William

J. Calhoun, minister to China, to Philander C. Knox, secretary of state (December 11, 1911), NA 893.00/892.

26. Keyte, *Passing of the Dragon*, pp. 81–84.

27. The remarks about Shensi in 1911–12 are based on: Keyte, *Passing of the Dragon;* Anna Holmberg, "Ko Lao Hui Participation in the Revolution of 1911—Shensi Province" (Master's thesis, Center for Chinese Studies, University of Michigan, 1969); Lust, "Secret Societies," pp. 194–95; Herbert Goffe, acting consul general in Hankow, to Jordan (April 4, 1912), FO 228/1841; quoting Shorrock of the Baptist Mission at Sian, Goffe to Jordan (July 10, 1912), FO 228/1841; Calhoun to Knox (December 11, 1911), NA 893.00/892; Roger Greene, consul general in Hankow, to Knox (January 19, 1912), NA 893.00/1104.

28. For a similar view, see Jean Chesneaux, "Secret Societies in China's Historical Evolution," in Chesneaux, ed., *Popular Movements and Secret Societies in China, 1840–1950*, pp. 19–21.

29. This account of the revolution in Kwangtung is based on: Edward Friedman, "Revolution or Just Another Bloody Cycle? Swatow and the 1911 Revolution," *Journal of Asian Studies* 29.2: 289–307 (February 1970); Winston Hsieh, "Triads, Salt Smugglers, and Local Uprisings: Observations on the Social and Economic Background of the Waichow Revolution of 1911," in Chesneaux, ed., *Popular Movements and Secret Societies in China, 1840–1950*, pp. 145–64; Lust, "Secret Societies," pp. 192–93; Rhoads, *China's Republican Revolution*, chaps. 9 and 10.

30. Examples are easily collected. See the case of Wusih under Ch'in Yü-liu, who had been an active revolutionary in Japan but organized a militia in 1911–12 to suppress organized peasant resistance to tax and rent collections. Yamashita, "Shingai kakumei," p. 157.

31. From a Chungking governmental proclamation of November 23, 1911, enclosed in Albert W. Pontius, consul in Chungking, to Knox (December 6, 1911), NA 893.00/980.

32. Schrecker, *Imperialism and Chinese Nationalism;* Sun E-tu (Zen), *Chinese Railways and British Interests, 1898–1911* (New York, 1954); Lee En-han, "China's Response to Foreign Investment in Her Mining Industry (1902–1911)," *Journal of Asian Studies* 28.1: 55–76 (November 1968); Mary Clabaugh Wright, "Introduction: The Rising Tide of Change," in Wright, *China in Revolution*, pp. 4–19.

33. Interesting eye-witness accounts can be found in the Morrison Papers: F. A. Larson to Morrison, Urga, November 20, 1912, MP item 144; T. A. Rustad to Morrison, Chinwangtao, November 5, 1912, MP item 151.

34. For details concerning the institutional changes, see Stanley F. Wright, *The Collection and Disposal of the Maritime and Native Customs Revenue since the Revolution of 1911* (Shanghai, 1927), pp. 1–9.

35. Jordan to Walter L. F. G. Langley, Peking, July 13, 1912, Jordan Papers, FO 350/8.

36. Mark Elvin, "The Mixed Court of the International Settlement at Shanghai (until 1911)," *Papers on China*, vol. 17 (Harvard University, December 1963), pp. 139–48.
37. The process of foreign possession of the Mixed Court is described in: Anatol M. Kotenev, *Shanghai: Its Mixed Court and Council* (Shanghai, 1925), pp. 169–78; Westel W. Willoughby, *Foreign Rights and Interests in China* (Baltimore, 1927), pp. 526–36; Col. C. D. Bruce, Chief of the Shanghai Settlement Police, to Morrison, Shanghai, July 8, 1913, MP item 176; "Memorandum on the Shanghai Extension, 10th January 1914," by G. E. Morrison, MP item 159; Jordan to Grey (March 26, 1914), FO 405/214.
38. Anatol M. Kotenev, *New Lamps for Old: An Interpretation of Events in Modern China and Whither They Lead* (Shanghai, 1931), p. 73. Kotenev, *Shanghai*, pp. 198–200, describes an effort by Yuan Shih-k'ai's government to recover some degree of jurisdiction in the Shanghai International Settlement.

    A mixed court in Amoy was similarly usurped by foreign consuls there during the revolution but was returned to Chinese hands in March, 1914. Jordan to Grey (April 27, 1914), FO 405/214.
39. Watanabe Atsushi, "En Seigai seiken no keizaiteki kiban" [The economic basis of the Yuan Shih-k'ai regime], *Chūgoku kindaika no shakai kōzō: shingai kakumei no shiteki ichi* (Tokyo, 1960), pp. 154–56; C. Ellsworth Carlson, *The Kaiping Mines (1877–1912)* (Cambridge, Mass., 1957), pp. 107–10.
40. G. E. Morrison, "The Chinese Government Guarantee of the Commercial Guarantee Bank of Chihli," September 3, 1913, MP item 132.
41. W. G. M. Müller, memorandum (February 26, 1912), FO 371/1313. This point became a major theme of the Reorganization Loan negotiations of 1912–13. It was reaffirmed by Foreign Secretary Grey himself at various points, for example: "Effective control to secure expenditure of money upon objects for which it was lent seemed to me essential. . . ." Grey to Jordan (September 19, 1912), FO 371/1322.
42. Jordan to Langley, Peking, March 25, 1912, Jordan Papers, FO 350/8.
43. Jordan to Langley, Peking, May 21, 1912, Jordan Papers, FO 350/8.
44. G. E. Morrison diary (December 31, 1912), MP item 95, reporting a conversation with Francis A. Aglen.
45. Charles W. Eliot to Tong [T'ang] Shao-yi, Tientsin (May 1, 1912), MP item 173.
46. Professor Mikesell, a highly regarded student of foreign aid programs with experience as a consultant to AID prescribes that ". . . foreign-assistance agencies should exert strong influence on monetary, fiscal, and trade policies of the recipient countries, even to the point of suspending aid when policies are widely at variance with those required for development progress. . . . [W]hen aid disbursement for specific programs are closely tied to the implementation of the projects and programs,

pre-agreed conditions can be enforced more or less automatically by varying the rate of disbursements." Raymond F. Mikesell, *The Economics of Foreign Aid* (Chicago, 1968), pp. 261–62.

The sort of analysis of the administration and consequences of foreign aid programs after World War II that I have in mind in my comparisons with China on the eve of World War I can be found in: Teresa Hayter, *Aid As Imperialism* (Harmondsworth, 1971); and Denis Goulet and Michael Hudson, *The Myth of Aid: The Hidden Agenda of the Development Reports* (New York, 1971).

47. A. Mitchie-Innes (?) to Morrison, Washington, D.C. (September 28, 1912), MP item 173.
48. Tsung-liang, "Sung-an yü chieh-kuan p'ing-i" [Comment on the Sung case and the loan], *Kuo-min yueh-k'an*, vol. 1, no. 1 (May 1913), p. 1.

Chapter 3

1. I have written about the process by which Yuan became president in "Yuan Shih-k'ai's Rise to the Presidency," in Wright, *China in Revolution*, pp. 419–42. In that article I cast doubt on Yuan's responsibility for the Peking mutiny of February-March, 1912. Although we have no confession from anyone who might have been responsible, I have been impressed by the number of people associated with Yuan who came to believe that *other* associates of Yuan (especially his son, Yuan K'o-ting) were responsible: Chang I-lin, *Hsin-t'ai-p'ing-shih chi* [Collection of Chang I-lin's works] (reprint ed., Taipei, n.d.), p. 69; Ts'ao Ju-lin, *I-sheng chih hui-i* [A lifetime's recollections] (Hongkong, 1966), pp. 74–77; G. E. Morrison diary (January 19, 1916), MP item 105. Banzai Rihachirō, a Japanese army colonel who observed at close hand both Yuan K'o-ting and Yuan Shih-k'ai on the first day of the mutiny, learned nothing concrete that would implicate either, but he subsequently inferred from the circumstances that subordinates of Yuan who feared for their positions if Yuan went south had something to do with the outbreak of the riots and that the mutiny soon got beyond anyone's control. Nakajima Masao et al., eds., *Zoku taiShi kaiko roku* [Supplementary volumes of memoirs about China], vol. 2 (Tokyo, 1941), pp. 823–25. The issue remains doubtful. A forceful statement denying Yuan's culpability, by a Chinese military officer who was there, occurs in Feng Yü-hsiang, *Wo ti sheng-huo* [My life] (Chungking, 1944), pp. 160–66. In any case, I believe the point made in the article stands: that the mutiny was not necessary to Yuan's acquiring the presidency or establishing the capital in Peking.
2. G. E. Morrison diary (March 10, 1912), MP item 92.
3. Paul S. Reinsch, minister in Peking, to William J. Bryan, secretary of state (December 1, 1913), NA 893.00/2049. Col. Banzai, who acted as an

adviser to Yuan during the presidency while representing the Japanese general staff, recorded in 1930 a similar appreciation of Yuan. Like some others, he was struck by Yuan's capacity for food and sex but stresses the discipline of his life, including his abstention from opium and alcohol. Banzai Rihachirō, *Rinpō o kataru* [Talks on China] (Tokyo, 1933), pp. 503–6.

4. Liang Ch'i-ch'ao, "Yuan Shih-k'ai chih chieh-p'ou" [An analysis of Yuan Shih-k'ai], YPSWC 12.34: 4–19. Huang Yen-p'ei's preface to Pai Chiao, *Yuan Shih-k'ai yü Chung-hua min-kuo* [Yuan Shih-k'ai and the Republic of China] (Shanghai, 1936), pp. 3–4. Ts'ao Ju-lin, *I-sheng chih hui-i*, pp. 114–15. Li Yuan-hung (June 7, 1916), FO 233/159.

5. Calhoun to Knox (November 12, 1912), NA 893.00/1515.

6. E. T. Williams, chargé d'affaires in Peking, to Knox (March 11, 1913), NA 893.00/1595.

7. Yen Hsi-shan, as paraphrased in Donald G. Gillin, *Warlord: Yen Hsi-shan in Shansi Province, 1911–1949* (Princeton, 1967), p. 19.

8. Citing Huang Yuan-yung's view of Yuan Shih-k'ai, Kuan Keng-lin's preface to Huang Yuan-yung, *Yuan-sheng i-chu* [Posthumous collection of writings of Huang Yuan-yung], vol. 1. T'ang Hsiang-ming, quoted in V. L. Savage, consul in Changsha, to Jordan (May 10, 1916), FO 228/2738.

9. Liu Feng-han, *Hsin-chien lu-chün* [The newly created army] (Taipei, 1967), pp. 12–13, 312–15; Schrecker, *Imperialism*, pp. 98–100, 113–17. Yuan's troops maneuvered to block the movement of German punitive expeditions in Shantung in 1899, to meet Italian threats there in 1899, and to confine German troops in 1900.

10. Jerome Ch'en, *Yuan Shih-k'ai*, 2d ed. (Stanford, 1972), p. 46.

11. For a detailed analysis of this process and a discussion of Yuan's role, see Schrecker, *Imperialism*, pp. 140–209.

12. My thoughts on factionalism have been much stimulated by Andrew James Nathan, "Factionalism in Early Republican China: The Politics of the Peking Government, 1918–1920" (Ph.D. diss., Harvard University, 1970), although the conclusions I draw may not correspond with his.

13. Liu Feng-han, *Hsin-chien lu-chün*, pp. 113–25.

14. For a description of Chiang Kai-shek's system, see Donald G. Gillin, "Problems of Centralization in Republican China: The Case of Ch'en Ch'eng and the Kuomintang," *Journal of Asian Studies* 29.4: 835–50 (August 1970).

15. Howard L. Boorman, ed., *Biographical Dictionary of Republican China* (New York, 1967–71), vol. 3, p. 330. *Tuan Ch'i-jui* (Shanghai, Kuang-wen shu-ch'ü, n.d.), appendix p. 1.

16. Chang I-lin, *Hsin-t'ai-p'ing-shih chi*, pp. 207–8.

17. Boorman, vol. 3, p. 302.

18. Boorman, vol. 3, p. 68.

19. Stephen Robert MacKinnon, "Yüan Shih-k'ai in Tientsin and Peking: The Sources and Structure of his Power, 1901–1908" (Ph.D. diss., University of California at Davis, 1971), p. 138, makes this point: ". . . in the recruitment and promotion of officers and men Yüan stressed professionalism, based on the foreign model, over combat experience or personal background and connections."

20. Ralph L. Powell, *The Rise of Chinese Military Power, 1895–1912* (Princeton, 1955), pp. 338–42; James E. Sheridan, *Chinese Warlord: The Career of Feng Yü-hsiang* (Stanford, 1966), pp. 5, 8; T'ao Ch'ü-yin, *Pei-yang chün-fa t'ung-chih shih-ch'i shih-hua* [Historical tales about the period of rule by the Peiyang warlords] (Peking, 1957), vol. 1, pp. 14–16.

21. The elevation of personal loyalties to the status of an organizing principle was apparently espoused and practiced in the mid-nineteenth century armies as a reform, in an effort to rectify the loss of responsiveness between troops and their commanders in the older Ch'ing armies. Kuhn, *Rebellion and Its Enemies*, pp. 122–48.

22. Arthur W. Hummel, ed., *Eminent Chinese of the Ch'ing Period (1644–1912)* (Washington, D.C., 1943), vol. 2, p. 688.

23. MacKinnon, "Yuan Shih-k'ai," p. 162.

24. For the case of Feng Yü-hsiang and his ability to assert the independence of his command in 1917, see Sheridan, *Chinese Warlord*, pp. 63–66.

25. Indications of this emerge from charts in Jerome Ch'en, "Defining Chinese Warlords and their Factions," *Bulletin of the School of Oriental and African Studies, University of London*, vol. 31, pt. 3 (1968), pp. 587–92, and in the orders for military postings issued by the presidency between 1912 and 1916, published in CFKP.

26. Sheridan, *Chinese Warlord*, p. 5. Powell, *Rise of Chinese Military Power*, p. 203, refers to "the clannishness of the Pei-yang clique," as a result of training in a Peiyang military school.

27. MacKinnon, "Yuan Shih-k'ai," pp. 229–30.

28. Pekin Shina Kenkyūkai, ed., *Saishin Shina kanshin roku* [Record of contemporary Chinese officials and gentry] (in two parts with separate pagination, Tokyo, 1918), pt. 2, pp. 392–95. Later, Peiyang scholarships were not granted as such. The responsibility devolved upon the provinces.

29. Gaimushō jōhōbu, ed., *Gendai Shina jinmeikan* [Biographical dictionary of contemporary China] (Tokyo, 1925), p. 270; Chou Hsun, *Shu-hai ts'ung-t'an* [Miscellaneous remarks about the Szechwan region] (reprint ed., Taipei, n.d.), p. 103; Des Forges, *Hsi-liang*, pp. 92, 165–66.

30. Werner, Foochow, to Alston (December 10, 1913), FO 228/1872; F. E. Wilkinson, consul in Foochow, to Jordan (January 12, and April 15, 1914), FO 228/1905; Jordan to Grey (May 3, 1916), FO 228/2738. Chiang Tso-pin (1884–1942), a graduate of the Japanese Army Officers' Academy and Sun Yat-sen's army vice-minister in 1912, is a similar case. He became Yuan's army vice-minister in 1912 and remained in the post until 1915.

31. Ts'ao Chü-jen, *Chiang Pai-li p'ing-chuan* [Critical biography of Chiang Fang-chen] (Hongkong, 1963), pp. 7–13; Boorman, vol. 1, pp. 312–17.

32. "Interview with Yuan Shih-k'ai" (February 7, 1916), MP item 135.

33. G. E. Morrison diary (March 31, 1912), MP item 92, quoting Aoki Norizumi.

34. "Memorandum of a Visit from Captain Ts'ai T'ing-kan, Nov. 16th, 1911" and "Memorandum. November 16th, 1911," MP item 147. Ts'ai and a foreign military aide to Yuan reported Yuan's attitude toward his appointment of Tuan Chih-kuei as acting Liang-hu governor-general in this vein.

35. Ts'ao Ju-lin, *I-sheng chih hui-i*, p. 112.

36. Interview with William R. Giles, as translated from the *Ya-hsi-ya jih-pao* (Peking), FO 233/158. For similar claims, see: Yuan's speech before the *Ts'an-i yuan* [National Deliberative Assembly], in *The China Year Book, 1913*, p. 500; his address to the *Cheng-chih hui-i* [Political Conference], December 15, 1913, in FO 228/1882 and CFKP 585: 1–6 (December 19, 1913); his statement on education in CFKP 1152 (July 23, 1914), rep. 39: 258.

37. Liu Feng-han, *Hsin-chien lu-chün*, p. 112; Boorman, vol. 2, pp. 136–37; Jerome Ch'en, *Yuan Shih-k'ai*, 2d ed., pp. 2, 34; Gaimushō jōhōbu, *Gendai Shina jinmeikan*, pp. 958–59. I follow Liu Feng-han and Gaimushō jōhōbu rather than Boorman and Jerome Ch'en in describing Hsu Shih-ch'ang's position at Hsiao-chan. S. A. M. Adshead, *The Modernization of the Chinese Salt Administration, 1900–1920* (Cambridge, Mass., 1970), pp. 49–50, notes Hsu's reform of Manchuria's salt administration, which Chang Chien regarded as the most efficient in the empire.

38. Liang Shih-i had originally been nominated for the examination by both the educational commissioner of Fukien and the president of the board of war. Chang Chih-tung was chief examiner for the first half of the examination. Liang emerged from the examination first of 191 aspirants. On the basis of entirely irrational political prejudices (his provincial origins and the coincidental correspondence of the characters of his name with elements from the names of Liang Ch'i-ch'ao and K'ang Yu-wei), he was deprived of his earned rank. Fang Tu Lien-che, "Ching-chi t'e-k'o" [The special examination in economics], in Wu Hsiang-hsiang, ed., *Chung-kuo hsien-tai-shih ts'ung-k'an*, vol. 3 (Taipei, 1961), pp. 1–44.

39. For Liang Shih-i's activities before the revolution, see Stephen R. MacKinnon, "Liang Shih-i and the Communications Clique," *Journal of Asian Studies* 29.3: 581–602 (May 1970); Arthur Lewis Rosenbaum, "Chinese Railway Policy and the Response to Imperialism: The Peking-Mukden Railway, 1895–1911," *Ch'ing-shih wen-t'i* 2.1: 58 (October 1969); Boorman, vol. 2, pp. 354–55.

40. Gaimushō jōhōbu, *Gendai Shina jinmeikan*, p. 1036; Boorman, vol. 1, pp. 409–13.

41. This account is based on Watanabe Atsushi, "En Seigai seiken," pp. 135–71. For an excellent biography, see Boorman, vol. 1, pp. 409–13.
42. For an illuminating study of the history of this company, see Albert Feuerwerker, "Industrial Enterprise in Twentieth-Century China: The Chee Hsin Cement Co.," in Albert Feuerwerker et al., eds., *Approaches to Modern Chinese History* (Berkeley and Los Angeles, 1967), pp. 304–41.
43. Watanabe Atsushi, "En Seigai seiken," pp. 148–57; Carlson, *Kaiping Mines*, pp. 80–96, 107–10.
44. Watanabe Atsushi, "En Seigai seiken," pp. 152–53, 165–68.
45. G. E. Morrison diary (April 7, 1912), MP item 93.
46. On Yuan's prerevolutionary diplomatic style and record, see: Lin Ming-te, *Yuan Shih-k'ai yü Chao-hsien* [Yuan Shih-k'ai and Korea] (Taipei, 1970); Schrecker, *Imperialism*; and Michael H. Hunt, *Frontier Defense and the Open Door: Manchuria in Chinese-American Relations, 1895–1911* (New Haven and London, 1973), especially pp. 152–78. On the possible connection between the failure of Yuan's diplomacy and his dismissal by the court, see: Ijūin Hikokichi, minister in Peking, to Komura Jutarō, foreign minister (January 2, and January 3, 1909); Takasu, consul in Changsha, to Komura (January 5, 1909); Brigadier General Aoki Nori-zumi to the chief of the general staff (January 5, 1909, two messages): Japan MFA film, MT 1.6.1.4–3, reel 110, pp. 1135–41, 1155, and 1188.
47. I have discussed the balance of forces and the general turn toward republicanism between October, 1911, and April, 1912, in "Yuan Shih-k'ai's Rise to the Presidency," in Wright, *China in Revolution*.
48. Watanabe Atsushi, "En Seigai—Hokuyō-ha seiken dasshu no michi" [Yuan Shih-k'ai—the path of the seizure of power by the Peiyang clique], *Rekishigaku kenkyū*, no. 258 (October 1961), pp. 36–37; Chang I-lin, *Hsin-t'ai-p'ing-shih chi*, pp. 213–14; Chang Kuo-kan, *Hsin-hai ko-ming shih-liao* [Historical sources of the 1911 Revolution] (Shanghai, 1958), pp. 304–7.
49. Adshead, *Modernization*, p. 68.
50. V. K. Ting (Ting Wen-chiang) to Morrison, Shanghai and Soochow, May 5, 1912, MP item 171.

Chapter 4

1. Li Shou-k'ung, *Min-ch'u chih kuo-hui* [The national assemblies of the early republic] (Taipei, 1964), pp. 33–38.
2. Roswell S. Britton, *The Chinese Periodical Press, 1800–1912* (Shanghai, 1933), p. 125.
3. W. H. Wilkinson, Chengtu, to Jordan (April 1, 1912), FO 228/1838; W. R. Brown, acting consul in Chungking, to Jordan (June 12, 1912), FO 228/1837; *Republican Advocate* (Shanghai), 1.30: 1187 (October 26, 1912). Since there was considerable turnover in newspaper publication,

272 Notes to Pages 77–80

counts during any one year vary. Rhoads, *China's Republican Revolution*, p. 246, reports sixteen newspapers in Canton in 1911 and close to thirty in 1912.

4. Prospectus and draft agreement for establishing a Chinese-language newspaper in Shanghai, by T. F. Millard, transmitted by G. E. Morrison (May 19, 1913), MP item 177. Millard was an experienced editor of an English-language magazine in Shanghai. He claimed that the figure was based on "careful investigation." On the other hand, he had an interest in minimizing the circulation of existing Chinese-language newspapers.

5. J. L. Smith, Tsinan, to Jordan (January 15, 1913), FO 228/1877.

6. Feng Yü-hsiang, *Wo ti sheng-huo*, p. 169.

7. Brown, Chungking, to Jordan (May 23, 1912), FO 228/1837.

8. Morrison to D. D. Braham, Peking, March 29, 1912, MP item 162.

9. Esherick, "Reform," pp. 465–66.

10. PDN, July 30, 1912, p. 1.

11. G. E. Morrison diary (February 6, 1913), MP item 96. Kwangtung's government tried to discourage celebrations of the lunar New Year in 1913, though not too successfully, even in Canton. Rhoads, *China's Republican Revolution*, pp. 252–53. A prefect in Hsiang-yang, Hupeh, forbade Chinese New Year celebrations in February, 1912. CTSTL, 1963, no. 2, p. 18.

12. *Min-kuo hsin-wen* (Shanghai), translated in *Republican Advocate* 1.31: 1219 (November 2, 1912). Among the issues at Peking University was the new chancellor. Liang Ch'i-ch'ao seems to have been someone the students tried to get. *Liang . . . nien-p'u*, p. 407.

13. CFKP 386: 1 (June 3, 1913).

14. Lo Jung-pang, ed., *K'ang Yu-wei*, pp. 38–39; Rhoads, *China's Republican Revolution*, p. 42; Daniel H. Bays, "Chang Chih-tung and the Politics of Reform in China" (Ph.D. diss., University of Michigan, 1971), chap. 3, p. 7.

15. Li Yun-han, "Huang K'o-ch'iang hsien-sheng nien-p'u kao" [Draft chronological biography of Huang Hsing], in Wu Hsiang-hsiang, ed., *Chung-kuo hsien-tai-shih ts'ung-k'an*, vol. 4 (Taipei, 1962), pp. 299–300.

16. F. E. Wilkinson, Nanking, to Jordan (March 7, 1912), FO 228/1836.

17. *North China Herald*, March 30, 1912, p. 847.

18. *Republican Advocate* 1.28: 1059 (October 12, 1912), 1.29: 1152 (October 19, 1912), 1.31: 1226 (November 2, 1912).

19. Kuo-fang yen-chiu-yuan, ed., *Kuo-fu ch'üan-shu* [Complete works of Sun Yat-sen] (Taipei, 1960), p. 528.

20. *Min-ch'üan pao* (Shanghai), translated in *Republican Advocate* 1.40: 1584 (January 4, 1913).

21. V. K. Ting to Morrison, Shanghai and Soochow, May 5, 1912, MP item 171. For an interesting account of women's activity in China in 1912 and 1913, see Gardner L. Harding, *Present-Day China: A Narrative of a Nation's Advance* (New York, 1916), pp. 38–67.

22. *Ta-kung-ho jih-pao* (Shanghai) (October 5, 1912), p. 5.
23. Pai Chiao, *Yuan Shih-k'ai yü Chung-hua min-kuo*, p. 41.
24. Ibid., pp. 52–55.
25. Ibid., pp. 57–58.
26. Ibid., p. 55.
27. Jordan to Grey (May 3, 1912), FO 371/1318.
28. Sun Yao, *Chung-hua min-kuo shih-liao* [Historical materials on the Republic of China] (reprint ed., Taipei, 1962), p. 281.
29. For example, spokesmen argued that representative government improved the government's ability to collect taxes and resist foreign encroachment. "I-hui cheng-chih lun" [On representative government], *Kuo-min yueh-k'an* (May 1913); Yeh Hsia-sheng, "Yü chih cheng-chien" [My political views], *Min-i tsa-chih* (Canton) (February 15, 1913).
30. For an understanding of the revolutionary movement and its achievements at the provincial level in these years, I have relied heavily on: Esherick, "Reform, Revolution and Reaction: The 1911 Revolution in Hunan and Hupeh"; Friedman, "The Center Cannot Hold"; Johnson, "China's 1911 Revolution in the Provinces of Yunnan and Kweichow"; Samuel Yale Kupper, "Revolution in China: Kiangsi Province, 1905–1913" (Ph.D. diss., University of Michigan, 1972); Mary Backus Rankin, *Early Chinese Revolutionaries: Radical Intellectuals in Shanghai and Chekiang, 1902–1911* (Cambridge, Mass., 1971); Edward J. M. Rhoads, *China's Republican Revolution: The Case of Kwangtung, 1895–1913;* Schoppa, "Politics and Society in Chekiang, 1907–1927"; and Sutton, "The Rise and Decline of the Yunnan Army, 1909–1925."
31. At one point Sun Yat-sen had been slated for this post in Peking. "Conversation with Ts'ai T'ing-kan. Feb. 1st, 1912," MP item 147. But even at that time, Morrison reported opposition to Sun on grounds of his lack of knowledge about China and his overly advanced views. By February 16, Morrison expected T'ang Shao-i to be prime minister. Morrison to D. D. Braham, Peking, February 16, 1912, MP item 161.
32. T'ang told the consortium representatives on February 27 that, in addition to the 2 million taels needed immediately in Nanking, he would require an additional 5 million taels for Nanking in March. This was apart from Peking's immediate needs. "The Financial Deadlock—The Four Ministers' Protest" (March 29, 1912), MP item 162. One British banker in China, E. G. Hillier, claimed T'ang's authority for the statement that T'ang spent 5 million taels during his trip to Nanking. G. E. Morrison diary (May 5, 1912), MP item 93. If T'ang did distribute that much, it seems that only 1 million taels of it went to Sun and that T'ang himself was not unrewarded, though at a lesser scale. The most circumstantial, though still indirect, account of the transaction that I have seen is by Arthur Pope of the Shanghai-Nanking Railway, who had worked closely with the revolutionaries during the Nanking phase of the revolutionary war. Arthur Pope to Morrison, Shanghai, May 10, 1912, MP item 158. The British consul in Nanking was told that the money

went to Sun, Wu T'ing-fang, the T'ung-meng hui, and the army in Nanking. F. E. Wilkinson, Nanking, to Jordan (May 19, 1912), FO 228/1836. When Yuan Shih-k'ai later raised the issue as an aspersion on the character of the recipients, Sung Chiao-jen admitted the substance of the transaction and argued only about the amount and its uses. *Min-li pao* (Shanghai), 860: 2 (March 12, 1913).

33. Ts'ai T'ing-kan to Morrison, Peking, January 5, 1914, MP item 183.

34. On Huang Hsing's reluctance, see *Min-li pao* 520: 3 (March 27, 1912) and 521: 2 (March 28, 1912). On the role of the military commanders in Nanking and their interest in keeping Huang Hsing in Nanking, see *T'ien-to pao* (Shanghai), April 3, 1912, p. 3.

35. On Chao Ping-chün's membership in the T'ung-meng hui, see *T'ien-to pao*, July 5, 1912, p. 3.

36. G. E. Morrison diary (July 15, 1912), MP item 94. Morrison reports here an hour and one-half interview with T'ang Shao-i in Tientsin. Nanking's nominee for Shantung was Po Wen-wei, who became the *tu-tu* of Anhwei, his home province. According to one pro-T'ung-meng hui newspaper in Shanghai, T'ang also undertook to support Nanking's nomination for Honan. *T'ien-to pao*, April 7, 1912, p. 3. If all the nominations had been accepted, Yuan would have had none of his own appointees in the military governorships of the home provinces.

37. Wang Cheng-t'ing had replaced Ch'en Ch'i-mei in the cabinet. Hsiung Hsi-ling's resignation as finance minister on the same day (July 14, 1912) as Sung Chiao-jen's, Wang Ch'ung-hui's, Wang Cheng-t'ing's and Ts'ai Yuan-p'ei's illustrates the multiplicity of issues and alignments surrounding T'ang Shao-i's break with Yuan. As with T'ang, Hsiung's departure apparently had to do with maneuvering in the negotiations for foreign loans. For an elaborate and partially speculative discussion of the politics of the resignation of T'ang Shao-i's cabinet, see K. S. Liew, *Struggle for Democracy*, pp. 163–68.

38. There are many sets of numbers for the soldiers at or near Nanking. One detailed breakdown is given in F. E. Wilkinson, Nanking, to Jordan (May 16, 1912), FO 228/1836. On Huang Hsing's brief reign in Nanking, see Li Yun-han, "Huang K'o-ch'iang," pp. 314–23.

39. *T'ien-to pao*, April 22, 1912, p. 3.

40. Ibid., May 10, 1912, p. 3, and May 21, 1912, p. 3.

41. These remarks were allegedly made by Yuan to representatives of the T'ung-i tang [Unity Party] and reported in the *Pei-ching jih-pao*. PDN, July 1, 1912, p. 4.

42. *Chung-hua min-pao* (Shanghai), August 25, 1912, p. 2; Martin Bernal, "Chinese Socialism to 1913" (Ph.D. diss., Cambridge University, 1966), pp. 306–22.

43. A good account is given in Li Shou-k'ung, *Min-ch'u chih kuo-hui*, pp. 53–59. See also Franklin W. Houn, *Central Government of China, 1912–1928: An Institutional Study* (Madison, 1957), p. 33.

44. PDN, August 29, 1912, p. 5.
45. A translation of some of Sun's remarks is given in Hsueh Chün-tu, *Huang Hsing*, pp. 141–42. Sun did not escape criticism from radicals for his endorsement of Yuan: *Min-ch'üan pao*, September 6, 1912, p. 1.
46. On Huang Hsing's role and his effort to bring various leading personalities, including Yuan, into the Kuomintang, see Li Shou-k'ung, *Min-ch'u chih kuo-hui*, pp. 65–69.
47. Speech by Sun Yat-sen, March 31, 1912, at the Nanking headquarters of the T'ung-meng hui: *Kung-ho yen-lun pao* (Shanghai), no. 1 (April 1912), pp. 75–83.
48. Kuo-fang yen-chiu-yuan, *Kuo-fu ch'üan-shu*, pp. 489–93, 497, 528.
49. Sun's surprise at Yuan's response is recorded in Ts'en Hsueh-lü, *San-shui Liang Yen-sun hsien-sheng nien-p'u* [Chronological biography of Liang Shih-i] (reprint ed., Taipei, 1962), vol. 1, p. 123.
50. For a different emphasis in evaluating the socially revolutionary meaning of T'ung-meng hui thought in these years, see Friedman, "The Center Cannot Hold" and *Backward Toward Revolution: The Chinese Revolutionary Party* (Berkeley, 1974), pp. 9–47. ᐧ
51. *Min-ch'üan pao*, quoted in *Republican Advocate* 1.32: 1257–58 (November 9, 1912).
52. CFKP 184: 9–10 (November 1, 1912).
53. *Ta-kung-pao jih-pao*, October 14, 1912, p. 3.
54. PDN, August 2, 1912, pp. 4–5; ibid., August 10, 1912, p. 4; Friedman, "The Center Cannot Hold," pp. 148–49, 188–89.
55. Ibid.; Rhoads, *China's Republican Revolution*, pp. 251–58.
56. May, Hongkong, to Harcourt (August 16, 1912), enclosed in colonial office to foreign office (September 26, 1912), FO 371/1322.
57. Hu Han-min (using pen name, Min-i), "Cheng-chien chih shang-ch'üan" [A discussion of political views], *Min-i tsa-chih* (November 15, 1912), pp. 4–6. Friedman, "The Center Cannot Hold," p. 127, notes an order issued when Ch'en Chiung-ming was military governor, instructing the county magistrates "to punish the gentry who oppress the villagers . . . ," but Friedman concludes that the magistrates were unable to carry out such an order. A similar fate met Liao Chung-k'ai's land tax bill. Ibid., pp. 202–21. Rhoads, *China's Republican Revolution*, pp. 257–58, concludes that, despite first steps taken toward a moderate land reform program, the Kwangtung government in this period was marked by "unconcern for and insensitivity to agrarian problems."
58. *Ta-kung-ho jih-pao*, October 16, 1912, p. 4.
59. Friedman, "The Center Cannot Hold," pp. 180–85; *Republican Advocate* 1.34: 1348 (November 23, 1912).
60. *Nihon gaikō bunsho*, combined vols. 44 and 45 (*Shinkoku jihen*), p. 38. E. Manico Gull to Morrison, Canton, July 20, 1912, MP item 174. Friedman, "The Center Cannot Hold," pp. 61–66.
61. Ibid., pp. 94–96, 157.

62. May, Hongkong, to Harcourt (July 23, 1912), FO 371/1322; Chinese Kuomintang, Central Committee for the Compilation of Materials on Party History, comp., *Ko-ming hsien-lieh hsien-chin chuan* [Biographies of martyrs and forerunners of the revolution], p. 311.

63. China, Maritime Customs, *Returns of Trade and Trade Reports*, 1912, pt. 2, vol. 4, p. 680. Fred W. Carey to Morrison, Canton, December 19, 1912, MP item 173. F. D. Cheshire, consul general in Canton, to Bryan (September 17, 1913), NA 893.00/1964.

64. PDN, July 17, 1912, p. 4; CFKP 210: 6–7 (November 27, 1912); Friedman, "The Center Cannot Hold," pp. 192–96.

65. Hu Han-min, "Cheng-chien chih shang-ch'üan." See also an interview in Maybon, *La République Chinoise*, p. 181; and a telegram to Yuan translated in Nara Kazuo, *Chūka minkoku daijiken to En Seigai* [The great event of the Republic of China and Yuan Shih-k'ai] (Tientsin, 1915), p. 408.

66. Yeh Hsia-sheng, "Yü chih cheng-chien."

67. From an earlier report by this British consular source, figures concerning plans for Changsha indicate a projected 40 children for each four-year lower elementary school. Estimating the maximum limits, I have taken the figure of 40 children per elementary school and have derived from George Barclay's figures on Taiwan's age composition in 1905 an estimate of 9.36 percent of total population for lower elementary school-age children. Using the 1912 census figures for Hunan (27,390,230), these assumptions translate into 33.9 percent of school-age children provided for in the 21,744 lower elementary schools in Hunan in 1913. Estimating the minimum limits, I have arbitrarily discounted the aim of 40 children per school to 30 and have derived from the age structure revealed by the 1953 census an estimate of 11 percent for school-age children. Using the same 1912 population figure for Hunan, these assumptions translate into 21.7 percent of school-age children provided for in these schools. J. L. Buck's age structure for south China in 1929–31 produces an intermediate estimate of 10.72 percent of total population at elementary-school age.

   Bertram Giles, consul in Changsha, to Jordan (January 29, 1913), FO 228/1869; George W. Barclay, *Colonial Development and Population in Taiwan* (Princeton, 1954), p. 14; Ho Ping-ti, *Studies on the Population of China, 1368–1953* (Cambridge, Mass., 1959), pp. 96–97; J. L. Buck, *Land Utilization in China* (Shanghai, 1937), pp. 376–77.

   Needless to say, the possibilities for error in these various assumptions are enormous. Also, actual attendance was overwhelmingly male; if boys alone are considered, the proportions provided for would be almost double.

68. This account of reform in Hunan is based on British consular reporting from Changsha: Bertram Giles, Changsha, to Jordan (April 26, July 30, October 25, 1912), FO 228/1837; Giles, Changsha, to Jordan (January 29, and April 29, 1913), FO 228/1869. Esherick, "Reform," chap. 3,

gives statistics showing Hunan's poor showing in the late Ch'ing development of primary schools compared with Chihli, Szechwan, and even Hupeh. For Hunan's comparative slowness as of 1907, see Hsuehpu tung-wu-ssu, eds., *Kuang-hsu 33 nien-fen: ti-i-tz'u chiao-yü t'ung-chi t'u-piao* [For the year 1907: first statistical tables on education] (reprint ed., Taipei, 1973), pp. 27–28. For politics in Hunan between 1911 and 1913, see Esherick, "Reform," pp. 478–95.

69. "Statistical Summaries of Chinese Education," Bulletin 16, vol. 2 (1923), p. 38, in Chinese National Association for the Advancement of Education, ed., *Bulletins on Chinese Education*, 1923 (Shanghai, 1923).

70. The British consul estimated that 150,000 Hunanese troops were dispatched from Changsha during the revolution. Giles, Changsha, to Jordan (February 28, 1912), enclosed in Jordan to Grey (March 31, 1912), FO 371/1317. The Peking army minister was said to put the number of Hunan troops at the end of the revolution at 90,000. Funatsu Shin'ichirō, consul in Changsha, to Uchida Yasuya, foreign minister (August 17, 1912), Japan MFA film, MT 5.1.10.5-1, reel 463, pp. 51–55. According to a Japanese report on provincial troop strengths in March, 1913, as compared to February, 1912, Hunan reduced her new-style forces by 80 percent (leaving, according to this report, about 10,000 soldiers in this category). The nearest competitor in reduction rates was Szechwan at 60 percent. General Staff, "Kakumei-go ni okeru Shina kakushō heiryoku zōgen ichi-ranbyō" [A table of changes in military strength in the Chinese provinces after the revolution], Japan MFA film, MT 5.1.10.5-1, reel 463, pp. 420–21.

On T'an Yen-k'ai's political motivations for disbandment, see Li Shih-yueh, *Hsin-hai ko-ming shih-ch'i liang-hu ti-ch'ü ti ko-ming yun-tung* [The revolutionary movement in the Hunan and Hupeh region in the period of the 1911 Revolution] (Peking, 1957), p. 113. I am grateful to Joe Esherick for bringing this point to my attention.

Hunan had reported a budget for the fiscal year beginning July, 1913, in which 40 percent of expenditures would go to the army. Her closest competitors among the home provinces for low military budget projections were: Chihli (43.9 percent), although this would not include national military expenditures for troops in Chihli, and a small separate budget for Peking's metropolitan district where 56.2 percent went to the military; and Chekiang with 44.5 percent. The highest proportions in these budgets were projected by Yunnan (75.1 percent) and Kwangtung (68.2 percent). All these other provinces had substantially larger total budgets than Hunan. The percentages are calculated from tables in Chia Shih-i, *Min-kuo ts'ai-cheng shih* [History of public finance under the republic] (Shanghai, 1917), vol. 1, pp. 81–84. As in all early republican budgetary figures, there is a degree of unreality in these tables. They are projections of expenditure within the artificial confines of provincial expenditure as distinct from national expenditure within the province.

The difference between the two types of expenditure seems to have been in practice merely a matter of bookkeeping. Chia Shih-i does not give figures on so-called national military expenditure within the provinces. Comparisons of proportions of projected expenditure may nevertheless indicate different emphases in provinces where former Peiyang troops were not present.

71. Giles, Changsha, to Jordan (August 9, 1913), FO 228/1869.
72. For an example, see Li Shih-yueh, *Hsin-hai ko-ming shih-ch'i liang-hu ti-ch'ü ti ko-ming yun-tung*, p. 111.
73. Giles, Changsha, to Jordan (April 26, 1912), FO 228/1837; Giles, Changsha, to Jordan (January 29, 1913), FO 228/1869; Li Shih-yueh, *Hsin-hai ko-ming shih-ch'i liang-hu ti-ch'ü ti ko-ming yun-tung*, pp. 107–10; Hu Han-min, "Cheng-chien chih shang-ch'üan," pp. 4–5.
74. *North China Herald*, November 22, 1913, report from Chen-chou (November 5, 1913). I correct here an obvious error in characters.
75. These assertions are primarily based on a survey of British and American consular reporting from the provinces in these years.
76. Pai Chiao, *Yuan Shih-k'ai yü Chung-hua min-kuo*, pp. 67–71.
77. Cited in a seventeen-page study of Kiangsu finances in the early republic: B. Twyman, consul at Chinkiang, to Jordan (October 31, 1914), FO 228/1904, pp. 5–6. By contrast, provincial revenues in Hunan rose greatly after the revolution. Esherick, "Reform," pp. 487–89, attributes the rise chiefly to increased salt taxes and inflation.
78. *Min-ch'üan pao*, June 2, 1912, p. 2.
79. Sun Yao, *Chung-hua min-kuo shih-liao*, pp. 149–50, 165–67.
80. Feng Yü-hsiang, *Wo ti sheng-huo*, pp. 160–64; interview with T'ang Shao-i in G. E. Morrison diary (July 15, 1912), MP item 94.
81. P'u Yu-shu, "The Consortium Reorganization Loan to China, 1911–1914: An Episode in Pre-War Diplomacy and International Finance" (Ph.D. diss., University of Michigan, 1950), p. 326.
82. Sun Yao, *Chung-hua min-kuo shih-liao*, p. 296. Jordan to Sir Charles Addis, Peking, April 10, 1916, Jordan Papers, FO 350/15.
83. For an analysis of Szechwan's fiscal relations with Peking in 1911, see W. H. Wilkinson, Chengtu, to Jordan (January 8, 1912), FO 371/1314. Hedtke, "Reluctant Revolutionaries," pp. 67–70, describes some of the external fiscal burdens carried by Szechwan in the late Ch'ing.
84. Harold Porter, acting consul general in Chengtu, to Beilby Francis Alston, chargé d'affaires in Peking (July 9, 1913), FO 228/1870.
85. G. E. Morrison diary (October 22, 1912), MP item 95. Morrison's attendance at cabinet meetings was unusual, not regular.
86. Sun Yao, *Chung-hua min-kuo shih-liao*, p. 296.
87. "Sung Chiao-jen hsien-sheng yen-shuo ssu" [A speech by Mr. Sung Chiao-jen], *Chung-hua T'ung-meng hui* [*Yueh chih-pu*] *tsa-chih* (Canton), September 11, 1912, pp. 5–6.
88. For an analysis of Liang Shih-i's part in the first years of the presidency,

see *Nihon gaikō bunsho*, 1914, vol. 2, pp. 778–82. (I assume from the context of this report that the currency units are Chinese dollars.) As regular sources of revenue were developed, Liang's stature in the government declined.

89. K'ang Yu-wei, "Fei-sheng lun," p. 514.

90. General Staff, "Shina jiji mondai no kenkyū" [A study of current questions in China], Japan MFA film, MT 1.6.1.62, reel 157, pp. 1751–57.

Chapter 5

1. *Min-li pao*, 796: 2 (December 31, 1912).

2. CFKP 210: 4–5 (November 27, 1912).

3. Jordan to Alston, Peking, November 9, 1912, Jordan Papers, FO 350/8. The words are Jordan's paraphrase, not a direct quotation from Yuan, but the sentiment was no doubt Yuan's.

4. *T'ien-to pao*, May 23, 1912, p. 4.

5. CFKP 210: 5–6 (November 27, 1912).

6. HHKMHIL, vol. 4, pp. 457–68. Gaimushō jōhōbu, *Gendai Shina jinmei-kan*, p. 217. Tahara Teijirō, comp., *Shinmatsu minsho Chūgoku kanshin jinmeiroku* [A biographical record of Chinese officials and gentry at the end of the Ch'ing and in the early republic] (Talien, 1918), p. 565. Huang Chi-lu et al., eds., *Ko-ming jen-wu chih* [Chronicles of revolutionary personalities], vol. 6 (Taipei, 1971), pp. 159–61. Ts'en Ch'un-hsuan, *Lo-chai man-pi* [Random notes from the study of Lo] (reprint ed., Taipei, 1962), pt. 1, p. 19. Amos P. Wilder, consul general at Shanghai, to Bryan (February 19, 1913), NA 893.00/1568. Werner, Foochow, to Jordan (May 15, May 22, August 9, August 31, September 30, October 10, and November 22, 1912), FO 228/1838. An extended criticism of P'eng Shou-sung, including charges of using secret societies, appeared in a T'ung-meng hui paper before Ts'en's mission: *Min-li pao* 656: 2 (August 10, 1912). P'eng held several important posts in the aftermath of the revolution in Fukien, but his major position came to be described as police commissioner.

7. This account of affairs in Shansi is based on the following: HHKMHIL, vol. 5, pp. 145–78; *Ko-sheng kuang-fu* [Restoration in the various provinces] (Taipei, 1962), vol. 1, pp. 252–55, 266; Chang P'eng-yuan, *Li-hsien-p'ai yü hsin-hai ko-ming*, pp. 172–75; Yen Hsi-shan, *Yen Hsi-shan tsao-nien hui-i-lu* [Yen Hsi-shan's memoirs regarding his early years] (Taipei, 1968), pp. 33–34, 41–42; *North China Herald*, March 23, 1912, pp. 798–99; "Nan-ching lin-shih cheng-fu kung-pao" [Gazette of the Nanking provisional government] (February 28, 1912), *Hsin-hai ko-ming tzu-liao*, CTSTL, 1961, no. 1, p. 197; *Republican Advocate* 1.44: 1752–53 (February 1, 1913). Li Ken-yuan, *Hsueh-cheng nien-lu* [Annual record of Li Ken-yuan] (reprint ed., Taipei, n.d.), pp. 57–58,

relates that he was asked to mediate this affair in Shansi but does not indicate how he did so, aside from seeing Yen Hsi-shan in Taiyuan. Donald Gillin errs, I think, in generalizing to other provinces Yen's deference to Yuan before the Second Revolution: Gillin, *Warlord*, p. 21.

8. Twyman, Chinkiang, to Jordan (October 31, 1914), pp. 7–8, FO 228/ 1904. Porter, Chengtu, to Alston (July 9, 1913), FO 228/1870. For further examples of the ineffectuality of Yuan's efforts to inject Peking's authority into the provinces through appointments, see Sutton, "Rise and Decline," p. 162, and Rhoads, *China's Republican Revolution*, p. 260.

9. Memorandum of a conversation with F. A. Aglen (January 21, 1913), inserted in G. E. Morrison diary, MP item 96.

10. *The China Year Book*, 1913, pp. 262–64. PDN, August 17, 1912, p. 4. *Ta-kung-ho jih-pao*, October 14, 1912, p. 3.

11. CFKP 243: 1–5 (January 9, 1913). *Republican Advocate* 1.42: 1673 (January 18, 1913). Ibid., 1.43: 1696–98, 1704 (January 25, 1913). PDN, January 11, 1913, p. 4. (Ch'en) Keng-fu, "Yuan tsung-t'ung kung-fu hsien-hsing ti-fang hsing-cheng kuan-t'ing tsu-chih ling chih p'ing-i" [Criticism of President Yuan's promulgation of the order on the organization of local administrative offices], *Min-i tsa-chih*, February 15, 1913, pp. 1–18. "Chung-kuo yao-chi" [Main events in China], *Min-i tsa-chih*, February 15, 1913, pp. 1–2, 10, 18. C. D. Jamieson, consul general in Canton, to Jordan (February 3, 1913), FO 228/1869. Smith, Tsinan, to Jordan (April 18, 1913), FO 228/1877.

12. *Ko-sheng kuang-fu*, vol. 1, p. 266; Nara Kazuo, *Chūka minkoku daijiken to En Seigai*, pp. 405–8. For Li Lieh-chün's own description of his modest reforms, see Li Lieh-chün, *Li Lieh-chün chiang-chün tzu-chuan* [Autobiography of General Li Lieh-chün] (Chungking, 1944), pp. 19–21. For examples of his repressive acts, which were in part responses to real threats to his power, see *Ta-kung-ho jih-pao*, October 7, 1912, p. 4; ibid., December 4, 1912, p. 5.

13. This point was made at the time by Li Ta-chao, "Ts'ai tu-tu heng-i" [A peevish discussion on behalf of doing away with the military governors], *Yen-chih* (Tientsin), no. 3 (July 1, 1913), pp. 1–2.

14. Wu T'ieh-ch'eng, "Chung-kuo yao-chi," *Min-i tsa-chih*, March 15, 1913, p. 7. In another version, the initiative for Wang's appointment as civil governor came from Li Lieh-chün and his entourage in an effort to forestall any appointment by Yuan, but Wang turned the tables on Li by seeking Yuan's formal endorsement. HHKMHIL, vol. 1, pp. 541–42, and vol. 4, p. 321. Kung Shih-tseng's version, which assigns the initiative to Wang Jui-k'ai and claims only that Li Lieh-chün agreed to give Wang an advisory role, which might later become a civil governorship, seems more likely and even so may be telescoping events taking place from June through December 1912 HHKMHIL, vol. 4, p. 338.

15. Wu T'ieh-ch'eng, "Chung-kuo yao-chi," *Min-i tsa-chih*, March 15,

1913, pp. 6–8. HHKMHIL, vol. 4, pp. 321–23. *Republican Advocate* 1.39: 1551 (December 28, 1912). Wang Jui-k'ai's own report (January 7, 1913) on the event to Yuan Shih-k'ai, which blames Li Lieh-chün's entourage for the fiasco and cites Li himself only for irresolution, is given in CTSTL, 1962, no. 1, pp. 120–21. Yuan may have tried to subvert Li's position by more devious means somewhat earlier in 1912. HHKMHIL, vol. 4, p. 337.

16. Hagi Motoba, secretary in Kiukiang, to Yoshizawa Shōkichi, consul general in Hankow (May 2, 1912), Japan MFA film, MT 5.1.10.5–1, reel 463, p. 471. Jordan to Grey (May 3, 1913), FO 228/1852. Greene, Hankow, to Calhoun (February 1, 1913), NA 893.00/1552. G. E. Morrison diary (January 15, and February 2, 1913) and a memorandum (January 21, 1913) inserted in the diary, MP item 96.
17. Jordan to Langley, Peking, November 27, 1912, Jordan Papers, FO 350/8.
18. CFKP 219: 6–8 (December 16, 1912).
19. Twyman, Chinkiang, to Jordan (April 10, 1913), FO 228/1870. For a reminiscence of the organization of the KMT victory in Hunan, which emphasizes the advantages of administrative power, see K. S. Liew, *Struggle for Democracy*, p. 183.

Proportions of population are anybody's guess in the middle of the period, between 1851 and 1949, that Ho Ping-ti has described as "practically a demographer's vacuum." Ho Ping-ti, *Studies*, p. 97. Elvin, "The Gentry Democracy in Shanghai, 1905–1914," pp. 78–80, presents comparatively reliable figures on voting and population for that portion of Shanghai served by the Chinese City Council. They indicate a registration of 4.1 percent of total population. The provincial figures on voters' registration seem to be of unequal reliability, some clearly inflated. For example, the Kwangsi figure amounts to 34.2 percent of the 1910 Customs estimate of the population, or 14.0 percent of the 1953 census, and surpassed in absolute number the registrations of Kiangsu, Chekiang, Anhwei, Hunan, Shantung, Honan, Szechwan, and Kwangtung, as well as several lesser provinces. Fincher, "Political Provincialism," p. 210, is mistaken, I think, in accepting the total figures at face value.

The Kiangsu figure of 1,939,692 registrants for the national assembly elections is surrounded by confirming evidence. Local reports from Nanking and Chinkiang describe local statistics of registrants and votes that, when extrapolated for the province as a whole, tend to confirm the provincial figure. As a proportion of the provincial government's estimate of population in 1912 (32,159,019), registrants were 6.0 percent. As a proportion of the 1953 census figure (47,457,000), they were 4.1 percent, or, reducing the Shanghai portion of that figure from its 1953 level of over 6,000,000 to a 1917 estimate of 1,500,000, they were 4.5 percent. In Hunan, where local self-government councils were particularly strong, registrants as officially reported would make up 8.3 percent of the 1912 census estimates and 6.9 percent of the 1953 population figure. A report from the small port town of Pakhoi (Pei-hai) in Kwangtung put registered voters at 2.3 percent of the local population. Friedman, "Revolution or Just Another Bloody Cycle?," pp. 304–5, reports a 1 percent registration in Swatow and a rural dominance in Kwangtung's elections.

I attempt here to achieve only a suggestion of the possible range, drawing on material found in the following: Ho Ping-ti, *Studies;* Elvin, "The Gentry Democracy in Shanghai, 1905–1914"; *The China Year Book*, 1914; Samuel Couling, *The Encyclopaedia Sinica* (Shanghai, 1917); Charles D. Tenney, consul in Nanking, to Knox (November 15, 1912), NA 893.00/1509; Tenney, Nanking, to Knox (December 19, 1912), NA 893.00/1529; *Republican Advocate* 1.36: 1435 (December 7, 1912); Cheshire, Canton, to Knox (January 20, 1913), NA 893.00/1544; Twyman, Chinkiang, to Jordan (January 16, and April 10, 1913), FO 228/1870; A. G. Major, acting consul in Pakhoi, to Jordan (April 14, 1913), FO 228/1874; as well as a quantity of other American and British reports.

20. *Ko-ming wen-hsien* 41: 419–21. M. S. Myers, vice-consul in Mukden, to Calhoun (February 13, 1913), NA 893.00/1551.
21. Noriko Kamachi (Tamada), "Sung Chiao-jen and the 1911 Revolution," *Papers on China*, vol. 21 (Harvard University, February, 1968), p. 220. For Sung Chiao-jen's views as Kuomintang leader, see "Sung Tun-ch'u hsien-sheng ta-cheng-chien" [The major political views of Sung Chiao-jen], *Kuo-min yueh-k'an*, May, 1913; *Ko-ming wen-hsien* 41: 259–89. Milton J. T. Shieh, *The Kuomintang: Selected Historical Documents, 1894–1969* (New York, 1970), pp. 41–51, translates a slightly edited version of one of Sung's articles as a Kuomintang manifesto of August 25, 1913. For a discussion of Sung's views in 1912 before the founding of the Kuomintang, illustrating his predisposition toward a centralized political structure, see K. S. Liew, *Struggle for Democracy*, pp. 162–63. For a glimpse of the election campaign, see Friedman, "The Center Cannot Hold," pp. 343, 345.
22. *Kuo-hui ts'ung-pao* (Peking), June, 1913, pp. 20–22. Other provincial leaders supporting this or similar proposals for a role in drafting the constitution were Ch'eng Te-ch'üan, Chu Jui, Hu Han-min, and T'an Yen-k'ai. Wu Hsiang-hsiang, *Sung Chiao-jen: Chung-kuo min-chu hsien-cheng ti hsien-ch'ü* [Sung Chiao-jen: precursor of Chinese democracy and constitutional government] (Taipei, 1964), p. 218.
23. Interview between Munakata Shōtarō and Sun Yat-sen, January 29, 1913, in Shanghai, *Nihon gaikō bunsho*, 1913, vol. 2, pp. 319–20. Sun is quoted as saying that neither he nor Huang Hsing were right for the presidency: "I as an individual believe that Yuan is a most fitting person [for the job]. Therefore I consider choosing him as the first-term [regular, as opposed to provisional] president well advised. . . . At present, only those who are not in touch with the state of our country's affairs

are in favor of the expulsion of Yuan Shih-k'ai." See also a public statement by Sun in Japan: Hsueh Chün-tu, *Huang Hsing*, p. 151. Hsueh generalizes about the KMT from Sun's position (mistakenly, I believe).

24. For Sung's public remarks about the premiership, the charge of ambition, and the presidency, see: *Min-li pao* 860: 2 (March 12, 1913); and *Ko-ming wen-hsien* 41: 289, 261, and 285. On the same charge during the Nanking government and on Sung's movements and remarks in early 1913, see: Li Yun-han, "Huang K'o-ch'iang," pp. 349 and 359; and K. S. Liew, *Struggle for Democracy*, pp. 186–88.

25. On the plan to oust Yuan Shih-k'ai, the following have been used: Tenney, Nanking, to Calhoun (January 29, 1913), NA 893.00/1538; Frank W. Hadley, vice-consul in Shanghai, notes (March 4, 1913), NA 893.00/1611; "Civil War between North and South: possibilities of" (March 14, 1913), FO 228/1861; Wu Hsiang-hsiang, *Sung Chiao-jen: Chung-kuo min-chu hsien-cheng ti hsien-ch'ü*, pp. 219–26; G. E. Morrison diary (March 19, 1913), MP item 96. For indications that shortly before his death Sung gave up his maximum goal (Yuan's full ouster), see *Republican Advocate* 1.51–52: 2066–67 (March 29, 1913).

26. *Ko-ming wen-hsien* 41: 359–62. The idea that the national assembly should meet outside Peking was broached as early as August, 1912. K. S. Liew, *Struggle for Democracy*, pp. 188–89.

27. For an account of Ying Kuei-hsing's relations with Peking, see *Nihon gaikō bunsho*, 1913, vol. 2, pp. 327–33. For background on Ying and Hung Shu-tsu, the culpable secretary to the prime minister, see: *Min-li pao* 873: 11 (March 25, 1913); Elvin, "The Gentry Democracy in Shanghai, 1905–1914," pp. 246–53a; Shen Yun-lung, *Hsien-tai cheng-chih jen-wu shu-p'ing* [Exposition and criticism regarding contemporary political personalities] (reprint ed., Taipei, n.d.), pp. 308–15. For the texts of the telegrams between Ying and Peking, see *Ko-ming wen-hsien* 6: 21–23. On the provocative character of Sung Chiao-jen's Nanking speech, see Li Yun-han, "Huang K'o-ch'iang," p. 359. Sung spoke for two hours and was heard by a reported audience of 3,000, including the Kiangsu military governor, Ch'eng Te-ch'üan. *Min-li pao* 858: 3 (March 10, 1913). Sung's public attacks on Yuan's government began in January, 1913, and gradually escalated. K. S. Liew, *Struggle for Democracy*, pp. 186–88.

28. See note 65 below.

29. For a version exonerating Yuan, see Shen Yun-lung, *Hsien-tai cheng-chih jen-wu shu-p'ing*, p. 315. For a version implicating Ch'en Ch'i-mei, see Kita Ikki, *Shina kakumei gaishi* [An unofficial history of the Chinese revolution] (Tokyo, 1916), pp. 138–40.

30. *Chen-tan min-pao* (April 4, 5, and 15, 1913), extracted and translated in W. H. Wilkinson, consul general in Hankow, to Jordan (April 23, 1913), FO 228/1873. Porter, Chengtu, to Alston (July 3, 1913), FO 228/1870.

W. H. Wilkinson, Hankow, to Jordan (April 11, 1913), FO 228/1873. On the reality of a plot to assassinate Yuan Shih-k'ai, see Boorman, vol. 2, p. 96.

31. For talk about KMT military strength and Yuan as being "an easy mark for a punitive expedition," see: E. Fraser, consul general in Shanghai, to Jordan (April 2, 1913), FO 228/1875; *Nihon gaikō bunsho*, 1913, vol. 2, pp. 335–37. For the retreat and the sources of discouragements, see: HHKMHIL, vol. 1. p. 206; *Nihon gaikō bunsho*, 1913, vol. 2, pp. 361–62, 363–64.

32. Li Shu-ch'eng in HHKMHIL, vol. 1, p. 206.

33. *Nihon gaikō bunsho*, 1913, vol. 2, p. 345.

34. Li Yun-han, "Huang K'o-ch'iang," p. 377; Fraser, Shanghai, to Jordan (May 11, 1913), FO 228/1875; Greene, Hankow, to E. T. Williams (May 28, 1913), NA 893.00/1738; *North China Herald*, July 19, 1913, p. 203; CFKP 466: 1 (August 22, 1913); *Nihon gaikō bunsho*, 1913, vol. 2, pp. 369–70.

35. Ibid., p. 345; Smith, Tsinan, to Alston (July 19, 1913), FO 228/1877; Chang Hsun to Yuan Shih-k'ai, Yenchow, May 7, 1913, MP item 178; marginal note reporting a conversation with W. H. Donald, written on a memorandum of September 18, 1913, MP item 142.

36. *Nihon gaikō bunsho*, 1913, vol. 2, pp. 421–24.

37. G. E. Morrison diary (April 28, 1913), MP item 97.

38. *Nihon gaikō bunsho*, 1913, vol. 2, pp. 340–41.

39. Ibid., p. 352.

40. Li Shih-yueh, *Hsin-hai ko-ming shih-ch'i liang-hu ti-ch'ü ti ko-ming yun-tung*, pp. 117–20; W. H. Wilkinson, Hankow, to Alston (July 8, 1913), FO 228/1873. Li's invitation was issued at least by April 7, 1913, as evidenced by Yuan's conversation with G. E. Morrison, recorded in his diary (April 7, 1913), MP item 97.

41. T'ao Ch'ü-yin, vol. 1, p. 180; Li Yun-han, "Huang K'o-ch'iang," p. 366.

42. So rewarding did this poorly organized arsenal attack prove to Peking's program that it has been suggested its Labor Party leaders were instigated by Yuan, though Yuan blamed Ch'en Ch'i-mei. I-ming, *Yuan Shih-k'ai ch'üan-chuan* [Complete biography of Yuan Shih-k'ai] (reprint ed., Taipei, n.d.), p. 94; Elvin, "The Gentry Democracy in Shanghai, 1905–1914," pp. 254–60; G. E. Morrison diary (July 1, 1913), MP item 97. Chao Ch'in, "Hsin-hai ko-ming ch'ien-hou ti Chung-kuo kung-jen yun-tung" [The Chinese labor movement in the period of the 1911 Revolution], *Li-shih yen-chiu*, 1959, no. 2, pp. 5–6, seems to accept the suggestion. Liang Yü-k'uei, "Kuan-yü Chung-hua min-kuo kung-tang ti hsing-chih wen-t'i" [The problem of the character of the Labor Party of the Republic of China], *Li-shih yen-chiu*, 1959, no. 6, p. 78, noting the leader's subsequent arrest and his execution in Peking on September 8, 1913, rejects the interpretation, despite his concern to deny the working-class character of the party.

43. *Liang . . . nien-p'u*, pp. 411–12.
44. Ibid., pp. 414–19.
45. Ibid., p. 412; Wu Hsiang-hsiang, *Sung Chiao-jen*, p. 219; *Republican Advocate* 1.43: 1696–98 (January 25, 1913).
46. A graphic picture is drawn in Huang Yuan-yung, vol. 2, pp. 128–35. First-hand evidence can also be found in G. E. Morrison diary (April 19, 1913), MP item 97.
47. G. E. Morrison diary (April 11, 1916), MP item 106.
48. *Liang . . . nien-p'u*, pp. 422–23.
49. Ibid., p. 402.
50. *National Review* (Shanghai), August 24, and September 14, 1912; Stanley F. Wright, *China's Struggle for Tariff Autonomy: 1843–1938* (Shanghai, 1938), pp. 424–25.
51. Jordan to Grey (May 18, 1912), FO 371/1319.
52. F. E. Wilkinson, Nanking, to Jordan (July 18, and July 26, 1912), enclosed in Jordan to Grey (August 5, 1912), FO 371/1321; Tenney, Nanking, to Calhoun (July 20, 1912), NA 893.00/1439; ibid. (July 27, 1912), NA 893.00/1436½; Funatsu, Nanking, to Uchida (August 23, 1912), Japan MFA film, MT 5.1.10.5–1, reel 463.
53. Jordan to Langley, Peking, September 21, 1912, Jordan Papers, FO 350/8. Edward Grey: ". . . if the loan does not contain proper guarantees for control of expenditure, it is a bad thing apart from any question connected with the six groups." Memorandum (September 11, 1912), FO 371/1322.
54. This theme runs all through the British diplomatic record of the negotiations. Jordan in June criticized the banks for having "little intention of placing salt under any foreign control" and for having "relaxed the provisions for superintending the expenditure of the advances." Jordan to W. G. M. Müller, Peitaiho, June 17, 1912, FO 350/8. An example of the bankers' attitude is the remarks of Charles Addis, manager of the London office of the Hongkong and Shanghai Bank and a director of the Bank of England, expressing his "delight" if the foreign office would agree to a relaxation of the conditions for renewing negotiations and his interpretation of the stress on supervision as some sort of German plot. Minutes (September 12, 1912), FO 371/1322.
55. Henry Bell to Morrison, London, March 19, 1913, MP item 139.
56. Minutes attached to Jordan to Grey (September 3, 1912), FO 371/1322.
57. An early example of this political use is given in Adshead, *Modernization*, p. 204. Adshead describes the first foreign inspector, Richard Dane, as "politically neutral," but one can accept this attribution only if policies of modernization and centralization as seen by a foreigner can be politically neutral. On Dane's politics and interventions, see ibid., pp. 97–98, 196.
58. W. G. M. Müller, in minutes attached to Jordan to Grey (March 25, 1912), FO 371/1316.

59. Jordan to Langley, Peking, March 25, 1912, Jordan Papers, FO 350/8.
60. Jordan to Grey (May 8, 1913), FO 405/211.
61. E. G. Hillier to Hsiung Hsi-ling, Peking, May 10, 1912, FO 371/1318.
62. Minutes (September 12, 1912), FO 371/1322. Earlier, "the advent of Dr. Morrison" was seen as "a new factor of paramount importance" in China's estrangement from the consortium. Minutes (August 27, 1912), FO 371/1321. Peter Lowe, *Great Britain and Japan, 1911–15: A Study of British Far Eastern Policy* (London, 1969), pp. 132–33, accepts this British evaluation. From the Morrison Papers, it appears rather that Morrison was asked upon his entering the Chinese government to help out on a project well under way. The basic arrangements for the Crisp loan were made before Morrison entered the government.
63. Adshead's study of the salt administration in the early twentieth century, in my view, accepts these claims too readily. The statistics it provides seem rather to show that, although centralized *reporting* of receipts improved with the addition of foreigners: (1) actual *collections* increased rather regularly between 1900 and 1922, with the greatest proportional advance before 1912, that is, before "reorganization"; (2) the decisive factor in increased *central receipts* was Yuan's unification of the country after the Second Revolution, rather than the foreign inspectorate (a decline set in with Yuan's demise, even as the foreign inspectorate matured); (3) the size of central *releases* of salt revenue related more to the size of foreign debt payments and the rising proceeds from the customs than to any foreign administrative contribution in the salt system. See Adshead, *Modernization*, tables, pp. 25 and 100. These questions are apart from the more important one: in what ways was it a benefit to Chinese society at this time to collect more salt taxes and to funnel more of the proceeds to the government in Peking? Very few, I should think.
64. Official pronouncements about trade and stability are common. Examples can be found in: "Minutes of Meeting between Mr. Tong Shao-yi, Mr. Alfred Sze, and the Group Representatives at the Premier's Office" (May 2, 1912), enclosed in Jordan to Grey (May 6, 1912), FO 371/1318; Jordan to Grey (June 20, 1912), FO 371/1319; Jordan to Langley, Peking, October 5, 1912, Jordan Papers, FO 350/8. Regarding Yuan's importance, Jordan at a crucial moment wrote that "his disappearance from public life would mean political and commercial chaos." Jordan to Grey (April 28, 1913), FO 450/211. For an account of British policy, see K. C. Chan, "British Policy in the Reorganization Loan to China, 1912–13," *Modern Asian Studies*, vol. 5, pt. 4 (October, 1971), pp. 355–72.
65. The date is derived from an analysis of three drafts of a note to the consortium found in the Morrison Papers. The first draft is dated March 5, 1913, but was probably composed between February 26 and February 28, 1913. The first two drafts assume that any agreement must be ac-

cepted by the national assembly. The third, emended by Yuan and dated March 11, deletes such references. "Letter from Chou Hsueh-hsi to E. G. Hillier, Esq, C. M. G., Senior Representative of the Sextuple Banks," three versions, MP item 96. At about the same time, the correspondence between Hung Shu-tsu, the prime minister's secretary, and Ying Kuei-hsing raised the question of Sung Chiao-jen's "destruction."

66. Foreign office to Hongkong and Shanghai Bank, London, April 16, 1913, and enclosure no. 1 in C. Addis to foreign office, London, April 16, 1913, FO 405/211.

67. Copy of a telegram (April 7, 1913), offering the option to Reuters of London, MP item 139.

68. G. E. Morrison diary (April 22, 1913), MP item 97; "Memorandum Regarding Finance, 8th May 1913," MP item 139; Chia Shih-i, *Min-kuo ch'u-nien ti chi-jen ts'ai-cheng tsung-chang* [Several finance ministers in the first years of the republic] (Taipei, 1967), p. 27.

69. A contemporary example of this conception of the issues is: Tsung-liang, "Sung-an yü chieh-k'uan p'ing-i" [A critical view regarding the Sung case and the loan], *Kuo-min yueh-k'an* (May 1913), pp. 2–3.

70. CTSTL, 1963, no. 2, pp. 34–48; *Ko-ming wen-hsien* 44: 39–47.

71. HHKMHIL, vol. 4, p. 340.

72. CTSTL, 1962, no. 1, pp. 43–46, 57–58, 65–66.

73. Kupper, "Revolution in China," pp. 329–42. My summary omits some complications in the sequence of events during the ten days before hostilities began, including vacillations on the part of Ch'en T'ing-hsun, the local military official who extended the invitation, and Li Yuan-hung, who was theoretically in charge of the movement of Li Ch'un's troops. Regarding the date of Li Lieh-chün's return and the first exchange of shots, I follow the most commonly used dates in the memoirs of revolutionary participants, though they do not always agree: HHKMHIL, vol. 4, pp. 309, 316, 324, 352. Contemporary counterrevolutionary accounts, including those of Li Yuan-hung and Ch'en T'ing-hsun, put Li Lieh-chün's arrival at Hu-k'ou on July 8 and the initiation of hostilities on July 12: CTSTL, 1962, no. 1, pp. 48, 59, 65. From the evening of the tenth, fighting was imminent (*Ko-ming wen-hsien* 44: 121) and the different dates for the first shots can probably be accounted for by differences in the initiation and outcome of early exchanges. The charge that Ch'en T'ing-hsun was bribed by Yuan Shih-k'ai is plausible. *Ko-ming wen-hsien* 44: 103.

74. *Nihon gaikō bunsho*, 1913, vol. 2, pp. 350–51.

75. B. G. Tours, consul in Nanking, to Jordan (May 8, 1913), FO 228/1874.

76. On the politics of the eighth division, see HHKMHIL, vol. 1, p. 203.

77. Smith, Tsinan, to Alston (July 23, and July 28, 1913), FO 228/2499; Tours, Nanking, to Alston (July 27, and July 29, 1913), FO 228/2500; Li Yun-han, "Huang K'o-ch'iang," pp. 337–38; CTSTL, 1962, no. 1, pp. 54, 60–63, 69–98.

78. *Nihon gaikō bunsho*, 1913, vol. 2, pp. 380–84.
79. *Ko-ming wen-hsien* 44: 349–51. CTSTL, 1962, no. 1, pp. 133–35.
80. E. Carleton Baker, consul in Chungking, to Williams (August 20, 1913), NA 893.00/1931; Porter, Chengtu, to Alston (October 10, 1913), FO 228/1870; Brown, Chungking, to Alston (October 1, and October 19, 1913), FO 228/1870.
81. Jordan to Grey (April 30, and June 5, 1913), FO 228/1852.
82. The British consul general in Canton in particular looked to Peking's intervention to settle his dispute with Canton over sale of materials to a Hongkong cement company. Jamieson, Canton, to Jordan (April 26, 1913), enclosed in colonial office to foreign office (June 21, 1913), FO 405/211.
83. Grey instructed Jordan that Britain must not "be expected to interfere or take any action in the case of internal troubles arising . . ." except to protect British subjects. Grey to Jordan (May 1, 1913), FO 405/211.
84. *Nihon gaikō bunsho*, 1913, vol. 2, p. 359.
85. Jordan to Langley, Peking, March 22, 1915, Jordan Papers, FO 380/13; Conyngham Greene, ambassador in Tokyo, to Grey (June 14, 1913), FO 405/211.
86. *Nihon gaikō bunsho*, 1913, vol. 2, pp. 370–71.
87. Ibid., p. 460.
88. H. A. Ottewill, consul in Wuhu, to Alston (August 24, 1913), FO 228/2501.
89. For an example of disappointment in "the present compromising policy of the government," see an editorial from the *Shen-chou jih-pao* as translated in *Republican Advocate* 1.46: 1838–39 (February 22, 1913).
90. CFKP 440: 1–2 (July 27, 1913).
91. Some accounts argue that Ts'ai O had opposed Yuan in the Second Revolution and was subsequently beguiled to Peking by the false promise of important positions, but instead was given meaningless posts. An example is Yü Eng-yang, *Yun-nan shou-i yung-hu kung-ho shih-mo chi* [Full record of Yunnan's uprising to protect the republic] (reprint ed., Taipei, n.d.), pp. 113–14. Although Ts'ai may have suffered some disappointments, this version fits neither Ts'ai's own testimony nor the significance of the posts he occupied in Peking. In May, 1913, Ts'ai thought a civil war should be avoided, since it would invite foreign aggression, but when it came, he supported Peking. CTSTL, 1963, no. 2, p. 74; CTSTL, 1962, no. 1, p. 121; Herbert Goffe, consul general in Yunnanfu, to Jordan (December 29, 1915), FO 228/2753. The nature of his Peking posts will emerge in subsequent chapters.
92. PDN, October 2, 1913.
93. Li Ta-chao, "Ts'ai tu-tu heng-i," pp. 10–12. My discussion of Li's views at this time is also based on other articles by Li in *Yen-chih*, and on Satoi Hikoshichirō, "Ri Daishō no shuppatsu: *Genchi*-ki no seiron o chūshin ni" [Li Ta-chao's point of departure: especially his political views in his *Yen-chih* period], *Shirin* 40.3: 12–15 (May 1957).

94. Li Shih-yueh, *Hsin-hai ko-ming shih-ch'i liang-hu ti-ch'ü ti ko-ming yun-tung*, p. 118.

Chapter 6

1. Pekin Shina kenkyūkai, *Saishin Shina kanshin roku*, pt. 1, p. 569; Giles, Changsha, to Jordan (January 7, 1914), FO 228/1903; Hunan Gazetteer Compilation Committee, ed., *Hu-nan chin-pai-nien ta-shih chi-shu* [Accounts of major events in Hunan over the last 100 years] (Changsha, 1959), pp. 335–36, which seems to err regarding T'ang Hsiang-ming's background.

   Between October and December, 1913, forty to fifty prominent officials and citizens were arrested and seven or more of them were shot. Though some had supported the break with Yuan, some had opposed it. None of them was among the real movers of Hunan's 1913 declaration of independence, who had left on Japanese ships.

2. A report of 136 pages about a 1915 journey through the northwest by Eric Teichman, enclosed in Jordan to Grey (October 16, 1916), FO 228/1957; Eric Teichman, *Travels of a Consular Officer in North-West China* (Cambridge, 1921), pp. 9–10.

3. Yuan's authority in Fengtien was dramatized by the execution in May, 1914, at Yuan's order of Chin Wan-fu, an associate of Chang Tso-lin's. The execution was for extortion, robbery, and blackmail, and was carried out over Chang Tso-lin's protests. Fred D. Fischer, consul general in Mukden, to Reinsch (May 12, 1914), NA 893.00/2129. There is further evidence of a Peking campaign to discredit Chang Tso-lin at this time. PDN, June 9, 1914, p. 4.

4. The population figure is based on the (so-called) 1912 census. Chang P'eng-yuan, *Li-hsien-p'ai yü hsin-hai ko-ming*, p. 16. The 1953 population of these provinces comes to over 390,000,000.

5. M. H. van der Valk, *Interpretations of the Supreme Court at Peking, Years 1915 and 1916* (Batavia, 1949), pp. 47–52.

6. G. E. Morrison diary (April 9, 1914), MP item 101; Julean H. Arnold, consul in Chefoo, to Bryan (May 27, 1914), NA 893.00/2136. Rhoads, *China's Republican Revolution*, p. 264.

7. Chang Ching-lu, *Chung-kuo chin-tai ch'u-pan shih-liao ch'u-pien* [The first volume of historical materials on modern Chinese publishing] (Peking, 1957), pp. 319–24, 325–30. CFKP 684: 1–7 (April 3, 1914).

8. *North China Herald*, August 30, 1913, p. 663.

9. *Nihon gaikō bunsho*, 1913, vol. 2, pp. 373–76. Wang Cheng-t'ing (C. T. Wang), Yale Phi Beta Kappa, Kuomintang deputy, vice-chairman of the upper house of the national assembly, chairman of the assembly's constitutional drafting committee, did not leave Peking until November 8, 1913, and then only at the urging of friends in the government. G. E. Morrison diary (November 14, 1913), MP item 99. Meanwhile, other

parties had been outlawed: the Socialist Party on August 9, the Freedom or Liberal Party (Tzu-yu tang) on August 30.

10. *Nihon gaikō bunsho*, 1913, vol. 2, pp. 575–77. CTSTL, 1963, no. 2, pp. 52–53. T'ao Ch'ü-yin, vol. 1, pp. 194–95. Alvin W. Gilbert, vice-consul in Nanking, to Williams (August 28, 1912), NA 893.00/1946; statement by Dr. N. W. Brown of Nanking (September 11, 1913), enclosed in Wilder, Shanghai, to Williams (September 11, 1913), NA 893.00/1938; Gilbert, consul in Nanking, to Williams (September 16, 1913), NA 893.00/1916; Gilbert, Nanking, to Williams (October 4, 1913), NA 893.00/1998; Gilbert, Nanking, to Williams (September 9, 1913), NA 893.00/1953; Gilbert, Nanking, to Reinsch (November 24, 1913), NA 893.00/2048. Tours, Nanking, to Jordan (January 8, 1914), FO 228/1909.

11. Dr. Buckens to Morrison, Chengchow, August 19, 1913, MP item 176; "The Blessings of the Republic of Honan," MP item 176; G. E. Morrison diary (September 11, 1913), MP item 98; ibid. (November 21, 1913), MP item 99.

12. Letter from Kaifeng (December 15, 1914), cited in Harry H. Fox, consul general in Hankow, to Jordan (January 13, 1915), FO 228/1945. For a study of Pai Lang's movement, see Friedman, *Backward Toward Revolution*, pp. 117–31, 144–64.

13. Li Shih-yueh, *Hsin-hai ko-ming shih-ch'i liang-hu ti-ch'ü ti ko-ming yuntung*, p. 123. Hunan Gazetteer Compilation Committee, *Hu-nan chinpai-nien*, pp. 334–35, describe the secret police and the instruments of torture employed in Changsha. For quotations from a contemporary Chinese newspaper regarding official repression in Honan in 1914, see Chin Ch'ung-chi, "Yun-nan hu-kuo yun-tung ti chen-cheng fa-tung-che shih shei?" [Who was the true initiator of the Yunnan National Protection movement?], in *Chin-20-nien Chung-kuo shih-hsueh lun-wen hui-pien, ch'u-pien: hsin-hai ko-ming yen-chiu lun-chi ti-i-chi (1895–1929)* [First collection of Chinese historical articles of the last 20 years: first volume of studies on the 1911 Revolution (1895–1929)], Chou K'ang-hsieh et al., eds. (Hongkong, 1971), p. 276.

14. Porter, Chengtu, to Jordan (January 14, 1914), FO 228/1904; E. W. Mead, acting consul general in Chengtu, to Jordan (October 24, 1914), FO 228/1904.

15. Schoppa, "Politics and Society in Chekiang," pp. 156–57; J. L. Smith, consul in Hangchow, to Jordan (January 26, and July 12, 1914), FO 228/1905; H. H. Bristow, acting consul in Hangchow, to Jordan (July 17, 1916), FO 228/1981.

16. *National Review*, August 31, 1912.

17. PDN, October 13, 1913, p. 3. Williams, Peking, to Bryan (October 13, 1913), NA 893.00/2004. On the climate of fear created by the secret police in Peking, see Chin Ch'ung-chi, "Yun-nan hu-kuo yun-tung," p. 276.

18. PDN, September 29, 1914, p. 4.
19. Ts'ao Ju-lin, *I-sheng chih hui-i*, p. 146.
20. CFKP 594 (December 28, 1913), rep. 20: 365. Li Ken-yuan, *Hsueh-cheng nien-lu*, p. 63.
21. *Nihon gaikō bunsho*, 1913, vol. 2, p. 429. Ikeda Yuji, "Sun Yat-sen's Pan-Asianism and Nationalism, Late 1913 through 1914" (seminar paper, Harvard University, 1963).
22. Ibid., pp. 6–13. Friedman, *Backward Toward Revolution*, pp. 53–54, 149–50.
23. HHKMHIL, vol. 4, pp. 343–44.
24. Friedman, *Backward Toward Revolution*, pp. 137–41. PDN: November 12, 1914, p. 6; November 20, 1914, p. 3; November 24, 1914, p. 5; December 9, 1914, p. 6. Yuan recognized Lung Chi-kuang as "barbarous," but approved his dislike of revolution. Colonel Banzai to the vice-chief of the general staff (December 23, 1915), Gaimushō 1.6.1.75, "Bessatsu: hanEn dōran oyobi kakuchi jōkyō" [Supplement: anti-Yuan disturbances and conditions in various places], vol. 1.
25. CFKP 715: 25–26 (May 4, 1914). Jane Cheng and Jean Chesneaux, "Chronologie Politique de la Chine Contemporaine: Période 1911–1919," MS., pp. 108, 115. Evidence that some Japanese had overplayed their hand with the Chinese exiles can be found in an interview, PDN, March 20, 1915, p. 4, and in H. H. Kung's remarkable charges against Sun Yat-sen, contained in his letter to G. E. Morrison, Peking, April 3, 1915, MP item 136.
26. The British minister in Peking saw the step as retrograde, since it would "affect, pecuniarily and from the point of view of their local prestige, a vast number of petty gentry and bourgeois throughout the country, and will range them on the side of his enemies." Jordan to Grey (February 9, 1914), FO 228/1883.
27. CFKP 563: 1–2 (November 27, 1914).
28. Albert Maybon, "La Situation Dans les Provinces Chinoises Voisines du Tonkin," *L'Asie Française*, no. 154 (January 1914), p. 12. Remarks of a similar tendency are quoted in Maybon, *La République Chinoise*, pp. 134–38. I am indebted to Ed Friedman for bringing Maybon's writings to my attention. For an extended discussion of Ts'ai O's views on matters of centralization, parliamentary government, and provincial autonomy, see Johnson, "China's 1911 Revolution," pp. 92–94.
29. Yuan's favorable view of Ts'ai O is recorded in: memorandum (December 3, 1913), inserted in G. E. Morrison diary, MP item 97.
30. Harold Zvi Schiffrin, "The 'Great Leap' Image in Early Chinese Nationalism," *Asian and African Studies* (Jerusalem), no. 3 (1967), pp. 104–7.
31. Liang Ch'i-ch'ao, "Kuo-hui chih tzu-sha" [The suicide of the national assembly], YPSWC 11.30: 14.
32. PDN, July 31, 1914, p. 5.

33. Sun Yao, *Chung-hua min-kuo shih-liao*, pp. 276–81. *Peking Gazette*, November 6, 1913, pp. 5–6. CFKP 585: 1–6 (December 19, 1913).
34. For example: Tai Chi-t'ao, "Ssu-cheng wang-kuo lun" [On selfish struggle and the fall of the country], *Min-ch'üan pao*, June 3, 1912, p. 2; Sun Yat-sen, "Sun Chung-shan hsien-sheng yen-shuo tsu" [A speech by Sun Yat-sen], *Min-i tsa-chih*, February 15, 1913, p. 2.
35. *Liang . . . nien-p'u*, p. 399. The associate was P'an Jo-hai.
36. *Min-ch'üan pao*, February 14, 1913, as cited in Li Shih-yueh, *Hsin-hai ko-ming shih-ch'i liang-hu ti-ch'ü ti ko-ming yun-tung*, pp. 110–11.
37. CFKP 628: 2–3 (February 5, 1914). Here Yuan purports to pass along proposals for the suspension of the provincial assemblies, as well as the arguments put forward in support of the proposals, to the Political Conference for a recommendation.
38. Sun Yao, *Chung-hua min-kuo shih-liao*, pp. 291–95. *Ta-kung-ho jih-pao*, February 22, 1914, p. 4.
39. Official charges against the local self-government organs can be found in: Pai Chiao, *Yuan Shih-k'ai yü Chung-hua min-kuo*, pp. 120–22; Sun Yao, *Chung-hua min-kuo shih-liao*, pp. 296–300; Huang Yuan-yung, vol. 2, p. 199.
40. Elvin, "The Gentry Democracy in Chinese Shanghai, 1905–1914," p. 60.
41. For a description of the revolution in Chekiang, see Rankin, *Early Chinese Revolutionaries*, pp. 214–26. A letter complaining about self-government abuses appeared in *T'ien-to pao*, May 27, 1912, p. 4. Similar complaints were registered from Nanking: *T'ien-to pao*, July 10, 1912, p. 2.
42. *North China Herald*, July 5, 1913, p. 24.
43. Ibid.
44. Elvin, "The Gentry Democracy in Shanghai, 1905–1914," p. 154.
45. Wilder, Shanghai, to Williams (October 4, 1913), NA 893.00/1996.
46. Elvin, "The Gentry Democracy in Shanghai, 1905–1914," pp. 260–61, accepts the thesis that the abolition of self-government was primarily directed at the dangerous example set by the powers of the Shanghai city council (not to be confused with the foreign "municipal council"). The proposition seems dubious to me because: (1) the Shanghai case was given no prominence in the official complaints about the self-government system, and (2) the recreation of urban local self-government was looked upon more favorably than it was for rural areas, and in the deliberations on the matter within the Peking government in 1916 before Yuan's death, the Shanghai example between 1912 and 1914 was cited as a good model for big cities. "Municipal Government of the South City of Shanghai" and "Local Self-Government: A Proposal of the Ministry of the Interior," papers of the Political Council (April 27, 1916), MP item 156.
47. Frank W. Hadley, Shanghai, "Notes on the Political Situation" (March 4, 1913), NA 893.00/1611.

48. *Ta-kung-ho jih-pao*, February 11, 1914, p. 3; ibid., February 16, 1914, p. 1.
49. "Report on Military Situation in South-East Honan," in Jordan to Grey (February 21, 1914), FO 405/214. J. T. Pratt, consul in Tsinan, to Jordan (April 9, 1914), FO 228/1913.
50. Giles, Nanking, to Jordan (March 27, 1916), FO 228/1982. Peking was delaying until the end of 1916 and perhaps on into 1917 before inaugurating a limited system in the capital area. PDN, March 1, 1916, p. 4.
51. Friedman, *Backward Toward Revolution*, p. 186, citing the *South China Morning Post* of March 21, 1916.
52. Schoppa, "Politics and Society in Chekiang," pp. 199–200, 308–9.
53. *Ko-ming wen-hsien* 46: 289–90.
54. CFKP 627: 1–2 (February 4, 1914) and 630: 1 (February 7, 1914).
55. CFKP 1094 (May 25, 1915), rep. 37: 816–18; CFKP (January 23, 1916), rep. 45: 906–7; CFKP (February 29, 1916), rep. 46: 1122–24. Chu Ch'i-ch'ien (minister of internal affairs), "Local Self-Government System. A Comparison of the Present System with the System Enforced during the late Ching Dynasty," MP item 156. F. E. Wilkinson, consul in Foochow, to Jordan (January 12, 1916), FO 228/1980; Giles, Nanking, to Jordan (April 24, and July 27, 1915), FO 228/1948. In Nanking, the electorate in 1915 was about one-tenth of what it had been in 1912.
56. CFKP 753: 7 (May 24, 1914).
57. Chia Shih-i, *Min-kuo ts'ai-cheng shih*, 1.1: 128–29.
58. *Liang . . . nien-p'u*, p. 427.
59. Kung-ch'üan Hsiao, "Administrative Modernization: K'ang Yu-wei's Proposals and Their Historical Meaning," *Tsing Hua Journal of Chinese Studies*, n.s., 8.1–2: 18–35 (August 1970). Ishikawa Tadao, "Shinmatsu oyobi minkoku shonen ni okeru rempō-ron to shōsei-ron" [Theories of federalism and the provincial system at the end of the Ch'ing and the early republic], *Hōgaku kenkyū* 24.9–10: 145–46 (September–October 1951). Esther Morrison, "The Modernization of the Confucian Bureaucracy: An Historical Study of Public Administration" (Ph.D. diss., Radcliffe College, 1959), pp. 1242–43. Johnson, "China's 1911 Revolution," pp. 93–94. Li Shou-k'ung, *Min-ch'u chih kuo-hui*, p. 72. Huang Yuan-yung, vol. 2, p. 9. *Ta-kung-ho jih-pao*, November 3, 1912, p. 3. *Min-kuo ching-shih wen-pien*, vol. 2, pp. 495–526. Schoppa, "Politics and Society in Chekiang," p. 106.
60. YPSWC 11.29: 120.
61. G. E. Morrison diary (April 4, 1916), MP item 106. "Notes on a meeting of the Political Conference" (April 4, 1916), MP item 156.
62. CFKP 735: 1–5 (May 24, 1914); CFKP 771: 4–5 (June 29, 1914); CFKP 772 (June 30, 1914), rep. 26: 352; CFKP 773 (July 1, 1914), rep. 27: 19.
63. Friedman, "The Center Cannot Hold," pp. 148–49. *Min-li pao* 587: 3 (June 2, 1912). *Ko-ming wen-hsien* 41: 262.
64. *Liang . . . nien-p'u*, pp. 425–28.

65. PDN, October 31, 1913, p. 5; *North China Herald*, December 20, 1913, pp. 911–12; PDN, December 12, 1914, p. 4.
66. Boorman, vol. 2, pp. 140–43. Gaimushō jōhōbu, *Gendai Shina jinmeikan*, pp. 903–4. PDN, February 23, 1916, p. 3.
67. Hu Ying-han, *Wu Hsien-tzu hsien-sheng chuan-chi* [Biography of Wu Hsien-tzu] (Hongkong, 1953), p. 11. Cheshire, Canton, to John Van A. MacMurray, chargé d'affaires in Peking (July 24, 1914), NA 893.00/2170; Cheshire to MacMurray (August 18, 1914), NA 893.00/2186. Jamieson, Canton, to Jordan (October 29, 1914), FO 228/1903.
68. Gaimushō seimukyoku, "Gendai Shina jinmeikan" [Biographical dictionary of contemporary China], Japan MFA film, SP47, reel SP-10, p. 1912. Des Forges, *Hsi-liang and the Chinese Revolution*, pp. 33 and 167. Han Kuo-chün, *Chih-sou nien-p'u* (reprint ed., Taipei, n.d.), pp. 32–41; and *Yung-i lu* (reprint ed., Taipei, in the same volume as the previous title but with separate pagination), pp. 55–61. Tours, Nanking, to Alston (October 28, 1913), FO 228/1874; Harold Porter, consul in Wuhu, to Jordan (October 23, 1915), FO 228/1953. Victoria Worley Bailie, *Bailie's Activities in China: An Account of the Life and Work of Professor Joseph Bailie in and for China—1890–1935* (Palo Alto, 1964), pp. 45–61. Col. Bruce to Morrison, Shanghai, November 10, 1913, MP item 176; Col. Bruce to Morrison, Shanghai, December 10, 1913, MP item 159.
69. On the factors in the fall of Hsiung's cabinet, see: *Nihon gaikō bunsho*, 1914, vol. 2, pp. 721–22; Huang Yuan-yung, vol. 2, pp. 209–11.
70. CFKP 767: 4–5 (June 25, 1914).
71. CFKP 653: 1–6 (March 3, 1914). PDN, July 31, 1914.
72. CFKP 734: 2–3 (May 23, 1914). PDN, June 19, 1914.
73. Huang Yuan-yung, vol. 2, pp. 254–58; PDN, October 24, 1914, pp. 3–4; CFKP 886 (October 23, 1914), rep. 30: 267; CFKP 888 (October 25, 1914), rep. 30: 286–87.
    In the midst of the antimonarchial movement of 1916, T'ang Shao-i told a Japanese diplomat a version of the reason for Wang Chih-hsing's execution that involved an elaborate series of coverups for Yuan's own crimes. Ariyoshi Akira, consul general in Shanghai, to Ishii Kikujirō, foreign minister (February 6, 1916), Gaimushō 1.6.1.75, "Bessatsu: hanEn dōran oyobi kakuchi jōkyō," vol. 3. T'ang had not been in the government at the time and was engaged in a propaganda war against Yuan when he told this story. Whatever the particular facts regarding Wang Chih-hsing's execution, the conspiracy theory could not apply to the many parallel cases. Legal proceedings against negligent or criminal officials, especially district magistrates, occurred in virtually all provinces and were acted upon by the central government.
74. Presidential order (December 2, 1913), CFKP 569: 1–7 (December 3, 1913), and many others subsequent to that date. *North China Herald*, March 14, 1914, p. 801. PDN: February 17, 1914, p. 4; August 15, 1914,

p. 4; September 16, 1915, p. 6; September 29, 1914, p. 4; October 1, 1914, p. 4; April 1, 1915, p. 4. Borst-Smith, *Mandarin and Missionary*, p. 180. Odoric Y. K. Wou, "The District Magistrate Profession in the Early Republican Period: Occupational Recruitment, Training and Mobility," *Modern Asian Studies*, 8.2: 217–45 (April 1974). Odoric Wou, "District Magistrate," p. 244, calls the changes growing out of the abolition of the old civil service examinations in 1905 and Yuan's system of December, 1913, "a fundamental revision of the process of magistrate recruitment and training." His discussion passes over the sharply differing practices of 1912 and most of 1913, for example, widespread local recruitment and appointment, which interrupted the regular development of the patterns he discerns.

In October, 1915, regulations for circuit examinations tied to school graduation but not function-specific with respect to post were issued. In contrast to the former examination structure under the empire, however, these examinations did not qualify one for a responsible administrative post, but only for the staff of an administrative official. CFKP 1221 (October 1, 1915), rep. 42: 47–50.

75. PDN: April 6, 1915, p. 4; May 1, 1915, p. 4. Yuan could also be cynical about the returned student. In a sullen mood in 1915, he told Morrison that, of the foreign-trained students he had met, only Wellington Koo and Wu Ch'ao-ch'u (C. C. Wu, sometimes transcribed Wu Ch'ao-shu, 1887–1934) knew how to apply their knowledge. G. E. Morrison diary (August 17, 1915), MP item 104.

76. CFKP 842 (September 8, 1914), rep. 29: 118; CFKP 855 (September 21, 1914), rep. 29: 248; CFKP (January 26, 1916), rep. 45: 1038–42.

77. Ts'ao Ju-lin, *I-sheng chih hui-i*, p. 108. I-ming, *Yuan Shih-k'ai ch'üan-chuan*, p. 118. CFKP 1221 (October 1, 1915), rep. 42: 25–35.

78. *Liang . . . . nien-p'u*, p. 427.

79. Liang Ch'i-ch'ao, "Min-kuo ch'u-nien chih pi-chih kai-ko" [Currency reform in the early republic], YPSWC 15.43: 13.

80. W. H. Wilkinson, Hankow, to Jordan (July 10, 1914), FO 228/1907. Pratt, Tsinan, to Jordan (July 6, 1914), FO 228/1913. CFKP 780 (July 8, 1914), rep. 27: 131. PDN: September 29, 1913, p. 3; June 9, 1914, p. 4; June 16, 1914, p. 6.

81. Chia Shih-i, *Min-kuo ts'ai-cheng shih*, 1.1: 60–61. One indication of the scale of funds from railway profits was the budgeting of over Ch$10 million as appropriations from net railway profits for the 1916 budget. CFKP (January 27, 1916), rep. 45: 1074–76.

82. P'u Yu-shu, "Consortium Reorganization Loan," pp. 591–94.

83. Adshead, *Modernization of the Chinese Salt Administration*, p. 100. Adshead interprets his data differently.

84. For details on Liang Shih-i's management of these domestic loans, see Jerome Ch'en, *Yuan Shih-k'ai*, 2d ed., pp. 149–50.

85. CFKP 590: 8–9 (December 24, 1913); CFKP 735: 6 (May 24, 1914).

86. Sun Yao, *Chung-hua min-kuo shih-liao*, p. 302.
87. The account of Kiangsu finances is based on: Tours, Nanking, to Alston (October 28, 1913), FO 228/1874; Cecil Kirke, acting consul in Nanking, to Jordan (May 4, 1914), FO 228/1909; Twyman, Chinkiang, to Jordan (July 8, and October 31, 1914), FO 228/1904; Giles, Nanking, to Jordan (January 30, April 24, July 27, and October 20, 1914), FO 228/1982; CFKP 847 (September 13, 1914), rep. 29: 155–67; CFKP 968 (January 18, 1915), rep. 33: 509–20.
88. Sutton, "Rise and Decline," p. 170.
89. Twyman, Chinkiang, to Jordan (October 31, 1914), FO 228/1904.
90. *North China Herald*, November 29, 1913, p. 621.
91. Lovat Fraser to Morrison, Slough, July 6, 1914, MP item 180.
92. Jordan to Grey (June 12, 1915), FO 228/1957. Jordan to Langley, Peking, June 13, and October 6, 1916, Jordan Papers, FO 350/15.
93. Jordan to Langley, Peking, February 8, and March 8, 1914, Jordan Papers, FO 350/12.
94. G. E. Morrison diary (January 11, 1912), MP item 91. Jordan to Grey (August 25, 1915), FO 228/2397.
95. Jordan to Grey (March 2, 1914), FO 228/1883. Yuan did not grant amnesties until two months later, and then only in limited cases. A general amnesty for contrite rebels was offered only in 1915.
96. Jordan to Langley, Peking, February 1, 1916, Jordan Papers, FO 350/15.
97. This paragraph is based on my reading of Morrison's diary and papers for the years of Yuan's presidency.
98. Kokuryūkai, ed., *Tōa shishi senkaku kiden* [Annals and biographies of pioneer patriots in East Asia] (Tokyo, 1933–36), vol. 2, p. 352. Ariga was a critic of Katō's methods, not of the larger aims of Japan's expanding position on the continent, as the biography in this volume brings out.
99. *Nihon gaikō bunsho*, 1913, vol. 2, pp. 354–58. A public protestation of his adherence to a scholarly role in China occurs in *Gaikō jihō* (Tokyo), 209: 14 (July 15, 1913).
100. *Gaikō jihō* (Tokyo), 205: 3 (May 15, 1913).
101. Ibid., 205: 5 (May 15, 1913).
102. Ibid., 203: 5–6 (April 15, 1913).
103. Ibid., 207: 106 (June 15, 1913). My interpretation of Ariga's views is also based on other of his reports and articles appearing in *Gaikō jihō*: 203: 92–97 (April 15, 1913), 204: 1–6 (May 1, 1913), 206: 94–97 (June 1, 1913), 208: 14–19 (July 1, 1913), 211: 10–19 (August 15, 1913), 212: 7–18 (September 1, 1913), 213: 15–24 (September 15, 1913), 215: 13–21 (October 15, 1913), 216: 12–22 (November 1, 1913), 225: 17–19 (March 15, 1914), and 228: 7–10 (May 1, 1914). I am grateful to Professor Hirano Ken'ichirō for alerting me to this source and for lending me his notes until I was able to read the originals.
104. Ibid., 213: 15–24 (September 15, 1913).
105. Ariga Nagao, "The function and law of election of Local Assembly (L. As.)" (April 11, 1916), MP item 156.

106. References to Yuan Shih-k'ai's interest in the French constitution include: Ts'ai T'ing-kan to Morrison, Peking, January 6, 1913, MP item 178; G. E. Morrison diary (January 9, 1913), MP item 96; Frank J. Goodnow to Nicolas Murray Butler, Peking, August 16, 1913 ("Miscellaneous Correspondence"), Goodnow Collection.

107. G. E. Morrison diary (July 21, 1914), MP item 102. James Bryce to Morrison, "The Atheneum" (probably written in China), August 7, 1914, MP item 180. Jordan to James Bryce, Peking, February 23, 1916, Jordan Papers, FO 350/15.

108. W. W. Rockhill to Ts'ai T'ing-kan, Litchfield, Conn., June 23, 1914, W. W. Rockhill Papers (Houghton Library, Harvard University), item 2203. *Proceedings of the American Political Science Association Held at Chicago, Ill., December 28 to 30, 1904* (Lancaster, Pa., 1905), pp. 5–14.

109. Goodnow to Butler, Peking, June 17, 1914 ("Miscellaneous Correspondence"), Goodnow Collection.

110. Gabriel A. Almond, "Introduction: A Functional Approach to Comparative Politics," in Gabriel A. Almond and James S. Coleman, eds., *The Politics of the Developing Areas* (Princeton, 1960), pp. 13–15.

111. *China's Constitution: Dr. Goodnow's Draft* and "The Legislative Powers of the Republic of China . . . ," MS. (54 pp.), Goodnow Collection.

112. Goodnow to Butler, Peking, July 23, and August 16, 1913 ("Miscellaneous Correspondence"), Goodnow Collection.

113. Charles E. Bigelow to Goodnow, New York, February 8, 1914, Goodnow Collection.

114. Morrison to Capt. Tsao, Peking, October 29, 1913, MP item 178. "Published in the Peking Gazette, October 31, 1913—by Frank Johnson Goodnow," MP item 133. "The Draft Constitution: Professor Goodnow's Criticisms" (printed), "Criticisms of the Draft Constitution" (MS.), "The Constitution and the President" (printed in the *Peking Daily News*, November 18, 1913), Goodnow Collection.

115. G. E. Morrison diary (November 23, 1913), MP item 99; Goodnow to Butler, Peking, January 2, and March 30, 1914 ("Miscellaneous Correspondence"), Goodnow Collection.

116. Goodnow to Butler, Peking, February 16, 1914 ("Miscellaneous Correspondence"), Goodnow Collection.

117. Goodnow to Butler, Peking, May 18, 1914 ("Miscellaneous Correspondence"), Goodnow Collection.

118. F. J. Goodnow, "The Parliament of the Republic of China," *American Political Science Review* 8.4: 560 (November 1914).

119. F. J. Goodnow, "Reform in China," *American Political Science Review* 9.2: 209–24 (May 1915). Similar thoughts were expressed in at least one newspaper article: clipping from an unidentified New York newspaper (December 13, 1914), Goodnow Collection.

120. There was more behind Goodnow's analysis than an adjustment of theory to his perception of Chinese realities, or a desire to justify Yuan's policies. One wonders whether he believed in his own scale for measuring

the progress of societies. A general mistrust of democracy and liberalism is detectable. It was not just that liberal institutions might not suit present Chinese conditions, though this was his "scientific" argument. They might not be so desirable even in the most developed country. At the same 1914 meetings of the American Political Science Association, he is reported to have commented on a paper about "Political Safeguards and Constitutional Guarantees" that Americans were the most lawless of people claiming to be civilized and that "emphasis should be placed on social duties rather than on individual rights." "News and Notes," *American Political Science Review* 9.1: 115 (February 1915). And yet he argued that a lack in China of the idea of individual rights was a reason for forgoing representative government. One is left with the impression that submission to authority was Goodnow's primary political value. He was made "a bit apprehensive" about the future in China when he heard in the summer of 1913 that Peking University students had the habit of forcibly ejecting professors and directors they disliked. His idea of a remedy was the application of force by public authorities. Goodnow to Butler, Peking, August 16, 1913 ("Miscellaneous Correspondence"), Goodnow Collection. His theories, not surprisingly, seem to have been a mixture of analysis and the projection of his class and professional anxieties.

121. Sudhindra Bose, "Remarks on President Goodnow's Paper," *American Political Science Review* 9.2: 225–26 (May 1915). Charles Beard's comment is noted in ibid., 9.1: 116 (February 1915).

Chapter 7

1. "Inaugural address of president to the Council of Government," December 15, 1913, FO 228/1852. This document purports to be a translation of a verbatim record of Yuan's speech to the Political Conference on December 15, 1913. Although I have not seen the original Chinese verbatim record, a comparison between this translation and the formal published text tends to support the authenticity of the translation as a faithful rendition of an unedited version of Yuan's remarks. I quote this translation in preference to the less personal, less defensive, and better organized published version, although I have made minor editorial changes in spelling and style. The published version can be consulted in CFKP 585: 1–6 (December 19, 1913).

2. Yen Hsi-shan, *Yen Hsi-shan tsao-nien hui-i-lu*, p. 45.

3. Jordan to Langley, Peking, March 8, 1914, Jordan Papers, FO 350/12. I-ming, *Yuan Shih-k'ai ch'üan-chuan*, p. 110, asserts that Yuan's small loan contracts with foreigners before World War I totaled Ch$200,000,-000. A rough calculation of the face value of all foreign loans and con-

tracts between 1912 and 1916, based on figures in Chia Shih-i, *Min-kuo ts'ai-cheng shih*, 2.4: 49–112, produces a total of Ch$1.14 bilion, or about $460 million in United States dollars of that time. Little of this passed into the hands of the Peking government. Some loan agreements were cancelled before payment in full. The railway contracts were commitments to future payments over a period of years. One-quarter of the total was the Reorganization Loan, of which less than a third actually went to the Chinese government. Nonetheless, some portion of these large sums did reach Peking—almost all of it before the outbreak of World War I.

4. A report of March 7, 1914. Sun Yao, *Chung-hua min-kuo shih-liao*, pp. 295–97.
5. Jordan to Grey (June 5, 1913), FO 228/1852. Parshotam Mehra, *The McMahon Line and After: A Study of the Triangular Contest on India's North-Eastern Frontier Between Britain, China and Tibet, 1904–47* (Delhi, 1947), pp. 153, 162. Tahara Teijirō, *Shinmatsu minsho Chūgoku kanshin jinmeiroku*, p. 404.
6. May, Hongkong, to Alston (August 18, 1913), with marginal notations and a draft reply, FO 228/2501; Jamieson, Canton, to Alston (August 18, 1913), FO 228/2501; Jamieson, Canton, to Jordan (July 22, 1914), FO 228/1903.
7. Alston to Grey (November 17, 1913), FO 405/212. An illuminating study of the affair of the cement companies appears in Friedman, "The Center Cannot Hold," pp. 265–79.
8. David G. Marr, *Vietnamese Anticolonialism, 1888–1925* (Berkeley, 1971), pp. 225–28.
9. W. H. Wilkinson, Hankow, to Jordan (April 11, 1914), FO 228/1907.
10. Jordan to Grey (November 27, 1915), FO 228/1918.
11. Kirke, Nanking, to Jordan (July 10, 1914), FO 228/1909. Giles, Nanking, to Jordan (January 30, 1915), FO 228/1948. Han Kuo-chün rebutted remarks about White Wolf with solicitude concerning British troubles in Ireland.
    Giles thought little of Ch'i Yao-lin, Han Kuo-chün's successor as Kiangsu civil governor, but was able to settle a couple of cases with him. Giles, Nanking, to Jordan (April 24, 1915), FO 228/1948.
12. G. E. Morrison diary (September 24, and October 8, 1914), MP item 103.
13. P'u Yu-shu, "Consortium Reorganization Loan," pp. 576–77. Jordan to Grey (March 23, 1914), FO 228/1883. G. E. Morrison diary (August 16, 1915), MP item 104.
14. Jordan to J. Langford Smith, acting consul general in Chengtu (July 23, 1915), FO 228/1942. The official in question was Keng Pao-k'uei of Kiangsu, whose father was said to have been killed by German troops during the Boxer Rebellion. Smith, Chengtu, to Jordan (June 22, 1915), FO 228/1942.

15. For the diplomatic details of the Mongolian separation, see Peter S. H. Tang, *Russian and Soviet Policy in Manchuria and Outer Mongolia, 1911–1931* (Durham, North Carolina, 1959), pp. 293–358. Owen Lattimore, *Nationalism and Revolution in Mongolia* (Leiden, 1955), pp. 30–35 and 48–52, analyzes the Mongolian motivations.

16. See translations or précis from the Chinese press in the *Republican Advocate* for November and December, 1912, and January, 1913.

17. *Republican Advocate* 1.37: 1475 (December 14, 1912), ibid. 1.38: 1505 (December 21, 1912), ibid. 1.39: 1548 (December 28, 1912). Porter, Chengtu, to Jordan (January 4, 1913), FO 228/1870. W. H. Wilkinson, Hankow, to Jordan (January 14, 1913), FO 228/1873. Yen Hsi-shan, *Yen Hsi-shan tsao-nien hui-i-lu*, p. 44, records his advocacy of a military response.

18. *Liang . . . nien-p'u*, p. 312. *Min-li pao* 752: 2 (November 15, 1912).

19. G. E. Morrison diary (November 12, 1912), MP item 95.

20. *Republican Advocate* 1.34: 1369 (November 23, 1912).

21. Li Yü-shu, *Wai-Meng-ku ch'e-chih wen-t'i* [The question of the administrative separation of Outer Mongolia] (Taipei, 1961), pp. 21–26. Peter Tang, *Russian and Soviet Policy*, p. 334.

22. My description of the Tibetan question relies on Lamb, *The McMahon Line*, pp. 426–54. The Russian government refused to accept the equivalency in imperialistic bargaining between Mongolia and Tibet. Its position was fortified by the Anglo-Russian convention of 1907.

23. For a detailed description of the proceedings of the Simla Conference, see Mehra, *The McMahon Line and After*, pp. 171–292. Mehra concurs in Alistair Lamb's rebuttal of the charge that Yuan agreed to send a delegate to the Simla Conference in return for British recognition of the republic. Lamb, *The McMahon Line*, p. 477.

24. Jordan to Langley, Peking, April 6, and June 15, 1914, Jordan Papers, FO 350/12.

25. G. E. Morrison diary (June 5, 1914), MP item 101.

26. "Memorandum. Feb. 20th, 1912," MP item 147.

27. Alston to Grey (August 15, 1913), FO 228/2500.

28. Aoki Norizumi to Terauchi Masatake, August 23, 1914, Terauchi Masatake Papers, item 12.1, Kensei Shiryōshitsu, Diet Library, Tokyo.

29. Jordan to Langley, Peking, June 29, 1916, Jordan Papers, FO 350/15.

30. Horikawa Takeo, *Kyokutō kokusai seijishi jōsetsu—nijūikkajō yōkyū no kenkyū* [An introduction to the history of Far Eastern international politics—a study of the Twenty-One Demands] (Tokyo, 1958), pp. 71–78. Ikei Masaru, *Nihon gaikōshi gaisetsu* [A survey of Japanese diplomatic history] (Tokyo, 1973), p. 119. Lowe, *Great Britain and Japan*, pp. 170–71. Jordan to Grey (May 29, 1914), FO 228/1883. The minister, Yamaza Enjirō, died suddenly, to be replaced by Hioki Eki.

31. "Memorandum," autumn 1915, by G. E. Morrison on China's entry into the war, MP item 150. Pratt, Tsinan, to Jordan (August 15, 1914), FO 228/1913. Lowe, *Great Britain and Japan*, p. 192. Yuan's offer to

participate in the taking of Tsingtao was also recollected by Banzai Rihachirō: Nakajima Masao, vol. 2, pp. 825–26.

32. Madeleine Chi, *China Diplomacy, 1914–1918* (Cambridge, Mass., 1970), pp. 20, 24. G. E. Morrison diary (November 9, 1914), MP item 103. PDN: October 3, 1914, p. 5; October 20, 1914, p. 4. Kirke, Nanking to Jordan (September 3, 1914), FO 228/1909. J. Paul Jameson, consul in Antung, to Reinsch (October 10, 1914), enclosed in Reinsch to Bryan (November 25, 1914), NA 893.00/2238.

33. Li Yü-shu, *Chung-Jih erh-shih-i-t'iao chiao-she* [Sino-Japanese negotiations over the 21 Demands], vol. 1 (Taipei, 1966), p. 235 (although Li would like to except Yuan and his private group from the praise); Lowe, *Great Britain and Japan*, pp. 220–58; and Madeleine Chi, *China Diplomacy*, pp. 28–61.

34. Marius B. Jansen, *The Japanese and Sun Yat-sen* (Cambridge, Mass., 1954), pp. 186–88. Horikawa Takeo, *Kyokutō kokusai seijishi jōsetsu— nijūikkajō yōkyū no kenkyū*, pp. 303–5.

35. Ibid., pp. 262–65. Lowe, *Great Britain and Japan*, pp. 220–58.

36. Jordan to Grey (May 5, 1915), FO 228/2308.

37. Ts'ao Ju-lin, *I-sheng chih hui-i*, p. 128. Ts'en Hsueh-lü, vol. 1, p. 255. Jordan to Grey (May 8, 1915), FO 228/2308.

38. The spread of the boycott and its effects are described by Kikuchi Takaharu, *Chūgoku minzoku undō no kihon kōzō—taigai boikotto no kenkyū* [Basic structure of the Chinese national movement: a study of antiforeign boycotts] (Tokyo, 1966), pp. 163–73. Evidence of possible connivance in the boycott by Yuan appears in G. E. Morrison diary (April 17, 1915), MP item 104. For Japanese-inspired charges that the authorities were tolerating anti-Japanese agitation, see *Shun-t'ien shih-pao* (Peking), August 4, and August 5, 1915, p. 2.

39. For a translation of the statement, see Hsueh Chün-tu, *Huang Hsing*, pp. 174–76.

40. "Anti-Japanese pamphlet issued in Hangchow," enclosed in Bristow, Hangchow, to Jordan (April 20, 1915), FO 228/1943.

41. PDN: March 10, 1915, p. 4; March 12, 1915, p. 4. See also an interview with Chang Yao-ching, PDN, March 20, 1915, claiming that after the beginning of the negotiations Japanese officials and merchants had offered money and weapons to provoke an occasion for further Japanese intervention in Shantung.

42. H. H. Kung to Morrison, Peking, April 3, 1915, MP item 136. Kung's motive in writing this letter may have been personal as well as patriotic. There is evidence that his relationship to Sun Yat-sen had placed him under suspicion of having revolutionary sympathies. He seemed to be attempting to dissociate himself from Sun's policies. An unsigned letter to Morrison, Peking, December 12, 1915, MP item 148, discussing Kung's marriage, Sun's marriage, and the attitudes of Kung and the Sung family generally.

For a discussion of Sun's behavior during the Sino-Japanese negotiations, see Jansen, *The Japanese and Sun Yat-sen*, pp. 188–93. Friedman, *Backward Toward Revolution*, pp. 87–103, describes the critical response to Sun's stance.

43. Greene, Tokyo, to Grey (March 10, 1915), FO 228/2307. Jordan to Grey (March 13, March 22, March 23, and March 26, 1915), FO 228/2307. The seriousness of Japanese planning for a military strike against Peking is evidenced in letters from a high army official of the time. Akashi Genjirō to Terauchi Masatake (February 3, February 22, and March 24, 1915), Terauchi Masatake Papers, items 6.44, 6.48, and 6.52.

44. G. E. Morrison, "Memorandum" (February 5, 1915), FO 228/2307.

45. Ts'ao Ju-lin, *I-sheng chih hui-i*, p. 129. Fei Hsing-chien (pseud. Wo-chiu chung-tzu), *Tuan Ch'i-jui* (Shanghai, 1921), pp. 43–44.

46. Recent versions of this view include: Madeleine Chi, *China Diplomacy*, p. 60; and Lowe, *Great Britain and Japan*, p. 251.

47. Ts'en Hsueh-lü, vol. 1, pp. 256–57, 264–66, 297. Ts'ao Ju-lin, *I-sheng chih hui-i*, p. 131. Chang I-lin, *Hsin-t'ai-p'ing-shih chi*, p. 39. A formal government statement, confessing failure, appeared in PDN, May 14, 1915, pp. 3–4. It was apparently written by Wellington Koo. G. E. Morrison diary (May 12, and May 13, 1915), MP item 104.

48. Madeleine Chi, *China Diplomacy*, p. 60. G. E. Morrison diary (May 20, 1915), MP item 104.

49. "Chung-Jih Man-Meng t'iao-yueh shan-hou hui-i lu" [Record of the conference on remedies for the Sino-Japanese treaty regarding Manchuria and Mongolia], 2 pts. (June 24 to July 31, 1915), Archives of the Ministry of Foreign Affairs, Institute of Modern History, Nankang, Taiwan, R090291. High officials from various Peking ministries participated. Ts'ao Ju-lin and Wellington Koo played leading roles. The conference held thirty meetings over a period of thirty-seven days.

50. G. E. Morrison diary (May 5, and May 28, 1915), MP item 104.

51. G. E. Morrison diary (June 23, 1915), MP item 104. The remark was made by Ts'ai T'ing-kan.

52. CFKP 726: 2 (May 15, 1914).

53. Sun Yao, *Chung-hua min-kuo shih-liao*, pp. 299–302.

54. CFKP 726: 2 (May 15, 1914).

55. Franklin Houn, *Central Government of China*, pp. 71–72.

56. The issue can be pursued in the following reports: Fraser, Shanghai, to Jordan (January 23, 1913), FO 228/1875; Walter J. Clennel, consul in Newchwang, to Alston (July 25, 1913), FO 228/1874; H. E. Fulford, consul general in Tientsin, to Jordan (March 3, 1914), FO 228/1913; Kirke, Nanking, to Jordan (October 13, 1914), FO 228/1909; Fulford, Tientsin, to Jordan (November 11, 1915), FO 228/1951; Pratt, Tsinan, to Jordan (April 5, 1915), FO 228/1953; annual report for 1915, Shanghai (February 4, 1916), NA 893.00/2356.

57. *Liang . . . nien-p'u*, p. 433.

58. "Inaugural address of president to the Council of Government," December 15, 1913, FO 228/1852.

59. van der Valk, *Interpretations*, pp. 3, 40–47, 152–59.

60. For a forceful expression of the hostile view by the civil governor of Kwangtung, see CFKP 983 (February 2, 1915), rep. 34: 79–80.

61. CFKP 702 (May 1, 1914), rep. 25: 21–22. For reports describing the effects of these decisions on the local situation, see: F. E. Wilkinson, Foochow, to Jordan (July 2, 1914), FO 228/1905; Giles, Nanking, to Jordan (January 30, 1915), FO 228/1948.

62. Yuan's educational policies can be studied through his presidential orders on the subject and in the regulations of the ministry of education in CFKP, especially: CFKP 735: 7 (May 24, 1914); CFKP 1152 (July 23, 1915), rep. 39: 258; CFKP 1161 (August 1, 1915), rep. 40: 7–19; CFKP 1302 (December 22, 1915), rep. 44: 887–88; CFKP (January 6, 1916), rep. 45: 15–16. See also: Shu Hsin-ch'eng, ed., *Chin-tai Chung-kuo chiao-yü shih-liao* [Historical materials on modern Chinese education], vol. 2 (Shanghai, 1928), pp. 49–61; T'ai Shuang-ch'iu and Huang Chen-ch'i, eds., *Chung-kuo p'u-chi chiao-yü wen-t'i* [The question of universal education in China] (Shanghai, 1938), passim; PDN: November 15, 1913, p. 5; July 15, 1914, p. 5; October 11, 1914, p. 1; March 25, 1915, p. 3; April 27, 1915, p. 3; and *North China Herald*, November 22, 1913, p. 608.

63. Mary Clabaugh Wright, *The Last Stand of Chinese Conservatism: The T'ung-Chih Restoration, 1862–1874* (Stanford, 1957), p. 4.

64. Shu Hsin-ch'eng, vol. 2, pp. 52–54. *Ta-kung-ho jih-pao*, February 2, 1914, p. 4. *North China Herald*, January 23, 1915, p. 264. On the intended elimination from primary school curriculum of the study of the classics per se during the liberal republic, see Ping Wen Kuo, *The Chinese System of Public Education* (New York, 1915), pp. 127–28, 131.

65. For Huang Hsing on the need to teach the traditional morality, see Chin Ch'ung-chi and Hu Sheng-wu, "Huang Hsing: Co-founder of the Republic of China," in Hsueh Chün-tu, ed., *Revolutionary Leaders of Modern China* (New York, 1971), p. 143. For an essay by Huang Hsing urging the contemporary relevance of loyalty and filial piety, see Wu Yen-yun, ed., *Huang liu-shou shu-tu* [Letters of resident-general Huang] (Taipei, 1962), pp. 2–3. See also *Min-li pao*, September 10, 1912, and *China Year Book*, 1913, p. 527.

66. CFKP 1301 (December 21, 1915), rep. 44: 838–39; CFKP (January 13, 1916), rep. 45: 429–30.

67. CFKP 1304 (December 25, 1915), rep. 44: 996–97. For background on the development of alphabets in China, see John de Francis, *Nationalism and Language Reform in China* (Princeton, 1950), pp. 33–38, although the scope of Chang I-lin's proposal is underestimated.

68. Regarding reduced funding for middle and professional schools and for universities in 1915, statistics are given in: Hiratsuka Masanori, *Kindai Shina kyōiku bunka shi* [A history of modern Chinese education and culture] (Tokyo, 1942), p. 206; Chinese Ministry of Education, Statistical Office, ed., *Ch'üan-kuo chiao-yü t'ung-chi chien-pien* [Abridged edition

of statistics on the nation's education] (Nanking, 1935), pp. 26–27. On the continuing growth at the primary level, see T'ai Shuang-ch'iu, *Chung-kuo p'u-chi chiao-yü wen-t'i*, pp. 30, 48. For descriptions of one active provincial response to the new policies, see Giles, Nanking, to Jordan (April 24, July 27, and October 20, 1915), FO 228/1948; Giles, Nanking, to Jordan (July 20, 1916), FO 228/1982. For some indication of provincial educational budgets, see Chia Shih-i, *Min-kuo ts'ai-cheng shih*, 1.1: 81–84, 90–92, 98–101. While the average provincial allotment for education was projected to exceed 6 percent of the 1916 provincial budget, Kwangsi allotted only 1.6 percent. Chihli allotted 12.7 percent, Fukien 10.2 percent, Kiangsu 10.2 percent, Hunan 8.8 percent, etc. On Kwangsi educational policies, see also *North China Herald*, May 23, 1914, p. 627.

Sidney D. Gamble, *North China Village*, pp. 5–6, discovered that 44 percent of the existing schools in Chihli's Ting county in 1928 had been founded during 1914 and 1915. Sun Fa-hsu, the county magistrate appointed by Yuan, was particularly capable. Tahara Teijirō, *Shinmatsu minsho Chūgoku kanshin jinmeiroku*, p. 352. Further, Ting was already a model area.

69. Gillin, *Warlord*, pp. 66–78. T'ai Shuang-ch'iu, *Chung-kuo p'u-chi chiao-yü wen-t'i*, p. 39. Another estimate would put in school 69 percent of Shansi children between ages six and fourteen in 1920: Cheng Tsung-hai, "Elementary Education in China," Bulletin 14, vol. 2 (1923), p. 6, in Chinese National Association for the Advancement of Education, ed., *Bulletins on Chinese Education, 1923* (Shanghai, 1923).

70. Ts'en Hsueh-lü, vol. 1, p. 231. PDN: June 27, 1914, p. 5; September 14, 1914, p. 4; November 6, 1914, p. 4; November 7, 1914, p. 4; December 14, 1914, p. 4; December 18, 1914, p. 6; December 23, 1914, p. 5; March 29, 1915, p. 4; February 2, 1916, p. 4; February 12, 1916, pp. 2, 4; February 21, 1916, p. 5. CFKP 594: 1 (December 28, 1913); CFKP 606: 1 (January 14, 1914). Jordan to Grey (November 26, 1915), FO 228/1918. For a description of the dictatorship's policies for economic development, see Kikuchi Takaharu, *Chūgoku minzoku undō no kihon kōzō—taigai boikotto no kenkyū*, pp. 156–62.

71. Bailie, *Bailie's Activities in China*, pp. 62–66. PDN: December 14, 1914, pp. 4, 6; December 23, 1914, p. 5; May 20, 1915, p. 4; January 11, 1916, p. 4; January 14, 1916, p. 4; February 20, 1916, p. 5. CFKP 822 (August 19, 1914), rep. 28: 1033–35; CFKP 1149 (July 20, 1915), rep. 39: 235; CFKP 1155 (July 26, 1915), rep. 39: 758–66. "Sugar Industry in Hupeh" (January 12, 1915), FO 233/157. J. B. Affleck, acting consul in Wuchow, to Jordan (January 25, 1915), FO 228/1953. Giles, Nanking, to Jordan (October 20, 1915), FO 228/1948.

72. Ting reported that his initial budget request of Ch$100,000, though approved by the ministry of finance, was turned down by the national assembly. In October, 1913, the new vice-minister of industry and com-

merce found him funds. V. K. Ting (Ting Wen-chiang) to Morrison, Peking, October 8, 1913, MP item 176. V. K. Ting to Morrison, Tsingshing mine, November 13, 1913, MP item 176.

73. CFKP (January 6, 1916), rep. 45: 34.

74. Ts'en Hsueh-lü, vol. 1, p. 272. PDN, September 14, and December 25, 1914. Giles, Nanking, to Jordan (January 30, 1915), FO 228/1948. Fox, Hankow, to Jordan (July 5, 1915), FO 228/1945. Kikuchi Takaharu, *Chūgoku minzoku undō no kihon kōzō—taigai boikotto no kenkyū*, pp. 159–67.

75. Chia Shih-i, *Min-kuo ts'ai-cheng shih*, 1.1: 69–70, 81–84, 98–101.

76. Richard Dane to Sydney Barton, Peking, October 25, 1913, FO 228/2504.

77. Liang Ch'i-ch'ao, "Yü chih pi-chih chin-yung cheng-ts'e" [My currency policy], YPSWC 12.32: 38. Liang Ch'i-ch'ao, "Min-kuo ch'u-nien chih pi-chih kai-ko" [Currency reform in the early republic], YPSWC 15.43: 12–13.

78. Ts'en Hsueh-lü, vol. 1, pp. 162–63, 179–82. George E. Anderson, consul general in Hongkong, to Knox (January 11, 1912), NA 893.00/1066. Cheshire, Canton, to Calhoun (October 31, and November 14, 1912), NA 893.00/1507 and 1508. John K. Davis, vice-consul general in charge in Canton, to Williams (November 21, 1913), NA 893.00/2057. *North China Herald* (August 1, 1914). Speculators, including foreign banks, profited from Peking's retirement schemes, but efforts were made to minimize this by-product of a necessary measure.

79. Ts'en Hsueh-lü, vol. 1, pp. 196–97, 202, 205, 250.

80. Willoughby, vol. 2, p. 1098. PDN, June 24, 1914, p. 5.

81. F. E. Wilkinson, Foochow, to Jordan (April 19, and July 19, 1915), FO 228/1943. F. E. Wilkinson, Foochow, to Jordan (January 12, 1916), FO 228/1980.

82. Admissions of borrowing from Japanese experience were understandably rare in the wake of the Twenty-One Demands. But for one frank allusion by Yuan's spokesman in monarchism (Yang Tu) to the special efficacy of the German and Japanese monarchs in the modern age, see Pai Chiao, *Yuan Shih-k'ai yü Chung-hua min-kuo*, pp. 191–92. At one point, Yuan attributed his centralizing policies to the influence of the Japanese example. PDN, April 28, 1916, p. 2.

83. Huang Yen-p'ei put Yuan's wives at fifteen or sixteen, in his introduction to Pai Chiao, *Yuan Shih-k'ai yü Chung-hua min-kuo*, p. 4. G. E. Morrison believed they had become twenty-four in the fall of 1914: Cyril Pearl, *Morrison of Peking* (Sydney, 1967), p. 305. For a pronouncement on the evils of sexual equality, see CFKP 807 (August 4, 1914), rep. 28: 55–56.

84. CFKP 860 (September 25, 1914), rep. 29: 291–92. An earlier presidential order said: "Naturally it would be inappropriate to establish a national religion [*kuo-chiao*], since this would do violence to the sentiments of the masses." CFKP 631.8 (February 8, 1914). The reference is to the divergent beliefs of the five nationalities. See also CFKP 563: 1 (November 27,

1913) and CFKP 631: 7 (February 8, 1914). Chow Tse-tsung's statement that Yuan "became an enthusiastic patron of the Confucian movement" seems to me misleading, since Yuan rejected the main demand of the Confucian Society. Chow Tse-tsung, "Anti-Confucianism in Early Republican China," in Arthur F. Wright, ed., *The Confucian Persuasion* (Stanford, 1960), p. 291.

85. *Republican Advocate* 1.29: 1152 (October 19, 1912). Cheshire, Canton, to Calhoun (October 31, 1912), NA 893.00/1507. *Ta-kung-ho jih-pao*, October 10, 1912, p. 4.

86. *Republican Advocate* 1.43: 1700 (January 25, 1913).

87. CFKP 1022 (March 14, 1915), rep. 35: 554. Kirke, Nanking, to Jordan (October 13, 1914), FO 229/1909.

88. PDN, January 16, 1914, p. 4.

89. PDN, January 24, 1914, p. 4; and January 30, 1914, p. 4. CFKP 631: 4–5 (February 8, 1914).

90. For a description of the ceremony, see Jerome Ch'en, *Yuan Shih-k'ai*, 2d ed., pp. 162–63. For Yuan's order generalizing the ceremony, a point absent from Ch'en's description, see CFKP 945 (December 21, 1914), rep. 32: 208. See also CFKP 631: 4–5 (February 8, 1914).

91. PDN, October 11, 1914, p. 1. CFKP 543: 1 (November 7, 1913). PDN: June 19, 1914, p. 5; June 25, 1914, p. 4; September 22, 1914, p. 4. CFKP 867 (October 3, 1914), rep. 30: 48. Huang Yuan-yung, vol. 2, pp. 247–48.

92. PDN, December 28, 1914, p. 4. Ts'ao Ju-lin, *I-sheng chih hui-i*, p. 153. CFKP 1295 (December 15, 1915), rep. 44: 535–36. CFKP (January 16, 1916), rep. 45: 571–72.

93. PDN, June 20, 1914, p. 5. Arnold, Chefoo, to Bryan (May 27, 1914), NA 893.00/2136. M. S. Myers, consul in Swatow, to Reinsch (April 20, 1914), NA 893.00/2123. Nelson T. Johnson, consul in Changsha, to Reinsch (January 11, 1916), NA 893.00/2352. Edwin S. Cunningham, consul general in Hankow, to Reinsch (January 3, 1916), NA 893.00/2349. Esherick, "Reform," p. 466.

94. PDN, April 9, 1915, p. 3. CFKP 967 (January 17, 1915), rep. 33: 481; CFKP 969 (January 19, 1915), rep. 33: 571–74; CFKP (May 25, 1916), rep. 49: 301–2. Friedman, *Backward Toward Revolution*, p. 164. The activity of the land survey administration belies Ts'ao Ju-lin's description of it as a device for controlling Ts'ai O. Ts'ao Ju-lin, *I-sheng chih hui-i*, p. 154.

95. CFKP 732: 1–5 (May 21, 1914).

96. Schoppa, "Politics and Society in Chekiang," pp. 171–74.

97. A correspondent (probably a missionary) from Chu-chou (June 19, 1914), enclosed in Jameson, Hankow, to Reinsch (June 26, 1914), NA 893.00/2160. A missionary resident in northern Hupeh reported in late 1914 after a local survey that, although two years previously Yuan was widely supported, no one had been heard speaking well of him for some

time. Letter from Dr. A. W. Lagerquist, China Inland Mission, Lao-ho-k'ou, enclosed in Julean H. Arnold, consul general in Hankow, to Bryan (December 14, 1914), NA 893.00/2248.

98. Jordan to Langley, Shanghai, January 1, 1915, Jordan Papers, FO 350/13.

99. In his study of worker activity around the 1911 Revolution, Chao Ch'in, "Kung-jen yun-tung," pp. 1–16, enumerates strikes in the early republic (twenty-four in 1912–13, eleven in 1914, eight in 1915, seventeen in 1916, twenty-one in 1917), but finds that workers enjoyed no autonomous political organization or expression in the period of Yuan's presidency.

100. John C. Donald to Morrison, Foochow, March 8, 1912, MP item 171.

101. Bertram Giles, Changsha, to Jordan (January 29, 1913), FO 228/1869.

102. Smith, Hangchow, to Alston (October 22, 1913), FO 228/1872. Schoppa, "Politics and Society in Chekiang," pp. 175–76.

103. Esherick, "Reforms" pp. 466–67.

104. CFKP 1297 (December 17, 1915), rep. 44: 623. *North China Herald*, September 20, 1913, p. 906. PDN: June 5, 1914, p. 4; July 25, 1914, p. 4; January 15, 1916, p. 4; January 22, 1916, p. 5.

105. Chia Shih-i, *Min-kuo ts'ai-cheng shih*, 1.1: 68, 1.2: 250–51.

106. CFKP 847 (September 13, 1914), rep. 29: 361–68. PDN, December 18, 1914, p. 5. Chin Ch'ung-chi, "Yun-nan hu-kuo yun-tung," p. 278, cites several instances from 1915 of merchant protests against Yuan's policies, particularly with respect to taxation. The instances come from Shantung, Kiangsu, Anhwei, Kwangtung, Yunnan and Shansi. For an analysis of the repressive character of Yuan's code for chambers of commerce, see Shirley S. Garrett, "The Chambers of Commerce and the YMCA," in Mark Elvin and G. William Skinner, eds., *The Chinese City between Two Worlds* (Stanford, 1974), pp. 220–21.

Chapter 8

1. Morrison to Louis E. Broome, Peking, March 31, 1916, MP item 184.

2. Edgar Snow, "A Conversation with Mao Tse-tung," *Life* 70.16: 46 (April 30, 1971).

3. Jordan to Grey (November 14, 1911), FO 405/205. G. E. Morrison diary (November 20, 1911), MP item 91.

4. G. E. Morrison diary (December 9, 1911), MP item 91.

5. Fei Hsing-chien, *Tuan Ch'i-jui*, p. 35. Chang I-lin, *Hsin-t'ai-p'ing-shih chi*, p. 41.

6. *K'ai-kuo kuei-mo* [Patterns in the inauguration of the republic], Committee on the Compilation of Documents on the Fiftieth Anniversary of the Founding of the Republic of China, eds. (Taipei, 1962), pp. 640–41.

7. For example, *T'ien-to pao*, May 13, 1912, p. 2, and in many other issues of this newspaper in May and June, 1912.

8. Jordan to Langley, Peking, June 1, 1914, Jordan Papers, FO 350/12.
9. *Chung-kuo T'ung-meng hui tsa-chih*, September 11, 1912, *cho-shu* section, p. 11.
10. "Notes on the political situation," Frank W. Hadley, Shanghai (March 4, 1913), NA 893.00/1611.
11. *Nihon gaikō bunsho*, 1914, vol. 2, pp. 743–45.
12. G. E. Morrison diary (September 25, 1915), MP item 104. The aide was Ts'ai T'ing-kan.
13. Report of a conversation with Ts'ai T'ing-kan, G. E. Morrison diary (May 26, 1915), MP item 104. Reportedly the remedy Yuan had in mind at that point was participation in the peace conference at the conclusion of the European war.
14. G. E. Morrison diary (August 17, 1915), MP item 104.
15. Jordan to Grey (December 22, 1911), FO 405/205.
16. Ts'ao Ju-lin, *I-sheng chih hui-i*, p. 132.
17. CFKP 554 (December 30, 1914), rep. 32: 319.
18. Pai Chiao, *Yuan Shih-k'ai yü Chung-hua min-kuo*, pp. 191–221. For a useful but inaccurate translation, see B. L. Putnam Weale (pseudonym of B. Lenox Simpson), *The Fight for the Republic in China* (New York, 1917), pp. 150–71.
19. "Inaugural address of president to the Council of Government," December 15, 1913, FO 228/1852. For a comment on this document, see note 1 to chapter 7. The published version contains similar remarks: CFKP 585: 2 (December 19, 1913).
20. *Papers Relating to the Foreign Relations of the United States*, 1915 (Washington, D.C., 1924), pp. 66–67.
21. PDN, March 14, 1916, pp. 5–6.
22. Ch'en Tu-hsiu, "Chiu-ssu-hsiang yü kuo-t'i wen-t'i" [Old thought and the problem of the national polity], *Hsin-ch'ing-nien* (May 1, 1917), Daian ed., 3: 207–9.
23. CFKP 1294 (December 14, 1915), rep. 44: 497.
24. Pai Chiao, *Yuan Shih-k'ai yü Chung-hua min-kuo*, p. 297. Reginald F. Johnston, *Twilight in the Forbidden City* (London, 1934), p. 114.
25. CFKP 1295 (December 15, 1915), rep. 44: 535–36. CFKP 1299 (December 19, 1915), rep. 44: 713. CFKP 1303 (December 23, 1915), rep. 44: 906.
26. Pai Chiao, *Yuan Shih-k'ai yü Chung-hua min-kuo*, pp. 194, 196, and 199. This appeal to constitutionalism should not, of course, be taken as a new-found enthusiasm on Yuan's part for constraints on his power. G. E. Morrison diary (August 17, 1915), MP item 104.
27. Harry H. Fox, consul general in Chengtu, to Jordan (April 7, 1914), FO 228/1904. For other reports expressing these themes regarding Szechwan, see: Porter, Chengtu, to Jordan (January 14, 1914), FO 228/1904; Fox, Chengtu, to Jordan (July 7, and August 22, 1914), FO 228/1904; Mead, Chengtu, to Jordan (October 24, 1914), FO 228/1904; PDN, December 2, 1914, p. 4.

28. Smith, Chengtu, to Jordan (January 4, April 14, June 22, July 15, and July 20, 1915), FO 228/1942. Mead, Chungking, to Jordan (July 27, 1915), FO 228/1942. Smith, Chengtu, to Jordan (February 1, 1916), FO 228/2753. Ch'en I is incorrectly referred to as Ch'en Huan in Sheridan, *Chinese Warlord*, pp. 55 et seq. Jerome Ch'en, "Defining Chinese Warlords," p. 586, notes the error.

29. Li Yü-shu, *Chung-Jih erh-shih-i-t'iao chiao-she*, vol. 1, pp. 246–52, 391–92. Able presentations of the more modest versions are: Kwanha Yim, "Yuan Shih-k'ai and the Japanese," *Journal of Asian Studies* 24.1: 63–73 (November 1964); Madeleine Chi, *China Diplomacy*, pp. 64–84.

30. G. E. Morrison diary (April 29, 1915), MP item 104. Morrison was told of Liang Ch'i-ch'ao's fear by Eugene Ch'en, who said he disabused Liang of this Japanese canard.

31. Odagiri Masunosuke, Japan's chief financial agent in Peking, told a British counterpart in early March, 1915, that the Japanese would support Yuan "as President or Emperor provided he submits to their direction." Jordan to Grey (March 3, 1915), FO 228/2307. It is evident from Japanese sources that the Japanese government did not feel, quite correctly, that Yuan at any stage submitted to its direction, although he did finally capitulate to its threat of force.

32. Jordan to Langley, Peking, October 20, 1915, Jordan Papers, FO 350/13. Jordan to Grey (October 27, 1915), FO 228/2397.

33. Madeleine Chi, *China Diplomacy*, p. 76. Slightly different versions are given in: Ts'en Hsueh-lü, vol. 1, p. 297; Kwanha Yim, "Yuan Shih-k'ai," p. 67.

34. "Memorandum Regarding the Activities of Kameizo Nishihara . . . ," MP item 133. On October 17, 1915, Uchida Ryōhei of the Kokuryūkai did propose to the Japanese prime minister a strategy of public welcome for Yuan's monarchical scheme, since its fulfillment was seen as hastening Yuan's fall. But the proposal came *after* Japanese knowledge of widespread Chinese opposition to Yuan's monarchy (indeed it was predicated on that fact); and, far from acting on Uchida's proposal, the Japanese government had already embarked on a policy of public disapproval of the monarchical movement. Usui Katsumi, *Nihon to Chūgoku—Taishō jidai* [Japan and China: The Taishō period] (Tokyo, 1972), pp. 90–91.

35. Jordan to Grey (August 25, 1915), FO 228/2397. Ts'ao Ju-lin, *I-sheng chih hui-i*, p. 132.

36. *Nihon gaikō bunsho*, 1915, vol. 2, pp. 48–56. At the same time, other papers, reportedly bribed by the monarchical movement, were quoting Japanese officials as though they favored the change.

37. G. E. Morrison diary (September 1, 1915), MP item 104. Obata Yukichi, chargé d'affaires in Peking, to Ōkuma (September 8, 1915), Japan MFA film, MT 1.6.1.75–1, reel 159, p. 208.

38. Madeleine Chi, *China Diplomacy*, p. 66.

39. Greene, Tokyo, to Grey (October 15, 1915), FO 228/2397.

40. Jordan to Grey (August 25, September 10, October 1, and October 10,

1915), FO 228/2397. Grey to Jordan (October 8, 1915), FO 228/2397. Jordan to Langley, Peking, September 7, and September 23, 1915, Jordan Papers, FO 350/13.

41. The change of attitude on the part of Liang Ch'i-ch'ao is expressed in: Liang Ch'i-ch'ao, "Hu-kuo chih i hui-ku-t'an" [Reminiscences of the fight against the monarchical movement], YPSWC 14.39: 88; and Liang Ch'i-ch'ao, "*Ta Chung-hua* fa-k'an tz'u" [Words on the occasion of the publication of the *Ta Chung-hua* (magazine)], YPSWC 12.33: 89–90. Others who expressed a disillusionment dating from about the same time include Ts'ai O and Ting Wen-chiang.

42. Chang I-lin, letter to Yuan Shih-k'ai, probably December 9 or 10, 1915, according to the author's description, though marked 1916: Chang I-lin, *Hsin-t'ai-p'ing-shih chi*, pp. 38–42.

43. Jordan to Langley, Peking, October 20, 1915, Jordan Papers, FO 350/13.

44. Goodnow wrote of seeing Yuan K'o-ting twice a week on a regular basis at the beginning of 1914, and there are evidences of a continuing closeness. Goodnow to Butler, Peking, January 2 and February 26, 1914 ("Miscellaneous Correspondence"), Goodnow Collection. G. E. Morrison diary (February 16, 1914), MP item 100.

45. Goodnow's private views are recorded in G. E. Morrison diary (July 16, July 28, and August 11, 1915), MP item 104.

46. On Goodnow as dupe, see Paul S. Reinsch, *An American Diplomat in China* (New York, 1922), pp. 172–73. On Goodnow as mercenary: G. E. Morrison diary (August 2, 1915), MP item 104, quoting W. H. Donald, who throws into the same category W. W. Willoughby, Goodnow's successor as constitutional adviser.

47. G. E. Morrison diary (July 28, August 11, August 17, and August 31, 1915), MP item 104. *Papers Relating to the Foreign Relations of the United States*, 1915, pp. 48–53. On Goodnow's monarchism, see also Noel Pugach, "Embarrassed Monarchist: Frank J. Goodnow and Constitutional Development in China, 1913–1915," *Pacific Historical Review*, 42.4: 499–517 (November 1973).

48. Dr. Frank J. Goodnow, "Republic or Monarchy?" in MP item 139. This typed copy was evidently given Morrison by Goodnow.

49. Pekin Shina kenkyūkai, *Saishin Shina kanshin roku*, pt. 1, p. 591. *Liang . . . nien-p'u*, p. 387. Wu Hsiang-hsiang, *Min-kuo cheng-chih jen-wu* [Political personages of the republic] (Taipei, 1964), pp. 69–85.

50. PDN, May 4, 1916, p. 5.

51. Goffe, Yunnanfu, to Jordan (January 9, 1916), FO 228/2753.

52. Fraser, Shanghai, to Jordan (March 27, 1916), FO 228/2753. Additional military men whom I have been able to identify on the list of Wen Tsung-yao, reported here, are: Wu Ping-hsiang, T'ang Tsai-li, and Chang Chen-fang.

53. Ts'ao Ju-lin, *I-sheng chih hui-i*, pp. 135–36. Hsu Tao-lin, ed., *Hsu Shu-cheng hsien-sheng wen-chi nien-p'u ho-k'an* [Collected writings and

chronological biography of Hsu Shu-cheng, published in one volume]
(Taipei, 1962), p. 162. Reinsch to Bryan (August 6, 1915), NA 893.00/
2304.

In his official biography, Liang Shih-i is presented as attempting to
resist the monarchy and never actively supporting it. Ts'en Hsueh-lü,
vol. 1, pp. 271–329. He may have held back in the early stages, but when
he gave his support he did so with great application. The revolutionaries
rightly considered him a major contributor to the monarchical effort.

54. "En sōtō teii ni soku subeshi to no fūsetsu ni kan-suru ken" [Report
regarding rumors that President Yuan will ascend the throne], enclosed
in Hioki Eki, minister in Peking, to Katō Kōmei, foreign minister (July
23, 1915), Japan MFA film, MT 1.6.1.75–1, reel 159, pp. 18–32.

55. Hsu Tao-lin, *Hsu Shu-cheng hsien-sheng wen-chi nien-p'u ho-k'an*, p.
159.

56. *Nihon gaikō bunsho*, 1915, vol. 2, pp. 24–25. Hsu Tao-lin, *Hsu Shu-cheng
hsien-sheng wen-chi nien-p'u ho-k'an*, pp. 162–68. "Notes of an Interview
with Liang Shih-yi" (February 23, 1916), MP item 135.

57. Obata to Ōkuma (September 6, 1915), Japan MFA film, MT 1.6.1.75–1,
reel 159, pp. 297–310.

58. Chang I-lin, *Hsin-t'ai-p'ing-shih chi*, pp. 70, 608–25.

59. Ts'ao Ju-lin, *I-sheng chih hui-i*, pp. 152–53, discusses Wang Shih-chen's
manner of expressing opposition.

60. *Nihon gaikō bunsho*, 1915, vol. 2, pp. 24–25. Takahashi Shinji, consul
in Nanking, to Ōkuma (September 9, 1915), Japan MFA film, MT
1.6.1.75–1, reel 159, pp. 210–11. "Hōkoku: Chūankai no teisei undō"
[Report: the monarchical movement of the Ch'ou-an hui], Japan MFA
film, MT 1.6.1.75–1, reel 159, pp. 221–27. The British representative in
Nanking began receiving the same information in October, 1915.

61. "Interview with Feng Kuo-ch'ang [*sic*]. Nanking, January 22nd, 1916,"
MP item 135. "Interview with Yuan Shih-k'ai" (February 7, 1916),
MP item 135. *Nihon gaikō bunsho*, 1916, vol. 2, pp. 105–6.

62. Japanese officials, particularly General Aoki Norizumi in Shanghai
from January, 1916, assiduously sought information on Feng Kuo-
chang's political preferences. Although for a time in March and April,
1916, Feng was thought to be favoring a Manchu restoration (which
Aoki and the Kokuryūkai had separately advocated in 1914), it was
concluded by the end of April that this was not the case. Gaimushō
1.6.1.75, "Bessatsu: hanEn dōran oyobi kakuchi jōkyō," vols. 6, 9, 11,
and 12.

63. Matsudaira Tsuneo, consul general in Tientsin, to Ōkuma (September
23, 1915), Japan MFA film, MT 1.6.1.75–1, reel 159, pp. 56–57.

64. E. C. Wilton, acting consul general in Canton, to Jordan (October 19,
1915), FO 228/2397.

65. "Hōkoku: Chūankai no teisei undō," Japan MFA film, MT 1.6.1.75–1,
reel 159, p. 222.

66. "Interview with Yang Cheng in the Arsenal, Shanghai" (January 30, 1916), MP item 135.
67. Wilton, Canton, to Jordan (October 19, 1915), FO 228/2397. PDN, May 8, 1916, p. 2.
68. Johnson, Changsha, to Reinsch (January 11, 1916), NA 893.00/2352.
69. Letter of A. W. Lagerquist, January 18, 1916, enclosed in Edwin S. Cunningham, consul general in Hankow, to Reinsch (January 24, 1916), NA 893.00/2352.
70. Bristow, Hangchow, to Jordan (October 28, 1915), FO 228/1943. Bristow, Hangchow, to Jordan (November 6, 1915), FO 228/2397.
71. Fox, Hankow, to Jordan (October 7, 1915), FO 228/1945. *Nihon gaikō bunsho*, 1916, vol. 2, pp. 10–11.
72. G. A. Combe, acting consul in Chefoo, to Jordan (November 8, 1915), FO 228/1942. Pratt, Tsinan, to Jordan (January 13, April 12, and October 9, 1916), FO 228/1983.
73. Cunningham, Hankow, to Reinsch (December 30, 1915), NA 893.00/2348.
74. Smith, Chengtu, to Jordan (February 1, 1916), FO 228/2753.
75. Liang Ch'i-ch'ao, "I-ts'ai so-wei kuo-t'i wen-t'i che" [How strange is the so-called problem of the national polity!], *Ta Chung-hua* (Shanghai), 1.8 (August 20, 1915). For an interpretation of Liang's position that stresses the importance of his distinguishing changes in the "form of the state" (*kuo-t'i*) from changes in the "political system" (*cheng-t'i*), see Chang P'eng-yuan, "Wei-hu kung-ho—Liang Ch'i-ch'ao chih lien-Yuan yü t'ao-Yuan" [Guarding the republic—Liang Ch'i-ch'ao's allying with Yuan and opposing him], *Chung-yang yen-chiu-yuan chin-tai-shih yen-chiu-so chi-k'an*, vol. 3, pt. 2 (December 1972), pp. 384–88.
76. An example of this line of thinking can be found in an interview with Shen Yun-p'ei: Obata to Ōkuma (September 6, 1915), Japan MFA film, MT 1.6.1.75–1, reel 159, pp. 253–59.
77. Chang I-lin, *Hsin-t'ai-p'ing-shih chi*, p. 41.
78. Albert W. Pontius, consul in Foochow, to Reinsch (March 11, 1916), NA 893.00/2371.
79. For some indictments of Yuan that raised these issues again in the context of the antimonarchical movement, see Huang Chi-lu, ed., *Hu-kuo chün chi-shih* [Records of the National Protection Army], vol. 1 (reprint ed., Taipei, 1970), pp. 67–82.
80. As late as July, 1915, Ts'ai O was reported to be standing in for Tuan Ch'i-jui as chairman of sessions of the council of generals-in-chief in Peking, when those in attendance included Feng Kuo-chang and Li Ch'un. *Shun-t'ien shih-pao* (Peking), July 10, 1915, p. 2.
81. Goffe, Yunnanfu, to Jordan (December 29, 1915), FO 228/2753. G. E. Morrison diary (January 20, 1915), item 104.
82. *Ko-ming wen-hsien* 6: 76.
83. Liang Ch'i-ch'ao, "Yuan Shih-k'ai chih chieh-p'ou," YPSWC 12.34:4–19.

84. PDN, April 28, 1916, p. 2.
85. For an excellent description of the Yunnan rising against Yuan, see Sutton, "Rise and Decline," chap. 7. See ibid., pp. 40–41, for the dimensions of the Yunnanese New Army at the end of the Ch'ing. For a detailed study that emphasizes the importance of the preparations by local officers, including the preliminary dispatch of troops toward Szechwan before Ts'ai O arrived, see Chin Ch'ung-chi, "Yun-nan hu-kuo yun-tung," pp. 261–83.
86. A. G. Major, acting consul in Chungking, to Jordan (April 29, 1916), FO 228/1980.
87. I follow here the judgment of Sutton, "Rise and Decline," chap. 7. This judgment is supported by a Japanese military analysis of the tactics of the National Protection Army in Szechwan, which are described as being marked by attacks initiated at night, sophisticated use of terrain, and effective political work with the opposing Szechwanese troops. The casualties inflicted on Peiyang troops are described as unexpectedly large. General Staff, "Shina jiken sankō shiryō, sono hachi" [Reference materials on the China incident, no. 8] (March 1916), Gaimushō 1.6.1.75, "Bessatsu: hanEn dōran oyobi kakuchi jōkyō," vol. 6.
88. R. Huntley Davidson (Friends Foreign Mission Association) to Morrison, Chengtu, January 31, 1916, MP item 184.
89. Smith, Chengtu, to Jordan (February 15, 1916), FO 228/2736. W. H. Hockman, Suifu (Hsu-fu, now I-pin), February 22, 1916, enclosed in Smith, Chengtu, to Jordan (March 5, 1916), FO 228/2736.
90. Liu Ts'un-hou, *Hu-kuo Ch'uan-chün chan-chi* [Record of the battles of the Szechwan National Protection Army] (Taipei, 1966), pp. 10–14. For Ts'ai O's low opinion of Liu Ts'un-hou's troops, see Liu Ta-wu, ed., *Ts'ai Sung-p'o hsien-sheng i-chi* [Posthumously collected works of Ts'ai O] (Shaoyang, 1943; reprint ed., Taipei, 1962), pp. 114–15.
91. Brown, Chungking, to Jordan (April 17, 1914), FO 228/1905. Mead, Chengtu, to Jordan (October 24, 1914), FO 228/1904; Mead, Chengtu, to Jordan (July 27, 1915), FO 228/1942.
92. Smith, Chengtu, to Jordan (April 22, 1916), FO 228/1979. The origins and actions of the "brigand" National Protection Army are also reported in: "Shina jōhō" [Intelligence on China], no. 16 (May 1916), General Staff, and Yamato Kugirō, secretary in Chengtu, to Ishii (April 29, 1916), both in Gaimushō 1.6.1.75, "Bessatsu: hanEn dōran oyobi kakuchi jōkyō," vols. 14 and 15. According to this Japanese intelligence, Hsiung K'o-wu, who had joined the Yunnan uprising, dispatched Leng Yü-ch'un and Sun Tse-p'ei to Szechwan with money to organize bandits and former soldiers of Hsiung's old Fifth Szechwanese Division in support of the anti-Yuan movement. Like Hsiung, both Leng and Sun were Szechwanese. Leng had headed the Nanking army hospital during the Second Revolution; Sun had been a regimental commander in the Fifth Szechwanese Division. Another organizer of popular forces was Yang Wei (or Yang Hsin-yeh), who was intimately associated with the Society

of Brothers and Elders and had been a chief of police in Chengtu in the aftermath of the 1911 Revolution. He reportedly had no direct connections with the Yunnan-based National Protection Army. For an account that emphasizes Yang's role at this time, see Yang Chao-jung, "Hsin-hai hou chih Ssu-ch'uan chan-chi" [Record of wars in Szechwan after the 1911 Revolution], CTSTL, 1958, no. 6, pp. 45–47. On Leng and Yang Wei, see Tahara Teijirō, *Shinmatsu Minsho Chūgoku kanshin jinmeiroku*, pp. 218 and 594.

93. Smith, Chengtu, to Jordan (March 21, 1916), FO 228/2736. Major, Chungking, to Jordan (April 2, 1916), FO 228/2736.
94. Smith, Chengtu, to Jordan (July 23, and August 17, 1916), FO 228/1979.
95. Agnes Smedley, *The Great Road: The Life and Times of Chu Teh* (London, 1958), pp. 114–15.
96. Liu Ta-wu, *Ts'ai Sung-p'o hsien-sheng i-chi*, pp. 114, 116. Goffe, Yunnanfu, to Jordan (telegram no. 18 and a letter, both January 26, 1916), FO 228/2753. Goffe, Yunnanfu, to Jordan (March 7, 1916), FO 228/2736. Smith, Chengtu, to Jordan (February 15, 1916), FO 228/2736. Dr. Rudd to Frank K. Pilson, Suifu (I-pin), March 24, 1916, enclosed in Goffe, Yunnanfu, to Jordan (April 27, 1916), FO 228/2738.

I feel that Sheridan, *Chinese Warlord*, pp. 56–63, though undoubtedly correct in his general picture of Feng Yü-hsiang's concern for his own military power, underestimates both Feng's and Ch'en I's readiness to try accommodation at an early stage with the National Protection Army. An accommodation took some time to work out. Meanwhile fighting occurred. But it appears from the documents cited above that Ts'ai O had good reason by early February, 1916, to hope that Ch'en and Feng would not defend Yuan's authority in Szechwan. Further, on the basis of internal evidence, a more probable dating than March 2 (as given in Sheridan, *Chinese Warlord*, p. 61) for the Ts'ai O telegram discussing the arrival of emissaries from Feng and Feng's attitude (text in Liu Ta-wu, *Ts'ai Sung-p'o hsien-sheng i-chi*, p. 116) is February 2. The telegram, dated the second of an unspecified month (apparently solar), cannot have been sent earlier than February or later than March, 1916. The text refers to the reading of a Peking telegram of "the 30th." Since there is no "30th" in February, it is unlikely (though barely possible) that the discussion is of a telegram from Peking that was a month old. Hence, February 2 seems the probable date of Ts'ai's message. This dating fits rather well Feng Yü-hsiang's own account of the events. *Ko-ming wen-hsien* 47: 248–55.

97. Smith, Chengtu, to Jordan (April 4, and April 9, 1916), FO 228/2736. Smith, Chengtu, to Jordan (May 26, 1916), FO 228/2737. *Nihon gaikō bunsho*, 1916, vol. 2, p. 110. *Yuan Shih-k'ai ch'ieh-kuo chi* [Record of Yuan Shih-k'ai's usurpation] (Taipei, 1954), pp. 306–14.
98. I-ming, *Yuan Shih-k'ai ch'üan-chuan*, p. 134. Major-general Machida, Peking, to General Staff (January 25, 1916), Gaimushō 1.6.1.75, "Bessatsu: hanEn dōran oyobi kakuchi jōkyō," vol. 3.

99. The sketches of events in various provinces during 1916, as I present them in this and the following paragraph, are primarily based upon a large number of contemporary American, British, and Japanese consular reports.

100. In his memoirs, Yen Hsi-shan explains the anomaly of his overlong adherence to Yuan as being in accord with Sun Yat-sen's wish that he preserve revolutionary strength in the north, rather than set it at risk. Yen dwells on the risk, stemming in effect from the weakness of his position both within the province and with respect to neighboring territory. Yen Hsi-shan, *Yen Hsi-shan tsao-nien hui-i-lu*, pp. 50–51. As discussed in chapter 5, Yen's position was indeed weak, but his loyalty to Yuan's policies went beyond what can be explained by this temporary weakness and suggests a genuine admiration of them. Gillin, *Warlord*, p. 21.

101. G. E. Morrison diary (June 6, 1916), MP item 106. Cyril Pearl, *Morrison of Peking*, p. 326, attributes the remark to Morrison himself, mistakenly, I believe.

102. Chang I-lin, *Hsin-t'ai-p'ing-shih chi*, p. 67.

103. Kwanha Yim, "Yuan Shih-k'ai," pp. 63–73. Madeleine Chi, *China Diplomacy*, pp. 75–84. Friedman, *Backward Toward Revolution*, pp. 167–89.

104. For an example of intimate Japanese assistance, see *Liang . . . nien-p'u*, pp. 474, 477–79.

105. Albert A. Altman and Harold Z. Schiffrin, "Sun Yat-sen and the Japanese: 1914–16," *Modern Asian Studies*, 6.4: 393–98 (October 1972). Ts'en Ch'un-hsuan, pt 1, p. 20. Wilton, Canton, to Jordan (February 19, 1916), FO 228/2736. Goffe, Yunnanfu, to Jordan (January 31, 1916), FO 228/2753. Goffe, Yunnanfu, to Jordan (March 4 and March 17, 1916), FO 228/2736. Goffe, Yunnanfu, to Jordan (May 30, 1916), FO 228/1985. Kirke, consul in Wuchow, to Jordan (April 28, 1916), FO 228/2738. *Nihon gaikō bunsho*, 1916, vol. 2, pp. 97–98, 110. Imai Yoshirō, consul general in Hongkong, to Ishii (February 14, 1916), Gaimushō 1.6.1.75, "Bessatsu: hanEn dōran oyobi kakuchi jōkyō," vol. 3. General Aoki, Shanghai, to General Staff (April 6, 1916), Gaimushō 1.6.1.75, "Bessatsu: hanEn dōran oyobi kakuchi jōkyō," vol. 8. Ts'en seems not to have returned to China before early April.

106. Jordan to Langley, Peking, February 29, 1916, Jordan Papers, FO 350/15. Adshead, *Modernization*, p. 204.

107. Hioki to Ishii (January 22, 1916), Japan MFA film, PVM 12–16, reel P23, p. 6550. Cabinet discussion of January 19, 1916, *Nihon gaikō bunsho*, 1916, vol. 2, p. 13.

108. Ibid., pp. 31–33. "Shina mokka no jikyoku ni tai-Shi teikoku no toru-beku seisaku" [Policy to be adopted by Japan toward the present situation in China], Japan MFA film, PVM 12–16, reel P23, pp. 6577–79. Efforts from April, 1916, onward by Ts'ao Ju-lin and Liang Shih-i to win Japanese support for Yuan included extravagant offers of favors

but were unavailing. Usui Katsumi, *Nihon to Chūgoku—Taishō jidai*, pp. 99–100.

Chapter 9

1. Goffe, Yunnanfu, to Jordan (July 22, 1916), FO 228/1985. Major, Chung-king, to Alston (December 5, 1916), FO 228/1980. Teichman, *Travels of a Consular Officer*, p. vi.
2. Jordan to Grey (June 21, 1916), FO 228/2737. Jamieson, Canton, to Jordan (June 6, 1916), FO 228/2737. Jordan to Langley, Peking, July 18, 1916, Jordan Papers, FO 350/15. Adshead, *Modernization*, p. 100.
3. For example, Franklin Houn, *Central Government of China*, p. 122; Powell, *Rise of Chinese Military Power*, pp. 78–80; and Jerome Ch'en, *Yuan Shih-k'ai*, rev. ed., pp. 214–15.
4. G. E. Morrison diary (January 20, 1915), MP item 104. See also Ts'ao Ju-lin, *I-sheng chih hui-i*, pp. 114–15, for a picture of Yuan as a tolerant boss.
5. For an example, see Yen Fu's evaluation of Yuan Shih-k'ai, as related in Benjamin Schwartz, *In Search of Wealth and Power: Yen Fu and the West* (Cambridge, Mass., 1964), pp. 223–24.
6. This picture emerges from the materials on events in Hunan during April and May, 1916, in Hunan Historical Materials Editorial Committee, eds., *Hu-nan li-shih tzu-liao* [Materials on the history of Hunan] (Chang-sha, 1960), vol. 1, pp. 127–47.
7. Pratt, Tsinan, to Jordan (April 12, 1916), FO 228/1983. Hayashi Kujirō, consul in Tsinan, to Ishii (March 27, March 29, April 1, April 18, and April 22, 1916), Gaimushō 1.6.1.75, "Bessatsu: hanEn dōran oyobi kakuchi jōkyō," vols. 6 and 9.
8. Pratt, Tsinan, to Jordan (October 9, 1916), FO 228/1983. *Ko-ming wen-hsien* 46: 255, 294, 327, 344.

   Although portions of the revolutionary forces in Shantung were commanded by Wu Ta-chou, who did not take orders from Chü Cheng and the Chinese Revolutionary Party contingent, this incident took place at Ch'ang-lo, which was under the *Min-chün*, or the Chinese Revolutionary Party group. Chiang Kai-shek's particular role in this affair is unclear, but he was appointed chief of staff in June, 1916, and spent some time in this capacity in Shantung. Pinchon P. Y. Lo, *The Early Chiang Kai-shek: A Study of His Personality and Politics, 1887–1924* (New York, 1971), pp. 29–30.
9. *Ko-ming wen-hsien* 46: 302–3.
10. Gillin, "Problems of Centralization," p. 850; Hung-mao Tien, *Government and Politics in Kuomintang China, 1927–1937* (Stanford, 1972), p. 4.
11. Chiang's style of repression, so similar to Yuan's though less national in scope, is described in Lloyd E. Eastman, *The Abortive Revolution:*

China under Nationalist Rule, 1927–1937 (Cambridge, Mass., 1974), pp. 6–9, 20–30.

12. Kuhn, "Local Self-Government," pp. 280, 284–87.
13. In a growing literature on the subject, among the most intimate and circumstantial accounts of this sort of behavior is Philip Agee, *Inside the Company: CIA Diary* (Harmondsworth, 1975).

Glossary

This character glossary of proper names and phrases excludes the names of provinces and major cities, terms and titles assimilated into English, persons with their own entries in the Hummel and Boorman biographical dictionaries, and persons who appear as authors in works cited.

Aoki Norizumi 青木宣純
Ariga Nagao 有賀長雄

Chang Chen-fang 張鎮芳
Chang Huai-chih 張懷芝
Chang Ming-ch'i 張鳴岐
Chang Shu-yuan 張樹元
Chang Yun-shan 張雲山
Ch'ang-lo 昌樂
Ch'ang-shou 常熟
Chan-hua 霑化
Chao Erh-feng 趙爾豐
Chao Ping-chün 趙秉鈞
Ch'en Ching-hua 陳景華
Ch'en Huan-chang 陳煥章
Ch'en I 陳宧
Ch'en I-fan 陳貽範
Ch'en T'ing-hsun 陳廷訓
Chen-chou 郴州
Ch'eng Te-ch'üan 程德全
cheng-chih hui-i 政治會議
Ch'i Yao-lin 齊耀琳
Chiang Kuei-t'i 姜桂題

Chiang Tso-pin 蔣作賓
Chiang Yen-hsing 蔣雁行
chiang-chün 將軍
Chiao Ta-feng 焦達峯
chien-kuo 建國
Chin Wan-fu 金萬福
Ch'in Yü-liu 秦毓鎏
Ch'ing 清
ching-chi t'e-k'o 經濟特科
ch'ing-hsiang 清鄉
Chin-pu tang 進步黨
chin-shih 進士
chiu-kuo 救國
chou 州
Chou Fu 周馥
Ch'ou-an hui 籌安會
Chü Cheng 居正
Chu Chia-pao 朱家寶
Chu Ch'i-ch'ien 朱啓鈐
Chu Jui 朱瑞
Chu-chou 株洲
chü-jen 舉人
Chung-hua min-kuo 中華民國
Chung-hua ti-kuo 中華帝國

319

chün-hsien 郡縣
chu-yin tzu-mu 注音字母

feng-chien 封建
fu 府

gagaku 雅樂
genrō 元老

Han Kuo-chün 韓國鈞
Hioki Eki 日置益
Ho Hai-ming 何海鳴
Hsiao-chan 小站
hsien 縣
Hsien 獻
hsien-sheng 先生
hsing-cheng tsung-chien 行政總監
hsiu-ts'ai 秀才
Hsu Chao-wei 徐兆瑋
Hsu Pao-shan 徐寶山
Hsu Shu-cheng 徐樹錚
hsun-an-shih 巡按使
Hua-hsin 華新
Huang Shih-lung 黃士龍
hui-kuan 會館
Hu-kuo chün 護國軍
Hung Shu-tsu 洪述祖
Hung-hsien 洪憲

I-chün 毅軍
Ishii Kikujirō 石井菊次郎

jiyū kyōwa 自由共和

Kai-chin t'uan 改進團
Katō Kōmei 加藤高明
Keng Pao-k'uei 耿葆煃
Kiangpei 江北
Ko-lao hui 哥老會
Ku Ao 顧鰲
Kuan Keng-lin 關賡麟

Kung-ho tang 共和黨
kuo-chia 國家
kuo-chiao 國教
kuo-hui 國會
kuo-min hsueh-hsiao 國民學校
kuo-shui t'ing ch'ou-pei ch'u 國稅廳
    籌備處

Lan T'ien-wei 藍天蔚
Lao-ho-k'ou 老河口
Leng Yü-ch'un 冷遹春
Li Ch'un 李純
Liang Ju-hao 梁如浩
Liang Tun-yen 梁敦彥
Liao Chung-k'ai 廖仲凱
li-fa yuan 立法院
likin 釐金
Lin-huai kuan 臨淮關
Liu Kuan-hsiung 劉冠雄
liu-shou 留守
Lo Lun 羅綸
Lu Chien-chang 陸建章

Ma An-liang 馬安良
Meng-tzu 蒙自
min-cheng-chang 民政長
min-chün 民軍
Min-chu tang 民主黨
min-kuo 民國

Ni Ssu-ch'ung 倪嗣沖
Nihon rikugun shikan gakkō 日本陸
    軍士官學校

Odagiri Masunosuke 小田切萬壽之
    助
Ōkuma Shigenobu 大隈重信

Pai Lang 白郎
pai-hua 白話
P'an Jo-hai 潘若海

Pei-hai 北海
Pei-yang 北洋
P'eng Shou-sung 彭壽松
p'ing-cheng yuan 平政院
Po Wen-wei 柏文蔚

Saigō Takamori 西鄉隆盛
Shen Yun-p'ei 沈雲沛
sheng 省
shen-shih 紳士
shen-shih kuo 紳士國
shih-kuan 史館
Sun Fa-hsu 孫發緒
Sun T'ien-sheng 孫天生
Sun To-yü 孫多鈺
Sun Tse-p'ei 孫澤沛

Ta-Ch'ing-kuo 大清國
T'ai-hsing 泰興
T'ang Hsiang-ming 湯薌銘
T'ang Tsai-li 唐在禮
tao 道
tao-yin 道尹
Teng Hsiao-k'o 鄧孝可
T'ien-an men 天安門
t'ien-hsia wei-kung 天下爲公
ti-fang pao-wei t'uan 地方保衛團
Ting 定
Tong King Sing (T'ang T'ing-shu) 唐景星 (唐廷樞)
ts'ai-cheng t'ing 財政廳
ts'an-cheng-yuan 參政院
ts'an-i-yuan 參議院
Tsung-she tang 宗社黨

tsun-yen 尊嚴
Tuan Chih-kuei 段芝貴
t'uan-lien 團練
tu-chün 都軍
T'ung-i tang 統一黨
T'ung-meng hui 同盟會
T'ung-wen kuan 同文館
tu-tu 都督
tzu-li 自立

Uchida Ryōhei 內田良平

Wang Chan-yuan 王占元
Wang Cheng-t'ing 王正廷
Wang Chih-hsiang 王芝祥
Wang Chih-hsing 王治馨
Wang Jui-k'ai 汪瑞闓
Wen Tsung-yao 溫宗堯
Wu Ping-hsiang 吳炳湘
Wu Ta-chou 吳大洲
Wu T'ing-fang 伍廷芳
wu hsiu-ts'ai 武秀才
Wu-pei hsueh-t'ang 武備學堂

Yamaza Enjirō 山座圓次郎
Yang Wei (Yang Hsin-yeh) 楊維 (楊莘野)
Yeh 葉
Yen Fu 嚴復
Yin-ch'ang 廕昌
ying 營
Ying Kuei-hsing 應桂馨
Yuan K'o-ting 袁克定
Yuan ta-t'ou 袁大頭

Works Cited

Archival and Manuscript Sources

China, Ministry of Foreign Affairs, Archives, Institute of Modern History, Academia Sinica, Nankang, Taiwan.

Goodnow, Frank Johnson, private papers (14,600 items), Eisenhower Library, Johns Hopkins University, Baltimore, Maryland. (Cited as Goodnow Collection.)

Great Britain, Foreign Office, Archives, Public Record Office, London (including the papers of Sir John Jordan). (Cited as FO.)

Japan, Ministry of Foreign Affairs, Archives at the Gaikō Shiryōkan, Tokyo (cited as Gaimushō), and microfilm at the Library of Congress, Washington, D.C. (cited as Japan MFA film).

Kuomintang, Archives, Ts'ao-t'un, Taiwan (consulted for its collection of early republican periodicals).

Morrison, George Ernest, private papers (uncataloged), Mitchell Library, Sydney, New South Wales. (Cited as MP.)

Rockhill, William W., private papers (3,000 items), Houghton Library, Harvard University, Cambridge, Massachusetts.

Terauchi Masatake, private papers (3,395 items), Kensei Shiryōshitsu, Diet Library, Tokyo.

United States, Department of State, Archives, National Archives, Washington, D.C. (Cited as NA.)

Published Sources

Adshead, S. A. M. *The Modernization of the Chinese Salt Administration, 1900–1920*. Cambridge, Mass.: Harvard University Press, 1970.

Agee, Philip. *Inside the Company: CIA Diary*. Harmondsworth: Penguin Books, 1975.

Almond, Gabriel A., and Coleman, James S., eds. *The Politics of the Developing Areas*. Princeton: Princeton University Press, 1960.

Altman, Albert A., and Schiffrin, Harold Z. "Sun Yat-sen and the Japanese: 1914–16," *Modern Asian Studies* 6.4: 385–400 (October 1972).

Bailie, Victoria Worley. *Bailie's Activities in China: An Account of the Life and Work of Professor Joseph Bailie in and for China—1890–1935*. Palo Alto: Pacific Books, 1964.

Banzai Rihachirō 坂西利八郎. *Rinpō o kataru* 隣邦を語る [Talks on China]. Tokyo, 1933.

Barclay, George W. *Colonial Development and Population in Taiwan*. Princeton: Princeton University Press, 1954.

Bastid, Marianne. *Aspects de la réforme de l'enseignement en Chine au début du XXe siècle: d'après de Zhang Jian*. Paris: Mouton, 1971.

Bays, Daniel Henry. "Chang Chih-tung and the Politics of Reform in China, 1895–1905." Ph.D. dissertation, University of Michigan, 1971.

Bergère, Marie-Claire. "The Role of the Bourgeoisie," in Mary Clabaugh Wright, ed., *China in Revolution: The First Phase, 1900–1913*. New Haven: Yale University Press, 1968.

Bernal, Martin. "Chinese Socialism to 1913." Ph.D. dissertation, University of Cambridge, 1966.

Boorman, Howard L., ed. *Biographical Dictionary of Republican China*. 4 vols. New York: Columbia University Press, 1967–71.

Borst-Smith, Ernest F. *Caught in the Chinese Revolution: A Record of Risks and Rescue*. London: T. F. Unwin, 1912.

———. *Mandarin and Missionary in Cathay*. London: Seeley, Service and Co., 1917.

Bose, Sudhindra. "Remarks on President Goodnow's Paper," *American Political Science Review* 9.2: 224–26 (May 1915).

Britton, Roswell S. *The Chinese Periodical Press, 1800–1912*. Shanghai, 1933.

Buck, J. L. *Land Utilization in China*. Shanghai, 1937.

Carlson, C. Ellsworth. *The Kaiping Mines (1877–1912)*. Cambridge, Mass.: Harvard University Press, 1957.

Chan, K. C. "British Policy in the Reorganization Loan to China, 1912–13," *Modern Asian Studies* 5.4: 355–72 (October 1971).

Chang Ching-lu 張靜廬. *Chung-kuo chin-tai ch'u-pan shih-liao ch'u-pien* 中國近代出版史料初編 [The first volume of historical materials on modern Chinese publishing]. Peking, 1957.

Chang, Chung-li. *The Chinese Gentry: Studies on Their Role in Nineteenth-Century Chinese Society*. Seattle: University of Washington Press, 1955.

Chang, Hao. *Liang Ch'i-ch'ao and Intellectual Transition in China, 1890–1907*. Cambridge, Mass.: Harvard University Press, 1971.

Chang I-lin 張一䴊. *Hsin-t'ai-p'ing-shih chi* 心太平室集 [Collection of Chang I-lin's works]. Reprinted in *Chin-tai Chung-kuo shih-liao ts'ung-k'an* 近代中國史料叢刊 [Library of historical materials on modern China], Shen Yun-lung 沈雲龍, ed., 1st ser., vol. 8. Taipei: Wen-hai ch'u-pan she, n.d.

Chang Kuo-kan 張國淦. *Hsin-hai ko-ming shih-liao* 辛亥革命史料 [Historical sources of the 1911 Revolution]. Shanghai, 1958.

Chang P'eng-yuan 張朋園. *Li-hsien-p'ai yü hsin-hai ko-ming* 立憲派與辛亥革命 [Constitutionalists and the Revolution of 1911 in China]. Taipei, 1969.

———. "Wei-hu kung-ho—Liang Ch'i-ch'ao chih lien-Yuan yü t'ao-Yuan" 維護共和～梁啓超之聯袁與討袁 [Guarding the republic—Liang Ch'i-ch'ao's allying with Yuan and opposing him], *Chung-yang yen-chiu-yuan chin-tai-shih yen-chiu-so chi-k'an* 中央研究院近代史研究所集刊, vol. 3, pt. 2 (December 1972), pp. 377–96.

Chao Ch'in 趙親. "Hsin-hai ko-ming ch'ien-hou ti Chung-kuo kung-jen yun-tung" 辛亥革命前後的中國工人運動 [The Chinese labor movement in the period of the 1911 Revolution], *Li-shih yen-chiu* 歷史研究, 1959, no. 2, pp. 1–16.

Che-chiang ch'ao 浙江潮 [Tides of Chekiang]. Tokyo, 1903.

Ch'en, Jerome. "Defining Chinese Warlords and their Factions," *Bulletin of the School of Oriental and African Studies, University of London* 31.3: 563–600 (1968).

———. *Yuan Shih-k'ai*. 2d ed. Stanford: Stanford University Press, 1972.

Ch'en T'ien-hua 陳天華. "Chin-jih ch'i fen-sheng-chieh chih jih yeh" 今日豈分省界之日耶 [Is this the time for provincial divisions?], *Min pao* 民報 1: 119–20 (November 1905).

Ch'en Tu-hsiu 陳獨秀. "Chiu-ssu-hsiang yü kuo-t'i wen-t'i" 舊思想與國體問題 [Old thought and the problem of the national polity], *Hsin-ch'ing-nien* 新青年 (December 14, 1917), Daian edition 3: 207–9.

Cheng, Jane, and Chesneaux, Jean. "Chronologie Politique de la Chine Contemporaine: Période 1911–1919." Manuscript.

Cheng-fu kung-pao 政府公報 [Government gazette]. Peking, 1912–28. Reprint ed., 1912–16, Taipei: Wen-hai ch'u-pan she, n.d. (Cited as CFKP.)

Chesneaux, Jean. "Secret Societies in China's Historical Evolution," in Jean Chesneaux, ed., *Popular Movements and Secret Societies in China, 1840–1950*. Stanford: Stanford University Press, 1972.

Chi, Madeleine. *China Diplomacy, 1914–1918*. Cambridge, Mass.: Harvard University Press, 1970.

Chia Shih-i 賈士毅. *Min-kuo ch'u-nien ti chi-jen ts'ai-cheng tsung-chang* 民國初年的幾任財政總長 [Several finance ministers in the first years of the republic]. Taipei, 1967.

———. *Min-kuo ts'ai-cheng shih* 民國財政史 [History of public finance under the republic]. 2 vols. Shanghai, 1917.

Chin Ch'ung-chi 金冲及. "Yun-nan hu-kuo yun-tung ti chen-cheng fa-tung-che shih shei?" 雲南護國運動的眞正發動者是誰 [Who was the true initiator of the Yunnan National Protection movement?], in *Chin-20-nien Chung-kuo shih-hsueh lun-wen hui-pien, ch'u-pien: hsin-hai ko-ming yen-chiu lun-chi ti-i-chi (1895–1929)* 近廿年中國史學論文彙編初編：辛亥革命研究論集第一集 [First collection of Chinese historical articles of the last 20 years: first volume of studies on the 1911 Revolution (1895–1929)], Chou K'ang-hsieh 周康燮 et al., eds. Hongkong, 1971, pp. 261–86.

Chin Ch'ung-chi and Hu Sheng-wu. "Huang Hsing: Co-founder of the

Republic of China," in Hsueh Chün-tu, ed., *Revolutionary Leaders of Modern China*. New York: Oxford University Press, 1971.

China, Maritime Customs. *Returns of Trade and Trade Reports*. 1912, vol. 4, pt. 2.

China Year Book, The. 1913, 1914, and 1916. London: George Routledge and Sons.

Chinese Ministry of Education, Statistical Office (Chiao-yü-pu t'ung-chi-shih 教育部統計室), eds. *Ch'üan-kuo chiao-yü t'ung-chi chien-pien* 全國教育統計簡編 [Abridged edition of statistics on the nation's education]. Nanking, 1935.

Chinese National Association for the Advancement of Education. *Bulletins on Chinese Education, 1923*. Shanghai, 1923.

Chin-tai-shih tzu-liao 近代史資料 [Material on modern history], comp. Chung-kuo k'o-hsueh-yuan chin-tai-shih yen-chiu-so chin-tai-shih tzu-liao pien-chi tsu 中國科學院近代史研究所近代史資料編輯組 [The group for compiling materials on modern history in the institute of modern history of the Chinese academy of sciences]. Series. Peking, 1954–66. (Cited as CTSTL.)

Chou Hsun 周詢. *Shu-hai ts'ung-t'an* 蜀海叢談 [Miscellaneous remarks about the Szechwan region]. Reprinted in *Chin-tai Chung-kuo shih-liao ts'ung-k'an*, Shen Yun-lung, ed., 1st ser., vol. 7. Taipei: Wen-hai ch'u-pan she, n.d.

Chow Tse-tsung. "Anti-Confucianism in Early Republican China," in Arthur F. Wright, ed., *The Confucian Persuasion*. Stanford: Stanford University Press, 1960.

Chung-hua min-pao 中華民報 [People's newspaper of China]. Shanghai, 1912.

Chung-kuo T'ung-meng hui [*Yueh chih-pu*] *tsa-chih* 中國同盟會 [粵支部] 雜誌 [Magazine of [the Kwangtung branch of] the T'ung-meng hui]. Canton, 1912.

Couling, Samuel. *The Encyclopaedia Sinica*. Shanghai, 1917.

de Francis, John. *Nationalism and Language Reform in China*. Princeton: Princeton University Press, 1950.

Des Forges, Roger V. *Hsi-liang and the Chinese Revolution*. New Haven: Yale University Press, 1973.

Deutsch, Karl W. *Nationalism and Social Communication: An Inquiry into the Foundations of Nationality*. New York: Wiley, 1953.

Eastman, Lloyd E. *The Abortive Revolution: China under Nationalist Rule*. Cambridge, Mass.: Harvard University Press, 1974.

———. *Throne and Mandarins: China's Search for a Policy during the Sino-French Controversy, 1880–1885*. Cambridge, Mass.: Harvard University Press, 1967.

Elvin, Mark. "The Administration of Shanghai, 1905–1914," in Mark Elvin and G. William Skinner, eds., *The Chinese City between Two Worlds*. Stanford: Stanford University Press, 1974.

———. "The Gentry Democracy in Chinese Shanghai, 1905–14," in Jack

Gray, ed., *Modern China's Search for a Political Form*. London: Oxford University Press, 1969.

———. "The Gentry Democracy in Shanghai, 1905–1914." Ph.D. dissertation, University of Cambridge, 1967.

———. "The Last Thousand Years of Chinese History: Changing Patterns in Land Tenure," *Modern Asian Studies* 4.2: 97–114 (April 1970).

———. "The Mixed Court of the International Settlement at Shanghai (until 1911)," *Papers on China*, 17: 131–59. Harvard University, East Asian Research Center, 1963.

Esherick, Joseph W. "Reform, Revolution and Reaction: The 1911 Revolution in Hunan and Hupeh." Ph.D. dissertation, University of California at Berkeley, 1971.

Fang Tu Lien-che 房杜聯喆. "Ching-chi t'e-k'o" 經濟特科 [Special examination in economics], in *Chung-kuo hsien-tai shih ts'ung-k'an* 中國現代史叢刊 [Library on modern Chinese history], Wu Hsiang-hsiang 吳相湘, ed., vol. 3. Taipei, 1961.

Fei Hsing-chien 費行簡 (pseud. Wo-chiu chung-tzu 沃丘仲子). *Tuan Ch'i-jui* 段祺瑞 [Tuan Ch'i-jui]. Shanghai, 1921.

Feng Tzu-yu 馮自由. *Ko-ming i-shih* 革命逸史 [Fragments of revolutionary history]. 2 vols. Taipei, 1953.

Feng Yü-hsiang 馮玉祥. *Wo ti sheng-huo* 我的生活 [My life]. Chungking, 1944.

Feuerwerker, Albert. *The Chinese Economy, 1912–1949*. Ann Arbor: Center for Chinese Studies, University of Michigan, 1968.

———. *The Chinese Economy, ca. 1870–1911*. Ann Arbor: Center for Chinese Studies, University of Michigan, 1969.

———. "Industrial Enterprise in Twentieth-Century China: The Chee Hsin Cement Co." in Albert Feuerwerker, Rhoads Murphey, and Mary C. Wright, eds., *Approaches to Modern Chinese History*. Berkeley and Los Angeles: University of California Press, 1967.

Fincher, John Howard. "The Chinese Self-Government Movement, 1900–1912." Ph.D. dissertation, University of Washington, 1969.

———. "Political Provincialism and the National Revolution," in Mary Clabaugh Wright, *China in Revolution: The First Phase, 1900–1913*. New Haven: Yale University Press, 1968.

Folsom, Kenneth E. *Friends, Guests, and Colleagues: The Mu-fu System in the Late Ch'ing Period*. Berkeley and Los Angeles: University of California Press, 1968.

Friedman, Edward. *Backward Toward Revolution: The Chinese Revolutionary Party*. Berkeley: University of California Press, 1974.

———. "The Center Cannot Hold: The Failure of Parliamentary Democracy in China from the Chinese Revolution of 1911 to the World War in 1914." Ph.D. dissertation, Harvard University, 1968.

———. "Revolution or Just Another Bloody Cycle? Swatow and the 1911 Revolution," *Journal of Asian Studies* 29.2: 289–307 (February 1970).

Gaikō jihō 外交時報 [Diplomatic review]. Tokyo, 1904–20.

Gaimushō jōhōbu 外務省情報部 [Information Division, Ministry of Foreign Affairs], ed., *Gendai Shina jinmeikan* 現代支那人名鑑 [Biographical dictionary of contemporary China]. Tokyo, 1925.

Gaimushō seimukyoku 外務省政務局 [Political Affairs Bureau, Ministry of Foreign Affairs]. "Gendai Shina jinmeikan" 現代支那人名鑑 [Biographical dictionary of contemporary China], on microfilm of the archives of the Japanese Ministry of Foreign Affairs, SP 47, reel SP 10, Library of Congress, Washington, D.C.

Gamble, Sidney D. *North China Villages: Social, Political and Economic Activities before 1933*. Berkeley: University of California Press, 1963.

Garrett, Shirley S. "The Chambers of Commerce and the YMCA," in Mark Elvin and G. William Skinner, eds., *The Chinese City Between Two Worlds*. Stanford: Stanford University Press, 1974.

Gillin, Donald G. "Problems of Centralization in Republican China: The Case of Ch'en Ch'eng and the Kuomintang," *Journal of Asian Studies* 29.4: 835–50 (August 1970).

———. *Warlord: Yen Hsi-shan in Shansi Province, 1911–1949*. Princeton: Princeton University Press, 1967.

Goodnow, Frank Johnson. "The Parliament of the Republic of China," *American Political Science Review* 8.4: 541–62 (November 1914).

———. "Reform in China," *American Political Science Review* 9.2: 209–24 (May 1915).

Goulet, Denis, and Hudson, Michael. *The Myth of Aid: The Hidden Agenda of the Development Reports*. New York: IDOC North America, 1971.

Han Kuo-chün 韓國鈞. *Chih-sou nien-p'u* 止叟年譜 and *Yung-i lu* 永憶錄. Reprinted in *Chin-tai Chung-kuo shih-liao ts'ung-k'an*, Shen Yun-lung, ed., 1st ser., vol. 9. Taipei: Wen-hai ch'u-pan she, n.d.

Harding, Gardner Ludwig. *Present-Day China: A Narrative of a Nation's Advance*. New York: The Century Co., 1916.

Hatano Yoshihiro. "The New Armies," in Mary Clabaugh Wright, ed., *China in Revolution: The First Phase, 1900–1913*. New Haven: Yale University Press, 1968.

Hayter, Teresa. *Aid as Imperialism*. Harmondsworth: Penguin Books, 1971.

Hedtke, Charles Herman. "Reluctant Revolutionaries: Szechwan and the Ch'ing Collapse, 1898–1911." Ph.D. dissertation, University of California at Berkeley, 1968.

Hiratsuka Masunori 平塚益德. *Kindai Shina kyōiku bunka shi* 近代支那教育文化史 [A history of modern Chinese education and culture]. Tokyo, 1942.

Ho, Ping-ti. *Studies on the Population of China, 1368–1953*. Cambridge, Mass.: Harvard University Press, 1959.

Holmberg, Anna. "Ko Lao Hui Participation in the Revolution of 1911—Shensi Province." Master's thesis, Center for Chinese Studies, University of Michigan, 1969.

Horikawa Takeo 堀川武夫. *Kyokutō kokusai seijishi josetsu—nijūikkajō yōkyū no kenkyū* 極東國際政治史序說～二十一箇條要求の研究 [An introduction to the history of Far Eastern international politics—a study of the Twenty-One Demands]. Tokyo, 1958.

Houn, Franklin W. *Central Government of China, 1912–1928: An Institutional Study.* Madison: University of Wisconsin Press, 1957.

Hsiao, Kung-ch'üan. "Administrative Modernization: K'ang Yu-wei's Proposals and Their Historical Meaning," *Tsing Hua Journal of Chinese Studies*, n.s. 8.1–2: 1–35 (August 1970).

Hsieh, Winston. "Triads, Salt Smugglers, and Local Uprisings: Observations on the Social and Economic Background of the Waichow Revolution of 1911," in Jean Chesneaux, ed., *Popular Movements and Secret Societies in China, 1840–1950.* Stanford: Stanford University Press, 1972.

Hsin-hai ko-ming 辛亥革命 [The 1911 Revolution], comp. Chung-kuo shih-hsueh hui 中國史學會 [Chinese historical association]. 8 vols. Shanghai, 1957.

Hsin-hai ko-ming hui-i-lu 辛亥革命回憶錄 [Memoirs of the 1911 Revolution], ed. Chung-kuo jen-min cheng-chih hsieh-shang hui-i ch'üan-kuo wei-yuan-hui wen-shih tzu-liao yen-chiu wei-yuan-hui 中國人民政治協商會議全國委員會文史資料研究委員會 [Committee on written historical materials of the national committee of the Chinese people's political consultative conference]. 5 vols. Peking, 1961–63. (Cited as HHKMHIL.)

Hsin-hai ko-ming tzu-liao 辛亥革命資料 [Materials on the 1911 Revolution], ed. Chung-kuo k'o-hsueh-yuan chin-tai-shih yen-chiu-so 中國科學院近代史研究所 [Institute of modern history of the Chinese academy of sciences]. Peking, 1961.

Hsin-min ts'ung-pao 新民叢報 [Renovation of the people]. Yokohama, 1902–8.

Hsu Tao-lin 徐道鄰. *Hsu Shu-cheng hsien-sheng wen-chi nien-p'u ho-k'an* 徐樹錚先生文集年譜合刊 [Collected writings and chronological biography of Hsu Shu-cheng, published in one volume]. Taipei, 1962.

Hsueh, Chün-tu. *Huang Hsing and the Chinese Revolution.* Stanford: Stanford University Press, 1961.

Hsueh-pu tsung-wu-ssu 學部總務司 [General affairs department of the ministry of education], eds., *Kuang-hsu san-shih-san nien-fen: ti-i-tz'u chiao-yü t'ung-chi t'u-piao* 光緒三十三年分: 第一次教育統計圖表 [For the year 1907: first statistical tables on education]. Taipei reprint, 1973.

Hu Han-min 胡漢民 (using pen name Min-i 民意). "Cheng-chien chih shang-ch'üan" 政見之商榷 [A discussion of political views], *Min-i tsa-chih* 民誼雜誌 [People's righteousness magazine], no. 1 (November 15, 1912).

Hu Ying-han 胡應漢. *Wu Hsien-tzu hsien-sheng chuan-chi* 伍憲子先生傳記 [Biography of Wu Hsien-tzu]. Hongkong, 1953.

Huang Chi-lu 黃季陸, ed. *Hu-kuo chün chi-shih* 護國軍紀事 [Records of the National Protection Army]. 4 vols. Taipei reprint, 1970.

Huang Yuan-yung 黃遠庸. *Yuan-sheng i-chu* 遠生遺著 [Posthumous collection of writings of Huang Yuan-yung]. 2 vols. Reprinted in *Chung-kuo hsien-tai shih-liao ts'ung-shu* 中國現代史料叢書 [Library of Chinese contemporary materials], ed. Wu Hsiang-hsiang 吳相湘, 1st ser. Taipei, 1962.

Hummel, Arthur W., ed. *Eminent Chinese of the Ch'ing Period (1644–1912)*. 2 vols. Washington, D.C.: United States Government Printing Office, 1943.

Hunan gazetteer compilation committee (Hu-nan sheng-chih pien-tsuan wei-yuan-hui 湖南省志編纂委員會), eds. *Hu-nan chin-pai-nien ta-shih chi-shu* 湖南近百年大事紀述 [Accounts of major events in Hunan over the last 100 years]. Changsha, 1959.

Hunan historical materials editorial committee (Hu-nan li-shih tzu-liao pien-chi wei-yuan-hui 湖南歷史資料編輯委員會), eds. *Hu-nan li-shih tzu-liao* 湖南歷史資料 [Materials on the history of Hunan]. Changsha, 1960.

Hunt, Michael H. *Frontier Defense and the Open Door: Manchuria in Chinese-American Relations, 1895–1911*. New Haven: Yale University Press, 1973.

Ichiko Chūzō 市古宙三. "The Role of the Gentry: An Hypothesis," in Mary Clabaugh Wright, ed., *China in Revolution: The First Phase, 1900–1913*. New Haven: Yale University Press, 1968.

―――. "Shisen horo undō no shunōbu" 四川保路運動の首脳部 [On the leaders of the railway protection movement in Szechwan], *Ochanomizu Joshi Daigaku jimbun kagaku kiyō* お茶の水女子大學人文科學紀要 6: 161–73 (March 1955).

Ikeda Yuji. "Sun Yat-sen's Pan-Asianism and Nationalism, Late 1913 through 1914." Seminar paper, Harvard University, 1963.

Ikei Masaru 池井優. *Nihon gaikōshi gaisetsu* 日本外交史概說 [A survey of Japanese diplomatic history]. Tokyo, 1973.

I-ming 佚名. *Yuan Shih-k'ai ch'üan-chuan* 袁世凱全傳 [Complete biography of Yuan Shih-k'ai]. Reprinted in *Yuan Shih-k'ai shih-liao hui-k'an hsu-pien* 袁世凱史料彙刊續編 [Supplement to the serial publication of historical materials on Yuan Shih-k'ai], ed. Shen Yun-lung 沈雲龍, vol. 7. Taipei: Wen-hai ch'u-pan she, n.d.

Ishikawa Tadao 石川忠雄. "Shinmatsu oyobi minkoku shonen ni okeru renpō-ron to shōsei-ron" 清末及び民國初年における聯邦論と省制論 [Theories of federalism and the provincial system at the end of the Ch'ing and in the early republic], *Hōgaku kenkyū* 法學研究 24.9–10: 129–59 (September–October 1951).

Jansen, Marius B. *The Japanese and Sun Yat-sen*. Cambridge, Mass.: Harvard University Press, 1954.

Johnson, William R. "China's 1911 Revolution in the Provinces of Yunnan and Kweichow." Ph.D. dissertation, University of Washington, 1962.

Johnston, Reginald F. *Twilight in the Forbidden City*. London: Victor Gollancz, 1934.

K'ai-kuo kuei-mo 開國規模 [Patterns in the inauguration of the republic], ed. Committee on the compilation of documents on the fiftieth anniversary of the founding of the Republic of China (Chung-hua min-kuo k'ai-kuo wu-shih-nien wen-hsien pien-tsuan wei-yuan-hui 中華民國開國五十年文獻編纂委員會). Taipei, 1962.

Kamachi, Noriko. "Huang Tsun-hsien (1848–1905): His Response to Meiji Japan and the West." Ph.D. dissertation, Harvard University, 1972.

Kamachi (Tamada), Noriko. "Sung Chiao-jen and the 1911 Revolution," *Papers on China* 21: 184–229. Harvard University, East Asian Research Center, 1968.

K'ang Yu-wei 康有爲. "Fei-sheng lun" 廢省論 [On abolishing the provinces], in *Min-kuo ching-shih wen-pien* 民國經世文編 [Republican essays on public affairs], vol. 2, pp. 509–22. Reprinted in *Chung-kuo hsien-tai shih-liao ts'ung-shu* [Library of Chinese contemporary materials], ed. Wu Hsiang-hsiang. 1st ser. Taipei, 1962.

Keyte, J. C. *The Passing of the Dragon*. London: Cary Press, 1925.

Kikuchi Takaharu 菊池貴晴. *Chūgoku minzoku undō no kihon kōzō—taigai boikotto no kenkyū* 中國民族運動の基本構造～對外ボイコットの研究 [Basic structure of the Chinese national movement: a study of antiforeign boycotts]. Tokyo, 1966.

Kita Ikki 北一輝. *Shina kakumei gaishi* 支那革命外史 [An unofficial history of the Chinese revolution]. Reprinted in *Kita Ikki chosaku shū* 北一輝著作集 [Collected works of Kita Ikki]. Tokyo, 1959.

Kokuryūkai 黑龍會 [Amur River society], ed. *Tōa senkaku shishi kiden* 東亞先覺志士記傳 [Annals and biographies of pioneer patriots in East Asia]. 3 vols. Tokyo, 1933–36.

Ko-ming hsien-lieh hsien-chin chuan 革命先烈先進傳 [Biographies of martyrs and forerunners of the revolution], comp. Chinese Kuomintang, central committee for the compilation of materials on party history (Chung-kuo Kuo-min-tang chung-yang tang-shih shih-liao pien-tsuan wei-yuan-hui 中國國民黨中央黨史史料編纂委員會). Taipei, 1965.

Ko-ming jen-wu chih 革命人物誌 [Chronicles of revolutionary personalities], eds. Huang Chi-lu 黃季陸 et al. 10 vols. Taipei, 1969–72.

Ko-ming wen-hsien 革命文獻 [Documents of the revolution], comp. Chinese Kuomintang, central executive committee, committee for the compilation of materials on party history (Chung-kuo Kuo-min-tang chung-yang wei-yuan-huî, tang-shih shih-liao pien-tsuan wei-yuan-hui 中國國民黨中央委員會黨史史料編纂委員會). Series. Taipei, 1953–.

Ko-sheng kuang-fu 各省光復 [Restoration in the various provinces], ed. Committee on the compilation of documents on the fiftieth anniversary of the founding of the Republic of China. 3 vols. Taipei, 1962.

Kotenev, Anatol M. *New Lamps for Old: An Interpretation of Events in Modern China and Whither They Lead*. Shanghai, 1931.

———. *Shanghai: Its Mixed Court and Council*. Shanghai, 1925.

Kuhn, Philip A. "Local Self-Government under the Republic: Problems of Control, Autonomy, and Mobilization," in Frederic Wakeman, Jr., and Carolyn Grant, eds., *Conflict and Control in Late Imperial China*. Berkeley: University of California Press, 1975.

———. *Rebellion and Its Enemies in Late Imperial China: Militarization and Social Structure, 1796–1864*. Cambridge, Mass.: Harvard University Press, 1970.

Kung-ho yen-lun pao 共和言論報 [Journal of republican opinion]. Shanghai, 1912.

Kuo, Ping Wen. *The Chinese System of Public Education*. New York: Teachers College, Columbia University, 1915.

Kuo-fang yen-chiu-yuan 國防研究院 [National defense academy], ed. *Kuo-fu ch'üan-shu* 國父全書 [Complete works of Sun Yat-sen]. Taipei, 1960.

Kuo-hui ts'ung-pao 國會叢報 [Journal of the national assembly]. Peking, 1913.

Kuo-min yueh-k'an 國民月刊 [Citizen's monthly]. Shanghai, 1913.

Kupper, Samuel Yale. "Revolution in China: Kiangsi Province, 1905–1913." Ph.D. dissertation, University of Michigan, 1972.

Kwok, D. W. Y. *Scientism in Chinese Thought, 1900–1950*. New Haven: Yale University Press, 1965.

Lamb, Alastair. *The McMahon Line: A Study in the Relations between India, China and Tibet, 1904 to 1914*. 2 vols. London: Routledge and Kegan Paul, 1966.

Lary, Diana. *Region and Nation: The Kwangsi Clique in Chinese Politics, 1925–1937*. London: Cambridge University Press, 1974.

Lattimore, Owen. *Nationalism and Revolution in Mongolia*. Leiden: E. J. Brill, 1955.

Lee En-han. "China's Response to Foreign Investment in Her Mining Industry (1902–1911)," *Journal of Asian Studies* 28.1: 55–76 (November 1968).

Levenson, Joseph R. "The Province, the Nation, and the World: The Problem of Chinese Identity," in Albert Feuerwerker, Rhoads Murphy, and Mary C. Wright, eds., *Approaches to Modern Chinese History*. Berkeley and Los Angeles: University of California Press, 1967.

Lewis, Charlton Miner, III. "The Opening of Hunan: Reform and Revolution in a Chinese Province, 1895–1907." Ph.D. dissertation, University of California, 1965.

Li Ken-yuan 李根源. *Hsueh-sheng nien-lu* 雪生年錄 [Annual record of Li Ken-yuan]. Reprinted in *Chin-tai Chung-kuo shih-liao ts'ung-k'an*, ed. Shen Yun-lung, 2d ser., vol. 15. Taipei: Wen-hai ch'u-pan she, n.d.

Li Lieh-chün 李烈鈞. *Li Lieh-chün chiang-chün tzu-chuan* 李烈鈞將軍自傳 [Autobiography of General Li Lieh-chün]. Chungking, 1944.

Li Shih-yueh 李時岳. *Hsin-hai ko-ming shih-ch'i liang-hu ti-ch'ü ti ko-ming yung-tung* 辛亥革命時期兩湖地區的革命運動 [The revolutionary movement in the Hunan and Hupeh region in the period of the 1911 Revolution]. Peking, 1957.

Li Shou-k'ung 李守孔. *Min-ch'u chih kuo-hui* 民初之國會 [National assemblies in the early republic]. Taipei, 1964.

Li Ta-chao 李大釗. "Ts'ai tu-tu heng-i" 裁都督橫議 [A peevish discussion on behalf of doing away with the military governors], *Yen-chih* 言治 [Statesman] 3: 1–12 (July 1, 1913).

Li Yun-han 李雲漢. "Huang K'o-ch'iang hsien-sheng nien-p'u kao" 黃克強先生年譜稿 [Draft chronological biography of Huang Hsing], in *Chung-kuo hsien-tai shih ts'ung-k'an*, ed. Wu Hsiang-hsiang. Vol. 4. Taipei, 1962.

Li Yü-shu 李毓澍. *Chung-Jih erh-shih-i-t'iao chiao-she* 中日二十一條交涉

[Sino-Japanese negotiations over the Twenty-One Demands]. Vol. 1. Taipei, 1966.

———. *Wai-Meng-ku ch'e-chih wen-t'i* 外蒙古撤治問題 [The question of the administrative separation of outer Mongolia]. Taipei, 1961.

Liang Ch'i-ch'ao. *Yin-ping-shih wen-chi: see Yin-ping-shih wen-chi.*

Liang Yü-k'uei 梁玉魁. "Kuan-yü Chung-hua min-kuo kung-tang ti hsing-chih wen-t'i" 關于中華民國工黨的性質問題 [The problem of the character of the Labor Party of the Republic of China], *Li-shih yen-chiu*, 1959, no. 6, pp. 73–78.

Liew, K. S. *Struggle for Democracy: Sung Chiao-jen and the 1911 Chinese Revolution.* Berkeley: University of California Press, 1971.

Lin Ming-te 林明德. *Yuan Shih-k'ai yü Chao-hsien* 袁世凱與朝鮮 [Yuan Shih-k'ai and Korea]. Taipei, 1970.

Liu Feng-han 劉鳳翰. *Hsin-chien lu-chün* 新建陸軍 [The newly created army]. Taipei, 1967.

Liu Kwang-ching. "The Limits of Regional Power in the Late Ch'ing Period: A Reappraisal," *Tsing Hua Journal of Chinese Studies*, n.s. 10.2: 176–223 (July 1974).

Liu Ta-wu 劉達武, ed. *Ts'ai Sung-p'o hsien-sheng i-chi* 蔡松坡先生遺集 [Posthumously collected works of Ts'ai O]. Reprinted in *Chung-kuo hsien-tai shih-liao ts'ung-shu*, ed. Wu Hsiang-hsiang, 1st ser. Taipei, 1962.

Liu Ts'un-hou 劉存厚. *Hu-kuo Ch'uan-chün chan-chi* 護國川軍戰記 [Record of the battles of the Szechwan National Protection Army]. Taipei, 1966.

Lo, Jung-pang, ed. *K'ang Yu-wei: A Biography and a Symposium.* Tucson: University of Arizona Press, 1967.

Lo, Pichon P. Y. *The Early Chiang Kai-shek: A Study of his Personality and Politics, 1887–1924.* New York: Columbia University Press, 1971.

Lowe, Peter. *Great Britain and Japan, 1911–15: A Study of British Far Eastern Policy.* London: Macmillan, 1969.

Lust, John. "Secret Societies, Popular Movements, and the 1911 Revolution," in *Popular Movements and Secret Societies in China, 1840–1950*, ed. Jean Chesneaux. Stanford: Stanford University Press, 1972.

MacKinnon, Stephen Robert. "Liang Shih-i and the Communications Clique," *Journal of Asian Studies* 29.3: 581–602 (May 1970).

———. "Yüan Shih-k'ai in Tientsin and Peking: The Sources and Structure of His Power, 1901–1908." Ph.D. dissertation, University of California at Davis, 1971.

Mao Tse-tung. *Selected Works of Mao Tse-tung.* 4 vols. Peking, 1965.

Marr, David G. *Vietnamese Anticolonialism, 1888–1925.* Berkeley, Los Angeles and London: University of California Press, 1971.

Maybon, Albert. *La République Chinoise.* Paris: Librairie Armand Colin, 1914.

———. "La Situation Dans les Provinces Chinoises Voisines du Tonkin," *L'Asie Française* 154: 9–14 (January 1914).

Mehra, Parshotam. *The McMahon Line and After: A Study of the Triangular*

Contest on India's North-Eastern Frontier between Britain, China and Tibet, 1904–47. Delhi: Macmillan, 1974.

Mikesell, Raymond F. *The Economics of Foreign Aid.* Chicago Aldine Publishing, 1968.

Min-ch'üan pao 民權報 [People's rights newspaper]. Shanghai, 1912.

Min-i tsa-chih 民誼雜誌 [People's righteousness magazine]. Canton, 1912–13.

Min-kuo ching-shih wen-pien 民國經世文編 [Republican essays on public affairs]. 4 vols. Reprinted in *Chung-kuo hsien-tai shih-liao ts'ung-shu,* ed. Wu Hsiang-hsiang, 1st ser. Taipei, 1962.

Min-li pao 民立報 [Independent people's newspaper]. Shanghai, 1910–13.

Morrison, Esther. "The Modernization of the Confucian Bureaucracy: An Historical Study of Public Administration." Ph.D. dissertation, Radcliffe College, 1959.

Nakajima Masao 中島眞雄 et al., eds. *TaiShi kaiko roku* 對支回顧錄 [Memoirs about China]. 2 vols. Tokyo, 1936.

———. *Zoku taiShi kaiko roku* 續對支回顧錄 [Supplementary volumes of memoirs about China]. 2 vols. Tokyo, 1941–42.

Nara Kazuo 奈良一雄. *Chūka minkoku daijiken to En Seigai* 中華民國大事件と袁世凱 [The great event of the Republic of China and Yuan Shih-k'ai]. Tientsin, 1915.

Nathan, Andrew James. "Factionalism in Early Republican China: The Politics of the Peking Government, 1918–20." Ph.D. dissertation, Harvard University, 1970.

National Review. Shanghai, 1910–16.

Nihon gaikō bunsho 日本外交文書 [Documents on Japan's diplomacy], comp. Gaimushō 外務省 [Ministry of foreign affairs]. Series. Tokyo, 1936–.

Nishikawa Masao 西川正夫. "Shisen horo undō—sono zen'ya no shakai jōkyō—" 四川保路運動〜その前夜の社會狀況 [Social conditions on the eve of the Szechwan railway protection movement], *Tōyō bunka kenkyūjo kiyō* 東洋文化研究所紀要 45: 109–74 (March 1968).

North China Herald and Supreme Court and Consular Gazette. Shanghai, 1870–1941.

Oikawa Tsunetada 及川恒忠. *Shina seiji soshiki no kenkyū* 支那政治組織の研究 [A study of the political organization of China]. Tokyo, 1933.

Pai Chiao 白蕉. *Yuan Shih-k'ai yü Chung-hua min-kuo* 袁世凱與中華民國 [Yuan Shih-k'ai and the Republic of China]. Reprinted in *Yuan Shih-k'ai shih-liao hui-k'an hsu-pien,* ed. Shen Yun-lung, vol. 14. Taipei: Wen-hai ch'u-pan she, n.d.

Papers Relating to the Foreign Relations of the United States, 1915, comp. United States Department of State. Washington, D.C.: United States Government Printing Office, 1924.

Pearl, Cyril. *Morrison of Peking.* Sydney: Angus and Robertson, 1967.

Peking Daily News. Peking, 1909–17. (Cited as PDN.)

Pekin Shina kenkyūkai 北京支那研究會 [The sinological association of Peking], ed. *Saishin Shina kanshin roku* 最新支那官紳錄 [Record of contemporary Chinese officials and gentry]. 2 parts with separate pagination. Tokyo, 1918.

Powell, Ralph L. *The Rise of Chinese Military Power, 1895–1912.* Princeton: Princeton University Press, 1955.

Proceedings of the American Political Science Association Held at Chicago, Ill., December 28 to 30, 1904. Lancaster, Pa.: Wickersham Press, 1905.

P'u, Yu-shu. "The Consortium Reorganization Loan to China, 1911–1914: An Episode in Pre-War Diplomacy and International Finance." Ph.D. dissertation, University of Michigan, 1951.

Pugach, Noel. "Embarrassed Monarchist: Frank J. Goodnow and Constitutional Development in China, 1913–1915," *Pacific Historical Review* 42.4: 499–517 (November 1973).

Rankin, Mary Backus. *Early Chinese Revolutionaries: Radical Intellectuals in Shanghai and Chekiang, 1902–1911.* Cambridge, Mass.: Harvard University Press, 1971.

Reinsch, Paul S. *An American Diplomat in China.* New York: Doubleday, Page and Co., 1922.

Reischauer, Edwin O., and John K. Fairbank. *East Asia: The Great Tradition.* Boston: Houghton Mifflin, 1960.

Republican Advocate. Shanghai, 1912–13.

Rhoads, Edward J. M. *China's Republican Revolution: The Case of Kwangtung, 1895–1913.* Cambridge, Mass.: Harvard University Press, 1975.

Rosenbaum, Arthur Lewis. "Chinese Railway Policy and the Response to Imperialism: The Peking-Mukden Railway, 1895–1911," *Ch'ing-shih wen-t'i* 2.1: 38–70 (October 1969).

Satoi Hikoshichirō 里井彦七郎. "Ri Daishō no shuppatsu: *Genchi*-ki no seiron o chūshin ni" 李大釗の出發:「言治」期の政論を中心に [Li Ta-chao's point of departure: especially his political views in his *Yen-chih* period], *Shirin* 史林 40.3: 1–39 (May 1957).

Scalapino, Robert A. "Prelude to Marxism: The Chinese Student Movement in Japan, 1900–1910," in Albert Feuerwerker, Rhoads Murphey, and Mary C. Wright, eds., *Approaches to Modern Chinese History.* Berkeley and Los Angeles: University of California Press, 1967.

Schiffrin, Harold Zvi. "The 'Great Leap' Image in Early Chinese Nationalism," *Asian and African Studies (Jerusalem)* 3.101–19 (1967).

Schoppa, Robert Keith. "The Composition and Functions of the Local Elite in Szechwan," *Ch'ing-shih wen-t'i* 2.10: 7–23 (November 1973).

———. "Politics and Society in Chekiang, 1907–1927: Elite Power, Social Control, and the Making of a Province." Ph.D. dissertation, University of Michigan, 1975.

Schrecker, John E. *Imperialism and Chinese Nationalism: Germany in Shantung.* Cambridge, Mass.: Harvard University Press, 1971.

Schwartz, Benjamin. *In Search of Wealth and Power: Yen Fu and the West.* Cambridge, Mass.: Belknap Press, 1964.

Shen Yun-lung 沈雲龍. *Hsien-tai cheng-chih jen-wu shu-p'ing* 現代政治人物述

評 [Exposition and criticism regarding contemporary political personalities]. Reprinted in *Chin-tai Chung-kuo shih-liao ts'ung-k'an*, ed. Shen Yun-lung, 2d ser., vol. 20. Taipei: Wen-hai ch'u-pan she, n.d.

Sheridan, James E. *Chinese Warlord: The Career of Feng Yü-hsiang*. Stanford: Stanford University Press, 1966.

Shieh, Milton J. F. *The Kuomintang: Selected Historical Documents, 1894–1969*. New York: St. John's University Press, 1970.

Shu Hsin-ch'eng 舒新城, ed. *Chin-tai Chung-kuo chiao-yü shih-liao* 近代中國教育史料 [Historical materials on modern Chinese education]. 4 vols. Shanghai, 1928.

Shun-t'ien shih-pao 順天時報 [Peking times]. Peking, 1901–26.

Smedley, Agnes. *The Great Road: The Life and Times of Chu Teh*. London: John Calder, 1958.

Snow, Edgar. "A Conversation with Mao Tse-tung," *Life* 70.16: 46–48 (April 30, 1971).

———. *Red Star Over China*. New York: Random House, 1938.

Spector, Stanley. *Li Hung-chang and the Huai Army: A Study in Nineteenth-Century Chinese Regionalism*. Seattle: University of Washington Press, 1964.

Sun E-tu (Zen). *Chinese Railways and British Interests, 1898–1911*. New York: King's Crown Press, 1954.

Sun Yao 孫曜. *Chung-hua min-kuo shih-liao* 中華民國史料 [Historical materials on the Republic of China]. Reprinted in *Chin-tai Chung-kuo shih-liao ts'ung-k'an*, ed. Shen Yun-lung, 2d ser., vol. 13. Taipei: Wen-hai ch'u-pan she, n.d.

Sutton, Donald Sinclair. "The Rise and Decline of the Yunnan Army, 1909–1925." Ph.D. dissertation, University of Cambridge, 1970.

Ta Chung-hua 大中華 [Great China]. Shanghai, 1915–16.

Tahara Teijirō 田原禎次郎, comp. *Shinmatsu minsho Chūgoku kanshin jinmeiroku* 清末民初中國官紳人名錄 [A biographical record of Chinese officials and gentry at the end of the Ch'ing and in the early republic]. Talien, 1918.

T'ai Shuang-ch'iu 邰爽秋 and Huang Chen-ch'i 黃振祺, eds. *Chung-kuo p'u-chi chiao-yü wen-t'i* 中國普及教育問題 [The question of universal education in China]. Shanghai, 1938.

Ta-kung-ho jih-pao 大共和日報 [Republican daily]. Shanghai, 1912–14.

Tang, Peter S. H. *Russian and Soviet Policy in Manchuria and Outer Mongolia, 1911–1931*. Durham, N.C.: Duke University Press, 1959.

T'ao Ch'ü-yin 陶菊隱. *Pei-yang chün-fa t'ung-chih shih-ch'i shih-hua* 北洋軍閥統治時期史話 [Historical tales about the period of rule by the Peiyang warlords]. 6 vols. Peking, 1957.

Teichman, Eric. *Travels of a Consular Officer in North-West China*. Cambridge: Cambridge University Press, 1921.

Tien, Hung-mao. *Government and Politics in Kuomintang China, 1927–1937*. Stanford: Stanford University Press, 1972.

T'ien-to pao 天鐸報 [The bell]. Shanghai, 1912.

Ting Wen-chiang 丁文江, ed. *Liang Jen-kung hsien-sheng nien-p'u ch'ang-pien ch'u-kao* 梁任公先生年譜長編初稿 [First draft of a chronological biography and sequentially arranged materials of Liang Ch'i-ch'ao]. Taipei, 1958. (Cited as *Liang . . . nien-p'u.*)

Ts'ao Chü-jen 曹聚仁. *Chiang Pai-li p'ing-chuan* 蔣百里評傳 [Critical biography of Chiang Fang-chen]. Hongkong, 1963.

Ts'ao Ju-lin 曹汝霖. *I-sheng chih hui-i* 一生之回憶 [A lifetime's recollections]. Hongkong, 1966.

Ts'en Ch'un-hsuan 岑春煊. *Lo-chai man-pi* 樂齋漫筆 [Rambling notes from the study of Lo]. Reprinted in *Chung-kuo hsien-tai shih-liao ts'ung-shu*, ed. Wu Hsiang-hsiang, 4th ser. Taipei, 1962.

Ts'en Hsueh-lü 岑學呂. *San-shui Liang Yen-sun hsien-sheng nien-p'u* 三水梁燕孫先生年譜 [Chronological biography of Liang Shih-i]. 2 vols. Reprinted in *Chung-kuo hsien-tai shih-liao ts'ung-shu*, ed. Wu Hsiang-hsiang, 4th ser. Taipei, 1962.

Tuan Ch'i-jui 段祺瑞 [Tuan Ch'i-jui]. Shanghai: Kuang-wen shu-ch'ü, n.d.

Usui Katsumi 臼井勝美. *Nihon to Chūgoku—Taishō jidai* 日本と中國～大正時代 [Japan and China: the Taishō period]. Tokyo, 1972.

van der Valk, M. H. *Interpretations of the Supreme Court at Peking, Years 1915 and 1916*. Batavia: University of Indonesia, Sinological Institute, 1949.

Wakeman, Frederic, Jr. "High Ch'ing: 1683–1839," in James B. Crowley, ed., *Modern East Asia: Essays in Interpretation*. New York: Harcourt, Brace and World, 1970.

Watanabe Atsushi 渡邊惇. "En Seigai—hokuyō-ha seiken dasshu no michi" 袁世凱～北洋派政權奪取の道 [Yuan Shih-k'ai—the path of the seizure of power by the Peiyang clique], *Rekishigaku kenkyū* 歷史學研究 258: 31–39, 21 (October 1961).

———. "En Seigai seiken no keizaiteki kiban—hokuyō-ha no kigyō katsudō" 袁世凱政權の經濟的基盤～北洋派の企業活動 [The economic basis of the Yuan Shih-k'ai regime: the industrial activity of the Peiyang clique], in *Chūgoku kindaika no shakai kōzō: shingai kakumei no shiteki ichi* 中國近代化の社會構造: 辛亥革命の史的位置 [The social framework of China's modernization: the historical position of the 1911 Revolution]. Tokyo, 1960.

Weale, B. L. Putnam (pseudonym of B. Lenox Simpson). *The Fight for the Republic in China*. New York: Dodd, Mead and Co., 1917.

Willoughby, Westel W. *Foreign Rights and Interests in China*. 2 vols. Baltimore: Johns Hopkins University Press, 1927.

Wou, Odoric Y. K. "The District Magistrate Profession in the Early Republican Period: Occupational Recruitment, Training and Mobility," *Modern Asian Studies* 8.2: 217–45 (April 1974).

Wright, Mary Clabaugh. "Introduction: The Rising Tide of Change," in Mary Clabaugh Wright, ed., *China in Revolution: The First Phase, 1900–1913*. New Haven: Yale University Press, 1968.

———. *The Last Stand of Chinese Conservatism: The T'ung-chih Restoration, 1862–1874.* Stanford: Stanford University Press, 1957.

Wright, Stanley F. *China's Struggle for Tariff Autonomy: 1843–1938.* Shanghai, 1938.

———. *The Collection and Disposal of the Maritime and Native Customs Revenue since the Revolution of 1911.* Shanghai, 1927.

Wu Hsiang-hsiang 吳相湘. *Min-kuo cheng-chih jen-wu* 民國政治人物 [Political personages of the republic]. Taipei, 1964.

———. *Sung Chiao-jen: Chung-kuo min-chu hsien-cheng ti hsien-ch'ü* 宋教仁: 中國民主憲政的先驅 [Sung Chiao-jen: precursor of Chinese democracy and constitutional government]. Taipei, 1964.

Wu Yen-yun 吳硯雲, ed. *Huang liu-shou shu-tu* 黃留守書牘 [Letters of resident general Huang]. Reprinted in *Chung-kuo hsien-tai shih-liao ts'ung-shu*, ed. Wu Hsiang-hsiang, 1st ser. Taipei, 1962.

Yamashita Yoneko 山下米子. "Shingai kakumei no jiki no minshū undō— Kō-Setsu chiku no nōmin undō o chūshin to shite" 辛亥革命の時期の民衆運動江浙地區の農民運動を中心として [Mass movements in the period of the 1911 Revolution, with special reference to peasant movements in Kiangsu and Chekiang], *Tōyō bunka kenkyūjo kiyō* 37: 111–218 (March 1965).

Yang Lien-sheng. "Ming Local Administration," in Charles O. Hucker, ed., *Chinese Government in Ming Times: Seven Studies.* New York: Columbia University Press, 1969.

Yeh Hsia-sheng 葉夏聲. "Yü chih cheng-chien" 余之政見 [My political views], *Min-i tsa-chih* (February 15, 1913).

Yen Hsi-shan 閻錫山. *Yen Hsi-shan tsao-nien hui-i-lu* 閻錫山早年回憶錄 [Yen Hsi-shan's memoirs regarding his early years]. Taipei, 1968.

Yim, Kwanha. "Yüan Shih-k'ai and the Japanese," *Journal of Asian Studies* 24.1: 63–73 (November 1964).

Yin-ping-shih wen-chi 飲冰室文集 [Collected essays from the Ice-Drinker's Studio]. Liang Ch'i-ch'ao 梁啓超. 16 vols. Taipei: Tai-wan Chung-hua shu-ch'ü, 1960.

Young, Ernest P. "Yuan Shih-k'ai's Rise to the Presidency," in Mary Clabaugh Wright, *China in Revolution: The First Phase, 1900–1913.* New Haven: Yale University Press, 1968.

Yü Eng-yang 廋恩暘. *Yun-nan shou-i yung-hu kung-ho shih-mo chi* 雲南首義擁護共和始末記 [Full record of Yunnan's rising to protect the republic]. Reprinted in *Yuan Shih-k'ai shih-liao hui-k'an hsu-pien*, ed. Shen Yun-lung. Taipei: Wen-hai ch'u-pan she, n.d.

Yu, George T. *Party Politics in Republican China: The Kuomintang, 1912–1924.* Berkeley and Los Angeles: University of California Press, 1966.

Yuan Shih-k'ai ch'ieh-kuo chi 袁世凱竊國記 [Record of Yuan Shih-k'ai's usurpation]. Taipei, 1954.

Index

Administrative court (*p'ing-cheng yuan*), 161
Aglen, Francis. *See* Inspector general of customs
Almond, Gabriel A., 173
American government, 71, 116, 123–24. *See also* Reinsch, Paul; Wilson, Woodrow
American Political Science Association, 172–73, 175
Anglo-Chinese Friendship Bureau, 173
Aoki Norizumi, 64, 186, 239
Ariga Nagao, 170–72, 174–75, 219

Beard, Charles, 176
Bell, Henry (general manager of Lloyds Bank), 126
Bose, Sudhindra, 176
British government: and Chinese domestic affairs, 128, 131, 133, 219; loans to China by, 47, 124, 126–27; and Tibet, 184–85; and Twenty-One Demands, 189; and Yangtze sphere of influence, 180. *See also* Jordan, John Newell
Bryce, James, 173

Canton, 41, 77, 203. *See also* Kwangtung
Carnegie Endowment for International Peace, 48, 172, 174
Censorate, 160–61, 226
Centralization: attitudes toward, 24, 93–94, 109, 115, 135–37, 172; derivation of, 82–83, 90; evaluation of, 167–68, 243–47; programs of, 148, 155–57, 160–67, 177–79, 250–51; Yuan's approach to, 105–6

Chang Chen-fan, 145, 310 n.52
Chang Chien, 129, 156
Chang Chih-tung, 59
Chang Hsun, 57, 146, 159, 187; and the queue, 78, 205; in the Second Revolution, 131–32, 139, 144; and Yuan Shih-k'ai, 57–58, 119, 121, 227
Chang Huai-chih, 56
Chang I-lin, 211, 220, 225, 231, 238
Chang Ming-ch'i, 227
Chang Shu-yuan, 57
Chang Tso-lin, 114, 142
Chang Yun-shan, 39–40
Ch'ang-shou (Kiangsu), 37
Chao Ping-chün, 86, 117–18
Chee Hsin Cement Company, 69
Chekiang, 133, 146; finances of, 164, 208; local militia in, 264 n.18; local self-government in, 36, 152–54; relations of, with Yuan Shih-k'ai, 140, 228, 237; rural protests in, 18–19
Ch'en Ch'i-mei, 131, 133, 147
Ch'en Ching-hua, 93
Ch'en Chiung-ming, 119, 132, 190
Ch'en, Eugene, 192, 238
Ch'en Huang-chang, 202
Ch'en I, 62, 217, 229, 236–37, 314 n.96
Ch'en I-fan, 180, 185
Chen, Ivan. *See* Ch'en I-fan
Ch'en T'ing-hsun, 287 n.73
Ch'en Tu-hsiu, 215
Ch'en Yu-jen. *See* Ch'en, Eugene
Ch'eng Te-ch'üan, 121, 130–31
Cheng-chih hui-i. See Political Conference
Chengtu, 38–39, 77. *See also* Szechwan
Ch'i Yao-lin, 299 n.11
Chiang Fang-chen, 62–63

103–4, 165, 200, 278–79 n.88; and the monarchical movement, 214–15, 220, 223–24, 311 n.53, 315–16 n.108; and the Twenty-One Demands, 189

Liang Tun-yen, 70, 212

Liberal Party, 289–90 n.9

Lin-huai-kuan (Anhwei), 131

Liu Kuan-hsiung, 62, 85–86, 140

Liu-shou. *See* Nanking residency general

Lo Lun, 38

Loans: Crisp, 103, 128; domestic, 165, 200; effects of, 118, 131, 133, 242–43; and foreign attitudes, 47–48, 285 n.54; purposes of, 85, 100, 103, 113; Reorganization Loan, 122–29, 135, 166, 179; in Yuan's dictatorship, 165, 179–80, 298–99 n.3

Local militia, 92, 97, 206–7, 264 n.18, 265 n.30

Local self-government. *See* Representative government

Localism, 20

Lu Cheng-hsiang, 71, 189, 225

Lu Chien-chang, 56, 102

Lu Jung-t'ing, 228, 237

Lung Chi-kuang, 140, 147, 158, 180–81, 237

Ma An-liang, 142

Ma Fu-hsiang, 142

MacKinnon, Stephen R., 59

Manchuria, 66, 71, 142, 188–89, 191–92, 289 n.4

Manchus: in the 1911 Revolution, 39–40, 42; and pensions, 124; and royalist movement after the 1911 Revolution, 78, 211–12, 227

Mao Tse-tung, 211, 247, 251, 260 n.19

Merchants: and the dictatorship, 167, 208–9; and other classes, 7–8, 11; in politics, 14–15, 41, 114, 259 n.15; and the Second Revolution, 136; and the Twenty-One Demands, 189–90

Mikesell, Raymond F., 266–67 n.46

Military forces (provincial): demobilization of, 96, 100–102, 125, 164; sizes and finances of, 100–102, 233, 277–78 n.70. *See also* Eighth Division, Nanking; Peiyang army

Military governor (*tu-tu*): emergence of, 31–32; and provincial reorganization, 110–11; revival of, in 1916, 158, 242; Yuan Shih-k'ai's views of, 107. *See also* General-in-chief

Min-chu tang. *See* Democratic Party

Mixed Court, Shanghai, 45–46

Model Army, 217–18, 225

Mongolia: and comment by Li Ta-chao, 137; opposition to Peking's policy toward, 122–23; and Outer Mongolia's separation, 43–44, 139, 182–84; in the Twenty-One Demands, 188–89

Morrison, George Ernest: as adviser to Yuan Shih-k'ai, 103, 128, 170–71, 286 n.62; and discussion with Feng Kuo-chang, 226–27; on Japan's manipulation, 219; on Yuan's monarchy, 210

Mutinies, 102, 111. *See also* Peiyang army

Nanking, 131–32, 143–44

Nanking central revolutionary government, 32–33, 44, 79, 85–86

Nanking residency general (*liu-shou*), 85–87

National assembly. *See* Representative government

National Protection Army (*Hu-kuo chün*), 233–37, 240, 248, 313 n.87

Nationalism: definition of, 16, 262 n.30; in the early republic and the Third World, 252; in education, 190–97; in the late Ch'ing, 17; and liberal politics, 82–83; and the Twenty-One Demands, 189–92; and Yuan Shih-k'ai, 74, 178–79, 206. *See also* Pan-Asianism; Provincialism

New Army (*Lu-chün*): and the gentry, 31, 34; in the 1911 Revolution, 30–31, 35, 39–40; personal influences in, 58; in the provinces, 23; social role of, 17–18, 30–31. *See also* Peiyang army

New Hunan (Hsin Hu-nan), 22

New Kwangtung (Hsin Kuang-tung), 22

Newly Created Army (*Hsin-chien chün*), 54, 56–59, 66

Newspapers: criticism of performance by, 105; growth of, 13, 77–78, 271–72 n.3; latitude of, in the liberal republic, 86–87; repression of, 93, 96, 138, 143

Ni Ssu-ch'ung, 139–40, 159, 223–25, 227

Nihon rikugun shikan gakkō. *See* Japan's Army Officers' Academy

1911 Revolution, 11, 27–49, 204, 211

Ningpo, 153